The Business of Tour Operations

Pat Yale

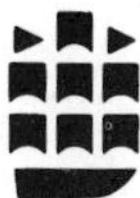

Longman Scientific & Technical
Longman Group Limited
Longman House, Burnt Mill, Harlow
Essex CM20 2JE, England
and Associated Companies throughout the world

First published 1995

British Library Cataloguing in Publication Data
A catalogue entry for this title can be obtained from the British Library.

ISBN 0-582-27797-3

Printed in Malaysia

CONTENTS

PREFACE

With the exception of ABTA's excellent manuals for tour operating trainees working towards the old COTOP exams, this is the first textbook to look in detail at the subject of tour operating as a business. It is aimed primarily at students on BTEC GNVQ Advanced Leisure and Tourism courses and on degree courses in Travel and Tourism, and Leisure, although students of business studies and marketing generally may also find parts of it useful.

The following people have kindly helped me by reading the text and commenting on it: Neil Taylor of Regent Holidays; Polly Davies of Marco Polo Travel Advisory Service; Tony Churchill, Rachel Millward, Sharon North, Kate Sallis and Barbara Turner of Soundwell College. Particular thanks are also owed to ex-Soundwell student Andy Veitch for providing me with a 'horse's mouth' description of a day in the life of a tour company resort representative and to Wendy Brown for all her help and understanding. I am immensely grateful to all of them for giving so generously of their time and energy. Of course, any mistakes or omissions are entirely my own.

1993 was a tricky time to be preparing a book on tour operating, as the new EC Package Travel Regulations threw the industry into turmoil over something as fundamental as the definition of a 'package holiday'. I have tried to ensure the information in this book is as up to date as possible. However, it is inevitable that changes will continue to take place as the dust settles. In any case, tour operating is a fast-changing business; no sooner is anything committed to paper than something else happens to render it redundant. I am grateful to *Travel Weekly* in particular for helping me keep track of recent changes.

Pat Yale, December 1994

Note: In September 1994, Owners Abroad changed its name to First Choice and rationalised its product range. The old Owners Abroad name has had to be retained when referring to events before September 1994. However, it should be remembered that Owners Abroad and First Choice are now one and the same company.

CHAPTER 1

Introduction to the business of tour operations

LEARNING OBJECTIVES

After studying this chapter you should be able to:

- **define the terms 'tour operator' and 'package holiday'**
- **describe the different categories of the tour operating business**
- **name the UK's largest tour operators**
- **explain the differences between tour operating and other businesses**
- **describe the relationships between tour operators and travel agencies, between tour operators and national tourist offices, and between tour operators and the travelling public**
- **understand the importance of vertical and horizontal integration to tour operating businesses**

INTRODUCTION

A **tour operator** is a person or company who purchases the different items that make up an inclusive holiday in bulk, combines them together to produce package holidays and then sells the final products to the public either directly or through travel agencies. The Package Travel, Package Holidays and Package Tours Regulations 1992 (known hereafter as the EC Package Travel Regulations) use the expression 'organiser' to refer to a tour operator.

Building on a definition originally developed by the Association of British Travel Agents (ABTA), the EC Package Travel Regulations define a 'package' as meaning:

> the pre-arranged combination of at least two of the following components when sold or offered for sale at an inclusive price and when the service covers a period of more than 24 hours or includes overnight accommodation:
>
> a) transport;
> b) accommodation;
> c) other tourist services not ancillary to transport or accommodation and accounting for a significant proportion of the package.

The expressions 'package holiday', 'package tour' and 'package travel' all have the same meaning. Package holidays can also be referred to as 'inclusive tours' (ITs), 'fully inclusive tours' (FITs), or, where they include flights, 'air inclusive tours' (AITs).

In 1994 the UK's three biggest tour operators were Thomson, Airtours and First Choice.

What tour operators do

The traditional package holiday is made up of three elements which are bulk purchased by tour operators:

- transport – flights, ferry crossings, etc.
- accommodation – rooms in hotels, self-catering apartments, etc.
- transfers – by coach, taxi, etc.

In the chain of distribution, tour operators can, therefore, be seen as the **wholesalers** of the travel industry, buying from its principals and reselling through its retailers, the travel agencies (*see* Fig. 1.1).

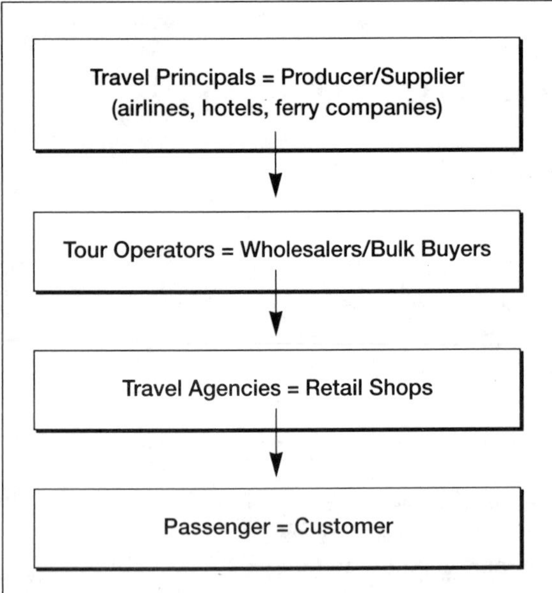

Fig. 1.1 The chain of distribution in the travel business

Why tour operators exist

There is a sense in which tour operators can be seen as redundant. In an age of easy international communication by telephone, fax or telex, and when computer technology makes information much easier to obtain, it might be argued that people could put their own holidays together perfectly well without operators (or agents) as intermediaries. Indeed, in the 1990s an increasing number of people were doing just that (*see* page 55). However, the travel and tourism business suffers from greater than usual difficulty in matching up supply with demand. For example, many of its products (hotels, restaurants, etc.) are small businesses attracting their clientele from a huge geographical catchment area. Without an unrealistically large advertising budget such enterprises could not hope to make contact with all of their potential clients. Instead, the operators do that for them by combining what they have to offer with the means of reaching it and advertising the two together.

As far as the customer (particularly the first-time customer) is concerned, there is also a problem in that they cannot know much about a particular hotel in, for example, Cyprus, and booking to stay there could be an expensive mistake. The operator, as intermediary, does the vetting for him/her and ensures that getting to the hotel, etc., will be as pain-free as possible. What's more, by virtue of its bulk-buying ability, the operator can often book the same hotel more cheaply than the client could on his/her own.

THE TOUR OPERATIONS PRODUCT

Most tour operators sell package holidays. The typical package holiday consists of three principal elements: transport, accommodation, and transfers between the airport and the accommodation. To be regarded as a package holiday these three elements must be sold at an **inclusive price**. If a consumer buys an air ticket from a travel agent one day, and then comes back to book a hotel and car hire the next day, this would not be a package holiday because it has not been 'prearranged' and is not offered for sale at an inclusive price. The EC Package Travel Regulations specifically state that invoicing for each of the three components of a prearranged package holiday separately would not prevent them from being regarded as a package for purposes of regulation.

Transport

The **transport** part of the package may involve:

- a seat on a charter or scheduled aeroplane
- a place on a ferry, hovercraft, hydrofoil or catamaran
- a berth or a cabin in a cruise ship
- a seat on a train
- a seat on a coach
- a hired car

Usually the transport part of a package is there to enable the client to get from his/her home to his/her holiday destination. However, in the following types of holiday, the transport itself is a crucial part of the experience:

- cruises
- coach tours
- luxury train trips, e.g. the Venice-Simplon Orient Express

- safaris
- self-drive holidays
- cycling tours
- boating holidays
- motorhome holidays
- horse-drawn caravan holidays

1. Air

Scheduled flights are those which operate to a fixed timetable regardless of the number of passengers. Often they are operated by the national 'flag carriers' (e.g. British Airways, Thai Airways, Air France, Alitalia). **Charter flight** departures are timed to fit the needs of the holiday market and may be cancelled if there are not enough bookings. Some charter airlines, like Britannia, are actually owned by the holiday companies, but a number of countries have been reluctant to permit charter flights because they want to protect their own scheduled airline. Cyprus, for example, continues to resist permitting British charter flights from any airports served by its national carrier, in order to protect Cyprus Airways. However, charter flights are increasing, even to long-haul destinations. In 1994, for example, charter services became available to the Cayman Islands, bringing down the cost of package holidays there.

By 1991 more scheduled than charter flights were being used for holidays. This situation came about as a) more people started to make their own travel arrangements, b) long-haul destinations became more popular and c) fly-drive arrangements became more common. Package holidays using seats on scheduled airlines are called **ITXs**. When seats on charter flights are used they are called **ITCs**.

2. Ship

Ferries and hovercraft are mainly used by UK passengers travelling to Europe. Like scheduled aeroplanes they operate to fixed timetables regardless of how many passengers there are, although the faster hovercraft, hydrofoil and catamaran services may have to be cancelled in bad weather.

It is still possible to travel further afield by boat (for example, the *Queen Elizabeth II* operates a timetabled service from Southampton to New York). However, these voyages on cruise liners would not normally be called 'ferry' trips.

3. Rail

Some clients prefer to reach destinations in Europe (e.g. the Costa Brava, the French Riviera, Switzerland) by train, because it's cheaper, because they enjoy seeing the scenery *en route* or because they dislike flying. A few tour operators, particularly ski holiday operators, organise rail transportation packages which may involve booking couchettes or sleepers for overnight journeys. Since Panorama axed most of its rail-transport packages in 1993, this market has been very small, although it may revive with the opening of the Channel Tunnel.

However, sometimes the train ride itself is the main feature of the holiday. In the 1980s an increasing number of operators featured tours in upmarket trains which were usually old, expensively restored and often pulled by steam engines. Examples of such trains are:

- the Venice-Simplon Orient Express, from Victoria to Venice
- the Al-Andalus Express which tours Seville, Granada and Cordoba
- the Palace on Wheels which tours Rajasthan in India
- the Copper Canyon Express, from Chihuahua to Los Mochis in Mexico
- the Bolshoi Express, from Moscow to the Baltic States and Uzbekistan
- the Eastern and Oriental Express, from Bangkok to Singapore

Not all train journeys which are part of the holiday experience are so luxurious. The Trans-Siberian Railway linking Moscow and Vladivostok is a travellers' institution but using it is hardly a glamorous experience.

4. Coach

Some clients prefer to reach destinations in Europe by coach, again perhaps because it is cheaper, because they enjoy seeing the scenery or because they dislike flying. For people in many parts of the country, coach travel also holds out the greatest hope of a local departure point; Cosmos alone has 260 departure points throughout the UK. Increasingly, operators offer luxury express coach services with videos, bars, toilets, air conditioning, drinks dispensers, fridges and double glazing. Hostesses on board look after clients and there are several drivers so that no overnight stops are needed – thus helping to keep costs down. For operators this is a tough business to be in, with particularly low profit margins. Since much of its clientele comes from the poorer end of the market, it is also a part of operating that was particularly badly affected by the recession. Perhaps rather surprisingly since they live furthest away from the Continent, northerners provide a disproportionately large number of coach holiday customers.

Competition comes from other similar companies but also from air-charter holidays; Cosmos believe holidaymakers will only opt for travelling by coach when they can save about £60 to £80 by doing so. Most people using coaches to reach their destination are travelling to camp and mobile home sites. This was a market in which ILG featured strongly, through NAT Holidays, Intasun Camping and Lancaster. After its collapse in 1991 the market contracted considerably.

COSMOS SUNLINK

SUNRIDER

CLUB CANTABRICA

TRAVEL EUROPE

SHEARINGS SUNSHINE EXPRESS

SUN EXPRESS (AIRTOURS)

Fig. 1.2 Some tour operators offering coach transport to holiday destinations in 1994

However, as with the train, the coach itself can form the basis of the holiday experience, with companies like Wallace Arnold specialising in extended coach tours. Coach tours are particularly popular with the older end of the holiday market.

5. Car

Some clients like to take their own cars on holiday, particularly if they're travelling to Northern Europe. When the Channel Tunnel starts running a full service in 1995 the number of people opting to take their car with them is likely to grow. At first, the increased popularity of self-drive holidays meant tour operators lost business to the ferry companies. However, operators soon began to put together 'self-drive packages', where the ferry bookings and/or motorail bookings are made for the client and prebooked accommodation vouchers are provided. Some clients prefer to hire the car, in which case the operators can arrange this too.

Accommodation

The accommodation part of the package may involve:

- a room in a hotel, guesthouse, bed and breakfast establishment or pension
- a self-catering apartment or villa
- a cabin in a holiday camp
- space for a tent or in a pre-erected tent
- a berth in a caravan
- a room in a chalet or hostel

1. Hotels

In some ways the hotel is the most important component of the package: once the client has selected a resort, he/she will then choose the particular holiday by comparing the hotels. The price of a holiday also reflects the type of hotel used: the more expensive the package, the more likely accommodation will be provided in a de luxe hotel with all sorts of facilities. Many standard packages use chain hotels – which will have much the same facilities no matter where they are in the world.

In most countries with a large tourist trade there are government hotel grading systems. Operators may use these gradings in their own descriptions of hotels or may develop their own system. Hotel prices are usually based on two people sharing a room, with supplements for any or all of the following:

- sea, lake or mountain views (or partial views)
- balconies
- terraces or patios
- private baths or showers
- single occupancy
- suites
- air conditioning

All except the smallest hotels will have restaurants, although the types of meals provided with any particular holiday will depend on what the operator has arranged. The biggest hotels will have restaurants offering **à la carte** menus, where clients can choose from a variety of options, as well as **table d'hôte** or **set menus**, where they will all be served the same meal. In popular seaside resorts buffets are increasingly replacing waiter service because they offer greater flexibility.

The following meal arrangements may be offered:

- Bed and Breakfast (BB) – room with breakfast
- Continental Plan (CP) – room with continental breakfast
- Half-Board (HB)/Modified American Plan (MAP)/Demi-Pension (DP) – bed, breakfast and one other meal
- Full-Board (FB)/American Plan (AP) – bed, breakfast, lunch and dinner

Just as the largest tour operators now have their own charter airlines to secure an adequate supply of flight seats, so some also own their own hotels in the resorts to secure a supply of beds as well (*see* page 60).

In large towns hotels may be open all year round. However, in European beach resorts they may only open from March to November, or even from April to October.

Apart from hotels, operators may offer serviced accommodation in:

- guesthouses or *pensions* – providing a more personal touch
- inns – usually with a bar on the premises
- hostels – providing basic, cheap accommodation
- motels – with plentiful parking space
- game lodges, e.g. Treetops in Kenya
- Greek tavernas
- *paradores* and *pousadas* – luxurious converted castles and mansions in Spain and Portugal respectively

2. Villas and apartments

Although some villas and apartments used by tour operators are privately owned and reflect their owner's taste in their decor, apartments are increasingly being built by large companies and are as standard in their design as chain hotels. Those built as part of large developments are more likely than private villas to be part of complexes with their own shops, swimming pools, etc.

Apartments come in several different sizes:

- studios which usually have a combined kitchen-living-room with a sofabed and can accommodate between one and three people
- one bed apartments which usually have a separate bedroom and a lounge/kitchen and can accommodate four or five people
- two bed apartments which usually have two separate bedrooms, a lounge and a separate kitchen and can accommodate between four and seven people

Prices for apartments are normally based on full occupancy, with supplements when they are hired by a smaller than maximum number of people.

Self-catering accommodation can also be provided in:

- country cottages or French *gîtes*
- private houses or flats
- caravans or motorhomes
- tents
- log cabins
- boats – longboats, river cruisers, houseboats, yachts, Turkish *gûlets*

Transfers

The third element of the traditional package holiday is the transfer between the airport and the hotel and vice versa. Normally this is by coach, although some upmarket packages will include transfers by taxi, and some multi-centre holidays will have transfers from town to town by scheduled flight. Operators usually charter coaches for transfer purposes, sometimes using a ground handler as the intermediary between themselves and the coach company. Some coach companies can be very large, with contracts to provide transfers in many different resorts.

In general, the business of providing transfers is fairly straightforward, although it may involve early morning and late night services. However, it can become more complicated, particularly when multi-centre holidays are involved, or where clients are being moved to islands in which case the coaches need to link up with scheduled ferry services.

However, the package holiday is much more than these three main components.

Other components of a package holiday

In addition to the basic components of package holidays, tour operators usually provide **representatives** at the UK and overseas airport to help their clients handle their travel arrangements, and a resort representative to welcome clients to their resort and help them with any problems that may arise. Sometimes the package will include some organised **excursions** as well. Purchasers of self-catering packages may find that a **welcome parcel** of basic groceries and maid service are included in the cost.

Almost all tour operators also sell **travel insurance**, and increasingly they make this a compulsory part of the purchase unless the client can show that they have taken out other insurance offering equivalent or better cover. There are two reasons for this: first, the profit margin on insurance sales is high, and second, it is very hard for an operator to turn its back on a client who has, for example, had an accident but has no insurance to cover the costs. Some companies do reserve the right to take no responsibility for clients who have not taken out their insurance but even if they are within their right to do this, it could still generate bad publicity. In the early 1980s Cadogan tried to get the cost of insurance included in brochure prices. However, other companies wouldn't agree to do the same; and with their products made to look uncompetitively expensive, Cadogan resumed offering it as an 'extra'. Travel agents also want to sell travel insurance because of the high commission rates, which means that for operators to leave clients without any choice of policy at all could damage the working relationship between operator and agent. In 1989 Redwing attempted to force clients to take out its insurance policy, but backed down when agents threatened not to rack its brochures. For the time being, therefore, insurance is likely to remain nominally optional.

As the travelling public becomes more sophisticated, tour operators are also selling packages with **options** to make them more flexible (for example, to extend the stay for an extra week, to add a week on the beach to a safari package, etc.). Finally, some operators also offer holidays tailor-made to a specific client's needs (*see* page 110).

Figure 1.3 shows the other features that go together to make up the total package holiday product. A quick look at this should show that alongside those features over which the operator has control (hotel, flight, etc.), there are many others ('airport not too congested', 'friendly locals') over which they have little, if any, control.

FEATURES OF THE TOUR OPERATOR'S PRODUCT

The product sold by the tour operator differs from that sold by most wholesalers in five crucial ways:

1 It is an *intangible* product that must be bought 'blind' because it cannot be seen, touched or experienced by the purchaser before consumption. Instead, tour operators prepare brochures which represent their products in words and pictures. The consumer makes his/her purchase on the basis of these words and pictures, supplemented with advice from either the tour operator or a travel agent. Inevitably words and pictures cannot give a complete impression of how any one particular client will experience the product, so sellers of travel products are often described as 'selling dreams'. What's more, the client uses up the product as he/she experiences it. In this way, buying a holiday is more like buying a bar of chocolate than a refrigerator; only memories are left behind afterwards. Since the product cannot be exchanged if faulty, the accuracy of the tour operator's brochure is vital to the sales process.

2 It is a *discretionary* product, meaning that clients do not have to buy it in the same way that they do food or fuel. During a recession clients may opt to forego a holiday altogether or trade down and buy a cheaper one. When finances are tight they may choose to spend the money that would have gone on a holiday on other consumer durables such as a compact disc player or new washing machine.

3 It is not a *heterogenous* product. You could buy a fridge like your neighbour's and expect it to look identical and operate in exactly the same way, but holidays are by their very nature varied. If

Product segment	Features
1 Destination	not too distant in flying time, clean, sandy beaches, reasonable certainty of sunshine, lively entertainment at night, good shops, reasonable prices, interesting excursions, friendly locals, safe to walk about, English widely spoken.
2 Originating airport	convenient local airport, car parking, not too congested, duty frees available.
3 Airline	flights at convenient time, reliable, good safety record, thoughtful, polite service, modern type of aircraft.
4 Coach transfers	clean, modern coaches, reliable, competent and friendly driver and courier.
5 Hotel	location: accessible to beach, shops, etc., staff trustworthy, English speaking, competent, friendly; facilities: well maintained, attractive decor, quiet at night, adequate public rooms, swimming pool, child care service, bar with good range of drinks at moderate prices, adequate size bedroom with balcony, sea view, comfortable beds, phone, colour TV, adequate cupboard space, wood (not wire) hangers, shower, toilet, shaver point, good lighting for make-up; restaurant/meals: good food, well cooked, served hot, adequate portions, good variety and choice, pleasant atmosphere, comfortable seating, flexible meal hours, fast, polite and friendly service.
6 Resort representatives	knowledgeable, competent, friendly, reliable, accessible.
7 Tour operator	price reflects good value for money, secure, reliable, offers guarantees, extras.
8 Travel agent	convenient, competent, reliable, friendly, pleasant 'shopping atmosphere', extra services provided (e.g. discounts, free transfers to airport, free insurance).
9 Miscellaneous	companionable fellow travellers with common interests; 'expectation': widening of general knowledge and interests, pleasant memories of experience.

Fig. 1.3 The total package holiday product

Source: *Marketing for Tourism*, Holloway and Plant, Pitman Publishing

you go to Greece in August, with the blazing heat and crowds of visitors, you will experience a different product from the one you discover in cooler, quieter May – even if you've booked into the same hotel, travelled on the same flight and used the same tour operator.

4 It is a *perishable* product. Although holidays don't go off in the same way as, say, yoghurts that have passed their sell-by date, a specific holiday is only saleable up to the date of the flight departure. If the flight takes off with empty seats, the tour operator which had contracted for them will lose money in the same way as the yoghurt seller. This explains the spate of late booking special offers – the tour operator's equivalent of the supermarket's 'reduced for quick sale' shelf.

5 Package holidays also suffer from *inseparability*, in that, as with other service industries, the behaviour of everyone involved in the product – from the chambermaid to the waiter to the resort rep – can have an effect on the outcome of the experience. This is markedly different from other consumer products: when we buy a washing machine, for example, our enjoyment of the product will not be reduced by the irritating behaviour of the plumber who installs it. The difference lies in the fact that we continue to get benefit from the washing machine after the plumber has left, while a holiday becomes nothing but memories once we return home.

The fact that tour operators are selling an intangible product has important consequences. They do not, for example, keep a stock of their products in the same way that other wholesalers do. Whether you go to a travel agency or to the office of the tour operator to buy your holiday you will not find a supply of airline seats or hotel rooms stacked up. Instead, the brochures represent the stock.

Since tour operators don't need to buy in actual

stock the capital costs of starting up a tour operations business are relatively low. This has made it easy for lots of small companies to develop; by 1994 there were 746 ABTA tour operators in the UK, compared with 506 in 1984. However, by the early 1990s the situation was changing, a fact highlighted by the collapse of Riva Travel. Riva was one of the companies set up after the collapse of the International Leisure Group in 1991 (*see* page 46) and retained some of the ILG staff. It was thought to offer a good product and had 60,000 advance bookings for the summer of 1993. However, in March 1993 it ceased trading, suggesting that it was becoming harder for a new company to establish itself in the market (*see* Fig. 1.4).

Reasons for the increasing difficulty included the fact that a new mass market operator would need to be able to match the market leaders' prices to attract enough business – at a time when profitability was not always the market leaders' highest priority and when the potential market was static or falling. Riva would probably have needed at least 180,000 bookings to be able to compete. Since the quality of the product offered by the market leaders had improved considerably since the early 1980s, the only way Riva could hope to cut into their business was by undercutting them – particularly difficult when it had made a loss of £5.4 million in its first year of trading and so started 1993 in a weak financial position. In addition, Riva was unable to persuade Lunn Poly or Thomas Cook to stock its brochures which made it hard to reach potential customers. It also meant other agents who were prepared to rack its products could dictate terms to the company (in other words, make them pay override commission on sales). Riva also thought that the ERM would ensure the pound's stability and therefore decided not to buy its currencies forward (*see* page 177), a decision which proved disastrous after the pound withdrew from the ERM and subsequently slumped in value after September 1992. Lastly, and perhaps most seriously, the cost of securing adequate bonding arrangements had risen enormously and the number of bond obligors willing to provide bonding had fallen.

Riva had started out aiming at an upmarket clientele, but had quickly switched to emphasising a mass-market product, 'Beachlife', which was in direct competition with the main operators' summer sun products. The lesson of its collapse might be that it's now almost impossible for a new company to start up in direct competition with the mass-market operators. However, even starting a new regional specialist operation is becoming more difficult as the mass-market operators increasingly spread their tentacles around the globe (for example, first Thomson and then Airtours moved in on Cuba, previously a specialist market), bringing their industrial muscle to bear to secure competitive prices which it would be hard for a newcomer to match.

- Difficulty in finding bond coverage at an affordable price.
- Problems in persuading the operator-owned multiple travel agencies to rack brochures.
- Extra cost of override commission to agencies prepared to stock brochures.
- Cost of buying necessary currencies forward.
- Impossibility of matching/undercutting the big operators' discounts and still making a profit.

Fig. 1.4 Why it was becoming harder for new operators to establish themselves by 1994

Ancillary services

Most tour operators sell ancillary products in addition to the basic package holiday. Figure 1.5 shows the ancillary products that may be available either in the UK or at the overseas resort.

THE MAIN CATEGORIES OF TOUR OPERATOR

For the general public, tour operators are companies, like Thomson, First Choice and Airtours, which provide **overseas holidays**. However, some operators, like Blakes Holidays, specialise in selling **domestic holidays**, i.e. holidays in the UK for UK residents. A third category of **incoming tour operators** sell holidays in the UK for overseas residents. These companies are probably the least familiar to UK customers because their

Optional ancillary services from the UK	**Optional ancillary services overseas**
Visas Insurance Travellers cheques/ foreign exchange Taxi to airport Discounted coach and rail fares Domestic air tickets Car hire Car parking at airport Hotel rooms at airport Travel goods e.g. maps, guidebooks, adaptor plugs	Excursions Car or bike hire Foreign exchange Ski equipment: skis/sticks boots lift passes ski school Sports facilities/ equipment Seats at events e.g. Oberammergau Passion Play

Fig. 1.5 Ancillary products sold by tour operators

brochures are not displayed in High Street travel agencies. Finally, a fourth category of operators specialise in specific markets: perhaps holidays for young people (The Club) or older people (Saga Holidays); holidays in Turkey (Metak) or the USA (Trek America); or holidays for people with special interests like bird-watching or rambling.

Tour operators who target the mass market are able to achieve the greatest turnover and are therefore likely to have the largest reserves to reinvest in the company. Ultimately they are likely to make the largest profits and can therefore afford to employ more specialist staff, such as solicitors, than more cash-strapped smaller or specialist operators.

Overseas tour operators

Overseas tour operators include household names like market leaders Thomson, First Choice and Airtours who between them sell around 70 per cent of all overseas package holidays from the UK, and smaller companies like Sunworld who sell just five per cent. Table 1.1 shows how three operators have increased their grip on the market since 1986, with Airtours expanding to fill the gap left by the demise of the International Leisure Group in 1991.

The 'Big Three's' grip on the market is partially concealed behind a plethora of different product names. Figure 1.7 shows the ownership and product names of Thomson, First Choice and Airtours.

Table 1.2 gives a more detailed picture of the tour operating market as it was in March 1994, showing how top placed Thomson Tour Operations Ltd was carrying nearly 100 times as many passengers as 40th placed Meridian Tours Ltd (since ceased trading). It also shows how there is a small cluster of 'second-tier' operators, with programmes of over 300,000 passengers carried annually: Avro, Iberotravel, Best Travel, Cosmosair, Aspro and Unijet Travel. But of these Avro is a seat-only specialist, while Aspro has now been absorbed into Airtours.

Most overseas tour operators offer a **summer sun** product of holidays to the Mediterranean for the period from April to October. Others also have a **winter sun** product covering October to March and sometimes supplementing a **winter ski** product of holidays to the ski resorts. The winter holiday products may make up a relatively small proportion of the company's overall profit but nevertheless help it keep everything ticking over throughout the year. Not surprisingly, if the figures for passengers carried are divided into separate sets of summer and winter seasons, the names of the top 40 companies change slightly to reflect those which have big seasonal rather than year-round programmes (*see* Table 1.3). It's also worth noting the comparatively small size of the winter programmes; for example, Thomson's 1993/4 winter programme was roughly half the size of its summer 1993 one.

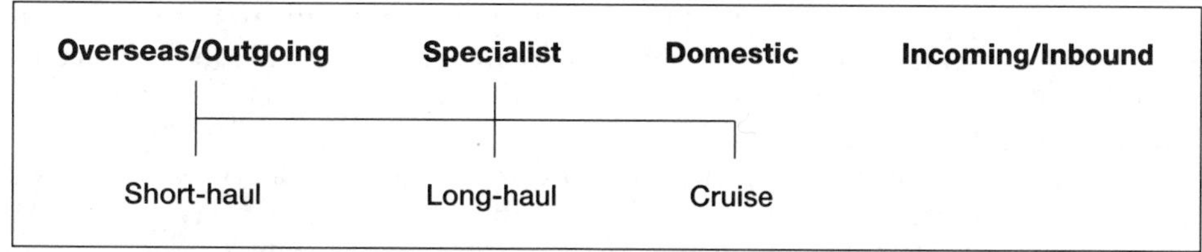

Fig. 1.6 Types of tour operator

Table 1.1 How the 'Big Three' tour operators took over the market, 1986–91*

Tour operator	*1986*	*1987*	*1988*	*1989*	*1990*	*1991*
Thomson	2773	3711	3864	4227	2936	3325
%	27.5	31.5	33.0	38.0	30.0	35.0
International Leisure Group (ILG)	1815	2121	2225	2113	1615	–
%	18.0	18.0	19.0	19.0	16.5	–
Owners Abroad**	–	353	702	834	1468	1805
%	–	3.0	6.0	7.7	15.0	19.0
Airtours	–	–	–	667	734	1520
%	–	–	–	6.0	7.5	16.0
Others	5495	5596	4917	3281	3034	2850
%	54.5	47.5	42.0	29.5	31.0	30.0
TOTAL:	10083	11781	11708	11122	9787	9500

(* figures indicate 000s of passengers)
(** now First Choice)

Parent Company	**Thomson Corporation**	**First Choice plc**	**Airtours plc**
Travel company	Thomson Travel Group	First Choice	Airtours
Main tour operating brands	Thomson Skytours *Portland	First Choice Freespirit Sovereign *Eclipse Direct	Airtours Aspro Tradewinds
Travel agents	Lunn Poly		Going Places
Linked airlines	Britannia (Airways) (39 planes)	Air 2000 (17 planes)	Airtours International + Inter-European Airways (16 planes)

(* direct sell)

Fig. 1.7 The UK's largest overseas tour operators in 1994

Some overseas tour operators only sell **short-haul** holidays, while others sell only **long-haul** holidays to exotic destinations more than five hours flying time from the UK. The biggest operators sell both long- and short-haul holidays and, increasingly, a range of more specialist products as well. For example, for summer 1994 Thomson offered 3 million holidays in 14 different brochures.

In 1993, almost all large overseas tour operators were members of ABTA, the Association of British Travel Agents. However, following the introduction of the EC Package Travel Regulations in 1993 it became apparent that ABTA's role would change and that a new organisation might need to be established to represent tour operators separately from travel agents. At the 41st ABTA Convention in

Table 1.2 Numbers of passengers carried by Britain's largest tour operators 1993–4

	Twelve months to March	*1994*	*1993*	*Percentage change*
1	Thomson Tour Operations Ltd	3,464,326	3,072,416	13
2	Airtours plc	1,912,142	1,534,163	25
3	Owners Abroad Holidays Limited*	1,569,706	1,569,387	0
4	Avro plc	777,578	541,043	44
5	Unijet Travel Limited	483,681	285,050	70
6	Iberotravel Limited	466,172	427,529	9
7	Cosmosair plc	382,954	367,997	4
8	Best Travel Limited†	353,360	445,632	(21)
9	Aspro Travel Limited	326,044	405,297	(20)
10	Owners Abroad Travel Limited*	271,488	328,269	(17)
11	Portland Holidays Limited	175,193	201,674	(13)
12	Kuoni Travel Limited	175,160	134,507	30
13	Virgin Holidays Limited	159,842	154,704	3
14	Sunset Holidays plc	148,759	104,860	42
15	Inspirations East Limited	136,594	110,719	23
16	British Airways Holidays Limited	131,553	123,612	6
17	Cresta Holidays Limited	131,044	102,401	28
18	Manos (UK) Limited	121,960	97,808	25
19	Hotelplan Limited	111,764	108,720	3
20	Balkan Holidays Limited	109,699	72,301	52
21	The Air Travel Group (Holidays) Limited	109,655	118,533	(7)
22	Olympic Holidays Limited	108,158	127,059	(15)
23	Crystal Holidays Limited	95,798	70,094	37
24	Thomas Cook Group Limited	86,108	45,235	90
25	The Globespan Group plc	73,384	65,654	12
26	Paris Travel Service Limited	73,172	37,334	96
27	Hayes and Jarvis (Travel) Limited	58,443	65,663	(11)
28	A T Mays Limited	54,014	4,878	1,007
29	Saga Holidays Limited	52,928	51,009	4
30	Skibound Limited	47,575	46,709	2
31	Beach Villas (Holidays) Limited	46,256	35,997	28
32	Sunseeker Leisure plc	45,594	47,798	(5)
33	Panorama Holiday Group Limited	45,404	35,656	27
34	Medchoice Holidays Limited (formerly Yugotours)	44,397	40,852	9
35	Cosmos Coach Tours Limited	42,900	38,013	13
36	Elvington Limited	41,401	36,683	13
37	Kosmar Villa Holidays Limited	40,094	29,949	34
38	Jetsave Limited	37,968	39,378	(4)
39	Brevis Marketing Services Limited	37,853	0	0
40	Meridian Tours Limited	37,838	45,836	(17)

Notes

- The above table shows passengers carried for the twelve months to March 1994 for the forty largest companies, ranked by passenger numbers.
- The figures for the year to March 1994 are generally comparable with previous periods but in a few cases there are distortions because of a change in ownership or licence cover. Carryings for Aspro Travel are included in those of Airtours plc after the December 1993 quarter.
- Figures in brackets represent a fall in traffic.

(*now First Choice) (†ceased trading)

Source: ATOL Business Monitor, CAA

Palma in May 1993 it was suggested that a new Tour Operators Trade Association could take over ABTA's tour operating trade association role if members voted to see it slimmed down to a regulatory body with limited functions.

Table 1.3 Number of passengers carried by major ATOL-holders, winter 1992/3 and winter 1993/4

	Winter season	*1993/4*	*1992/3*	*Percentage change*
1	Thomson Tour Operations Limited	1,169,233	1,003,777	16
2	Airtours plc	691,855	509,865	36
3	Owners Abroad Holidays Limited*	462,034	382,683	21
4	Avro plc	271,838	221,941	22
5	Unijet Travel Limited	189,981	90,086	111
6	Iberotravel Limited	146,785	109,812	34
7	Cosmosair plc	128,186	111,953	14
8	Owners Abroad Travel Limited*	82,688	93,424	(11)
9	Kuoni Travel Limited	81,012	76,368	6
10	Crystal Holidays Limited	70,162	55,091	27
11	Virgin Holidays Limited	66,489	69,139	(4)
12	Best Travel Limited†	64,544	98,369	(34)
13	British Airways Holidays Limited	64,206	56,642	13
14	Hotelplan Limited	60,427	60,102	1
15	Cresta Holidays Limited	50,868	46,337	10
16	A T Mays Limited	50,623	1,953	2,492
17	Portland Holidays Limited	45,597	52,498	(13)
18	Thomas Cook Group Limited	40,736	35,132	16
19	Sunset Holidays plc	39,985	17,919	123
20	Skibound Limited	37,685	37,568	0
21	Paris Travel Service Limited	36,382	26,505	37
22	Hayes & Jarvis (Travel) Limited	32,077	33,694	(5)
23	The Air Travel Group (Holidays) Limited	31,607	39,186	(19)
24	Aspro Travel Limited (December 1993 quarter only)	28,134	107,106	(74)
25	Saga Holidays Limited	26,473	23,458	13
26	Inspirations East Limited	24,487	54,380	(55)
27	Olympic Holidays Limited	23,349	20,409	14
28	Cunard Line Limited	19,824	15,973	24
29	Travelscene Limited	19,067	18,585	3
30	Panorama Holiday Group Limited	18,050	14,459	25
31	Bladon Lines Travel Limited	16,883	19,269	(12)
32	Balkan Holidays Limited	16,628	14,958	11
33	Airlink International Limited	16,549	14,228	16
34	Beach Villas (Holidays) Limited	16,134	10,082	60
35	Manos (UK) Limited	15,660	3,176	393
36	Kosmar Villa Holidays Limited	14,122	4,246	233
37	Brevis Marketing Services Limited	12,717	0	0
38	The Air Travel Group Limited	11,701	12,110	(3)
39	Travelsphere Limited	11,613	13,407	(13)
40	RCI Europe Limited	11,356	5,613	106

Source: ATOL Business Monitor, CAA
(* now First Choice) (†ceased trading)

Table 1.4 Passengers carried by Britain's largest ATOL-holders, summer 1992 and summer 1993

	Summer season	*1993*	*1992*	*Percentage change*
1	Thomson Tour Operations Limited	2,295,093	2,088,639	11
2	Airtours plc	1,220,287	1,024,298	19
3	Owners Abroad Holidays Limited*	1,107,672	1,186,704	(7)
4	Avro plc	505,740	319,102	58
5	Iberotravel Limited	319,387	317,717	1
6	Aspro Travel Limited	297,910	298,191	0
7	Unijet Travel Limited	293,700	194,964	51
8	Best Travel Limited†	288,816	347,263	(17)
9	Cosmosair plc	254,768	256,044	0
10	Owners Abroad Travel Limited*	188,800	234,845	(20)
11	Portland Holidays Limited	129,596	149,176	(13)
12	Inspirations East Limited	112,107	56,339	99
13	Sunset Holidays plc	108,774	86,941	25
14	Manos (UK) Limited	106,300	94,633	12
15	Kuoni Travel Limited	94,149	58,139	62
16	Virgin Holidays Limited	93,354	85,565	9
17	Balkan Holidays Limited	93,071	57,343	62
18	Olympic Holidays Limited	84,809	106,650	(20)
19	Cresta Holidays Limited	80,176	56,064	43
20	The Air Travel (Group) Holidays Limited	78,048	79,347	(2)
21	British Airways Holidays Limited	67,347	66,970	1
22	The Globespan Group plc	63,203	53,997	17
23	Hotelplan Limited	51,337	48,618	6
24	Thomas Cook Group Limited	45,372	10,103	349
25	Medchoice Holidays Limited (formerly Yugotours)	39,578	37,047	7
26	Sunseeker Leisure plc	37,797	37,007	2
27	Elvington Limited	37,093	33,298	11
28	Paris Travel Service Limited	36,790	10,829	240
29	Cosmos Coach Tours Limited	34,836	31,905	9
30	Jetsave Limited	31,273	29,616	6
31	Channel Islands Travel Service Limited	30,759	33,654	(9)
32	Beach Villas (Holidays) Limited	30,122	25,915	16
33	Preston Travel (CI) Limited	29,122	4,897	495
34	Panorama Holiday Group Limited	27,355	21,197	29
35	Meridian Tours Limited†	26,941	33,936	(21)
36	Saga Holidays Limited	26,455	27,551	(4)
37	Hayes and Jarvis (Travel) Limited	26,367	31,969	(18)
38	Kosmar Villa Holidays Limited	25,972	25,703	1
39	Crystal Holidays Limited	25,636	15,003	71
40	The Air Travel Group Limited	25,204	28,340	(11)

Source: ATOL Business Monitor, CAA
(*now First Choice) (†ceased trading)

DOMESTIC TOUR OPERATORS

Tour operators have played a relatively small part in the UK domestic holiday market, largely because good communication systems mean that it is easy for people to make their own arrangements; if a family plans a seaside holiday in Blackpool they may well choose to drive there and will only need to make one phone call to secure their accommodation. Even if they travel by coach or train they can buy the necessary tickets direct from the principal without difficulty. As a result, few hotels have thought it worthwhile to market themselves through operators, a procedure which would dilute some of their profits. Holidaymakers also feel happier about making arrangements to holiday at home because there are none of the problems of different languages and currencies to worry about.

However, some parts of the domestic holiday market have been more routinely packaged, especially holidays to outlying islands like the Isle of Man and the Channel Islands where arrangements must be made for ferry or flight bookings as well as for accommodation. Tour operators like Wallace Arnold also have a long history of offering packaged coach tours of the UK where, once again, individuals might think the difficulty of arranging the different hotels and transport themselves would be too great.

Those packaging domestic products are often suppliers of one component trying to make it easier for the public to buy their products; so British Rail offers Goldenrail and Superbreak holidays to boost its leisure traffic. Many hotels also package minibreaks, including transportation, to make their rooms more inviting. However, after the EC Package Travel Regulations became law in 1993, some hotels considered abandoning packaging because they thought it would be too expensive to arrange the requisite protection for their customers' money (*see* page 241).

In the UK, the main types of domestic holiday involve:

- hotels or guesthouses
- holiday camps – Butlin's, CenterParcs, etc.
- self-catering
- camping or caravanning
- boating
- coach tours
- minibreaks
- special interests and activities

Few domestic tour operators are members of ABTA, although some belong to alternative trade associations like the Channel Islands Tour Operators Group, CITOG.

WALLACE ARNOLD
CRYSTAL HOLIDAYS
SHEARINGS
NATIONAL EXPRESS HOLIDAYS
BLAKES HOLIDAYS
HAVEN
HOSEASONS
GOLDEN RAIL
SUPERBREAK HOLIDAYS
RAINBOW HOLIDAYS

Fig. 1.8 The UK's largest domestic tour operators in 1993

A closer look at Superbreak Holidays

Superbreak was formed out of the old British Transport Hotels group of 34 properties which were privatised in 1983. Originally it was called Shortbreak Mini-Holidays Ltd and featured 83 hotels in 64 locations. In the last 10 years it has expanded to feature 550 hotels (including some in the de Vere, Edwardian and Copthorne hotel chains) in 300 locations, as far afield as the Channel Islands and Ireland. In 1994, Superbreak won *Travel Weekly's* Travel Industry Globe award as the best operator of UK short break holidays.

SPECIALIST TOUR OPERATORS

To define the expression 'specialist tour operator' is tricky because some such operators are very small and cater for very specific niches in the market (e.g. birdwatchers), while others are very large operations, handling thousands of clients every year. Typical of the latter might be a company like Nielson, who handled 40,000 winters sports customers over the 1993/4 winter season. In the 1980s there were an increasing number of specialist tour operations as holidaymakers became more sophisticated and demanding in their needs. However, successful specialist operators often expand their sphere of business so that they became less specialised as time goes by. In 1992, for example, Spanish holiday specialist Mundi Color announced a new programme to Portugal, and in 1993 India specialists Cox and Kings offered train trips in Russia. By the late 1980s many large tour operators also produced more specialised programmes in addition to their main summer and winter sun products, e.g. Thomson Holiday's 'Simply Greece' and Airtours' 'Cuba' programmes.

Many of the smaller specialist operators are members of the Association of Independent Tour Operators (AITO) instead of ABTA.

It's worth noting that many companies specialising in one particular country are either owned by that country's government or national airline, or have a very close link with the government. Until 1991 Yugotours was a typical example. Before the outbreak of civil war in what was Yugoslavia, Yugotours was a state-owned tour operator, offering a programme of holidays throughout the country. When the country split up into separate republics, 'Yugotours' became the property of rump Yugoslavia, the states of Serbia and Montenegro. To

Type of specialisation	Area	Typical company
One country	Italy Spain	Citalia Mundi Color
One area	Far East Caribbean South America	Oriental Magic Caribbean Connection Journey Latin America
One type of terrain	Lakes and mountains	Inghams
One age group	Youth market Senior citizens	The Club Saga Holidays
One type of holiday	Safaris Short breaks	African Safari Club Time Off
One type of accommodation	Self-catering Small hotels	Meon Villas Abercrombie and Kent
One generating area	Day trips from local area	Baker Dolphin coach tours (Avon area)
One type of transport	Coach transport	National Express Holidays
One specialist interest	Walking Boating Birdwatching	Ramblers Holidays Blakes Holidays Ornitholidays
'Adventure' holidays	Lengthy overland trips	Encounter Overland

Fig. 1.9 Types of specialist tour operator

survive it was forced to change its name to Med Choice, and although it continued to feature holidays to the newly independent state of Slovenia, it diversified into offering holidays to other Mediterranean destinations as well. Another example is Italian specialist Citalia, which is owned by CIT, the Italian State Railways Board.

Before the collapse of most of the Communist states at the end of the 1980s, holidays in Eastern bloc countries were tightly controlled by the individual governments concerned. For example, Intourist was in charge of all holidays throughout the old USSR. Although it allowed Thomson and other Eastern bloc specialist companies like Regent Holidays and Progressive Tours to sell a few packages, most holidays to the USSR had to be bought direct from Intourist. Similar state-owned companies operated in other Eastern bloc countries (e.g. Cedok in the old Czechoslovakia and Polorbis in Poland). These companies are now being privatised and must carve out new niches for themselves in the changed conditions of the 1990s. For example, in 1994 Cedok announced that it would cease offering package holidays to the Czech Republic and would instead concentrate on arranging group tours and on business and incentive travel.

A closer look at Regent Holidays

Set up in 1970, Regent Holidays is a small ABTA-bonded tour operating business, specialising in 'holidays for thinking people' to what were until recently the countries of the eastern bloc. A private limited company, Regent Holidays operates out of two offices: one on the Isle of Wight concentrating on the non-eastern bloc countries and one in Bristol handling the traffic to the Communist and ex-Communist countries.

In 1970 Regent started by selling holidays to Albania which was then closed to independent travellers. Soon it was offering trips to Iceland and the German Democratic Republic (GDR), now eastern Germany. During the 1970s business was slow to pick up; in 1975, Regent handled perhaps just 500 clients a year. However, in the 1980s it expanded more rapidly and was soon featuring around 12 or 13 different countries a year, including the Soviet Union, Northern Cyprus and Cuba. With the break up of the Soviet Empire into the separate states of the CIS, Regent found itself featuring even more countries. Indeed, by 1993 it was offering tours to 25 different 'countries'. In 1994 it initiated tours to Uzbekhistan, one of the breakaway states of the old Soviet Union.

Because of the particular countries it chose to feature, Regent has always had to be adaptable and ready to deal with excess paperwork and delay. When it started in business many of the countries it featured would only let in guided groups of tourists; alternatively they were associated with the sort of off-putting bureaucracy that made most people prefer the safety of going in a group. However, that situation was already changing, even before the collapse of the Berlin Wall in 1989 heralded a new era of fewer visas and easier travel in Eastern Europe. By 1982 even China had started to ease the restrictions previously imposed on independent travellers. At the same time, the travel industry changed and matured as more people went abroad and came home feeling more confident and ready to try going it alone. Regent has reacted to these trends by creating an increasing number of tailor-made itineraries, and by selling flight-only arrangements to places like Moscow and Istanbul.

The opening up of Eastern Europe might be expected to have helped a company like Regent which had offered tours there for so many years and had so much experience of working the systems. In fact, the opposite has been the case; as arrangements became easier to make, so the mainstream operators moved in, particularly to popular towns like Prague and Budapest. In the same way, as soon as charter flights to Cuba became available in 1992, first Thomson and then Airtours moved in on the country, offering bulk-bought, mass-market prices it would be hard for Regent to beat.

Regent continues to do particularly well in countries which, for one reason or another, are not ready for the bigger operators. For example, in 1993, its programmes to the Baltic States (Latvia, Lithuania and Estonia) and to Vietnam were particularly popular. The Baltic States appeal to a wide range of people (some of whom remember the countries from their days of independence before the Second World War) and the abolition of visa requirements for British citizens has also made visiting them easier. However, the Baltic States were always among the most heavily regulated of the Eastern bloc countries, and whereas there were always some private rooms available for rent in Hungary and Czechoslovakia, there were none in the Soviet Union. This of course means that it will take years to develop a range of accommodation to suit all visitors. In addition, very few people there speak western languages, making independent travel a continued problem. In such circumstances bigger operators are unlikely to want to launch new programmes yet. Vietnam already appears in many Far East operators' brochures, but usually as a fixed add-on itinerary to, for example, visits to Thailand or Hong Kong. Holidaying there remains expensive because of the lack of direct charter flights and continued government bureaucracy. When parting with large sums of money, the public generally prefer to deal with an ABTA-bonded operator, which puts Regent in a strongly competitive position.

Regent needs to feature a wide range of countries to allow for external circumstances which may mean that some cannot be offered in any particular year. For example, after the Tiananmen Square massacre in 1989, bookings to China slowed to a trickle, and those to Mongolia (usually reached via China) vanished. In 1992 anarchic conditions in Albania meant that it had to be removed from brochures. Fortunately a new charter flight which offered easier access to Cuba took up some of the slack.

Regent is a company with a very clear market. In the past it made unsuccessful efforts to diversify into Zimbabwe and Colombia, but they probably didn't work because the company was too closely associated with Eastern bloc countries in the public's mind.

By 1993 Regent Holidays employed seven staff and handled roughly 5,000 clients a year. However, it remains a small tour operator. All of its staff regularly travel to the countries it features to keep their product knowledge up to date, but there are no overseas resort representatives and no plans for regular weekly departures. 'Brochures' continue to be mainly two-colour leaflets focusing on individual countries. Regent Holidays' three directors intend it to stay small so that it can continue to offer clients a very personal service. After many years in which it felt that its turnover did not justify the cost of computerisation, in 1992 it finally took the plunge and installed a Worldspan booking system, a great help with its 'tailor-made' packaging.

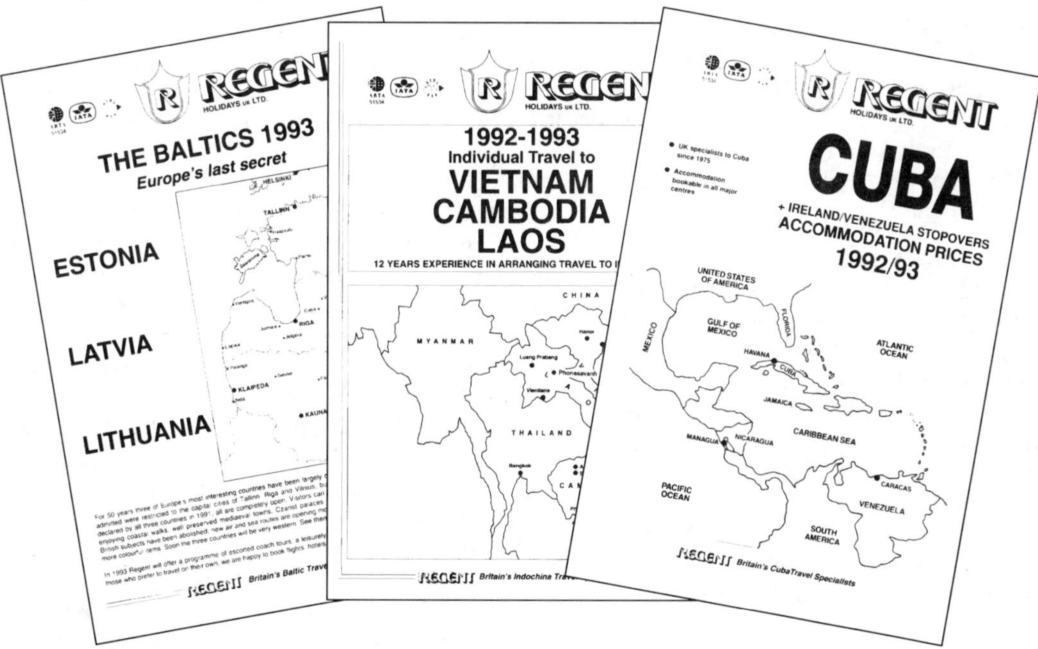

Fig. 1.10 A selection of Regent Holidays' brochures
Courtesy: Regent Holidays

INCOMING TOUR OPERATORS

Incoming (or inbound) tour operators differ from domestic operators in that they handle arrangements inside a country for tourists coming from elsewhere. So in the UK, incoming tour operators put together tours of Britain for visitors from overseas. Sometimes incoming operators are called inbound tour operators or ground handlers.

Incoming operators offer a range of services which may include:

- a 'meet and greet' service for people arriving at airports or other termini
- negotiating with coach companies and hoteliers
- organising excursions
- specialist services, e.g. catering for the needs of the UK's Japanese visitors

From the point of view of the overseas purchaser, using an incoming operator avoids problems with language, different laws and cultures, etc. It also means that all the arrangements can be paid for in one go instead of having to be billed as separate items.

In the early 1980s the UK had about 300 incoming operators. Few of them are household names because they sell their products through the overseas travel trade. Most of them were dealing with cultural tours and courses for foreign language students. Roughly a quarter of them are members of the British Incoming Tour Operators Association (BITOA). Some of the UK's incoming tour operators who are also members of BITOA are:

Albatross Travel Group	Queensberry Travel Service
British Rail International	Quest International Tours
Evans Evans Tours Ltd	Redwing Coaches
Golden Gateway Travel	Travelsave Tours
Holiday Club Pontin	World Link Travel
Jet Travel	
London Handling	

British overseas tour operators often work very closely with foreign incoming tour operators who also act as ground handling agents.

A closer look at Albatross Incoming Tours

Set up in 1985, Albatross is owned by an Austrian and an Australian and has three branches, two in the UK and one in Salzburg. Albatross Tours offers Continental coach packages to UK and overseas operators; Albatross Incoming Tours (based in a converted church) offers tours of the UK and Ireland to domestic and overseas operators; and Albatross Salzburg handles conference and incentive travel, and ground handling services for incoming operators to Austria. Director Erich Sibermayr previously worked in hotels and ground handling for incoming operators. Albatross handles about 3,000 group bookings a year, an increasing number of them from ex-Eastern bloc countries, and now employs 18 full-time staff, taking on extra help over the high season. It places great emphasis on high standards of customer care, carefully inspecting all hotels they feature and constantly looking for possible new products.

INDEPENDENT CONTRACTORS AND PRODUCER-OWNED COMPANIES

Apart from this categorisation of operators into four broad types, it is also possible to subdivide them into two main blocks: those which are completely independent entities, free to negotiate contracts with whichever producers they see fit; and those which are owned by the producers of one component of their packages and therefore have much less room for manoeuvre, the packages being intended to sell the company's surplus capacity. All the UK's biggest operators are independent contractors, although it could be argued that some have become less independent as they have become more vertically integrated and, therefore, more concerned to fill their own aircraft seats (*see* page 63). However, some of the traditional producer-owned companies also generate considerable business. Among them are:

Product name	*Producer company*
British Airways Holidays	British Airways
Goldenrail/Superbreak	British Rail
Wallace Arnold	Wallace Arnold Coaches

BRITISH AIRWAYS	**BRITISH AIRWAYS HOLIDAYS**
AIR FRANCE	**AIR FRANCE HOLIDAYS**
IBERIA	**MUNDI COLOR**

Fig. 1.11 Examples of airline-owned tour operating companies

With the exception of Hoverspeed, P&O European Ferries and Sally Line, all the companies operating ferries out of the UK also offer their own extensive holiday programmes, with Stena Sealink's being the largest. Hotels, too, often operate their own holiday programmes, although the tougher bonding requirements of the 1993 EC Package Travel Regulations may persuade some of the smaller ones to drop out of the market.

A closer look at the ferry-owned operations

In 1993, both Hoverspeed and P&O European Ferries sold their holiday operating arms to Travelscene, preferring to concentrate on offering transportation and to let specialist operators handle the business of creating inclusive tours based on their sailings. P&O, in particular, believed it was better to concentrate its efforts on fighting off competition from the Channel Tunnel, and suspected it would probably obtain the same amount of package-holiday trade through other companies which already used its crossings. In 1994, Travelscene sold P&O Holidays on to the Bridge Group and scrapped Hoverspeed European Holidays altogether. In 1992 Sally Line had handed its tour operating side to Novotours, but when that collapsed it resumed running Sally Holidays itself, only to sell it on again, this time to Keycamps, in 1993.

Most of the other large-scale ferry operators out of the UK continue to run their own tour packages (usually short breaks or ski-drive holidays), regarding this as a way of encouraging sales of off-peak capacity. Britanny Ferries, one of the first ferry companies to offer inclusive tours as well as simple sailings, calculates that 18 per cent of its passengers have bought one of its own package holidays and is increasing the scope of its programmes. Stena Sealink, Color Line and Scandinavian Seaways all believe their packages are profitable and bring in extra traffic. In the case of the long-sea-crossing carriers, producing their own holidays is a particularly good idea because in a pooled brochure featuring holidays with short-sea-crossing carriers, their prices (which have to cover overnight accommodation) tend to look uncompetitively high.

Difficulties for ferry companies wanting to double-up as tour operators include:

a) lack of specialist expertise
b) in Sally's case, a limited range of possible routes – Stena Sealink probably does well because it has crossings to many more ports
c) the increasing need to concentrate all financial and marketing resources on fighting off the threat posed by the Channel Tunnel
d) the general traffic-depressing impact of the recession
e) difficulty in persuading travel agents to rack their holiday brochures

In 1993/4 ski-drive packages seemed hardest to sell, and both North Sea and Brittany Ferries withdrew their programmes. At the same time, however, Stena Sealink chose to launch a new ski-drive programme, arguing that it would help boost sales in the January/February low season lull.

THE MARKET

The UK has roughly 38 million people between the ages of 4 and 65 who are potential holidaymaking clients for tour operators. By 1990 the average full-time manual worker had four weeks annual paid holiday, and 27 per cent of the workforce had five weeks. However, the recession of the early 1990s squeezed many families' net disposable income, with a detrimental effect on the numbers actually taking holidays. In 1988 12.6 million overseas package holidays were sold, but since then the number

Table 1.5 1985–90 Purpose of overseas holiday visits

Purpose of visit	*1985*	*1986*	*1987*	*1988*	*1989*	*1990*
Inclusive tour	8.5	10.7	12.0	12.6	12.6	11.4
Other holidays	6.4	7.2	7.7	8.1	9.3	9.9
Visiting friends & relatives	2.6	2.7	3.1	3.2	3.5	3.9
Total holidays:	17.5	20.6	22.8	23.9	25.4	25.2

Table 1.6 UK Residents' leisure travel – purpose of visit, 1990

Purpose of visit	*No. of visits*		*No. of days*		*Spending*	
	(billions)	*percentage*	*(billions)*	*percentage*	*(£bn)*	*percentage*
Holidays	21.3	84	261.4	78	6.8	88
Visiting friends & relatives	4.0	16	74.1	22	0.9	12
Total	25.2	100	335.5	100	7.7	100

Table 1.7 Average overseas holiday expenditure by UK residents 1990

Purpose of visit	*Spend per visit (£)*	*Average length of stay (days)*	*Spend per day (£)*
Holidays	320.1	12.3	26.1
Visiting friends & relatives	235.3	18.7	12.6
Overall average:	307.3	13.3	23.1

has been declining slowly. In 1990 11.4 million packages were sold, in 1991 only 10.5 million; of these as many as 2.5 million may have been 'flight-only' arrangements. But the overall number of holidays taken overseas has fallen far less dramatically and Table 1.6 shows how the number of independent holidays taken abroad continued to rise even after 1988 when the number of package holidays started to fall. This probably reflects the greater confidence of travellers who may have taken packages in the past but now feel ready to make their own arrangements.

There is some evidence to suggest that people now see holidays as a necessity rather than a discretionary product. Faced with a squeeze on their finances as a result of the recession, many seem to have reacted by reducing the length of their holiday, trading down to a cheaper product and taking less spending money with them rather than by going without altogether.

The potential UK holiday market splits into three slightly overlapping segments:

The youth market (16–30)

Young, unmarried people have the fewest commitments and therefore the highest level of discretionary income, worth perhaps £30 billion a year. However, during the early 1990s this age group was particularly badly affected by unemployment and low wages. The number of people in this age bracket is also shrinking; by 2000 the number of 16 to 24-year-olds is expected to have declined by 12 per cent.

The younger end of this age bracket includes the 'student' market – which usually takes its holidays in peak periods, may be able to spend more than two weeks away, but tends to have relatively little money. At the opposite end of the spectrum are those in their late twenties with good jobs and no children. These people are frequently high spenders, able to take their holidays at any time of year, perhaps travelling to long-haul destinations and taking several holidays or minibreaks a year.

Operators catering specifically for the youth

market include The Club, Twenties, and Contiki. Many of the overland tour companies also aim primarily for young people.

The family market (25–50)

This age group is the bedrock of the tour operating business, and most of the summer and winter sun brochures are aimed at it. The middle age bracket often has the highest level of actual income (perhaps £112 billion) but also the highest level of fixed outgoings in the form of mortgages, school fees, clothing for children, etc. They tend to take holidays to coincide with school holidays and will often be very price conscious, and happy to switch destinations from one to another if it's cheaper.

In 1993 the Henley Centre for Forecasting suggested that 66 per cent of families surveyed with children under five had cut down on their holiday expenditure in the preceding 12 months. This suggests there may be plenty of pent-up desire for holidays waiting to be met when the recession ends.

The 'Third Age' market (50 upwards)

The over-50s represent a huge amount of potential spending power (perhaps £108 billion), largely because they have often waved goodbye to their children and paid off mortgages and other financial commitments. In addition, the over-50s hold 70 per cent of all savings, may benefit from matured insurance policies and may inherit up to £8 billion a year. An increasing number of over-50s are taking early retirement and/or may benefit from occupational pensions. This is a growth market: during the 1990s the number of over-50s will increase by 9 per cent; by 2001 they will have increased by 31 per cent, while the number of people in their late 50s will have risen by 15 per cent; by 2027 over-55s may make up as much as 33 per cent of the population. Over-50s can usually take their holidays at any time of the year and are responsible for 43 per cent of all tourism expenditure. This is the only age group which still takes more holidays at home than abroad.

Nevertheless, the market divides into those who are relatively young and healthy and those at the extreme end of the age scale who may be prevented from taking holidays by age and/or infirmity. There is also considerable poverty in this age group, especially among those who retired before 1979 and who live alone on a state pension in rented accommodation. Car ownership and usage also declines as people age.

The biggest company specialising in holidays for senior citizens is direct-sell Saga Holidays. However, most of the large operators have their own specialist products, often featuring long-stay winter holidays in warmer countries where the cost of the holiday will not be much more than the cost of staying at home and paying heating bills. Coach tours and lakes and mountains holidays are also particularly popular with the older age group.

THE RELATIONSHIP BETWEEN TOUR OPERATORS AND TRAVEL AGENCIES

Ninety per cent of overseas package holidays from the UK are sold through British travel agencies which can be viewed as a distribution system for an intangible product. When a travel agent agrees to sell a tour operator's products, an *agency agreement* will be drawn up, setting out the formal relationship between the two sides. The travel agent then becomes an official agent of the tour operator and is paid commission in return for their services. The average payment will be about 10 per cent of the holiday cost, although bigger travel agencies with more muscle are often able to secure bigger payments ('overrides') for bulk sales.

Until the end of 1993, the 1965 Stabiliser agreement (*see* page 40), ensured that ABTA tour operators were only able to sell their products through ABTA travel agencies. However, even then it was never the case that all ABTA travel agents stocked the brochures of all ABTA tour operators. Now, with more than 7,000 travel agencies in the UK, it would be prohibitively expensive for operators to even think of supplying all of them with brochures and sales support. Different agencies also vary enormously in their productivity, so that perhaps 80 per cent of bookings might be coming from 20 per cent of agents. Only the biggest operators, therefore, have intensive distribution systems covering most of the agencies. Smaller ones go for selective distribution to particularly productive agents instead.

Increasingly, agents also pick and choose which operators' products they want to sell. In the mid-1970s, most travel agencies stocked the brochures of most tour operators. However, as more and more companies were formed in the 1980s it became unrealistic to think any one agent could know the contents of all the brochures. Since agents also earned higher levels of commission from companies for whom they made a lot of sales, the biggest travel agency chains began to narrow down the number of operators with whom they made sales agreements. For example, by 1994 the largest branches of Thomas Cook racked no more than 500 different brochures, and most effort went into selling the products of just 35 'premium' suppliers who qualified for preferential treatment in racking position, etc. In the aftermath of the shake-up caused by the EC Package Travel Regulations, the Stabiliser agreement was abandoned, allowing travel agents even greater flexibility over which brochures they choose to stock.

To enable travel agents to sell their products, tour operators have to supply them with regular brochure deliveries and an efficient reservations system. Traditionally, larger tour operators also employed field sales representatives to visit the travel agencies which sold their products, to check they were receiving brochures and to supply point of sales materials, window displays, etc. The sales reps also handled any queries the agents had and sometimes arranged training sessions for them as well. However, in April 1993 Owners Abroad axed its field sales team, followed in May 1993 by Thomson who decided to concentrate their resources on the biggest agents by supplying them with individual account managers to handle any problems. Smaller agencies' problems are now dealt with over the phone.

In 1986 72 per cent of holidays were booked through independent travel agencies. However, by 1993 that figure had fallen to 53 per cent as ownership of the largest multiple travel agencies became concentrated in the hands of the biggest tour operators (in 1994 nearly one-third of the 7,010 ABTA travel agencies were wholly or partially owned by tour operators). Thomson had owned the Lunn Poly chain since 1972 when it had relatively few branches. By 1994, however, Lunn Poly was by far the largest multiple agency, with 714 branches countrywide controlling 25 per cent of the retail market. Although it continued to sell a range of tour operators' products, smaller agencies and operators were increasingly anxious that it might decide to sell only Thomson holidays. In 1992, Airtours bought the Pickfords chain of 325 travel agencies (now renamed Going Places), then controlling 10 per cent of the retail market; sales of Airtours' packages through Pickfords shot up by 34 per cent after the company started paying Pickfords' staff a £3 bonus for every Airtours booking they made. In May 1993 Thomson retaliated by offering Lunn Poly counter staff £3 and branch managers £1 for every Thomson booking they made.

British travel agents sell a range of products developed by different, competing tour operators. To encourage individual agents to sell their particular products, smaller tour operators sometimes offer incentives like Marks and Spencer vouchers with every sale. They also provide thanks and encouragement to travel agents by offering discounted holidays (often two for the price of one) and educational trips for their staff. However, in 1994 there were signs of operators taking a more aggressive approach, offering agencies higher commission if they would agree not to rack rival products.

The importance of the link between operators and agents was highlighted in late 1993 when it was the 10 per cent discounting policy sparked off by Thomas Cook and picked up by the other multiples that led to a rush of early bookings for summer 1994. Such big price cuts were possible because the multiples are able to negotiate commissions of more than 10 per cent and can pass part of their sales commission on to the public in discounts. In any case, most such discounts depend on the client buying the agency's own travel insurance, offering hefty sales commission, meaning that insurance sales often effectively subsidise cuts in holiday prices.

In general, the working relationship between tour operators and travel agents is a happy one. However, policies that may suit one side of the equation aren't always so convenient for the other. For example, the combined efforts of operators and agents to reverse the trend towards late booking by offering incentives for early bookers brought about a rush of early bookings for summer 1994 when agents were still trying to handle late bookings for the summer 1993 and advance bookings for winter 1993/4 (i.e. they ended up handling three seasons simultaneously). Agents frequently complain about operators' price cutting tactics as well, since these can lead to their earning less commission on more work.

DIRECT SELL TOUR OPERATIONS

Although most tour operators make the majority of their sales through travel agencies, some, particularly specialist operators, still prefer to deal directly with the public. In 1990, 19 per cent of inclusive tours were sold without travel agents acting as intermediaries, but by 1994 this figure had fallen to 14 per cent of the total. By dealing directly with the public, operators are able to save the average 10 per cent commission they would have paid the travel agent for making the booking. In theory this cost saving can then be passed on to the customer. However, without the 'shop window' of High Street travel agencies to bring their product to the public's attention, direct sell operators are obliged to spend more on advertisements and other publicity to get their message across. What's more, in the 1990s travel agencies used heavy discounting to attract early bookers in a sluggish market; by doing this they tended to undercut the price advantages direct sell operators could offer. It also seems that most clients who want to make a telephone booking prefer to call a local travel agent.

Direct sell operators are not always completely separate from the companies using travel agencies. Among the best-known, Portland Holidays, for example, is part of the Thomson group, while Eclipse Direct (previously Tjaereborg, Sunfare and Martin Rooks) is part of First Choice.

Companies can move from being entirely direct sell to retailing through agencies too. For example, after Seasun, a direct sell operator set up in 1979, bought Tentrek which dealt through agencies in 1989, the combined company Seasun Tentrek steadily built up its agency sales, before going into liquidation in 1993. In 1994, 45 specialist operators who had not previously sold their products through travel agencies signed agreements to do so with agents selected to be members of a new AITO 100 Club.

The relationship between tour operators and national tourist offices (NTOs)

Tour operators often work hand-in-glove with the national tourist offices whose promotional efforts supplement their own. For example, when a national tourist office runs a high-profile national television or newspaper advertising campaign, companies with programmes to that country can expect to pick up extra bookings (*see* Chapter Nine). Conversely where there is no national tourist office, operators may have an uphill struggle to get across the message that the country is worth visiting. Until 1993, for example, Indonesia didn't have a UK tourist office and operators found it hard to interest the public in venturing beyond Bali. National tourist offices are also a useful source of information and contacts for operators interested in starting up a new programme. Without such an office their work may be made much harder.

Occasionally, however, a national tourist office can actually stand in the way of an operator's plans. This happened in 1993 when Airtours produced a dedicated Cayman Islands brochure, only to have the tourist office reject the idea of charter flights to the Islands. (After considerable adverse publicity, the tourist office rescinded its objections.)

The relationship between the tour operator and the public

When a holidaymaker buys a package holiday from a tour operator he/she enters into a contract with that tour operator regardless of whether he/she made the purchase through the intermediary of a travel agent or not. This means that it is the tour operator rather than the travel agent to whom he/she will have to turn for redress if something goes wrong with the holiday. He/she must also turn to the tour operator even when the principal is at fault: for example, if there is no room available for the holidaymaker in the hotel he/she had booked, he/she will need to sue the tour operator responsible for arranging the room rather than the hotelier.

SETTING UP A TOUR OPERATING COMPANY

Setting up a new tour operating company is relatively easy because:

a) no specific licences are required to set up in business, although an Air Travel Organiser's Licence (ATOL) will be necessary before the operator can start selling its own air packages.
b) no stock is required because of the unique nature of the product on sale (*see* above)

Starting a new tour operating company can be seen as a creative business requiring imagination and strong nerves, so it has tended to attract entrepreneurial characters with strong personalities, most of them men. Among the best known are Harry Goodman (founder of ILG and Intasun), Freddie Laker (whose Skytrain Holidays evolved out of his original transatlantic Skytrain business), Roland Castro (who set up Time Off), Vic Fatah (founder of Sunmed and managing director of Inspirations) and Noel Josephides (ex-Chair of AITO and managing director of Sunvil Holidays).

Company ownership

Behind the household names of some of the UK's biggest operators can lie big international companies, often based overseas. The parent company can lend financial backing for advance payments, etc., which can then be repaid when cash starts to flow later in the season. Being part of a larger organisation also allows for economies of scale and therefore for lower prices and greater competition.

The spate of tour operator failures in the early 1990s and increasing uncertainty about ABTA's future make being part of a bigger group which can offer greater security a key selling point. However, companies remain surprisingly coy about admitting their exact ownership – which often turns out to be international. This is what some of them said in their 1993 and 1994 brochures:

> COSMOS
> 'As part of a large international travel group . . .'
>
> NEILSON
> 'Neilson is part of Iberotravel Ltd, a company within a major international organisation specialising in tourism.'

In comparison, Inghams is refreshingly open:

> . . . Inghams is part of Swiss-owned Hotelplan International, one of Europe's largest and most respected holiday companies with offices throughout the continent and in all main countries of operation. Hotelplan, in turn, is the holiday subsidiary of MIGROS, one of Switzerland's largest and most successful companies employing over 50,000 people and generating an annual turnover in excess of £5 billion.'

THE MARKETPLACE FOR TOUR OPERATIONS

In Great Britain in the 1990s the concept of the **free market** as the perfect business environment held sway. In this free market, competition was believed to lead both to benefits for consumers and to greater efficiency and therefore greater profits for businesses. In theory, businesses should operate within a perfect market with the following features:

- There are a large number of competing organisations.
- Each business produces only a small proportion of the industry's total output.
- There are no barriers preventing entry to the market.
- Because all the organisations are producing the same goods or services there is no need for branding or advertising.
- Both producers and consumers are assumed to have a perfect knowledge of the market.

In fact, tour operators function in a marketplace characterised by **oligopoly**, with a small number of companies controlling much of the supply of holidays. Indeed, in the late 1980s and early 1990s, the growth of these companies through mergers and changes of ownership raised fears that a true monopoly situation might be emerging. A **monopoly** exists when:

- there is only one business organisation
- its demand curve matches the industry's demand curve
- the business is able to set prices for the market
- barriers prevent new, competing businesses from entering the market

- there is little need for branding or advertising because the firm is producing a single product.

Monopolies are seen as undesirable because, without competition, a company is in a position to increase prices and otherwise act against the consumer's interest if it thinks it can increase its profits by so doing. To guard against this, the Fair Trading Act of 1973 arrived at a definition of a monopoly which could be used as a practical test and created the Monopolies and Mergers Commission (MMC) to investigate potential monopolies. According to the Fair Trading Act a monopoly exists when:

- a business has or is likely to have control of 25 per cent of a specific market, or
- the total assets of the merged organisation exceed £5 million.

This sort of monopoly is called a 'scale monopoly'. A 'complex monopoly' exists when:

- at least 25 per cent of a particular type of goods or services is supplied by two or more unconnected companies or groups of companies who, intentionally or otherwise, conduct their affairs in such a way that they prevent, distort or restrict competition in the supply of goods or services.

If, after a MMC investigation, a business is found to be operating as a monopoly, the Secretary of State for Trade and Industry can order actions to change the situation. He or she would usually justify this by claiming that the monopoly situation worked against the general public interest.

Horizontal and vertical integration

In the 1980s, the biggest tour operators consolidated their position in the market by a process of **horizontal** and **vertical integration** with other travel companies. Vertical integration takes place when two companies at different levels on the chain of distribution (*see* page 2) merge; *backward integration* takes place when the tour operator buys companies which contribute to its packages, whereas *forward integration* occurs when it buys companies at the retail level (*see* Fig. 1.12). In travel, vertical integration has been a way for tour operators to gain control both of the individual components of their packages and of their sales outlets. In contrast, horizontal integration takes place when two companies on the same level of the chain of distribution merge. In travel this has often allowed a strong company to swallow up weaker competition.

1. Vertical integration

Thomson Holidays began the integration process in 1972 when it was formed out of an amalgamation of Universal Skytours, Riviera Holidays, Gay Tours and Luxitours. Lord Thomson had already bought Britannia Airways which became part of the same company, ensuring that the new holiday company had guaranteed control over a source of flight seats (by 1992 Britannia supplied flight seats for 80 per cent of Thomson holidays). At the same time Lord Thomson also bought Lunn Poly, then a small chain of retail travel agents, now the largest chain of all. In doing so he also guaranteed a source of sales outlets for Thomson Holidays which now had a grip on all three levels of the chain of distribution: namely a principal, a wholesale division and a retail outlet.

During the 1980s the biggest tour operators gradually gained control over the charter airlines, which are sometimes called 'holiday airlines' in consequence. Thomson now owns Britannia Airways, First Choice owns Air 2000, Airtours owns Airtours International and Cosmos owns Monarch. The charter airlines started out with a cheap and cheerful image, but standards of service on the wholly-owned airlines have tended to improve since they reflect on the image of the tour operator: in-flight meals are getting better and increasingly several classes of service are available as on scheduled airlines.

Tour operators have preferred buying charter airlines to buying hotels. In the 1970s Clarksons did buy some hotels but wasn't able to manage them profitably. This was problematic because it hadn't separated out the hotel management side of the business from the general tour packaging side with the result that losses from the hotels dragged down the profits from packaging. At the same time Thomson also bought up hotels in Tunisia, Spain and Malta but managed them under a separate overseas hotel development division. Even so, Thomson soon pulled out of hotel management, believing it to be a task best left to experts; in the 1990s Thomson preferred to work closely with favoured hoteliers rather than own hotels outright

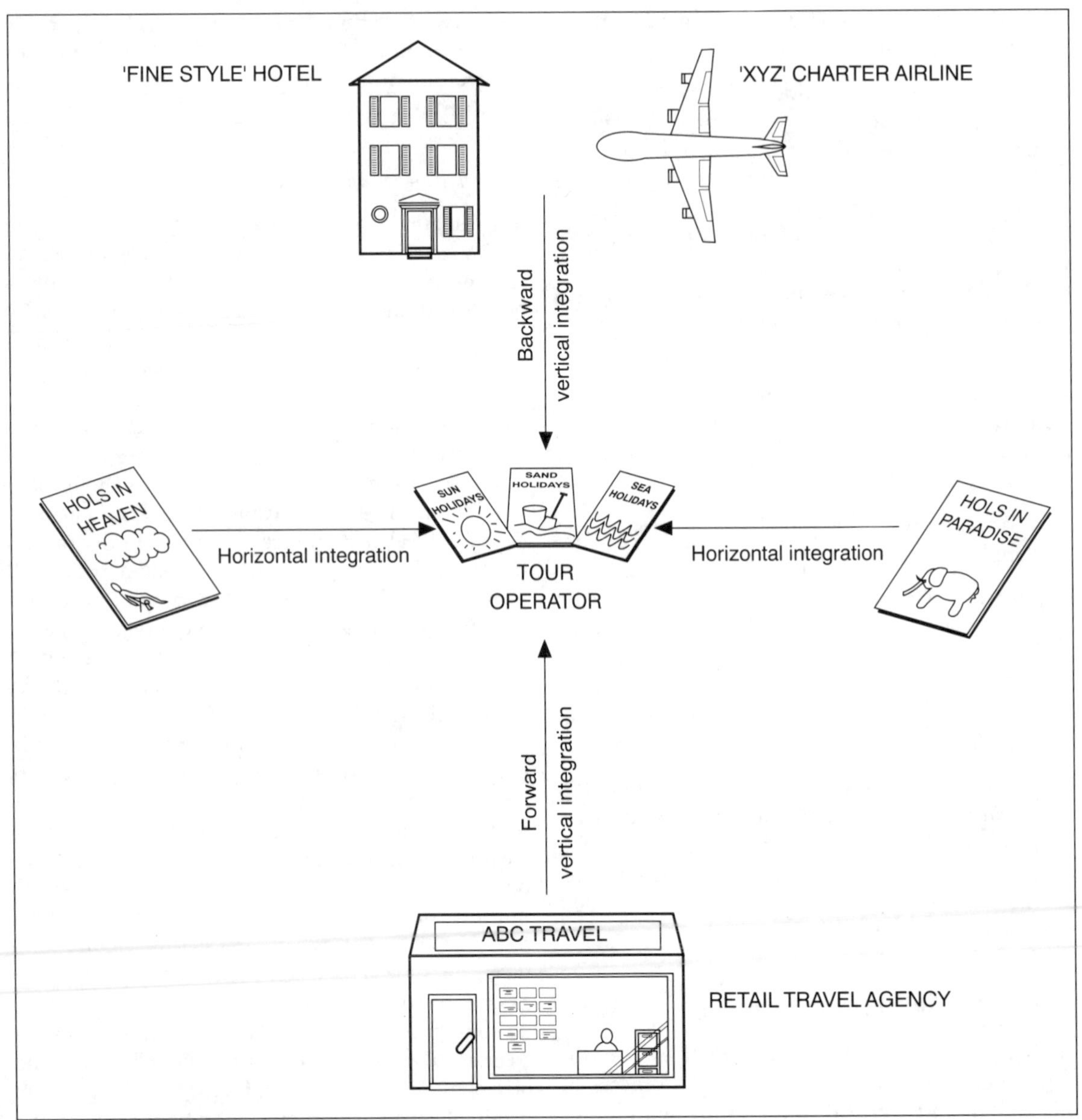

Fig. 1.12 How integration works in the travel business

(*see* page 62). However, in 1993, rapidly-expanding Airtours decided to invest £10 million in eight hotels in Majorca, Portugal, Spain and other year-round European holiday destinations. A special hotel division was set up to handle the new purchases. In general, the industry continued to believe that buying hotels was dangerous because of their non-transferability; although it gave them control over every aspect of the package, there was always a risk that a destination would fall from favour, leaving the operator with hard-to-fill hotels and apartment blocks. In contrast, charter flights can always be re-routed away from unpopular destinations to those which are more fashionable.

Although the Thomson Travel Group has never given Lunn Poly a monopoly on sales of its package holidays, the rest of the industry has lived in fear of this, and in 1992 Airtours bought the

Pickfords travel agency chain, thus ensuring a secure sales outlet for its own holidays. Airtours, too, had its own airline, Airtours International, and so, once again, a market leader had control of all three levels of its chain of distribution. In 1993, in the face of this development, Owners Abroad (owners of Air 2000) arranged a tie-up with Thomas Cook which ensured all three of the largest tour operators owned their own airline and had a formal link with one of the largest retail travel agency chains. However, in the case of the Owners Abroad–Thomas Cook tie-up, which left Owners Abroad controlling 21.4 per cent of Thomas Cook, this was not complete vertical integration because the operator had not obtained complete control of the retail outlet. In 1993 Airtours also purchased the Hogg Robinson leisure travel business, acquiring another 214 travel agency outlets to add to the 334 Pickfords branches. (The Hogg Robinson and Pickfords chain have been renamed Going Places.)

A smaller but expanding tour operator, Inspirations, had tried to buy Pickfords before Airtours did. In 1993 it announced a deal with AT Mays, the travel agency chain with strong representation in the north of the UK. In a variation on normal vertical integration, it agreed to buy 100 agencies which would be franchised as AT Mays shops in return for a guarantee that all Inspirations brochures would be given rack space as a preferred operator. The company hoped that this deal would enable it to protect its distribution outlets in a way that would not alarm other agents who also stocked its brochures. In 1993 Inspirations also bought air seat broker Goldcrest to provide itself with a stake in the aviation business too.

In 1993 the Office of Fair Trading set up an inquiry into the implications of increased vertical integration in the travel industry. Its task became all the more urgent when Owners Abroad attributed a large part of a slump in profits to the increased sales of Thomson holidays through Lunn Poly and of Airtours products through Pickfords – as both companies offered agents cash incentives to switch-sell to their products.

2. Horizontal integration

The process of integration has also proceeded horizontally, with large tour operators buying up other tour operators to improve their market share and reduce competition. In 1981 the Rank Organisation bought out OSL/Wings and in 1983 Owners Abroad bought Falcon Holidays. In 1989 Thomson Holidays purchased the Horizon Travel Group and Owners Abroad added Tjaereborg to its portfolio. In 1989 Owners Abroad also bought Sunward Holidays, adding Redwing (Enterprise, Sovereign and Martyn Holidays) in 1989. At the end of 1992, Airtours, the UK's third largest tour operator, made a bid to take over Owners Abroad, its second largest, a bid which was rejected by Owners Abroad shareholders. In 1993 Airtours bought out both Aspro and Tradewinds.

When looking for similar companies to buy, tour operators have not always restricted their sights to the UK. For example, in 1994 Owners Abroad announced that its latest acquisition would be International Travel Holdings, the largest tour operating company in Canada, with a 25 per cent share of the Canadian IT market. In choosing ITH, Owners argued that it had selected a company whose peak season coincided with the UK low season, thus helping the company's year-round cash flow. ITH specialises in Caribbean holidays and Owners Abroad could also use its expertise to help in expanding its own long-haul interests. In 1994, Airtours also acquired SAS Leisure, Scandinavia's biggest tour operating company.

In theory, horizontal integration leads to economies of scale (for example, in functions like personnel and purchasing) and thus to cost savings and price reductions. The cost savings may also enable a company to become more competitive, allowing it to develop a better range of products for its clients and to achieve better quality control over its products. The buy-out may also reinforce its corporate image in the public mind. However, the Airtours bid for Owners Abroad raised worries that the end result would leave two giant companies, Thomson and the newly expanded Airtours, holding such a large share of the holiday market that they would form a virtual duopoly, with enormous power to manipulate prices. Although the Monopolies and Mergers Commission (MMC) had not objected to Thomson's buy-out of Horizon, the Office of Fair Trading advised that the Airtours bid for Owners Abroad should still be referred to the MMC. As grounds, it argued that the merger would be anti-competitive, giving a single company control of between 25 and 30 per cent of the market.

However, Trade and Industry Secretary Michael Heseltine rejected this advice and the merger only failed to go ahead because Owners Abroad shareholders preferred the offer made by Thomas Cook.

By 1993, however, there were sufficient concerns over the consequences of increased vertical integration in the travel industry for the Office of Fair Trading to launch an inquiry. However, in 1994 OFT concluded that no action needed to be taken since holiday prices had not risen significantly and consumers still had plenty of choice.

The consequences of increased vertical integration in the travel business

In 1993, it was too early to know what the long-term consequences of increased vertical integration in the travel industry would be. However, there were already some clues:

- Owners Abroad claimed that it had lost a significant amount of its trade through Lunn Poly, Pickfords and Hogg Robinson after all three travel agency chains started offering staff financial incentives to switch-sell to products of their parent companies.
- Smaller operators were increasingly anxious that they would lose rack space in travel agencies as the multiples concentrated their attentions on the products of their owner companies and of their 'preferred' operators. For example, in 1993 Lunn Poly only had arrangements to sell the products of 147 ABTA tour operators (out of a total 746). What's more, an average Lunn Poly Holiday Shop actually stocked the brochures of about 80 operators. Even more crucially, up to a fifth of the rack space in a typical shop was devoted to Thomson products which also had the best eye-level positions on the shelves. In 1993 Thomas Cook had a 'premier selection' scheme, encompassing 30 tour operators, some of whose products were overbranded with a 'Thomas Cook Holidays' logo. Shortly after the tie-up with Owners Abroad was completed, Thomas Cook announced that it would be replacing Sunworld as its 'Thomas Cook Summer Sun' supplier with Enterprise, an Owners Abroad product (Falcon Flights and Sovereign were already overbranded as 'Thomas Cook' products). In 1993 the Association of Independent Tour Operators discussed levying its members to pay for its own shop to showcase members' products, fearing that otherwise most of them would be squeezed out of agencies altogether. Instead, it decided to create the AITO 100 Club, an elite group of agencies which would stock members' brochures.
- The stronger the grip the multiple agencies have on the market, the stronger their ability to dictate the commission levels operators must pay to guarantee themselves rack space. By 1989, operators wanting to sell through Lunn Poly generally had to agree to pay 15 or 16 per cent commission instead of the industry average of 10 per cent. In a complex agreement to safeguard its position in 1994, Cosmos was believed to have agreed to pay 15 per cent commission to 45 agencies during the peak booking months of September, October, January and February provided they would publicise 10 per cent discounts off its holidays. Inevitably, it is hard for smaller operators to increase their commission levels without putting up their prices and reducing their competitiveness in relation to bigger operators with greater ability to absorb price increases.
- From the consumer's point of view, there were fears that:
  a) they would be given biased information without necessarily realising it, as travel agents increasingly tried to promote the products of their parent companies. In July 1993 Airtours responded to this criticism by positioning signs in all branches of Pickfords and Hogg Robinson (now Going Places) explaining that they were wholly owned by the operator. Lunn Poly and Thomas Cook were slow to follow suit.
  b) the holiday market would become less competitive, with small operators forced out of business by the difficulty of marketing their products, and independent travel agencies vanishing, unable to compete with the sales power and sometimes predatory behaviour of the multiples.

Why smaller operators continue to survive

In such difficult circumstances, the survival of so many small operators might seem surprising. However, these operators still offer benefits it is hard for their mass-market rivals to beat:

- Smaller companies often specialise in niches for which specific expertise is required. It would be hard, for example, for the mass-market operators to know as much about any one activity as a company which offers nothing but holidays featuring that activity.
- Smaller companies may also handle parts of the world (much of Africa, South America and Eastern Europe) perceived as too 'difficult' to be worth the larger companies' while.
- Smaller companies are often able to build on a reputation for quality and exclusiveness. Some holidaymakers who wouldn't dream of buying a Thomson or Airtours package will nevertheless buy those of smaller companies they regard as more select.
- Because they are dealing with a smaller number of customers, smaller companies may be able to offer a more personal service, in some cases even producing newsletters for past clients.

THE TOUR OPERATING COMPANY

Tour operating companies vary enormously in size. Some consist of just half a dozen staff looking after all the different functions, from choosing the destinations to preparing the brochures, themselves. However, companies like Thomson, Airtours and First Choice are vast and divide into two separate divisions, one based in the UK, the other distributed round the destinations they feature.

The UK-based division deals with:

- brochure production
- holiday reservations
- product promotion
- financial matters
- personnel
- day-to-day administration
- payments to overseas staff, hoteliers, airlines, etc.
- correspondence to do with holidays

The overseas-based division deals with:

- day-to-day running of the holidays
- actioning the flight and room manifests
- looking after clients while they're abroad
- liaising with hoteliers, ground handling agents, etc.
- arranging and selling excursions
- running any overseas office
- liaising with the UK head office

The make up of a large tour operating company

The managing director

The managing director co-ordinates the various parts of the company. Ultimately all heads of department report to the managing director.

The accounts department

A financial controller or company accountant is usually in charge of the accounts department which has responsibility for recording all financial dealings for payments within the UK and for foreign currency payments overseas; controlling the flow of cash in and out; making approved payments; and monitoring the overall financial position. The accounts department will receive:

a) holiday deposits made at the time of booking – usually about 10 per cent of the total cost
b) balance payments usually paid about eight weeks before the holiday is due to commence, or at the time of booking in the case of a late booking
c) insurance premiums paid at the time of booking
d) any financial support for promotions, for example, from national tourist offices
e) revenue from sales of ancillary products like travel bags and videos

From these takings the accounts department will have to pay for:

a) operational costs for flights, accommodation, transfers, excursions, etc.
b) salaries
c) office costs – rent, heat, light, etc.
d) communication costs – telephones, fax, telex, etc.
e) computer costs – maintenance/support, paper, etc.
f) sales expenses, e.g. for the brochure
g) promotional and advertising costs
h) travel agents' commission on sales
i) costs of running overseas activities
j) recruitment costs – advertisements, etc.
k) training
l) staff uniforms, etc.

Most of the operational costs are paid through an

agent. For example, airlines are often paid for flight seats through an air broker.

The administration department

The administration department handles all the background paperwork and office functions, including:

a) staffing the reception and switchboard
b) looking after office maintenance, cleaning, etc.
c) providing secretarial services, often for all the other departments
d) making sure stationery stocks are maintained
e) looking after the telephones, faxes, telexes, word processors, personal computers and other office machinery
f) handling the post
g) despatching documents to clients
h) sending computer printouts (flight manifests, rooming lists, tickets, etc.) to the relevant departments

In the largest companies the computer may be running 24 hours a day, seven days a week, and shiftwork will be required to staff it. Sometimes a separate data processing department looks after everything to do with the computer.

The reservations department

The reservations department looks after *actual bookings* – processing them, liaising with accounts over payments, liaising with administration over documentation and dealing with all queries and changes to holidays. Sometimes reservations may be a function of the administration or sales and marketing departments.

The sales and marketing department

The sales and marketing department is responsible for developing and promoting the tour operator's product. In order to generate sales it must develop a product to suit its clients' needs, produce and distribute a suitable brochure, promote the overall product and liaise with travel agents to encourage sales. Its functions include:

a) carrying out product and market research
b) developing a suitable product
c) producing the brochure(s)
d) arranging despatch and distribution of the brochure(s)
e) organising promotions, including advertising and special events
f) co-ordinating agency sales, providing sales reps, etc.

The overseas department

The overseas manager is in charge of recruiting, training and placing the resort representatives. He/she also arranges staff uniforms and ensures smooth communications between the resorts and the UK.

The staff in the resorts are usually in weekly contact with the departments in the UK: with accounts to sort out invoices for payment and to get updates on costs; with administration for information on problems, to discuss client questionnaires, etc.; and with overseas to offer reports on flights, hotels, excursion sales, problems, etc.

Contracting of hotels and flight seats is usually a function of the overseas department, although Thomson now has a purchasing division to handle this. Overseas representatives may also provide pictures of accommodation for use in brochures and report on new resorts, hotels, etc.

Support services

Apart from the travel agents who sell their products, tour operators depend on a network of other support services as well. Some of these support services are provided by the private sector, others by the public sector (i.e. they are funded by local or central government).

Private sector support services

These include:

- Airports and ports
- Guide and timetable publishers
- Insurance companies
- Banks
- Travel trade press
- Guides
- 'Meet and greet' services
- Marketing companies
- Computer services

- Education and training services
- Property consultants/timeshare developers

Public sector support services

- Airports and ports
- Passport and visa offices
- Health and immunisation centres
- National tourist offices
- Regional tourist boards
- Tourist information centres
- Education and training providers

QUESTIONS AND DISCUSSION POINTS

1 Why did the number of tour operators increase so steeply during the 1980s?

2 What do you think would be the results of having two very large tour operators, both of them owning a chain of retail travel agencies, dominating the UK holiday market?

3 What advantages do you think specialist tour operators might offer over larger, more comprehensive companies? What disadvantages might they suffer from?

4 Find out the typical cost per head of a two week package holiday to Majorca in August. What other products might consumers choose to spend a similar sum of money on?

5 Look at the list of private and public sector support services and discuss the ways in which each of the listed services is of use to operators.

ASSIGNMENTS

1 You work for a small public relations company which has been asked to promote a local tour operator. Find one tour operator with an office in your locality. Collect copies of their brochure(s) and produce a chart analysing the product they are offering. Your chart should show whether they are overseas, domestic, incoming or specialist operators or a combination of several types.

2 Once you have done this, examine the brochure in more detail to find out which destinations are being featured. What market do you think the company is aiming for? What kind of transport to the destinations is being offered? Is the accommodation in hotels, self-catering apartments or something else? If the operator is specialising, what are they specialising in? Does the company have any unique selling points? Use the information you have collected to write a press release for local newspapers and magazines, drawing attention to the company. (Some information about writing press releases can be found on page 209.)

3 You are invited to talk about the company on local radio. You decide you need practise in radio interviewing techniques. In pairs, draw up a list of questions you might expect to be asked about the company and the answers you would like to give. Then record a practice interview to last no longer than five minutes.

CHAPTER 2

The development of tour operating as a business

LEARNING OBJECTIVES

After reading this chapter you should be able to:

- **list the factors necessary for the growth of a mass holiday market**
- **explain how the first tour operators went into business**
- **describe how the holiday market has developed and changed during the twentieth century**
- **explain the main features of the tour operating market in the first half of the 1990s**

INTRODUCTION

Although there have always been some travellers, the package holiday as we know it is a relatively recent innovation, dating back only as far as the latter half of the nineteenth century. Mass overseas holidaymaking is an even more recent phenomenon. Until the 1960s the number of people travelling abroad rose fairly slowly. Since then the expansion has been extraordinary.

Holidaymaking was slow to develop because its growth was dependent on a number of factors. According to Maslow's hierarchy of needs (*see* Fig. 2.1) people only consider luxuries like holidaymaking after their more fundamental needs have been met, so there could be no mass holidaymaking until the majority of people were adequately housed and fed, and had paid holidays, providing them with time and money to go away. An adequate transport and accommodation infrastructure also had to have evolved to make it possible for people to get away and stay away. There also had to be methods of carrying money abroad and agreements that people should be allowed to cross frontiers.

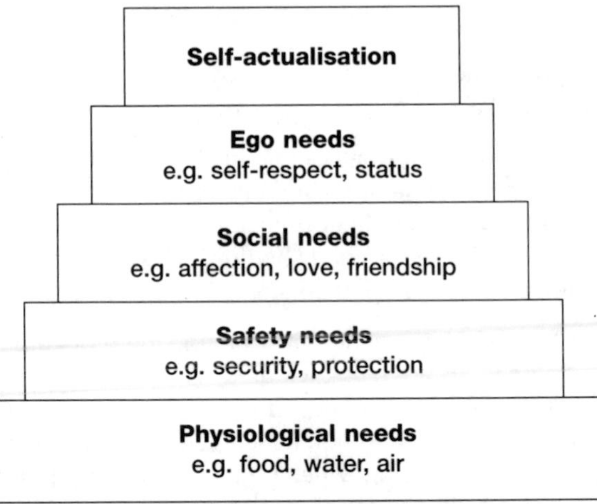

Fig. 2.1 Maslow's hierarchy of needs

HOW IT ALL BEGAN

Throughout history there have always been some travellers: soldiers, traders, pilgrims, nomads, etc. However, the concept of travel for travel's sake and the idea of holidays as times when you travelled away from home are relatively new ones. The word 'holiday' is derived from the medieval 'holy day', usually a saint's feast day when people might stop work to celebrate but when they normally stayed put in their villages. In the past people seem to have travelled because they had to. Today they do so because they want to.

The first people to have travelled for pleasure were, of course, the wealthy, who had the time and money to enjoy their leisure and put it to active use. In the seventeenth and eighteenth centuries the idea of the 'Grand Tour' evolved. The sons of the wealthy set off to explore the Continent, travelling through France and Italy and back via Switzerland, Germany, Austria and the Netherlands, sometimes taking five years to complete their trip. Their tours were seen as an extension of their education and they often travelled with a tutor who could help them study the history and languages of the countries through which they passed. The Grand Tour was about cultural exploration; lakes and mountains only belatedly appeared on itineraries, beaches never. It was only at the end of the eighteenth century that seaside resorts began to develop as a fashionable élite decided bathing in the sea and taking the sea air were healthy pastimes. Then the Napoleonic Wars at the end of the eighteenth century put an end to the Grand Tour by making Continental travel offputtingly dangerous.

By the end of the nineteenth century the increased trade stemming from the Industrial Revolution and the growth of the British Empire had led to a burgeoning middle class. The number of people with the time and money to travel for pleasure began to grow. Improvements in the road network and the development of the railways also provided the physical infrastructure necessary for travel to become a pleasure rather than a lengthy and much to be avoided ordeal.

Thomas Cook and the first package holidays

Thomas Cook is the man usually credited with creating the modern package holiday. Born into a poor Leicester family in 1808, he was a keen supporter of the British Temperance Movement which encouraged working people to drink less and become better educated with a view to improving their lives. Like so many of the men who have helped create the modern travel industry, Cook had an entrepreneurial spirit and an eye to the main chance. In 1841 he organised a day trip to a Temperance Society meeting in Loughborough. Six hundred people travelled to Loughborough in the open-topped carriages of the newly-opened Midland Railway on what is generally regarded as the first package tour, albeit a day trip: although no accommodation was needed, it did require a wholesaler (Thomas Cook) buying tickets from a principal (Midland Railway) and reselling them to get people to a specific event, just as operators today sell trips to football matches, etc.

In 1845 Cook decided to branch out on his own, selling tours for personal profit rather than to help

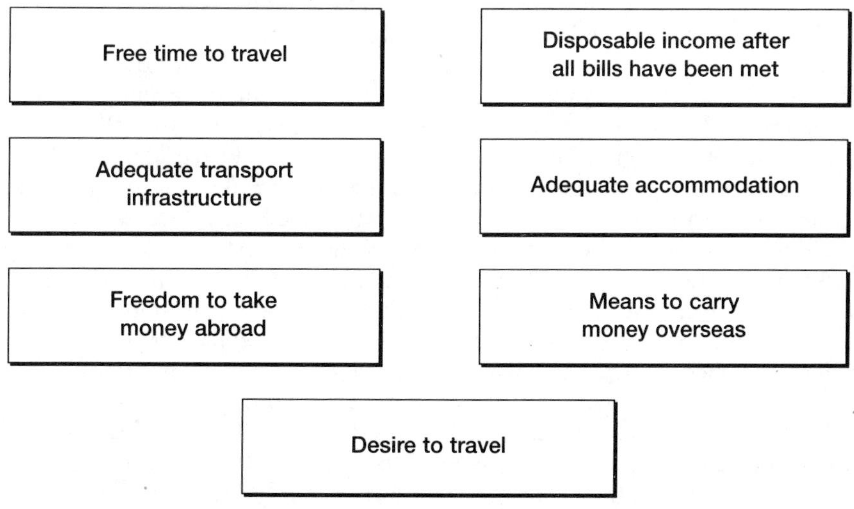

Fig. 2.2 Prerequisites for mass holidaymaking

the Temperance Movement. The tour he organised to Liverpool in 1845 incorporated more of the features of a modern package holiday. Cook produced a guidebook for the people travelling on his tour. He also arranged day trips to nearby attractions like Caernarvon Castle and Mount Snowdon. In those days travelling from Leicester to Liverpool involved using four different private railway companies, but Cook was able to buy all the necessary tickets and resell them with accommodation at all-inclusive prices. Later he chartered entire trains and travelled with his tourists, giving rise to the term a 'Cook's Tour'.

Over the next few years Cook went on to develop the idea of the 'circular ticket', an all-inclusive ticket from one destination to another, regardless of how many different railway companies might be used to travel between them. He persuaded most of the different railway companies to recognise his tickets and offer him discounts which he could then pass on to the client. Many of his excursions were to seaside towns which had been brought within day-trip reach of the big industrial towns by the railways. In 1851 he was also responsible for arranging for about 165,000 people to travel from the Midlands to the Crystal Palace in Hyde Park to see the Great Exhibition, a showcase for the best that British industry then had to offer.

Until the early 1860s, Thomas Cook restricted his activities to domestic tours and day trips, but his market was gradually cut from under him as the railway companies jumped on the bandwagon and started to withdraw his franchises and to run their own trips. In 1855, therefore, Cook offered an escorted tour from Harwich to the Hook of Holland, then down the Rhine to Strasbourg and back to Paris for the Great Exhibition there. He followed up this success by launching tours to Switzerland and the Bernese Oberland. By the 1860s, he was offering what would be recognisable as modern package holidays; escorted tours inclusive of rail and ferry travel and accommodation. Obviously these overseas tours were more expensive than the domestic ones, so whereas Cook had started out selling day trips to the working classes, he now moved into arranging holidays for the new middle classes, and particularly for women. Alongside the 'circular ticket' for train travel, Cook also developed the hotel coupon which could be used to pay for accommodation, and the 'circular note' which could be exchanged for foreign currency – the original travellers cheque.

From 1860 onwards, Thomas Cook himself played an increasingly backseat role, ceding the running of the family business to his son John Mason Cook who became his partner in 1864. In 1865 the Cooks moved from Leicester to London and set up shop at 98 Fleet Street, selling ancillary travel products like bags, telescopes and water purifiers to help cover the increased overheads. Above the shop, John Mason Cook also managed the Temperance Hotel. By now the family had started selling trips to the United States (for example, tours of the Civil War battlefields) from Liverpool and Glasgow. After the Suez Canal was opened in 1869 John Mason Cook also set up offices in Cairo and Alexandria to handle the traffic through Suez to the Far East. Egypt became a base for tours to Palestine, Lebanon, Syria and Iraq which involved rather upmarket camping. In 1872 the Cooks offered their first round the world tour which involved travelling across the Atlantic in a screw-driven and sail steamship, across the States by rail and stagecoach, across the Pacific to Japan by paddlesteamer, then on to China, Singapore, India and Ceylon, across the Indian Ocean to Aden, back up the Red Sea and Suez to Egypt and home via Brindisi.

In 1879 Thomas Cook retired and John Mason Cook took the business over completely. By then more and more people were travelling as the British Empire expanded. Many of Cook's passengers were what we would call business travellers but there were also many emigrants going in search of a new life in America or Australia. However, arranging travel around the world in the 1880s was a very different matter from what it is today. Alexander Graham Bell only invented the telephone in 1876 and there were no computers or faxes and only the simplest typewriters, making communication slow and tricky. To get round these difficulties John Mason Cook expanded the travel newspaper, *The Excursionist*, which his father had established in 1851, bringing out French, German, Indian and Australian editions describing what the company could do for its readers. *The Excursionist* was therefore a prototype brochure.

1808	Thomas Cook born in Melbourne, Derbyshire.
1818	Left school to become apprentice woodturner.
1828	Became Baptist missionary. In 1829, travelled 2,692 miles (2,106 of them on foot) around England.
1832	Married daughter of Rutland farmer and moved to Market Harborough as woodturner. Joined Temperance Movement and became secretary to South Midlands Temperance Association.
1841	Moved back to Leicester. Arranged rail excursion from Leicester to temperance rally in Loughborough, carrying 570 passengers for 1/- return.
1842–4	Organised summer excursions for temperance societies and Sunday schools.
1845	Started organising excursions on full-time basis, earning commission on sales from Midland Railways, e.g. arranged for 350 passengers to travel from Leicester to Glasgow for one guinea return, taking a train to Manchester and then a ferry from Fleetwood to Ardrossan, with entertainments laid on in Glasgow and Edinburgh.
1855	Took people from Leicester to Paris to visit Great Exhibition.
1856	Organised first tour of Europe.
1864	Went into partnership with son, John Mason Cook.
1865	Crossed Atlantic for first time to prepare for tours of States. Moved company's head office to London.
1872	Completed round-the-world tour in 222 days.
1878	John Mason Cook became sole manager of business. Thomas Cook placed on fixed annual salary.
1892	Ended life blind in Leicester. Died in Thorncroft, Stonegate on 18 July.

Fig. 2.3 The life of Thomas Cook

1834	John Mason Cook born in Market Harborough.
1864	Became partner to father, Thomas Cook.
1865	Took charge of London head office of Thomas Cook business, and of *The Excursionist* newspaper.
1866	Travelled to United States to sort out problems which had arisen over agreements made by his father in 1865. Arranged 41 sets of rail tickets to cover the entire United States and Canada.
1868	Great Eastern Railway Company put him in charge of passengers on their route to the Continent via Harwich. Cook liaised with Dutch, Belgian and German rail authorities to sell their tickets – in one month, sold 500 rail tickets.
1870	Became agent for routes through Germany via Brenner Pass to Italy (during the Franco-German war this was only route to popular Riviera). When war ended, French also appointed him agent for their tickets. Became agent for Nile passenger services.
1873	Opened Cairo office.
1875	First Norwegian operations. Bought Vesuvius railway.
1877	Opened hotel in Luxor. By then was agent for boat services along Nile to Third Cataract.
1880	Visited India, setting up offices in Bombay and Calcutta and organising rail ticket issue.
1884	Government employed Cook to arrange General Gordon's transport to Sudan.
1885	Helped organise pilgrim traffic from India to Saudi Arabia.
1891	Wrote *The Business of Travel, a Fifty Years' Record of Progress*.
1894	Established 'Egypt Limited' to handle all Thomas Cook company's different business interests in Egypt e.g. mail services along Nile.
1898	Organised travel arrangements for German Emperor's visit to Holy Land.
1899	Died at Mount Felix in Walton-on-Thames. Three sons took over Thomas Cook business.

The Times obituary wrote that:

> his real work consisted in breaking down the obstructiveness of foreign railway managers and even governments, and in making journeys all over the world possible and easy to anyone who chose to buy a bundle of coupons at Ludgate Circus.

Fig. 2.4 The life of John Mason Cook

1871	First bank holidays in the UK.
1919	First International Labour Conference in Sweden suggested adding the idea of paid holidays to its agenda.
1925	Bill to introduce holidays with pay blocked in the House of Commons.
1936	International Labour Organisation finally discussed paid holidays. British delegates abstained on final vote.
1938	**Holidays with Pay Act** passed. Ministry of Labour could arrange paid holidays with employers' agreement.
1945	14 million British workers became entitled to paid holidays.
1993	EC ruled that workers should be entitled to minimum four weeks paid holiday. Britain challenged this.

Fig. 2.5 The growth of paid holidays

Passports

Passports are documents which identify a person and allow him/her to leave his/her own country and return to it. Sometimes they are all that is required to enter and leave a foreign country as well. However, in some cases the passport must be endorsed with a **visa**, or permit, before it is possible to enter or leave another country. Visas are usually valid for a limited period of time.

Nowadays travellers take it for granted that they need a passport, but this was not always the case. For example, it was only in 1868 that visitors to the Vatican began to be asked for passports. In 1870 France and Belgium started to ask visitors for passports. Thomas Cook protested to the French Foreign Minister that passports were an impediment to travel and in 1872, with the ending of the Franco-Prussian War which had made all foreigners the object of suspicion, France stopped asking for them again. By then, however, the idea had taken root, and by 1888 Spain, Russia, Bulgaria, Romania and Serbia were all demanding them.

Soon such uncertainty was attached to the need for passports that the Cooks had to reassure clients that they didn't need them to visit the Isle of Wight (although until 1920 they *did* need them for the Channel Islands).

Many countries were also asking visitors for visas. The outbreak of the Second World War meant that most European countries would only let in foreigners with passports and visas. After the war, however, visa requirements for most Europeans were relaxed. Indeed, in 1937 the French government allowed weekend visitors to Paris to come and go without passports; in 1939 they extended this to allow British visitors to travel throughout France on just an identity card.

In January 1993 most countries which belonged to the then European Community (now the European Union) scrapped requirements for EC citizens to show passports at their borders. Britain continues to require passport checks at borders. Visas continue to be needed for travel to most non-European countries, although even there steps have been made to ease the bureaucracy. In the early 1980s, the USA agreed to accept a signed waiver form from British holidaymakers on short visits in place of a formal visa. Since the collapse of the Berlin Wall in 1989, visa requirements for Eastern European countries have also been eased or dropped altogether.

THE EXPANSION OF THE TOUR BUSINESS

From the beginning, tour operating was a low profit industry and at first Thomas Cook made little money from his business, despite having a virtual monopoly. Even in the 1880s John Mason Cook ran sidelines in importing ostrich feathers from Sudan and sausage skins from India to boost takings. But as more and more people wanted to travel it was inevitable that others would follow in Cook's footsteps. Between the 1850s and 1880s Henry Gaze ran a similar business. In 1872 Georges Nagelmackers created the *Compagnie des Wagons-Lits et des Grands Express Européens* to provide luxury Continental train travel, and in 1883 he developed the original Orient Express which linked Paris with Istanbul, going on to create the Blue Train from Paris to Rome via the French Riviera. In the 1880s Quintin Hogg set up the Polytechnic Association to arrange tours for students. The Methodist Sir Henry Lunn also started organising ski holidays. In 1891 American Express launched its own version of the traveller's cheque. Nevertheless in the first quarter of the twentieth century the travel business was still completely dominated by the Cook business, carried on after John Mason died by Thomas Cook's grandsons, Frank, Ernest and Thomas. In 1928 the business was sold to the Wagons-Lits company with the result that during the Second World War its headquarters, then in Brussels, fell into enemy hands. To make sure that could never happen again, the government nationalised Thomas Cook after the war and it wasn't until the 1970s that it became a private company again.

The changing nature of the product

In 1920 the Thomas Cook company offered the first flights to Paris and by the 1930s the company was also offering flying-boat holidays to the Mediterranean and Madeira. In 1939 it even offered a round-the-world tour by flying boat, costing £475 for 30 days. However, the high cost meant such trips remained the preserve of the wealthy. Then in 1938 the government passed the Holidays With Pay Act which guaranteed for the first time that most of the working population would have the time and the money to take at least a short holiday. Companies like the Co-op Holidays Association and the Workers Travel Association helped young people to go abroad, sewing fertile seeds for the future. By the outbreak of the Second World War, therefore, the idea of having a holiday had taken a firm hold in the UK. Even during the war, Thomas Cook continued to advertise holidays to areas outside the war zones.

1921	700,000	
1955	3,000,000	
1972	3,000,000	(ITs)
1978	4,500,000	(ITs)
1985	8,500,000	(ITs)
1986	10,600,000	(ITs)
1987	12,000,000	(ITs)
1988	12,600,000	(ITs)
1989	12,500,000	(ITs)
1990	11,400,000	(ITs)
1991	10,500,000	(ITs)
1992	12,500,000	(ITs)

(IT = inclusive tour)

Fig. 2.6 The number of British package holidaymakers travelling overseas

Developments after the Second World War

After the Second World War a number of factors facilitated the rapid expansion of the holiday market. These were:

- the greater prosperity of the population at large
- paid holidays for many workers
- excess aeroplanes put to a new use after the war
- technical improvements in aircraft which made it possible to fly further and faster
- a greater sense of democracy and equality fostered by the war effort
- better education
- better packaging of the opportunities by operators
- spread of television, bringing images of the rest of the world to almost every household

The ending of the war put in place some of the last pieces of the jigsaw of mass holidaymaking. First, a large number of old Dakota planes came on the market and could be used for flying holidaymakers; when Vladimir Raitz founded Horizon Holidays he was using army surplus planes.

The war had also brought about changed social attitudes. So many people had been affected by it, at home and abroad, that old hierarchical ideas about society had been undermined. In the new more democratic atmosphere that followed, what had previously been thought of as luxuries for the wealthy began to be seen as desirable for the population as a whole. Many people had travelled overseas during the war and came home with an enduring interest in other countries. These new attitudes fed through into a greater demand for overseas holidays which were also suited to the confident new mood brought about by the end of rationing in July 1954.

This new demand could not be supplied immediately. For example, most hotels on the Continent were grand places, well suited to the old travelling classes but less appropriate for a new generation of holidaymakers. At first little investment capital was available to adapt the hotels or build new ones, but gradually the situation changed. Previously hoteliers had been happy to wait for payment until a room was actually filled. Now as they borrowed money to develop their properties they began to require advance payment. Some even overbooked rooms to ensure they wouldn't be left empty if a client didn't materialise.

Immediately after the war, most people continued to travel abroad by train, and the Creative Tour Agents Conference (a group consisting of Sir Henry Lunn, the Polytechnic Association, Wayfarers and the Workers Travel Association) started to organise charter train trips. However, the war had revealed the potential of air flight, and in 1949 the appearance of the quicker, cheaper jet airliner meant that the days of the old turbo-prop planes were numbered. Entrepreneurs like Vladimir Raitz quickly spotted the potential for reusing the old planes to provide 'charter' flights at reduced prices to take more people further afield. In 1949 when he set up Horizon Holidays he challenged Thomas Cook's claim to have invented the package holiday, offering something which would seem much more familiar to a modern holidaymaker. In 1950 Horizon Holidays used a DC3 to carry 32 holidaymakers to Corsica at a cost of £32 10/- inclusive of return flights, transfers, tented accommodation and full board meal arrangements. For the first time holidays along the Mediterranean coast were brought within reach of ordinary working people.

But before air travel could take off on a mass scale, its costs still had to be brought down, something that took longer than it might have done because of a government ruling that reduced-price charter flights should only be available to members of special affinity groups or societies. High air fares guaranteed that most people continued to go abroad by train or steamship well into the 1950s. Nevertheless by 1952 Vladimir Raitz's Horizon was offering charter flights to Palma, by 1954 it was operating to Alghero and Perpignan (for the Costa Brava), by 1955 it was flying to Malaga and by 1956 to Tangier and Oporto. In 1952 the airlines introduced the first 'tourist fares', but it wasn't until 1958 that the first 'economy fares' appeared.

Competition between the tour operators and the airlines

After the war, the emerging tour operators and the airlines were in competition with each other, and regulations were designed to stop operators poaching what was traditional airline business. These rules included:

a) insisting that clients stay a fixed or minimum length of time at their destination
b) imposing minimum or maximum advance booking periods
c) establishing minimum prices for selling inclusive tours (ITs)
d) saying that only certain types of passenger (e.g. affinity groups) could book on charter flights

But during the 1960s and 1970s there was intense pressure on the airlines to bring fares down, first to Mediterranean holiday destinations and then later to destinations further afield. In the 1960s and 70s the charter airlines introduced cheap Advance Booking Charters (ABCs) which had to be booked and paid for *x* number of weeks in advance. The scheduled airlines retaliated by introducing Advanced Booking Excursion fares which operated on similar lines. In September 1977 Freddie Laker introduced his Skytrain which offered cheap standby air fares from Gatwick to New York, forcing the scheduled airlines to cut their fares on the transatlantic routes and opening the way to package holidays in the United States.

Currency allowances and travellers cheques

For holidaymakers to travel overseas they also had to be able to take money out of Britain to spend abroad. In 1945 every adult was allowed to export £100 without referral to the Bank of England for permission. There was also a £50 allowance for each child. Both Thomas Cook and American Express quickly established travellers cheque systems to enable them to carry their money safely.

THE CHANGING TRAVEL MARKET OF THE 1960S

In the 1950s and 60s it was easy for a tour operator to start up a business just by booking a few hotel rooms and seats on aeroplanes, and paying for both after the clients had taken their holiday. But as more people became involved, it grew harder for anyone to make a profit and ingenuity was required to find ways to keep costs to a minimum. Increasingly, hoteliers and airlines began to demand payment in advance. To attract clients, more had to be spent on brochures and publicity. Tour operators were forced to turn to the banks for funding to cover the period between the holidays being planned and sold. Bigger operators were in a strong position to dictate terms to hoteliers, and encouraged the building of huge skyscrapers which could accommodate vast numbers of high season clients in places like the Costa Brava.

Although more people were interested in travelling overseas to the guaranteed sun of the Mediterranean in the 1960s, tour operators still had to contend with three psychological obstacles: fear of flying, and dislike of foreigners in general and of foreign food in particular. Fear of flying is, of course, something that still troubles some would-be travellers. However, in the early days of mass holidaymaking it had less to do with phobia and more to do with consciousness that the planes being used to transport people were often elderly, ex-wartime stock, with uncomfortable layouts. What's more, some of the airports used did not have a particularly good safety record. Far-sighted tour operators gradually recognised that what was needed were new, purpose-built aircraft, designed with the needs of civilian holiday traffic in mind. In the meantime some of them offered 'trial flights' at rock-bottom prices, using up last-minute unsold stock as a way of allowing first-time travellers to 'sample' the product and perhaps overcome their apprehension.

The problem of the dislike of foreigners was something of a paradox given that people wanted to travel to foreign countries. However, it makes better sense when it is understood that what many holidaymakers wanted was the chance to soak up the sun on a pleasant beach rather than an opportunity to meet strangers. Few people were interested in learning about, let alone experiencing foreign customs, especially when it came to their hotels and restaurants. A general wariness was not helped by the overbooking of hotels which was a regular feature of holidays in the early 1960s and which could easily be blamed on perfidious foreign hoteliers. Eventually the big operators got to grips with these problems by investing in brand-new properties, some of which they managed themselves and some of which they oversaw. The passing of the 1968 Trade Descriptions Act meant that operators began to clamp down on overbookers, offering to compensate customers who were inconvenienced and then passing on the cost to the hoteliers. The role of resort representatives was also upgraded so that they offered more than a 'meet and greet' airport service and became available to help smooth clients' difficulties and explain local customs to them.

People's dislike of foreign food also had to be acknowledged, and some companies even sent catering experts out to their hotels to teach the chefs how to prepare and cook food that would be palatable to British clients. The biggest breakthrough probably came when hotels started to provide buffet breakfasts and lunches which cut down on labour costs and the cost of rejected food while also fitting in with holidaymakers' greater desire for flexibility.

But signs that tour operating could come unstuck came in the early 1960s when some smaller companies collapsed as the market grew more competitive. In 1964 Fiesta Tours went bust, followed by Omar Khayyam Tours in 1965.

Technological change

Technological developments continued to shape the tourism business. For example, in 1969 Boeing built the first 747 or jumbo jet, making it possible to fly further in less time. Long-haul destinations thus began to look more realistic possibilities for holidays. In 1969 the Anglo-French Concorde also made its maiden flight (it didn't enter commercial service until 1976), although this plane has only ever had limited impact on the tour operating business, mainly as transport for expensive day-trip excursions.

Development of consumer protection

At first the holiday market grew up in haphazard, uncontrolled fashion. But by the mid-1950s, steps to regulate it began to be taken. In 1955 the Association of British Travel Agents (ABTA) was set up as a trade association to represent both travel agents and tour operators, and to provide a forum for discussing industry-wide issues. In 1960 the Civil Aviation (Licensing) Act created the Air Transport Licensing Board (ATLB). All British airlines were required to get a licence from the Board before they could start operating. A provision of obtaining a licence was that the operator had to charge a minimum price for an inclusive holiday involving air transport. This minimum price always had to be more than the lowest scheduled return fare, so that the holiday companies couldn't undercut the scheduled airlines. In 1971 the role of policing air transport licences passed to the Civil Aviation Authority (CAA), with whom it remains.

In 1965 in an attempt to ward off looming government regulation of the industry, an ABTA conference established 'Operation Stabiliser' which decreed that tour operators who belonged to ABTA could only sell their holidays through travel agencies which also belonged to ABTA and vice versa. The rationale behind this was that it would make it easier to control the industry and that the pubic would be able to regard ABTA membership as a guarantee of security. In effect 'Stabiliser' created a 'closed shop' which was said to be in the interests of all the parties in the holiday transaction: the operators, the agents and the consumers.

In 1967 the Tour Operators Study Group (TOSG) was set up to represent the leading tour operators and to provide another forum for discussing common interests. TOSG also lobbied governments at home and abroad when it saw a threat to tour operators' interests. While ABTA tried to regulate members' financial worthiness, the TOSG never interfered in its members' affairs. However, in 1970 TOSG members agreed that holidays should be bonded: they would pay cash to a third party to be used to repatriate and reimburse holidaymakers if they ceased trading. The 22 members of the TOSG paid 5 per cent of their turnover into a Trust Fund to create a pool of more than £5 million. This scheme was later extended to include all ABTA tour operators and from 1973 the CAA required that all those applying for Air Transport Organiser's Licences (ATOLs) should be bonded, using their own capital rather than clients' deposits to pay for the bonds.

Under the 1971 Civil Aviation Act the CAA was required to issue Air Transport Organiser's Licences (ATOLs) to anyone wanting to offer flights to the public. The CAA quickly lifted the ruling that only affinity groups could book charter flights, at least in the winter, and this led to a rapid expansion in the market for winter holidays; the first winter holidays were started by Harry Chandler with a trip to the Algarve. In 1973 the ruling on affinity groups was scrapped altogether.

GROWTH OF THE PACKAGE HOLIDAY MARKET IN THE 1970S

In 1965 roughly one million people travelled on package holidays to Western Europe. In 1970 the Air Transport Licensing Board received 3,151,798 applications for route licences. Since applications had to be made separately for outward and return flights, this suggested that tour companies were planning to carry 1,575,899 passengers. Already by 1970 the ATLB applications show that four companies had established a grip on the market (*see* Table 2.1).

Table 2.1 Licence applications to the ATLB, 1970

Company name	*No. of seats*	*Total*	*Percentage of applications*
Clarkson's	494,434		
Thomson	301,696		
Horizon	246,804		
Cosmos	206,224		
		1,249,158	40
Lunn Poly	167,655		
Global	162,382		
Hickie Borman/Milbanke	131,659		
Blue Cars (Blue Sky)	127,436		
Sunair	121,760		
		710,892	22
		1,960,050	62

Of the entire holiday market in 1970, only 9 per cent continued to travel by coach.

The onset of recession

Just as everything was going so smoothly, in 1973/4 the Arabs woke up to the power they could wield through their control of much of the world's oil supplies. In 1974 the price of oil more than doubled, with knock-on effects for all aspects of travel. As fuel prices rose, so holiday prices were forced up too, with several consequences. In the short-term some tourist receiving countries like Greece saw a dip in their visitor arrival figures (*see* page 252). The price rises also helped fuel a shift away from hotels in favour of cheaper self-catering accommodation. However, in the longer-term, the number of inclusive tours sold continued to rise steadily.

Some tour companies found it harder to weather the storm than others. In the early 1970s a spate of tour operator failures, climaxing in the collapse of Court Line, tested the consumer protection already put in place. A lethal blend of factors combined to push companies out of business:

- Some companies had grown too quickly, borrowing too much money to finance their development.
- Companies engaged in a cut-throat price war to try and squeeze out the competition. Ultimately this meant they were earning very low profits per passenger carried.
- Soaring fuel prices helped bring about a recession, leading some people to forego holidays altogether or to trade down to cheaper ones.
- Poor management decisions exacerbated all these difficulties.

The Court Line/Clarkson's episode

In 1974 Clarkson's, the UK's largest tour operator, was owned by Court Line, a conglomerate with interests in everything from tankers to aircraft. As well as Clarkson's, Court Line also owned Horizon, 4S, 4S Sports and Airfare. In July 1974 it became apparent that Court Line was in difficulties, and the Labour Government agreed to buy its shipbuilding businesses for £24 million, hoping that this would enable the tour operating businesses to continue to trade through the summer. Later Court Line denied that it had ever agreed that that would be enough to safeguard the situation and there were claims that Tony Benn, then Secretary of State for Industry, had been more interested in an opportunity to nationalise the shipbuilding industry than in the fate of the tour operating companies. In any case, it soon became apparent that £5–10 million would be needed to wind the company down slowly. On 16 August 1974 Court Line went into liquidation at the height of the tourist season. With it went Clarkson's Holidays, Horizon Holidays, Halcyon Holidays, Associated Travel and Leisure Service and Court Travel, leaving 39,000 passengers stranded overseas, and 100,000 people booked on holidays they were unlikely to be able to take. In addition another 50,000 passengers booked on Court Line flights chartered by other operators faced disruption to their plans.

Why did Court Line collapse?

In a leading article, *The Times* said:

> it must be assumed . . . that the basic problems of running a high-volume, low-margin business at a time of unpredictable cost increases and economic uncertainty were fatally exacerbated by the company's decision to assume the businesses of Clarkson's and Horizon Holidays within the past year. What then seemed an enlightened move by a giant of the industry to preserve the reputation of that industry must now be judged an act of financial suicide.

Since the mid-1960s, Clarkson's had been involved in a price war with Thomson, then the second largest operator, with the result that holidays were being sold at a loss. When the company got into difficulties Court Line bought it, together with Horizon Holidays, a move which seemed wise at the time but became less so as the oil crisis made it impossible to plan ahead for any part of the conglomerate's businesses – oil tankers, aviation or tour operating. Clarkson's low profits left it with little scope to cushion the impact of the oil crisis which exacerbated the situation by forcing up fuel prices just as families started to cut back on expenditure, especially during the three-day week of 1974. In 1973 the floating pound had forced operators to collect currency surcharges at the airports. In

1974 they were forced to collect fuel surcharges too, a move that was very unpopular with the travelling public.

What happened after the crash?

The Court Line planes at Luton airport were impounded and 3,000 staff (1,200 of them working for the airline, 1,800 for the tour operating companies) lost their jobs. Other companies did their best to pick up the lost bookings; for example, Harry Goodman doubled his profits in 1974 by taking over many of the lost hotel bookings. Thomson laid on an extra 20,000 'square deal' holidays to Spain and Portugal, while Blue Sky added 2,000 to Majorca.

This was the first major test of the bonding systems put in place to protect customers against the loss of their money if a tour operator collapsed. Court Line's ABTA bond, worth £3.3.million, was called in and deposited in a Trust Fund administered by the TOSG. Within ten days the CAA, ABTA and TOSG had spent £1 million on repatriating 39,000 holidaymakers amid accusations that some hoteliers had evicted clients when they heard that the operator had ceased trading. Although the Foreign Office was asked to help out, some tour company representatives simply abandoned their clients, who flew back to the UK claiming that they hadn't eaten for 24 hours. By the end of August almost everyone had been repatriated, with ABTA officials working almost non-stop to arrange this.

Court Line assets to be liquidated included tankers, several aircraft, Caribbean hotels, a number of properties and the shipbuilding interests which were to be sold to the government. Travel agents were holding about £5 million in deposits and advance payments for holidays, and there was uncertainty over whether they could refund this 'pipeline' money to the clients or whether it formed part of the Court Line assets to be disbursed by the liquidators. Ultimately there was no money left to compensate most of those who had booked and paid for holidays but hadn't actually set out on them. The Tour Operators Study Group stepped in to fill the gap and was given a government indemnity to protect it against further claims. One of the Trust's directors even settled the bills of Spanish hoteliers. The government made a pre-election pledge to compensate those who had lost out and set up the Air Travel Reserve Fund with £5 million of Treasury money which was to be recouped through a levy on future holidaymakers. Between 1975 and 1977 the government levied two per cent of tour operators' turnovers to make up the shortfall. On 22 August Cosmos Tours upped its bond to twice the CAA's statutory requirement to forestall future problems.

The Court Line episode led to extension of the bonding system. In future ABTA members were required to pay in a bond of no less than 10 per cent of their turnover. The old Air Travel Reserve Fund was replaced by the Air Travel Trust which was supposed to make up any shortfall. Non-ABTA tour operators could be asked to pay up to 15 per cent of their turnover to the CAA as a bond. The TOSG continued to administer its own Trust Fund.

Before Court Line collapsed staff had been talking about the necessity of a 30–35 per cent across-the-board price increase to bring the tour operating business back into the black. Hoteliers who had got their fingers burnt in 1974 also became much more interested in advance payment. Nevertheless, the industry has always remained so competitive that the oft-talked of price increases have been slow to materialise.

After Court Line

The next biggest test of the bonding system came in February 1982 when Freddie Laker's Skytrain collapsed, taking with it his Skytrain Holidays operation. This time the bankers called in their debts before the peak holiday season, thus avoiding the risk of leaving thousands of holidaymakers stranded in the resorts. The 52,000 claims made by people booked on Skytrain Holidays were met from the Laker bond, topped up by the Air Travel Reserve Fund. However, passengers booked on Skytrain scheduled flights to the States were not protected by any bond scheme.

GROWTH OF THE HOLIDAY MARKET IN THE 1980S

In 1979 Margaret Thatcher became Prime Minister, ushering in an era of renewed enthusiasm for capitalist enterprise. Although the decade started and ended with recession, many of the actions of the

Table 2.2 Return passengers licenced by the CAA, 1977–9

	Company Name	*April 1979*	*April 1978*	*April 1977*
1	Thomson Travel	734,000	631,000	679,000
2	Silver Wing Surface Arrangements Ltd	360,552	249,340	211,920
3	Cosmos Air Holidays Ltd	342,000	261,000	300,000
4	Horizon Midland Ltd	304,000	206,000	170,000
5	Laker Air Travel Ltd	174,000	174,000	141,200
6	Global of London (Tours & Travel) Ltd	137,150	104,100	91,825
7	Intasun North Ltd	135,000	90,000	55,000
8	Owners Services Ltd	134,600	110,780	132,300
9	Intasun Ltd	130,950	82,500	50,000
10	Blue Sky Holidays Ltd	128,300	86,875	75,000
11	Thomas Cook Ltd	105,002	100,176	63,566
12	Martin Rooks & Co. Ltd	100,000	70,450	70,000
13	Saga Holidays Ltd	96,000	80,000	na
14	Arrowsmith Holidays Ltd	95,000	95,000	103,000
15	Inghams Travel Ltd	94,600	84,750	52,300
16	Ellerman Lines Ltd	90,850	71,293	53,535
17	Tjaereborg Ltd	81,000	na	na
18	Yugotours Ltd	75,000	50,000	50,000
19	Pontinental (Holiday Services) Ltd	67,500	72,000	67,500
20	Jetsave Ltd	60,550	70,050	na
21	Wings Ltd	60,000	na	na
22	Vingresor/Club 33AB	55,000	na	na
23	Exchange Travel Holidays Ltd	54,000	na	na
24	Wardair (UK) Ltd	52,000	53,000	na
25	Overseas Air Travel Ltd	na	62,250	na
Totals		3,667,054	2,804,564	2,366,146

Source: CAA

Conservative Government contributed towards a climate in which tour operating would flourish. For example, in 1980 exchange controls on the amount of money individuals could take out of the country were lifted, making it easier for people to travel wherever they wanted for as long as they wanted. Until then people were only allowed to take limited amounts of money out of the country (*see* Fig. 2.7). When they bought foreign currency, the amount purchased was recorded in the back of their passport. Anyone wanting to exceed the permitted allowance had to apply to the Bank of England for special permission to do so.

The amount of paid holiday firms gave their employees continued to rise, and increasing numbers of people were able to take more than one annual vacation, leading to expansion of the winter sun and winter ski markets. Increasingly people also topped up their two weeks in the sun with shorter second holidays, encouraging the growth of the city breaks market.

Cheaper air fares and longer paid holidays also contributed to a gradual expansion in the market for long-haul destinations. At first, specialist

Year	**Per adult**
1945	£100
1966–70	£50
1970–77	£300
1978	£500
1979	£1000
1980	no limit

Fig. 2.7 Changes in the foreign exchange allowance, 1945–80

companies looked after the demand but, as it grew, so the big tour operators moved in, adding new worldwide brochures to their existing ones. The Caribbean and Gambia both benefited from a growing number of winter sun seekers, while countries like Thailand were soon receiving almost too many visitors for their own good. Nevertheless, in 1993 only 11 per cent of package holidays sold through travel agencies were to long-haul destinations, up from 4 per cent in 1987.

As at 31 December	Members of ABTA Tour Operators' Class
1983	484
1984	506
1985	511
1986	544
1987	648
1988	673
1989	699
1990	697
1991	657
1992	647

Fig. 2.8 Rising and falling – the number of ABTA tour operators in business, 1983–92

Merger mania

During the 1980s more and more of the tour operations market became concentrated in the hands of a few big companies. For example, the Owners Abroad company steadily expanded by buying other companies: in 1983 it bought Falcon Holidays, in 1988 Tjaereborg and Sunfire Travel, in 1989 Sunward Holidays and in 1990 Redwing which owned Enterprise, Sovereign and Martyn Holidays. In 1988 Thomson Holidays, then the biggest operator, bought Horizon Holidays, then the third biggest, from Bass, thereby securing 35 per cent of the total package holiday market. And in 1993 Airtours expanded by buying Aspro Holidays and Tradewinds. Such expansion wasn't restricted to the UK. In 1994 Owners Abroad announced plans to buy International Travel Holdings, Canada's largest tour operator.

The number of companies also grew rapidly, from 506 in 1984 to 746 in 1994. Although this was sometimes because new market opportunities had been identified, this was not always the case; for example, in 1990 only eight operators offered African holidays, but by 1993 70 operators had crowded into the market despite the fact that the number of potential purchasers hadn't risen to match the increased supply.

The Thomson/Horizon merger

In May 1987 Bass, the breweries to hotels group, bought Horizon Holidays (including Orion Air) for £94.8 million, following up this purchase by buying Wings/OSL in August 1987. However, by August 1988 it was obvious that it was making a loss on the tour operating part of the business even though Orion was profitable. It therefore agreed to sell Horizon (with Wings/OSL) to the International Thomson Organisation for £75 million. The deal was announced on 19 August 1988. In buying Horizon, Thomson Travel secured 35 per cent of the package holiday market against ILG's 20 per cent, British Air Tours' 6 per cent and Owners Abroad's 5 per cent. Merged with Orion, Britannia Airways became the world's biggest charter airline.

At the time of the merger, Thomson and Horizon had the following assets:

	THOMSON	HORIZON
Aircraft		
737s	27	8
767s	8 (2 on order)	–
A320s	–	2
No. of airports served	15	8
Travel agencies owned	439 (Lunn Polys)	17 (Horizon Travel Centres)

Since the deal was worth more than £30 million and in theory gave Thomson a technical monopoly of more than 25 per cent of the market, the Office of Fair Trading considered referring it to the Monopolies and Mergers Commission for approval. Thomson's offer to Bass was unconditional, so it would have been obliged to resell Horizon had the MMC ruled against it. For ILG, Harry Goodman lodged an objection to the takeover with the OFT, claiming it would destabilise the industry and represented 'an unprecedented concentration of power' in the package holiday market. The Consumers' Association also lodged an objection to the narrowing of consumer choice.

Thomson argued that the whole overseas holiday market was made up of independent holidaymakers as well as those on packages. When the independent travellers were taken into account, its share of the overall foreign holidays market fell to 22.9 per cent against ILG's 10.4 per cent and Redwing's 2.6 per cent. Thomson also argued that because it was relatively easy to set up a new tour company it could never hope to monopolise the market completely. Finally it claimed it was looking ahead to the post-1992 Single European market which might result in Continental travel companies targeting the UK for expansion.

Thomson's arguments were accepted and the merger with Horizon was allowed to take place. Horizon continued to exist as a separate brand name, although the Horizon Travel Centres were merged with the Lunn Poly chain. In 1993 Thomson announced the closure of Horizon's head office in Birmingham.

Niche marketing

Another feature of tour operating in the 1980s was **niche** marketing. In the early days it was assumed that the same type of product would suit most types of customer. However, as more people travelled more often, the market began to divide into segments. The biggest companies still tried to service everyone, even where they produced discrete products for discrete parts of the overall market (senior citizens, young people, coach travellers, etc.), but an increasing number of specialist companies also emerged to cater for identified niches in the market (ramblers, birdwatchers, etc.).

Moving into recession again

While the number of tour operating companies expanded rapidly in the 1980s, that didn't necessarily mean there were big profits to be made out of the business, as constant price wars between the biggest companies held profit levels down and accustomed the consumer to the idea of cheap holidays. Indeed in the summer of 1987 the CAA suggested that the top 30 tour operating firms had, between them, made losses of £25 million on the year. Although Thomson still turned in a pre-tax profit of £43 million, that was considerably down on the £60 million it had made in 1986.

By 1988 the market was stagnating under the impact of rising interest rates and mortgage costs, and incipient recession. The travelling public's enthusiasm was also dented by well-publicised delays at airports in 1988 and by fears over aircraft safety. In 1989, with the recession deepening, the situation worsened. In February 1989 Thomson dropped 600,000 out of 3 million planned holidays, saying the market was 20 per cent smaller than it had anticipated. Redwing, too, reported a 10 per cent drop in bookings and laid off 50 staff, claiming this was due to improved computerisation of bookings and administration.

Despite this, tour operators continued to engage in price-cutting tactics. When the Gulf War broke out in January 1991 it was the last straw for some companies. Uncertainty caused would-be holidaymakers to delay making bookings, and once again the consumer protection system was pushed to its limits when the International Leisure Group (ILG), then the country's second largest tour operator, collapsed in the spring of 1991. As more small companies followed it into liquidation, the gap that allowed non-air, non-ABTA operators to trade without bonding was highlighted when Land Travel, a coach tour operator, collapsed in 1992, leaving customers stranded and with no hope of compensation. The EC Package Travel Regulations which became law in January 1993 were designed to prevent such situations in the future by insisting that *all* operators of inclusive tours be bonded or insured against failure.

MORE LONG-HAUL HOLIDAYS
MORE SHORT BREAK HOLIDAYS
MORE SPECIALIST HOLIDAYS
MORE SELF-CATERING ARRANGEMENTS
MORE SELF-DRIVE PACKAGES
MORE FLY-DRIVE AND FLY-CRUISE HOLIDAYS
MORE 'UNPACKAGED' PACKAGES

Fig. 2.9 Trends in tour operating in the early 1990s

Table 2.3 The UK's largest tour operators in the mid-1980s

	Company	*April 1986*	*April 1985*	*April 1984*
1	Thomson Travel Ltd	2,100,000	1,313,366	954,529
2	Intasun Holidays Ltd	1,226,900	880,438	na
3	Horizon Holidays Ltd	591,180	409,270	544,000
4	Rank Travel Ltd	405,485	323,200	365,600
5	British Airways Holidays Ltd	391,517	296,418	533,569
6	Cosmos Air Holidays Ltd	250,000	225,000	300,000
7	Pendle Travel Services Ltd	244,699	127,000	90,000
8	Best Travel Ltd	240,000	188,250	88,000
9	Yugotours Ltd	220,000	160,000	120,000
10	Falcon Leisure Group Ltd	202,500	130,000	118,500
11	Portland Holidays Ltd	175,618	233,255	128,387
12	Sky Tours Ltd	150,000	na	na
13	Martin Rooks & Co. Ltd	121,553	115,546	na
14	Redwood Travel Ltd	112,000	87,000	51,938
15	Thomas Cook Ltd	108,850	160,554	204,800
16	Tjaereborg Ltd	100,000	115,000	115,000
17	Schools Abroad Ltd	88,200	111,000	90,525
18	Saga Holidays plc	87,500	87,500	87,500
19	Owners Abroad Aviation Ltd	85,500	57,000	97,250
20	Pegasus Holidays (London) Ltd	76,500	73,750	65,500
21	CIT (England) Ltd	57,912	*	na
22	Olympic Holidays Ltd	57,011	62,500	88,441
23	Sol Holidays (AE) Ltd	55,085	95,000	*
24	Hourmont Ltd	50,000	55,000	50,000
25	Blue Sky Holidays Ltd	na	218,909	219,610
26	Global of London (Tours and Travel) Ltd	na	190,000	174,000
27	Arrowsmith Ltd	na	85,575	87,250
28	Wardair (UK) Ltd	**	65,000	75,000
29	Holiday Club International Ltd (HCI)	*	60,426	126,000
30	Carousel Holidays Ltd	*	57,303	95,000
31	Hards Travel Service Ltd	*	54,000	89,412
32	Paris Travel Service Ltd	*	50,000	*
33	Zebra Holidays Ltd	na	50,000	*
	Totals	7,198,010	6,137,260	5,876,263

(* represents less than 50,000 passengers licenced)

Source: CAA

The collapse of International Leisure Group (ILG)

On 8 March 1991 International Leisure Group (ILG), Britain's second largest tour operator, went into liquidation with debts of around £500 million. It was the worst failure in the travel industry since Court Line had collapsed in 1974. Although the decision to cease trading in March (rather than waiting until the summer season got into its swing) meant that fewer clients were stranded in the resorts, the scope of Air Europe's chartering operation meant that more flights were disrupted than when Laker went bust in 1982.

In addition to Air Europe, the following tour companies all ceased trading as parts of ILG:

Intasun	Lancaster
Intasun Skiscene	Select

Global	Coach Europe
Club 18-30	NAT

ILG: The background

International Leisure Group was the brainchild of Harry Goodman, a flamboyant entrepreneur from humble origins who started his first tour company, Sunair, when he was just 26. In 1971 he sold Sunair for £70,000, buying Intasun, a combined tour operating and travel agency business, for £25,000. After selling the agency arm of the business, he began building up the tour operation, taking advantage of Court Line's failure in 1974 to snatch up many of the lost bookings and double his profits for the year. When Laker Holidays collapsed he was again quick to scoop up disappointed customers.

Until 1981 Goodman concentrated on cheap, no-frills 'sun, sea, sand and sex' holidays, notoriously developing the Club 18–30 product which didn't even pretend to be offering anything more sophisticated to its young customers. In 1981 ILG was floated on the Stock Exchange and Goodman was soon sitting on a £30 million fortune.

However, in March 1987 Goodman took ILG off the stock market to become a private company once more. By then he had decided to expand Air Europe's operations to make it a combined charter and scheduled airline in competition with British Airways. He claimed it was impossible for him to do this while ILG remained a public company because of the stock market's short-term outlook. His plan was to use the planes for scheduled services during the peak morning and evening rush hours, and for holiday charters during the remainder of the day. By 1989 Air Europe had a fleet of cost-effective, modern 737s and 757s which offered an award-winning service to passengers and was the second largest carrier flying out of Gatwick airport. However, to finance the operation Goodman had borrowed enormous sums at a time when interest rates were cripplingly high.

ILG: The crash

During the winter of 1991 the uncertainty caused by the Gulf War meant that the business passengers supposed to fill Air Europe's scheduled flights stopped travelling at the same time as the holidaymakers supposed to fill the charter flights postponed booking summer holidays. ILG found itself with a serious cash flow problem and needed a further short-term loan of £40 million to see it through to May when final holiday payments would start to come in. However, the consortium of banks to whom ILG was indebted was reluctant to lend him any more money. Goodman discussed a merger between Air Europe and Dan Air but this came to nothing. Lloyd's was prepared to advance another £25 million if Goodman could find a matching sum from elsewhere. The situation was not helped by the fact that Goodman had sold 49 per cent of ILG to the Swiss businessman Werner Rey whose Omni Holdings ceased trading in February 1991, making the banks even more nervous.

Tickets for Air Europe flights continued to be sold until eight hours before the company ceased trading but the CAA claimed that to have revoked its licence would simply have precipitated the crash. An attempt was made to find a buyer for the tour companies which were believed to be fundamentally profitable, and for Air Europe's routes and airport landing slots. However, this was not successful. ILG's £60 million bond was then called in and the TOSG set to work to try and find alternative flights for disappointed customers and to sort out repayments for those booked on the charter flights and package holidays. Air Europe's scheduled services were not covered by the ABTA bond.

ILG: The aftermath

The collapse of the UK's second largest tour operator put enormous strain on ABTA and existing bond arrangements. The situation was not helped by the fact that the Gulf War and recession claimed other victims, including companies which had specialised in holidays to Turkey, Israel and Egypt, all countries whose tourism industry was devastated by the war. By 1992 ABTA's continued existence in its present form was even under question.

However, as far as customers were concerned the bonding and repatriation arrangements worked very well. Other companies also rushed to pick up the would-be travellers left high and dry by ILG's demise, so few people ultimately lost their holidays. The financial fall-out took longer to sort out. In mid-1993 the courts were still trying to decide what should happen to monies paid to agents for ILG holidays which was still with the agents when

ILG collapsed (so-called 'pipeline' payments). Some agents held on to this money as part settlement of money owed to them by ILG, or even repaid it to clients to stop them losing it. However, the administrators believed it should be paid into a pool of assets to be divided up amongst the creditors. By July 1993, the Air Travel Trust estimated that the eventual shortfall on funds which would have to be met from insurance would be about £12.7 million.

Four new companies quickly emerged from the ashes of ILG: The Club (successor to Club 18-30), Sunworld, Novotours and Riva Travel, which employed ex-ILG chair Harry Goodman as a consultant. However, by mid-1993 both Novotours and Riva had, in turn, ceased trading.

In 1994, Harry Goodman issued a writ for damages against British Airways, claiming that the airline had helped to force ILG into liquidation, in particular by spreading malicious rumours about Air Europe.

INTO THE 1990S

The demise of ILG did not signal the end of the cut-throat competition among the biggest operators. Looking to the future, the biggest operators struggled to build up their share of the holiday market, sometimes making that a higher priority than simply increasing their profits. Since 1989 Airtours had been steadily building up its position, so that by 1991 it was ready to step into ILG's shoes as Thomson's main competitor. Owners Abroad, too, had been expanding its market share, and by 1991 these three operators between them held 70 per cent of the entire package holiday market. Since the market was no longer growing the only way these companies could further expand their market share was by merging (hence Airtours' 1993 attempt to buy out Owners Abroad which ultimately failed, *see* below) or undercutting each other's prices. So although the first edition of, say, a Thomson brochure would be realistically priced, later editions would usually contain hefty discounts as its rivals undercut it.

By 1993 the marketplace exhibited contradictory signs. On one hand, the worst recession since the 1930s had caused it to stagnate as potential customers either went without holidays or traded down to cheaper ones, but, on the other, travelling abroad (which had once seemed frightening and unusual) had become more or less routine for many people who were therefore much more prepared to make their own arrangements and travel independently. Although the 10.5 million packages sold in 1991 suggested that the much-heralded 'death of the package holiday' was still some way off, nevertheless operators were being forced to become increasingly imaginative in what they offered in order to hang on to their customers. On top of this, some people at least were becoming more conscious of environmental issues and the impact their holidays had on the resorts to which they travelled. The implications of this were considerable since much of the post-war tourism boom had been based on the assumption that people would continue to be happy with shoddy high-rise hotels in over-developed resorts. Smaller, specialist operators were in some ways best placed to capitalise on these new tendencies. However, they found it difficult to compete on price terms with the bigger companies, and the holidaymaking public continued to put most emphasis on low prices when choosing their holiday – despite their purported interest in 'green' issues. Indeed in a speech to the press in January 1993 Noel Josephides, Chair of the Association of Independent Tour Operators, described the British holiday market as the 'cheapskate of the EC', citing German market leader TUI's evidence that the Swiss, Italians and Germans spent twice as much as the British on their holidays and were motivated in their choices by quality rather than price.

In 1992 the European Community became a single market for trading purposes which meant it would be legal for Continental travel companies to move in on the British holiday market. Already the Swiss company Kuoni has been very successful here, although the Danish direct-sell operator Tjaereborg did less well, succumbing to a buy-out by Owners Abroad in 1988.

In 1993 the EC Package Travel Regulations became law (*see* Chapter Ten). These laid down new arrangements for bonding holidays intended to prevent any tour operating companies trading without protection against failure. In the immediate aftermath there was considerable confusion about exactly who was defined as an 'organiser' by the regulations and, particularly, about the new arrangements for bonding holidays. In 1993 the ability of some smaller, newer companies to raise the requisite bonds looked in doubt and it seemed likely that some operators (for example hotel chains) might have to stop offering package arrangements. Taking advantage of this situation, Kuoni announced that it would be interested in expanding by buying small, successful 'niche' operators which were not able to secure suitable bonding. ABTA's own role was once again called into question and it seemed likely that a new trade association representing tour operators alone would eventually emerge.

1974	Collapse of Court Line and Clarkson's.
1989	Thomson buys Horizon Holidays from Bass.
1991	Gulf War leads to failure of several small and/or specialist companies. International Leisure Group collapses.
1992	EC Single Market comes into effect.
1993	Introduction of EC Package Travel Regulations, with new bonding arrangements.
	Failure of Airtours' bid to buy Owners Abroad. Airtours buys Aspro Holidays instead.

Fig. 2.10 Important dates in tour operating history since 1974

1993: THE 'BIG THREE' TOUR OPERATORS

At the start of 1993, Thomson had roughly 30 per cent of the package holiday market, while Owners Abroad and Airtours had between them perhaps another 33-4 per cent. Cosmos had 6 per cent of the market, and Aspro, Unijet and Sunworld 5 per cent each. All the other companies held smaller percentages of the market which had therefore become just as top-heavy as it was in 1988 when Thomson/Horizon had 38 per cent of the market, ILG had 14 per cent, and Airtours, Cosmos and Owners Abroad had another 35 per cent between them.

The next section looks at two of the 'Big Three' – Owners Abroad and Airtours.

Owners Abroad/First Choice

Unlike Thomson and Airtours, Crawley-based Owners Abroad, the UK's second largest holiday company, started out in 1972 as an air seat wholesaler, rather than a fully-fledged tour operator. Eventually it established its own charter airline, Air 2000, and then started buying existing tour operating companies to fill its seats; by 1993 Air 2000 had 15 Boeing 757s and two A320s with another two on order. Unfortunately, as other tour operators increasingly developed their own airlines, it became harder for Owners to sell its seats so easily. In the 1990s, Owners Abroad needed to become better established as a tour operator in its own right, but was not helped by its relative anonymity, the larger company concealed behind individual product names like Falcon Holidays, Sovereign and Enterprise. In addition, some of those products appeared to be in competition with each other, reflecting the piecemeal way in which they had been acquired: both Falcon Holidays and Enterprise, for example, offered mass market family products. After fighting off a hostile takeover bid from Airtours in the first half of 1993, Owners Abroad saw its profits plummet and attributed part of this loss to 'directional selling' of Thomson and Airtours products by the wholly-owned agency chains, Lunn Poly, Pickfords and Hogg Robinson (*see* page 28).

In 1993 Owners Abroad announced changes which would mean the old leisure division which used to supervise tour operating and seat wholesaling being scrapped in favour of a new tour operating division which would oversee an aviation division looking after both Air 2000 and the seat wholesaling business. In future, providing seats for Owners Abroad's own tour operating products will take precedence over providing seats for the wholesaling division. A new product service division was also created to improve the quality of Owners' tour programmes and to look after the overseas operation.

In 1994 Owners Abroad changed its name to First Choice and rationalised its product range (*see* Fig. 2.11). By then it had been overtaken as the UK's second largest tour operator by Airtours.

Airtours

One of the conspicuous success stories of the early 1990s was Helmshore-based Airtours, set up in 1989 but the country's third biggest operator by 1993. Despite some hiccoughs (for example, an unsuccessful foray into the US ski market in

OWNERS ABROAD

'The UK's Second Largest Holiday Company'

Owners Abroad Group PLC

Owners Abroad Group PLC

Air 2000 Ltd
Charter Airline

Owners Abroad Services Ltd

Owners Abroad Overseas Ltd

Owners Abroad Aviation Ltd
Seat Wholesaler

Owners Abroad Tour Operations Ltd

Fraser Marr Financial Services Ltd
Insurance & School Fee Planning Specialist

Press Office	**'Direct Sell' Brands**	**Owners Abroad Travel Ltd**
071 757 5777 or 0293 588111 (from 21/9/92)	Mainstream and specialist holidays to a range of long and short haul destinations as well as flight only programmes	MARTIN ROOKS OWNERS ABROAD SUNFARE TIMSWAY TJAEREBORG

Owners Abroad Holidays Ltd	**Through Agent 'ABTA' Brands**	**Press Office**
ENTERPRISE	A mainstream brand with a broad appeal providing a wide range of popular sun, lakes, and mountains and ski holidays.	
FALCON	A brand which provides popular family holidays and flights to a wide range of resorts at highly competitive prices.	
MARTYN	Market leader to Portugal plus specialist programmes to Greece, Cyprus, Madeira and Canary Islands.	(0293) 588415 or (0293) 588405
SOVEREIGN	A leading brand offering high quality sun and activity holidays differentiated through superior service.	
SUNMED	The market leader in low cost holidays to Greece and Turkey aimed primarily at young people.	
TWENTYS	The UK's largest specialist youth brand serving the holiday needs of the 18–24 age group.	
OLYMPIC	A brand focused by destination specialising in quality holidays to Greece and Cyprus.	(0536) 770575

(a)

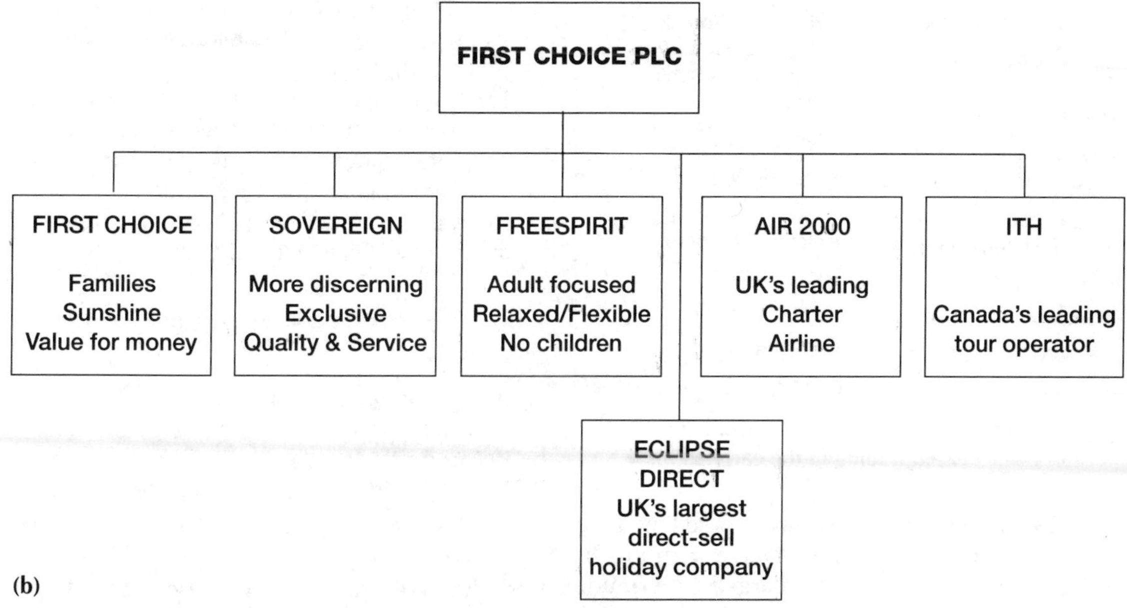

Fig. 2.11 Company structure of (a) Owners Abroad plc, 1993 and (b) First Choice, 1994
Courtesy: First Choice

1989/90), by 1991, when it set up Airtours International Aviation to guarantee itself a source of flights seats, Airtours had become the UK's fastest growing operator.

Initially Airtours had a rather downmarket image, highlighted in 1992 when a MORI survey found that 58 per cent of agents received more complaints about Airtours than any other company; in part this may have been because it was trying to step into ILG's shoes, in part because the UK recession meant many holidaymakers were trading down to cheaper products, notorious for generating complaints. However, by 1993 Airtours had started to reposition itself further upmarket, a fact reflected on the front covers of its brochures which became more sophisticated and stylish, and by the launch, in 1994, of a specialist cruising brochure. In 1994 Airtours also purchased the long-haul company Tradewinds to act as a springboard for the launch of its own more upmarket products.

In 1992 Airtours bought the Pickfords chain of travel agencies from National Freight Corporation (NFC) to ensure itself a sales outlet. It then went on to buy the Hogg Robinson retail travel agencies and a smaller competitor, Aspro Holidays (in 1994 Pickfords and Hogg Robinson were renamed Going Places). Had its 1993 bid to buy Owners Abroad succeeded, it might even have overtaken Thomson to become the UK's largest operator.

More business failures

Company failures continued throughout the early 1990s as increasing competition coincided with a stagnant, recession-hit market; indeed between March 1992 and March 1993 24 licensed operators went bust, the largest number in a single year since the Air Travel Trust was set up in 1975. Because of the bonding arrangements, ABTA was forced to bail out clients of many of these companies, leaving it strapped for cash by 1992, and struggling to find new ways to reassure the public that their holiday payments were safe and which wouldn't leave it so exposed to weak companies. However, even the existing bonding arrangements were exposed as inadequate in July 1992 when Bath-based coach-tour operator Land Travel collapsed, leaving 2,000 clients in need of repatriation and £2 million owed to creditors. Land Travel was not an ABTA member which meant few people who had booked holidays but not travelled were likely to recover their money. The company had been in business for 18 years but

The International Leisure Group companies	Airbreak – Airbreak Ltd, Next Holidays, Peter Pan Travel, Suntan Tours
Riva Travel	Flight Seekers
Novotours	Land Travel
Seasun Tentrek	Zenith Holidays
Transglobal	Number 1 Airtours
DHG (UK) – Flights Delight/Turkish Delight	Tempo Travel
Impact	Sunseekers
Meridian	Cypriana
Grecian	

Fig. 2.12 Going, going, gone – some of the tour operators who ceased trading in the early 1990s

by 1992 was offering holidays at prices so low there was almost no room left for making a profit. In August 1993 its directors were charged with fraud.

Airtours bids for Owners Abroad

In January 1993 Airtours, the UK's third biggest tour operator, made a bid to buy Owners Abroad, its second largest. It did this just days before Owners Abroad shareholders were due to consider a bid by Thomas Cook to buy 10.3 per cent of the company. Despite suggestions that two of Owners Abroad's directors had approached Airtours to discuss the possibility of a merger, this was a 'hostile' bid which was not welcomed by Owners Abroad's board of directors.

Why did Airtours want to buy Owners Abroad?

a) It would have given it a 27 per cent market share, enough to compete with Thomson's 32 per cent share.
b) It should have been possible to achieve economies of scale and cost reductions across the two companies.
c) The combined company would have had greater clout to negotiate better deals with hoteliers.
d) Airtours sells well in the north of England, Owners Abroad in the south, so the combined company would have achieved a better geographical spread of sales.

What potential difficulties could there have been?

a) While tour operating had always been Airtours' core business, Owners Abroad was primarily a seat wholesaler. They therefore had very different strategies and objectives.
b) The two companies flew different aircraft, making it difficult to take advantage of economies of scale, for example in buying spare parts.
c) The two companies used different computer reservations systems which could have slowed the process of integration.

Why did Thomas Cook want a link with Owners Abroad?

a) Because it wanted help with developing its own package tour operation.
b) Because it saw the Lunn Poly/Thomson and Pickfords/Airtours links as threatening its own potential sales.

Had the bid succeeded, Thomson and Airtours/Owners Abroad would have controlled 60 per cent of the package holiday market between them. What's more because of their links with Lunn Poly and Pickfords, the two companies would have been able to exert a stranglehold over the market, by refusing to shelve the brochures of rival companies in their agencies, for example. This might have led to a reduction in competition and to price rises as far as the travelling public was concerned. However, had the bid succeeded it is possible that Thomson would have responded by launching a price war against Airtours/Owners Abroad as it did against Clarkson's in the early 1970s. Price wars lead to lower prices for consumers, but to lower profits for the companies concerned and to lower dividends for their shareholders. In 1974 a price war had contributed to the eventual collapse of Court Line and Clarkson's (*see* page 41).

Because an Airtours/Owners Abroad link-up would have given the company more than 25 per cent of the market there was a risk that the Office of Fair Trading would have referred the deal to the Monopolies and Mergers Commission as a technical monopoly. (According to the Fair Trading Act of 1973 a business has a monopoly if it has or is likely to have control of 25 per cent of a particular market, or if the total assets of a merged organisation exceed £5 million.) However, when Thomson bought Horizon from Bass in 1988 that merger was not referred to the MMC; Thomson argued that its share of the entire UK holiday market, taking into account domestic holidays, independent holidays and so on, was still only 11 per cent. It also argued that there were so few barriers to entering the tour operations market that it would still be unable to suppress competition. After six weeks' deliberation, the Office of Fair Trading nevertheless advised that the Airtours/Owners Abroad merger should be referred to the MMC. However, their advice was overruled by Trade and Industry Secretary Michael Heseltine.

In March 1993 Thomas Cook finally made a rival bid for a 12.5 per cent stake in Owners Abroad. Shareholders accepted this offer and the Airtours bid failed, probably because the price offered was too low and because it was harder for it to quantify the supposed benefits of the better management it promised than it was for Owners' management to quantify the benefits of a tie-in with Thomas Cook. Ultimately Owners Abroad ended up with a 21.4 per cent share in Thomas Cook.

However, in July 1993 Owners Abroad reported an unexpected slump in profits of almost 50 per cent. Owners' management claimed that holiday sales in May, June and July had been disappointing, hence the change in its profits forecast. It explained this fall in sales by saying that the recession had forced clients to trade down to cheaper holidays when Owners tended to sell more upmarket packages. It also suggested that its sales through Lunn Poly had fallen by 48 per cent and through Pickfords by 38 per cent since Thomson and Airtours had started offering incentives to agency staff to sell their own products. Owners Abroad chair Howard Klein resigned, and there were calls for the one-year rule (forbidding a company to repeat a bid within a year of a previous offer) to be waived because shareholders had been misled. There were also calls for the Thomas Cook chief executive Christopher Rodrigues to step down as director of Owners Abroad since it was thought that Thomas Cook had a vested interest in blocking any further bids to take over Owners Abroad. Largely as a result of this, the Office of Fair Trading announced an inquiry into the consequences of increased vertical integration in the travel business.

What Owners Abroad gained from the tie-up with Thomas Cook

There were several benefits to Owners Abroad from their successful union with Thomas Cook:

a) Thomas Cook's major shareholder is the German company LTU which has its own tour operating arm, LTU Touristik. Working with LTU Touristik, Owners Abroad would hope to increase its bargaining clout with European hoteliers.
b) It would also be possible for the two companies to save money by pooling some of their resources. For example, in Corfu where the British and Germans arrive on different days, both companies could make use of the same transfer coaches. In some resorts they would also be able to combine their operations and use one office instead of two.
c) LTU has its own in-house airline, so there would be possible savings in bulk purchase of spare parts, aviation fuel, maintenance contracts, insurance, etc. When either company needed to replace its aircraft, better deals with the aircraft manufacturers could be negotiated.
d) Smaller savings would also be possible through the joint purchase of office equipment like paper for brochure production.
e) Owners Abroad would expect to see increased sales of its own products through the Thomas Cook shops.

The aftermath

In the meantime Airtours invested £20 million in buying up Cardiff-based Aspro Holidays, which held three to four per cent of the market. In doing so it gave itself access to Aspro's strength out of regional airports and to its links with major destinations in the eastern Mediterranean, like Crete and Cyprus. At the time of the purchase Aspro was pursuing legal action against Owners Abroad, claiming that it was behind a 'dirty tricks whispering campaign', aimed at suggesting to potential Aspro clients and hoteliers that the company was about to collapse. Since the purchase, Airtours has, in turn, been pursuing action against Aspro's original owners, arguing that the company had been overvalued at the time of sale.

A CLOSER LOOK AT CRUISING

Until the 1950s, shipping was really about liners which operated timetabled passenger services from one point to another: for example, from Britain to

New York, or from Britain to South Africa. However, as soon as air transport became a realistic and much faster alternative, the days of the great cruise liners were numbered. Crucially, in 1957 for the first time more people crossed the Atlantic by air than did so by liner. By the 1960s cruising was emerging as a possible alternative way of using the ships. However, it was not always easy for shipping companies simply to switch from offering A to B services to offering cruises because:

a) many of their ships were too large for the relatively shallow ports of, for example, the Caribbean;
b) the ships were designed to be economic when sailing at speed rather than when cruising in more leisurely fashion.

The 1973/4 oil crisis also dealt a serious blow to the emerging cruise companies. However, some companies were already investing in new purpose-built cruise ships and, at the same time, Greek, Norwegian and Russian companies stepped in to launch entirely new fleets. Cunard offered the first fly-cruise to the Mediterranean in response to the problem that most people's holidays were of limited duration and they were reluctant to spend the majority of them getting to and from their chosen destination and the sun.

In the early 1970s cruising suffered from two 'image' problems: it was seen as expensive and as appealing only to the elderly. During the 1970s tour operators had tried to reverse the decline in passenger numbers by chartering cruise ships to provide their own cruise products; however, in trying to bring down prices they also tended to reduce standards which proved counterproductive. By 1985 the number of British holidaymakers buying cruises had slumped to about 75,000. Ironically it was falling air fares which helped to reverse the decline. As air fares to the USA were progressively reduced in the 1980s, fly-cruises to the Caribbean, with its more youthful image, became possible. By 1992 the number of cruise passengers had crept back up to about 230,000 (*see* Table 2.4). When general tour operators include cruises in their packages nowadays, they tend to do it by bulk-buying berths on normal cruises and leaving the cruise companies to run the programme.

The biggest cruise market is out of America: in particular out of Miami to the Caribbean. Since the Americans set high standards for safety and hygiene, older ships which could not match up to their expectations have gradually been squeezed out. But cruising remains a labour-intensive and therefore potentially expensive business. To help

Table 2.4 Cruising from the UK, 1986–92

	1986	*1987*	*1988*	*1989*	*1990*	*1991*	*1992*
Total UK residents taking cruise	91,500	128,500	152,140	168,400	186,490	193,010	228,728
Ex UK cruises	40,900	51,440	50,300	52,650	47,230	65,678	66,866
Fly-cruises							
– Caribbean	19,960	26,600	32,900	45,950	60,840	73,484	84,428
– Mediterranean	24,850	31,250	30,650	34,800	44,320	15,643	30,407
– Scandinavia/Baltic	580	6,850	4,850	7,350	7,250	6,997	6,068
– Far East	350	1,250	1,650	2,240	2,480	2,703	2,875
– West Coast US/ Trans-Panama Canal	290	1,500	3,160	4,010	4,370	6,410	8,928
– Other areas	520	2,100	8,250	9,150	6,230	7,217	9,899
Line voyages (e.g. Southampton to New York)	na	2,050	11,820	1,680	3,720	5,300	4,600
Round the world	4,050	2,410	2,290	2,980	2,970	3,675	5,094
River cruises	na	3,050	6,270	7,590	7,080	5,903	9,563

Source: PSARA

keep costs down in the 1990s, the big cruise companies employ a high percentage of foreign crew who are prepared to accept lower wages than Europeans.

THE DEATH OF THE PACKAGE HOLIDAY?

As the travelling public grew increasingly confident in the 1990s and as the amount of information available to help them make their own travel arrangements expanded, there were frequent predictions of the imminent death of the package holiday. These predictions were fuelled by figures that showed the number of package holidays sold rising from 8.5 million in 1985 to 12.6 million in 1988, before falling back to 11.4 million in 1990 and 10.5 million in 1991. It was thought that 2.5 million of the 1991 'packages' could have been 'flight-only' deals which would support the argument that the number of people travelling independently was increasing. However, 1991 was an exceptional year because of the Gulf War, and in 1992 the number of packages sold rose again to 12.6 million despite the recession.

It is undoubtedly true that more people are travelling independently. However, it is probably premature to read the last rites for the package holiday. After all, for people with children it remains the best way of ensuring everything goes smoothly at the busiest times of year. For many (although not all) destinations it remains the case that tour operators can negotiate cheaper deals with their bulk-buying power than individuals can on their own, so that some people will buy a package even when they don't intend to use any or all of the accommodation, just to take advantage of the cheap fares.

Shrewd tour operators who have seen the way the wind is blowing have also reacted by building greater flexibility into their 'packages', while still offering clients the benefit of their bulk-buying powers. Self-drive deals with accommodation vouchers are now commonplace, and some companies, like Kuoni and Regent Holidays, are as happy to arrange tailor-made 'packages' as to sell off-the-shelf arrangements. Obviously this is a time-consuming and skilled business, requiring an in-depth knowledge of destinations on the part of the organiser, so such arrangements are unlikely to be cheap. They do, however, give the holidaymaker the peace of mind that comes from knowing everything has been sorted out in advance that truly independent travellers rarely have. In some ways, it is the agent rather than the operator who is most threatened by a move towards tailor-made packages since agency staff rarely have the requisite knowledge to put 'packages' together themselves. What's more, if they did so, they would risk becoming 'organisers' under the terms of the EC Package Travel Regulations and would have to make expensive bonding arrangements accordingly.

Even among those people booking conventional packages, the desire for greater flexibility means that an increasing number of deals involve self-catering; in 1987 only 24 per cent of people booking through travel agencies opted for self-catering, but by 1993 that proportion had risen to 44 per cent. Conversely, the proportion of hotel packages fell from 63 per cent in 1987 to 47 per cent in 1993.

QUESTIONS AND DISCUSSION POINTS

1 Why did the real boom in package holidays only come after 1945 when Thomas Cook had run his first excursion in 1841?

2 Discuss the ways in which the 'Big Three' operators (Thomson, Airtours, First Choice) have established their grip on the market.

3 Compare the success of Thomson's bid to take over Horizon Holidays in 1988 with the failure of Airtours' bid to take over Owners Abroad in 1993. Why do you think the former succeeded while the latter failed?

ASSIGNMENTS

1 You work for a national broadsheet newspaper. It is 9 March 1991, the day after the International Leisure Group collapsed, and your paper is getting ready to run lengthy background features on issues raised by the failure. You are asked to research the earlier collapse of Court Line/Clarkson's and to write a 500-word article highlighting the similarities and differences between the two events. Remember that newspaper articles need to be pithy and sharp, so make sure you use suitable language and structure your sentences and paragraphs appropriately.

2 You work for First Choice in the product development section. Conscious of changes in the marketplace, your manager has asked you to look into the latest trends and provide a report outlining what is happening in terms of changing demographics, net disposable income, attitudes to the environment, confidence about travelling, desire for independence, etc.

3 On the basis of that report, he/she then asks you to look ahead and make suggestions for ways in which First Choice should change and develop its product range to take account of the changes. Your suggestions should appear in an attached appendix, with reasons given for each suggestion.

CHAPTER 3

Putting the package together

LEARNING OBJECTIVES

After reading this chapter you should be able to:

- **list the stages involved in putting together a programme of package holidays**
- **explain the differences between commitment, allocation and *ad hoc* arrangements in the contracting of bed space**
- **describe the differences between time series charters, part charters and *ad hoc* arrangements in the contracting of flight seats**
- **discuss the pros and cons of operators owning their own charter airlines**
- **understand the role of ground handlers in organising transfers, excursions, etc.**
- **discuss the importance of quality control for package holidays**

INTRODUCTION

As we have already seen, tour operators act as wholesalers, collecting together rooms in hotels, seats on planes and transfers to and from airports, pricing them for individual passengers and producing brochures with all the details to sell the new products to potential clients. Before doing this they must first decide what destinations they would like to feature, a task carried out by product development departments of marketing divisions in large operations, or by all-purpose staff in smaller ones.

Once this has been done they will have to decide on the size of the programme they would like to offer. Only then can they get down to the nitty gritty of negotiating prices and signing contracts for beds, seats, transfers and all the other bits and pieces that go to make up the standard package holiday.

PLANNING A PROGRAMME OF PACKAGE HOLIDAYS

The planning of a programme of package holidays has to be started well in advance of brochure production. Typically, a company will start planning between 12 and 18 months before the first expected departure to allow time for contracting beds and seats, production of the brochure and a marketing push. If the purchase of hotels or airlines is involved then planning may have to start as part of an overall corporate strategy two to three years before the actual holidays involved. A summer sun brochure must be ready in the late summer or early autumn of the year preceding the departures, winter sun and winter ski brochures in the preceding summer. Consequently companies have to make critical decisions about prices long before the holidays actually take place, a process which entails considerable risk.

Deciding on the product

Once a company has been established for a number of years the bulk of its programme will be fairly fixed. Unless poor sales or external circumstances force them to abandon a destination they alread
feature, they will mainly be looking at marg
changes to the programme, bringing in a fe
hotels in familiar resorts, a few new resor
established destinations, and perhaps
new destination. Such changes will
lighted on the front cover of the
first few pages. So in summ
highlighting new program
both in Italy, a country i
was promoting new
and Costa de Almer

already featured, and to Egypt, a country which had not appeared in the summer 1992 brochure.

When deciding to launch a new product, an operator may be influenced by outside factors. So, for example, in 1993 several operators (including Twickers World and Speedwing) decided to take advantage of a new summer WST charter flight to Eilat to offer summer holidays to Israel, normally thought of as a winter holiday destination from the UK.

If the new resorts slot easily into the general pattern of the operator's programme, they can expect them to sell without difficulty to a regular clientele. When it moves away from the usual programme, however, it can be very much harder, as eastern bloc specialists Regent Holidays found when they tried to launch programmes to Colombia and Zimbabwe, countries with which they were not associated.

It is obviously easier for larger operators, with their mass-buying clout, to launch unexpected destinations. So, for example, in 1992 Thomson developed a new programme to Cuba. Although it already had a strong presence in the Caribbean, Cuba's image sat a little uneasily with its general mass-market image. To set the ball rolling, Thomson offered some excellent start-up offers to Cuba, at loss-leading prices which it could afford to bear because of its size. Despite some initial sales resistance, Cuba was thought enough of a success to merit inclusion in 1993 brochures too.

However, it doesn't *automatically* follow that large operators can make a success of a new destination if they have timed their introduction of it wrongly. In the late 1980s most of the big tour operators launched programmes of beach holidays in Mexico, hitherto featured mainly as a sightseeing destination in upmarket long-haul brochures. Two resorts were favoured: Acapulco on the Pacific coast and Cancun in the Yucatan on the Caribbean side of the country. Unfortunately, at the time there were no direct flights from the UK to Mexico, and many visitors concluded that they had flown halfway round the world for something they could ave got more cheaply and conveniently nearer to me. Mexico lapsed from favour until 1993 when mson and Airtours made another attempt to k the market, using new British Airways direct s into Mexico City and their own charter to Cancun. In contrast, in 1993 Thomson to drop its two-year-old programme of Cuban holidays which it had found impossible to sell despite a strong presence in other parts of the Caribbean.

Nor is it the case that countries always co-operate with operators' schemes. In 1993 Airtours was interested in introducing charter-based holidays to the Cayman Islands but found its path blocked by the islands' tourism authorities who were concerned that charter flights would encourage low-budget holidaymakers to visit a destination which was actually very expensive, something they doubted Airtours would highlight in its brochures. The Cypriot authorities also bar the way to seat-only charters because they want to protect Cyprus Airways', the national carrier, business.

When moving into a new area, an operator may decide to run a small test programme before becoming too involved. So in winter 1992/3 Wallace Arnold, a coach tour operator franchised to offer coach tours to Euro Disney, added a small number of self-drive holidays to its coach tour brochure. When this proved successful, it launched a fully-fledged standalone self-drive brochure ('Way-Ahead Holidays by Car') for 1993.

For a small operator launching a new destination, the first 100 bookings are usually hardest to secure. No matter how obscure the destination there will usually be 10 to 50 people prepared to book for a range of idiosyncratic reasons. However, once 100 people have travelled there, usually from all different parts of the country, word will start to spread. At that point it will usually be possible to get the media interested, after which building bookings up to 500 should be much easier.

Of course operators with successful programmes could just repeat them without alteration. However, fashions change and a resort which was popular one year may not be the next. Also, a programme with no changes to it can quickly look stale; in particular it will have little publicity value in a media world which is always in search of novelty and new angles. Thirdly, in an uncertain world, diversification avoids the risk of an entire programme falling foul of some external hiccough, as happened with well-established Transglobal in 1991 when the Gulf War rendered its entire programme of holidays to Israel, Egypt and Turkey unsaleable. Fourthly, in a highly competitive business environment no operator wishes to be caught on the hop. This has led to a situation where if one operator introduces a new destination, it can be overwhelmed by the rush in the following year as other operators hasten to include it in their brochures to make sure they don't miss out on the latest moneyspinner. This was what happened to Cyprus in 1992.

Deciding the product mix

Once an operator has decided on the destinations and resorts it wants to feature, it must then decide what type of accommodation to offer, in what proportions and on what dates. Again, fashion will have a lot to do with this. For example, in the early 1980s there was a huge increase in the amount of self-catering accommodation on offer, as operators responded to a recession-inspired demand for lower priced holidays by featuring more apartments and villas and fewer hotels.

Decisions on what to feature, when and where must be decided by market research (*see* Chapter Nine), by keeping in touch with what competitors are doing and by listening to feedback from clients and staff in the resorts. Inevitably it is easy to make

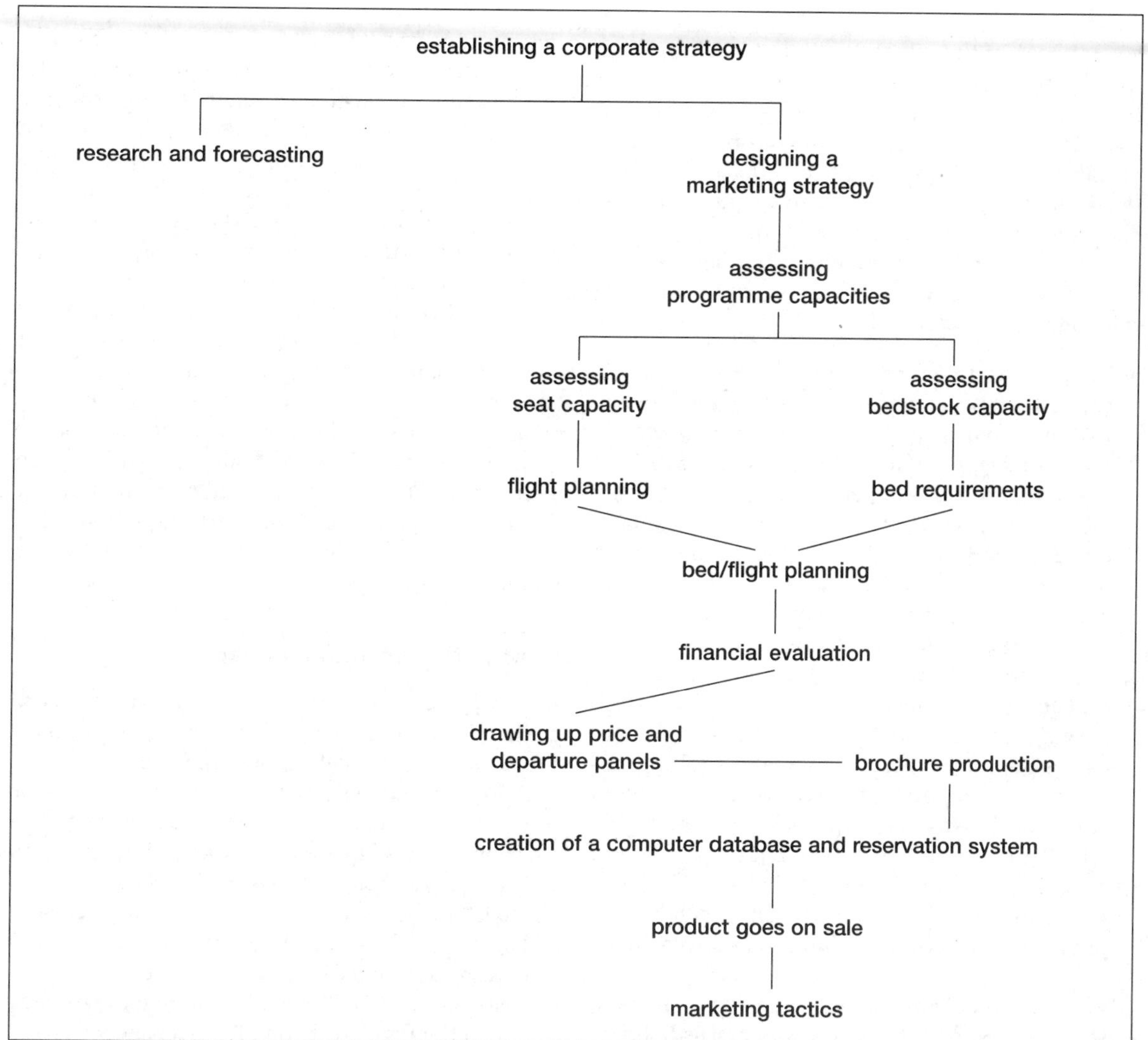

Fig. 3.1 Logical sequence for constructing and marketing an air-inclusive tour

mistakes. In 1993, for example, operators overestimated the demand for Spain and underestimated the demand for holidays in the Eastern Mediterranean, leading to discounting of Spain and a scramble to secure extra seats and accommodation in Greece, Turkey and Cyprus.

Other forecasting problems

Having decided what destinations it wants to feature, an operator also has to make difficult forecasting decisions about the likely size of the market before going ahead with contracting flight seats and hotel beds. Forecasting can never be an exact science, especially given that it must be done so far ahead of the actual departure dates, when so much can happen to alter the basis of even the best forecast. For these reasons it has been argued that tour operating calls for staff with strong entrepreneurial skills and the nerve to stick with their decisions when times get tough or alter them at short notice as circumstances require.

When operators were planning holidays for winter 1993/4 these were some of the immediate dilemmas they faced:

1 When interest rates were high, the overall market was adversely affected by the fact that people with high mortgages found their net disposable income squeezed. However, by the start of 1993 interest rates had dropped sharply, helping home owners but putting the squeeze on people, many of them elderly, who relied on their savings for an income. It was difficult to know how many would-be holidaymakers would be pushed out of the market or forced to trade down by this.
2 By March 1993 the pound had slumped 22 per cent in value against the dollar since July 1992, making the United States significantly more expensive for British holidaymakers. This coincided with reports of attacks on tourists in America. It was hard for operators to assess whether to buy dollars forward at poor rates and charge higher prices in the hope that clients would travel anyway, or to wait and hope the pound would recover its value as the year wore on.
3 A similar problem applied to the French market, still the most popular with UK overseas holidaymakers. Again, by March 1993 the pound had lost 13.5 per cent in value against the French franc, making France significantly more expensive for British visitors. However, it was widely believed that domestic circumstances in France would force interest rate cuts there and that these would in turn reduce the value of the franc, restoring some of the pound's lost value. Once more operators had to decide whether to buy French francs ahead at high cost and pass the price on to consumers or to assume that the value of the franc would fall again and price accordingly.

CONTRACTING

Putting together the holiday programme involves contracting flight seats, hotel beds, seats on transfer coaches and lots of smaller details. Contracting is a specialist skill involving knowledge of UK and overseas law, and language abilities. Large companies will therefore have a whole department devoted to contracting, often as a subsection of the overseas department. However, in 1993 Thomson created a new purchasing division to take over responsibility for purchasing holiday components from the old disbanded overseas department. A contracts manager will probably have responsibility for working out seat and bed requirements. Smaller companies, however, will not be able to afford the luxury of a separate department in which case much of the contracting will be carried out by the managing director. All contracting will need to be completed by June or July when the brochure will usually go to print.

Contracting accommodation

If an operator is already established in a resort, contracting bed space will be relatively straightforward. Often it will involve renewing contracts with known contacts. However, when an operator moves into a new resort it may take months to finish contracting all the required rooms. Big operators are usually in the best position to negotiate the cheapest rates. However, sometimes smaller specialist companies may be able to build on their long-term credibility to get better rates.

The contractor will need to secure enough beds to match the flight seats on offer. He/she will have to ensure that they are contracted at a price that will enable the company to compete with other tour operators, while also ensuring that financial risk to the company is kept to a minimum. He/she will also need to gather information to go in the brochure, check that old details remain true and organise whatever meals will be required in each hotel. Large companies will send their own contractors to negotiate directly with the hoteliers in the resorts, although smaller ones may have to use a local ground agent as an intermediary, or even do much of the legwork themselves.

It is important to remember that when it comes to contracting for hotel space a company will often be competing with buyers from other European tour operators; if they are prepared to pay more for rooms, this can force prices up for British buyers too. However, sometimes the largest operators contract for all the rooms in a hotel, in which case there is no competition over prices. Operators often prefer to secure exclusive British occupancy of a hotel, because this makes it easier for them to control rates, with no risk of being undercut by the competition. Hoteliers, on the other hand, may prefer to spread their risk around competing companies. As hotels have grown bigger it has inevitably become harder for any single operator to expect to fill all the rooms.

Beds can be contracted in three different ways, each involving different risks to the operator and therefore being suited to different markets.

1 Commitment

A tour operator may agree to buy a specific number of beds for the season regardless of how many it actually manages to sell. The higher the percentage of beds they make a commitment to in this way, the lower the price the hotelier is likely to accept. In a good year, this can be very profitable. However, in a bad year it may mean the operator paying for lots of beds it is ultimately unable to sell. Although unsold beds are less costly than unsold flight seats, commitment offers little flexibility and is therefore only really appropriate in established resorts with a mass market. Even when an operator does opt for commitment they are unlikely to commit for 100 per cent of their bed requirements.

In a well-established resort the hoteliers may be able to help fill committed bed spaces in a bad year. However, tour operators are also put under considerable pressure to commit hotels to specific targeted markets to avoid conflict between, for example ,elderly couples who find themselves in a hotel full of young late-night partygoers. This can make for tough decisions in slow-selling resorts.

2 Allocation

Alternatively, a tour operator may agree to an allocation of rooms in hotels which will be put on sale up to a specified date. On the 'release date' the rooms revert to the hotelier to fill if still unsold. Although 'release dates' are usually three to four weeks before the holiday date, well-established companies can often negotiate later dates which facilitate handling late bookings; in 1993 Kuoni announced that it had negotiated three-day release dates with 200 hotels worldwide and hoped to extend the agreement to 400 hotels by 1994.

If rooms are required after the release date, the tour operator will have to phone, fax or telex out to the resort to regain the room. This is more costly in administrative terms, but less risky than being left with unsold beds. Because allocation leaves the hotelier with more uncertainty, beds contracted in this way will be more expensive than those gained through commitment. What's more, where hoteliers know they cannot rely on rooms being sold they may be tempted to double-book to be on the safe side. Operators can try and prevent this by building penalty clauses for double-booking into the contracts.

Large tour operators may take some rooms on allocation to top up their committed beds. Long-haul and specialist tour operators also tend to go for allocation rather than commitment. Allocation is less appropriate where the operator wants to be sure a hotel will only be filled with one type of customer.

3 Ad hoc *rooms*

Finally, operators can contract beds as and when they are required by phone, fax or telex to the resort. Administratively, this is the most costly method. However, it involves no risk to the operator. Many upmarket and specialist operators will opt for *ad hoc* arrangements, although almost all companies will have had to resort to it at some time when, for example, overbooking has occurred and alternative rooms must be found in a hurry. Increasingly, sophisticated computer reservation systems are making *ad hoc* bookings easier to arrange, so this method of 'contracting' is likely to become more popular.

Problems can arise when hoteliers are reluctant to agree contract prices that operators believe will make their packages marketable. This was a particular difficulty in Cyprus during the summer of 1993. In 1992 Cyprus had been *the* place to go, after a year in which fears engendered by the Gulf War had effectively wiped it off the map. In fact Cyprus was so popular that hotels ended up double-booking rooms, something that hadn't been a problem in Mediterranean resorts for 10 years. As operators rushed to secure beds in 1992, it was assumed the enthusiasm would continue; property developers moved in to build new hotels and apartment blocks to fill the gaps revealed by the rush in 1992, and existing hoteliers put up their prices. Few operators were able to beat them down, and summer 1993 saw the number of visitors to Cyprus slump by 20 per cent. The situation was hardly helped when sterling's devaluation against the Cypriot pound forced some smaller operators to resort to surcharging. Late in the season, faced with unsold rooms, some hoteliers did agree to discount rates, but most operators felt this was too late in the day; people who had seen early brochure editions had been put off by high prices, and the sort of clients attracted by sudden late offers were not always those the Cypriots actually wanted to encourage. When it came to negotiating for summer 1994, therefore, British operators were keen to persuade Cypriot hoteliers to reduce their prices; some companies like Manos, however, dropped Cyprus from their programmes, citing uncompetitive hotel rates as the reason.

Hotel ownership

The cost of accommodation usually represents a high proportion of a package holiday price, so as tour operators have increasingly looked for opportunities to control their suppliers it might have seemed logical that more would have started to buy hotels in popular resorts outright to gain complete control over their bedstock. In fact this has not happened much at all, although in 1986 Owners Abroad bought into a Lanzarote hotel and in 1993 Airtours announced a major investment in eight European properties.

The problem tour operators face when they buy a hotel is that their investment cannot be moved if the destination falls from favour for any reason. The risk can be minimised by buying property in an area which is popular for holidays all year round. However, particularly for smaller operators, buying hotels outright represents a high-risk strategy.

After a short-lived move into hotel ownership in the 1970s, Thomson now prefers to concentrate on building up a good relationship with specific hotels. In 1988 it launched its 'Sun' branding concept which originally applied to chosen Spanish hotels but now encompasses favourites in Greece too. A 300-point specification covering quality of food, levels of service and entertainment, etc. was drawn up and then Thomson entered negotiations with hoteliers who were prepared to maintain those standards in return for the extra effort that Thomson would put into marketing them. Hoteliers are offered considerable incentive to maintain standards because Thomson can always drop them from the programme if they don't. Given the company's considerable clout, this would be a serious blow.

CONTRACTING FLIGHT SEATS

Whereas hotel rooms are usually contracted in the resort, flight seats are normally contracted in the UK, either directly from the airline or through an air broker. The contractor will need to ensure the number of seats available matches the number of beds for sale and that prices are competitive with those offered by other operators. Once contracts are signed operators usually have to hand over 10 per cent of the total cost. The balance will be paid just before or after the flight departure.

Airline ownership

The easiest way for a tour operator to gain control over a stock of air seats is to own its own airline, so by the mid-1990s all three of the biggest tour operators owned a charter airline: Thomson had Britannia

Airways, Airtours had Airtours International and First Choice had Air 2000. Actually owning an airline is not as high-risk a strategy for big operators as buying into hotels, because if a destination falls from favour they can re-route the aircraft to those which have become more popular. If necessary, they can also subcontract surplus seats to other operators. Interestingly some of the big operator collapses have involved companies which were trying to expand their airline operations, as Laker did in 1982 and ILG did in 1991.

Owning the airline also gives the operator greater say over standards of service on board which can make a lot of difference to the overall way a holiday is perceived. Inevitably, standards have been rising steadily. Nowadays charter airlines may well offer two classes of service like scheduled carriers. In 1992 Britannia Airways introduced its 'Royal Service' which offers extras like free newspapers and complimentary 'baby packs' with nappies, baby wipes, tissues and a bib. On its long-haul services it also features in-flight movie entertainment and an Airborne Flightmaster which plots the aircraft's movements (International Leisure has a similar 'Airshow' system). The charter airlines are also upgrading their fleets, with Monarch and Air 2000 concentrating on Airbus A320s and Britannia on Boeing 757s and 767s.

However, owning your own charter airline is not always a bed of roses. In particular, it can make the decision to consolidate that much harder. If summer bookings are slow in April one way to handle this is to delay the start of the flight series. If they're slow in May, one option is to consolidate flights rather than have them flying half empty. In the past that decision would have been made even if it meant some small charter airlines were put out of business. However, when the same company that offers the holidays also owns the airline, such decisions mean consigning their own aircraft to expensive time on the ground. In such circumstances operators may resort to discounting even when that doesn't fit their overall strategy for selling the programme; in other words, the needs of one part of a group can be sacrificed to those of another. When Airtours introduced a new skiing programme into the flat market of winter 1993/4 (a market it had already failed to break into once before), one reason it gave for doing so was the need to make as much use as possible of its eight aircraft.

Most charter airlines started with aircraft suitable for short-haul flights, but as the long-haul market has expanded, fleets have had to be upgraded. By 1993 both Thomson (Britannia Airways) and Unijet (Leisure International) had bought Boeing 767s able to fly to Florida without refuelling *en route* in Maine, and Airtours was considering investing in similar aircraft. In 1988 Britannia also started operating flights to Australia, a move followed by Airtours in 1994.

Even when an operator does own its own airline it may still need to buy in seats from other airlines on routes where it doesn't have enough seats or doesn't fly the right planes. So in 1992 Airtours was buying seats on Monarch and Air 2000 to operate its programmes to Orlando because Airtours International didn't own any long-haul aircraft. When Airtours bought Aspro in 1993 it acquired Aspro's own airline, Inter-European Airways, thus increasing its own seating capacity.

Of course, most operators don't own their own airlines and must therefore buy their flight seats from scheduled or charter airlines.

Scheduled flights

Scheduled airlines offer timetabled services around the world which operate regardless of the number of passengers booked on them, unlike charters

THOMSON	OWNERS ABROAD	AIRTOURS
Britannia Airways	*Air 2000*	*Airtours International*
Boeing 757s Boeing 767s	Airbus 320s Boeing 757s Boeing 757-200ERs	MD-83s Boeing 757s Boeing 767s Airbus A320s

Fig. 3.2 The charter airlines of the 'Big Three' operators, 1993

- Seats with more leg-space
- Seat pitch of 30 inches
- Seats reclining by as much as 5' 5"
- Meals served on good quality, reusable trays
- Free wine, buck's fizz or soft drinks
- Free ice cream
- Free in-flight entertainment
- Free amenity kits with slipperettes and eyeshades
- Fold-up aisle armrests for easier access
- Washrooms suitable for disabled travellers
- Free newspapers

Fig. 3.3 Possible features of charter airlines in the 1990s

which may be consolidated if there are not enough reservations to justify flying. They also offer greater flexibility than charter airlines for creating 'open-jaw' packages (where the client flies into one destination and out of another), and for designing packages for different durations than the standard one, two or three weeks.

In the past, relatively few operators used scheduled flights which were usually more expensive than charters. However, by the early 1990s competition on many routes, particularly outside Europe, had brought scheduled air fares down, making them more attractive to operators. Indeed in some cases scheduled air fares had been brought down so much that it was questionable whether a charter operator would want to try and compete. Typical of such a situation is Australia. Fares to Australia from the UK used to be prohibitively high. In 1988 Britannia Airways introduced a charter service to nine destinations in Australia and New Zealand which Ausbound used to create cheap package holidays. However, by 1993, scheduled fares had fallen so much that new companies wanting to enter the market were likely to be better off buying scheduled seats with no risk of consolidation than using charters.

Some tour operating companies are actually owned by the airlines. British Airways has a long history, dating back to the 1960s, of involvement in tour operating, both on long-haul and short-haul routes. In the mid-1980s, it part-owned Enterprise, Sovereign, Flair and Redwing Holidays. However, in 1990 all these were sold and only the long-haul company, Speedbird, was retained. In 1992 Speedbird was relaunched as *British Airways Holidays* which now offers long-haul and city break holidays. Inevitably this means most of the holidays use British Airways flights, although the brochure states that 'in order to offer a wider choice on some routes, or to create the most effective itinerary of connecting flights, certain holidays are operated with airlines other than British Airways', including charter flights to Egypt, Kenya and Florida.

Tour operators owned by scheduled airlines are able to offer a full range of airline services, including upgrades to Club or First Class for sizeable supplements. British Airways Holidays is even able to offer upgrades to Concorde for holidaymakers to New York, Washington or Barbados, although with price supplements of more than £1,000 one-way. In addition, it also offers a range of free or discounted connecting flights on the British Airways domestic route network for passengers joining holiday departures.

When operators are offering ITX packages using scheduled air services, they will contract a specific number of seats for specific dates. If these have not been sold they will be released back to the airline, usually one month before departure. ITXs are usually more expensive than ITCs and are mainly offered by specialist or upmarket operators. However, increasingly long-haul operators are making use of scheduled flights, particularly on routes where intense competition is keeping prices down. For example, 15 different carriers operate services between London and Bangkok, and in 1993 Hayes and Jarvis started using a Philippine Airlines scheduled service to Bangkok in place of the charter service direct to Phuket it had been using since 1990.

Operators offering tailor-made holidays often use scheduled flights and may book them through a computer reservations system like Galileo, buying seats as and when needed. As the EU's air liberalisation moves get into their stride and more scheduled airlines start operating new routes in Europe, bringing prices down, charter airlines may become less important to the package tour market in which case more holidays may be booked on a one-off basis like flight-only arrangements. On the other hand, air brokers are now free to charter seats from European carriers as well as British ones.

Charter flights

Because they don't have to operate to a regular schedule, charter airlines can be more flexible than scheduled ones: if a destination is selling badly, flights can be dropped or consolidated; if one is doing unexpectedly well, the operator will look round for extra charter capacity to contract.

Most tour operators offer ITC packages using charter flights to keep prices down. However, customers only really want to fly on charters when there is a significant price differential between them and the scheduled equivalents which are still thought of as offering better service and standards of comfort. As price margins narrow, so operators are becoming more interested in using scheduled services.

When it comes to contracting the required number of charter seats for their holidays operators have three possible ways of proceeding.

1 Time-series charters

The operator may contract for a 'time charter' or 'whole-plane' charter whereby they charter whole aircraft for specific times, perhaps for one day a week, or for one season, or for one year. Doing this involves considerable risk of being left with unsold seats, so the operators must then make as much use of the aircraft as possible in the time available, leading to complicated flight patterns. To avoid flying with empty seats, charter flight operate on a 'back-to-back' basis, flying out to the resort with one group of passengers and back again with another. Companies which operate all year round can eliminate the problem of 'empty legs' at the start and end of the season when one planeload of passengers must be flown out to the resort without there being another group waiting there to be flown back and vice versa. Otherwise losses can be reduced by using the empty seats to offer discounted spring and autumn breaks of unusual durations. Nevertheless, this system allows the operator considerable flexibility over where the planes should fly.

Operators can pass on some of the cost of a time charter by subcontracting days or times when they can't use the plane to other operators. For example, night flights might be subcontracted out to another company as a 'series charter'. In the summer of 1993, Unijet subcontracted space on its two Leisure International Airways non-stop charters to Orlando and Montego Bay to seven other operators.

In return for a guaranteed block booking, companies can sometimes dictate terms to an airline. For example, in 1993 Jetsave signed a two-year agreement with American charter airline, World Airways, to cover flights to Orlando during the peak nine-week summer season when flight seats are always hard to come by. In return, World Airways agreed not to work with any other UK operator during the two-year period.

2 Part charters

Some operators will not want to contract for the whole aircraft but will opt for a 'part charter' or 'allocation' instead. Again, this can be for set days or weeks or for a longer period of time. However, the operator will only have responsibility for filling a smaller portion of the aircraft. Even when an operator owns its own airline it may part charter some seats to other operators to reduce the risk of flying with empty seats.

3 Ad hoc *chartering*

Smaller operators may prefer to buy seats on specific routes on specific dates for a fixed price. Alternatively they can part charter some seats and buy others on an *ad hoc* basis. As computer technology improves, more and more small operators are opting for *ad hoc* arrangements which they can make themselves as and when they need to.

Air brokers

Air brokers specialise in matching operators with available flight seats and can be very helpful in tracking down seats when they're in short supply. They can also help offload excess seats which aren't selling well.

In 1972 Owners Abroad started out primarily as a seat-broking company, with its own airline, Air 2000, and its flights operated through Owners Abroad Aviation (OAA). Because broking has been such an important part of its business, it has not been unusual for clients of competitor Airtours to find themselves flying on Air 2000 services. Many small operators also make use of Air 2000 and were traditionally seen as clients rather than competitors by the company. By 1993 Owners Abroad was selling 3.3 million air seats a year, one million of them to other operators, many of them seat-only operators like Unijet. In contrast, seat broking has always been incidental business for Thomson and Airtours. However, after a rethink of company strategy in 1993, Owners Abroad lost interest in air broking except to supply its own needs as a tour operator. OAA disappeared, and an Air 2000 broking department took over the business of arranging flights for Owners Abroad (now First Choice) products.

Some air brokers are specialists who are not themselves involved in tour operating at all. Some buy and sell flight seats, while others simply organise contracts for other operators. For example, Gatwick-based Flight Directors organises contracts for companies like seat-only operators Avro and Flights Company, and acts as general sales agent for some overseas charter airlines. By 1992 it was broking about one million seats a year. In the past air brokers worked closely with specific airlines, but increasingly they concentrate on building up relationships with particular operators instead. So Goldcrest, which is owned by Inspirations, Grecian and the Airbreak administrators, is primarily interested in securing seats for Cosmos.

Foreign charter companies

Even before 1992, operators were already working with foreign carriers on the transatlantic routes. For example, Jetsave had an exclusive contract with American carrier World Airways. However, in 1992 the Single Market made it possible for European charter operators to fly in and out of Britain, a move welcomed by some smaller operators who feared the big operator-airlines would start charging steep prices to outsiders. In 1993 Avro and Cosmos formed a seat-broking company called First Aviation and discussed the possibility of bringing so-called 'second-tier' operators into an alliance to use their seats and seats contracted with foreign charter companies like Spanish Centennial, Air Europa, LTE, TAP, Air Colombus and Oasis. A particular advantage to operators of working with foreign charter companies is that they can often negotiate contracts just for the peak July to September period whereas UK airlines want them to commit themselves to the longer season from May to September. However, for historical reasons foreign carriers rarely have the best-timed slots at British airports and cannot always fly at times to suit the British market.

Flight scheduling

Schedules for the busy summer flights season are agreed at a huge meeting of the airlines in November. Where airlines have been operating a route for some time they will have first refusal over their usual take-off time. However, airlines operating new routes will have to haggle for slots, either by trading them with other airlines or by negotiating with the Scheduling Committee. At the moment, operators then print precise flights times in their brochures. Over the ensuing year or so these times often alter, and the EC Package Travel Regulations allow for them to do so by 12 hours before compensation must be paid to the customer. Instead of this system, a banding arrangement has been proposed. Were this proposal to be accepted, precise times would not be printed in the brochures. Instead, flights would be allocated to four bands (perhaps Band A midnight to 6 a.m.; Band B 6 a.m. to midday; Band C midday to 6 p.m.; and Band D 6 p.m. to midnight). Clients could then be notified of precise timings once these had been confirmed, thereby reducing some of the irritation caused by alterations.

Airline meals

In-flight meals are supplied by the airlines, but the tour operator will agree a budget for them and discuss what should be provided when contracting for seats. Inevitably, the more expensive the package, the better the in-flight meals are likely to be.

Although in general scheduled airlines are thought of as offering higher standards, some charter carriers now offer perfectly good food, while some scheduled carriers, especially from ex-Eastern bloc or Third World countries, continue to offer very mediocre meals.

CHARTERING CRUISE SHIPS

Some companies include cruises in their programmes and contract space on ships from the companies who own them as if they were hotels. Sometimes demand can force the cruise company itself to sub-contract space on alternative vessels. Some companies are happy to charter the necessary berths and then leave the cruise company to organise everything else. Others, however, take over the running of the ship right down to stocking the library and games room.

CONTRACTING HIRE CARS, ETC.

Although contracting for beds and flight seats is the most important function of a contracting department, contractors will also need to ensure that the right transfers from the airports to the hotels have been arranged, that 'extras' like car hire have been organised, and that items like travel bags and baggage labels will all arrive in good time for each departure.

Tour operators hire cars in the resorts by using their bulk-buying muscle to negotiate better rates with big name companies like Avis and Hertz than the clients could get themselves if they waited until they reached the resort to make a booking. More rarely, they may make arrangements with cheaper local companies.

THE ROLE OF GROUND HANDLING AGENTS

Ground handling agents are local individuals or companies who may deal with hoteliers, airport officials, local coach companies and even the local police on behalf of overseas operators. They have the advantage of knowing the local language and laws, and will also have good local contacts to draw on. Even the largest operators will make some use of ground handling agents to sort out some of their local arrangements, but agents are obviously most important to smaller companies which don't have their own staff in the resorts to organise excursions, etc. In some cases ground handling agents may even provide resort representatives for a company. Several different UK tour operators will often use the same overseas ground handling agent.

In most countries operators can choose between a range of ground handling agents and will use client feedback and resort rep's comments to alert them if the one they are using is not up to scratch. However, in the old Communist countries the state provided ground handling services, as it provided everything else, eliminating any possibility of competition and making it impossible for operators to force improvements by changing agent. This continues to be the case for operators to China who still depend on the services of the monopoly agent, China International Travel Service or CITS. Operators trying to put tailor-made products together have particular problems since CITS continues to be better equipped to deal with the groups it was accustomed to in the past than with individuals.

Excursions

Ground handling agents are often responsible for the programmes of optional excursions most operators sell to customers in a resort. These have become increasingly sophisticated and may range from simple day trips to surrounding attractions to two- to four-day side trips away from the resort, to explore the Tunisian desert, for example. There are even nightlife excursions with the cost of food, drink and folkloric entertainment thrown in.

The amount of information brochures provide about optional excursions varies enormously. Quite often there is no more than an indication of the names of the excursions, with the previous season's price, even when quite a lengthy trip is involved. This is all Sunworld had to say about its Tunisian excursion programme for 1993/4:

> **Excursions** (*prices are approximate and based on Winter 92/3*):
> 2-day Safari £53; Tunis & Carthage (full day) £15; Hammamet & Nabeul (half day) £3; Kairouan (half day) £9; Bedouin Feast (evening) £15.

Long-haul brochures sometimes provide more information (*see* Fig. 3.4).

Excursions are usually booked and paid for in the resorts and one of the rep's jobs is to publicise them at the welcome party and take bookings. Usually, details of excursions are also displayed on a noticeboard or in a file of information at the operator's desk in the hotels. Sometimes excursions can be booked and paid for in the UK (this is more usual with long-haul products). Thomson allows people to prebook its most popular excursions on the basis of a £5 deposit, with the balance payable in the resort. This both helps people budget for the full cost of their holiday and avoids the risk of disappointment if a particular excursion is sold out.

On coach touring holidays, excursions are usually included in the price; sometimes, however, this is made to appear lower by turning many of the excursions into optional extras. On cruise holidays shore excursions must almost always be booked and paid for on the ship; prices vary from an average £15 in the Mediterranean to nearer £60 in the Caribbean.

CREATING AND MAINTAINING A QUALITY PRODUCT

Producing a holiday programme is not just a question of selecting the right destinations, contracting the right components and then pricing them

Egypt Excursion Packages

These excursion packages can be pre-booked and paid for in the UK before you travel.

Luxor

Apart from sunbathing and enjoying the bazaar like atmosphere in Luxor there is so much to do.

£34 per adult, £17 per child under 12.

***The West Bank:** A half day excursion across the Nile visiting The Valleys of the Kings and Queens Deir El Bahari and Nobles Tomb.

***Luxor and Karnak Temples:** A half day excursion to Luxor Temple and to Karnak a superb example of architecture depicting life around 1600 BC.

Please note that for passengers taking a Nile cruise during their stay these excursions are included in their itineraries.

If you also wish to visit Abu Simbel during your stay in Luxor, you would need to spend at least four nights in Luxor to comfortably cover all the sightseeing.

Balloons over Egypt

£151 per person.

Now you can experience a completely new perspective as you drift gently in a hot air balloon over the Temple of Queen Hatshepsut on the West Bank, the River Nile and the ancient city of Luxor.

Flights take place twice each day, at dawn and in the late afternoon when the winds are most favourable. The duration can be from 45 minutes to 2 hours. You should allow 4 hours from the pick up point to the return to your hotel. A sumptuous breakfast is served at the end of the morning flight and high tea following the afternoon flight.

Please note the balloons only operate from October to May.

Cairo

Any Kuoni passenger spending a minimum of three nights in Cairo may pre-purchase the following excursion package:

£23 per adult, £11 per child under 12.

***Pyramids at Giza.** A half day visit to the Pyramids and Sphinx (excludes Cheops Pyramid).

***Egyptian Museum.** Half day visit to one of the most fascinating museums to be found anywhere in the world, it's like history coming alive (excludes the Mummies Room).

Abu Simbel

£114 per person from Aswan.
£174 per person from Luxor.

The most magnificent of all the four colossal statues of Ramses II, faces the sun so that on the birthday of Ramses the sun's rays strike through the temple to fall on the forehead of the seated Pharaohs inside. The incredible feature of Abu Simbel is that the Temples were originally built on the river bank. With the construction of the Aswan High Dam the water level rose and the temples would have been lost if it were not for the UNESCO project to painstakingly move stone by stone and resurrect the temples above the new high water. This optional excursion includes a tour of approximately one hour of the temples.

This excursion may be carried out by air or overland at the same price depending on local conditions. If travelling from Luxor it should be noted that long delays may occur in Aswan on the return journey.

Fig. 3.4 How Kuoni described its Egyptian excursions for 1993

Courtesy: Kuoni

accordingly. In a highly competitive market, ensuring you have produced a *quality* product is also vital, particularly as the public is becoming more demanding and quicker to complain if their holiday fails to live up to expectation.

One way to assess the quality of a programme is by the responses to the customer questionnaires most operators hand out, which ask questions about everything from the service in the hotel to the smiliness of the rep. Most operators take these seriously and will rectify problems identified, sometimes even dismissing staff who aren't up to scratch. In 1993 Sovereign announced that it would drop hotels from its programmes which scored below a fixed minimum.

Another, more negative, way to assess a programme is by the number of complaints received. Of the big three operators, Thomson has perhaps the best record, with a complaints ratio of just one per cent of bookings; this compared with Airtours' at 2.5 per cent. Of course, the gravity of the complaints will vary considerably, and Airtours claim that 75 per cent of those complaining about its products nevertheless say they will book with the company again, suggesting they cannot be particularly serious.

Some companies depend on feedback from their own staff in the resorts although this is a very hit and miss approach. Bales expects all tour managers and escorts to prepare a detailed report on each tour which should include details on crucial matters like the punctuality of guides and coach drivers which might be overlooked by a UK-based office but which can make a lot of difference to client satisfaction with a holiday.

A product's quality can also be assessed through external judgement. For example, in 1993 Airtours threatened to sue the Consumers' Association magazine, *Holiday Which?* after it had placed the operator third from bottom in a survey of readers' views of holiday companies (Airtours claimed that the *Holiday Which?* readership profile didn't match that of its usual clients). However, in a MORI poll, 58 per cent of travel agents also claimed that Airtours was the company about which they received most complaints. Since then, Airtours has taken steps to reposition itself further upmarket; notoriously, it is the cheapest holidays that give rise to most complaints.

Maintaining standards is hardest when operators feature a wide variety of destinations, some of them with very different standards of living from the UK, and when they are dependent on people like hoteliers who the company does not directly employ. It is made even more difficult by the fact that the British package holiday market is so price-led; it's hard to improve standards *and* keep prices down simultaneously. Nevertheless most operators are conscious of the need to maintain standards, and the EC Package Travel Regulations have made this even more imperative by limiting operators' ability to renounce liability for many aspects of their packages. In 1993 Thomson restructured the company to separate contracting from the day-to-day running of the holidays, which should make it easier to identify and deal with problems as they occur; this is especially important as Thomson doesn't pay override commissions to agents and needs to offer a consistently high quality product so that agents will continue selling it.

The bigger companies have been most willing to consider formal methods of ensuring high or consistent standards, often through structured in-house training schemes. Smaller companies still tend to shy away from undertaking such initiatives, claiming that the cost far outweighs any possible benefit to them. Nevertheless, the Association of Independent Tour Operators (AITO), whose members are mainly small tour operators, has drawn up a 'Quality Charter' to which members must subscribe. The charter defines 'quality' as 'providing a level of satisfaction which, based upon the holiday information provided by the tour operator, aims to meet or exceed a customer's reasonable expectations, regardless of the type of holiday sold or the price paid.' Figure 3.6 shows the AITO Quality Charter and the ways in which members hope to achieve 'the quality alternative'.

Hotel grading systems

Most European countries have a nationally regulated hotel grading system, designed to give a consistent indication of a hotel's quality. Such systems vary considerably, however, and may only measure such tangible things as the number of bathrooms, while overlooking ambience, decoration and the standard of service.

Tour operators prefer to use their own grading systems, designed to offer consistency across a range of countries whose grading systems may

. . . . by giving us your

1. With which British Airways Holidays programme did you travel?

a) ☐ Worldwide b) ☐ Florida c) ☐ America & Canada
d) ☐ Cities d) ☐ Golf e) ☐ Other ________

2. What was your departure date from the UK?

(Day/Month) ________________

3. What class did you travel in?

a) ☐ Traveller (economy) b) ☐ Club
c) ☐ First d) ☐ Concorde

4. What was your main holiday destination?

____

5. Did you book with a travel agent? ☐ YES ☐ NO

6. How did you hear about us?

a) ☐ Friends/Family b) ☐ Travel Agent
c) ☐ Previous Experience d) ☐ Advertisement
e) ☐ Brochure Mailing f) ☐ Other

7. With which airline(s) did you fly?

a) ________________ b) ________________

8. In the last 5 years, how many British Airways Holidays have you taken?

a) ☐ none b) ☐ one c) ☐ two d) ☐ three +

If one or more, which British Airways Holidays programmes have you travelled with previously?

____

9. Please rate your satisfaction with the flight.

	Excellent ☺	Good ☺	Fair ☺	Poor ☹
Check-in service	☐	☐	☐	☐
Cabin staff's he]p & attitudes	☐	☐	☐	☐
Baggage Reclaim service:				
UK	☐	☐	☐	☐
Overseas	☐	☐	☐	☐
Overall in-flight experience	☐	☐	☐	☐

10. Please provide the names and location of the hotel(s) at which you stayed during your holiday (main hotels, if more than two).

	Hotel Name	Location
Hotel 1	________	________
Hotel 2	________	________

Please rate these hotel features individually:

(Hotel I ☐ Hotel 2 ☐)

	Excellent ☺	Good ☺	Fair ☺	Poor ☹
Hotel service	☐	☐	☐	☐
Food	☐	☐	☐	☐
Amenities	☐	☐	☐	☐
Cleanliness	☐	☐	☐	☐
Hotel location	☐	☐	☐	☐
Hotel overall	☐	☐	☐	☐

Any other comments ________________________________

Fig. 3.5 British Airways Holidays customer service questionnaire

indicate different things. Thomson, for example, has its 'T' grading system (*see* page 15), Airtours its 'A' system and Cosmos its diamonds. Sometimes they also show the country's own grading evaluation for comparison. This is what Cosmos has to say about its diamond grading system:

> Official category rating systems do not represent a consistent method of comparing accommodation standards from one country to another or even, on occasions, within the same country and we therefore show this information only as a general guide . . . We have, however, allocated to each hotel . . . our own 'Diamond' rating based both on our personal knowledge of each property (at the time of going to press) and, most importantly, your own views. Cosmos 'Diamond' ratings are our guide to your accommodation and cover, for example, aspects such as facilities, service, food, comfort and location, taking account of the different characteristics and emphasis on each aspect between hotel and apartment accommodation. The ratings are awarded on a scale of 1 to 5, representing a range from basic good value without frills to above average accommodation offering that extra touch of comfort. Not all accommodation within the same rating will necessarily offer the same facilities . . . but we think you will find these a useful guide.
>
> (Courtesy: Cosmos)

Other holiday grading schemes

Holidays are sometimes graded in other ways and to indicate considerations other than simple quality.

opinion of this one

11. Please rate the other features of your holiday.
(Enter N/A if service not included)

	Excellent ☺	Good ☺	Fair ☺	Poor ☹	N/A
Brochure information and accuracy	☐	☐	☐	☐	☐
Reservations service	☐	☐	☐	☐	☐
Information supplied in your travel pack	☐	☐	☐	☐	☐
Overseas representatives' service	☐	☐	☐	☐	☐
Airport/hotel transfers	☐	☐	☐	☐	☐
Car rental	☐	☐	☐	☐	☐
Optional excursions	☐	☐	☐	☐	☐

12. Which of the following British Airways Holidays would you be interested in?

a) ☐ Worldwide b) ☐ Florida c) ☐ America & Canada
d) ☐ Cities e) ☐ Golf

In order to assist us with our future planning, it helps us to know what different types of people think about our holidays.
The information below will of course be strictly confidential.

13. Which age bracket do you fall into?

a) ☐ 16–24 b) ☐ 25–34 c) ☐ 35–44
d) ☐ 45–54 e) ☐ 55–64 f) ☐ 65 +

14. How many children do you have under 12?

a) ☐ none b) ☐ one c) ☐ two d) ☐ three +

15. Which best describes the type of job you do?

a) ☐ management b) ☐ professional c) ☐ office/retail
d) ☐ skilled worker/tradesman e) ☐ retired f) ☐ other

16. Into which income bracket does your combined income fall?

a) ☐ under £15 000 b) ☐ £15–25 000 c) ☐ £25–40 000
d) ☐ £40 000 + e) ☐ not prepared to answer

17. Which national newspapers and magazines do you read regularly? (please list)

____

____

18. Please rate your overall satisfaction with your holiday?

a) ☐ Excellent b) ☐ Good c) ☐ Fair d) ☐ Poor

19. How likely are you to book with us again?

a) ☐ Very likely b) ☐ Quite likely c) ☐ Not likely

20. Any additional comments?

____

____

____

____

____

____

Some activity holidays, for example, will be graded according to their difficulty to ensure people don't embark on ventures they are not fit enough to handle. This is how Himalayan Kingdoms grades its 'treks and expeditions among the world's highest mountains':

> **Mild**: up to 5 days walking in total. Usually 4 to 6 hours walking a day, with the occasional steep path. A walking holiday with plenty of time for sightseeing.
>
> **Moderate**: More remote country and the occasional 6 or 7 hour day, but not more than 5 days consecutive walking unless on popular trails. Relatively low-altitude treks.
>
> **Vigorous**: Up to 7 days consecutive walking through wild country, including high passes (sometimes snow-covered) between 12,000 and 16,000 ft. Sometimes a 7 or 8 hour day.
>
> **Strenuous**: Challenging long distance treks for the fit enthusiast. Sometimes more than 7 days consecutive walking and at least one pass over 16,000 ft. Often very rarely visited areas.
>
> (Courtesy: Himalayan Kingdoms)

Alongside the grading of the hotels used in the programme, winter ski programmes usually have maps which grade the local ski runs according to the degree of expertise needed to use them. Ski runs are usually labelled as suitable for beginners, intermediate or advanced skiers, and the maps are colour-coded to indicate which runs are which.

Grading schemes are sometimes designed to

THE AITO QUALITY CHARTER

AITO is an association of independent companies specialising in particular areas or types of holiday and sharing a common dedication to high standards of quality and personal service. AITO defines 'quality' as "providing a level of satisfaction which, based upon the holiday information provided by the tour operator, aims to meet or exceed a customer's reasonable expectations, regardless of the type of holiday sold or the price paid".

THIS IS HOW WE AIM TO ACHIEVE IT:

ACCURATE BROCHURES

AITO members ensure that their brochures clearly and accurately describe the holidays and services offered.

PRODUCT IMPROVEMENTS

AITO members listen to their customers and welcome suggestions for improving standards. All customers receive a post-holiday questionnaire.

PROFESSIONAL SERVICE

AITO members are committed to high standards of personal service, maintained by the thorough training of employees.

FINANCIAL SECURITY

AITO takes care to ensure that all members comply with current Government Regulations regarding the protection of clients' money.

EXCLUSIVE MEMBERSHIP

AITO has strict membership criteria which must be satisfied before new companies are allowed to join. All members must adhere to a rigorous Code of Business Practice which governs their operational conduct.

ENVIRONMENTAL ISSUES

AITO is committed to raising the level of environmental awareness within the industry.

AND, AS A LAST RESORT, in the unlikely event that a dispute between an AITO member and customer cannot be resolved amicably, AITO's low-cost Independent Dispute Settlement Service may be called upon by either side to bring the matter to a speedy and acceptable conclusion.

THE ASSOCIATION OF INDEPENDENT TOUR OPERATORS

THE QUALITY ALTERNATIVE

Fig. 3.6 The AITO quality charter – creating 'the quality alternative'

Courtesy: AITO

reflect a particular programme. So Neilson grades its hotels with outline mountain peaks, while The Imaginative Traveller uses cartoon camels to indicate the overall style and standard of its adventure holidays (*see* Fig. 3.7). Club Med uses two to four tridents to grade its holiday villages in terms of comfort and setting.

FIRE, SAFETY AND HYGIENE STANDARDS OVERSEAS

The EC Package Travel Regulations make it even more important that tour operators ensure that the hotels they feature offer high standards of safety and hygiene, not just to protect their clients but also to protect themselves from being sued if something goes wrong. The main problem is that, even within Europe, different countries have different standards and set different rules; so far, although the EC has issued a Recommendation on Hotel Fire Safety, even the Single Market has not managed to impose conformity in precautions, and consumer watchdogs like the BBC's *Watchdog* programme and the Consumers' Association magazine *Holiday Which?* have frequently highlighted hotels where fire precautions, and pool and balcony safety don't meet UK standards.

The bigger companies therefore carry out their own fire and safety audits in hotels they intend to feature. In theory this should mean that hotels which don't come up to scratch are dropped. However, this can be problematic in countries like Greece and Portugal where many properties fall short of UK standards.

When carrying out a safety audit, these are the main things operators should be looking for:

Fire safety precautions

- Where the hotel has more than 25 bedrooms, there should be more than one protected staircase in case one becomes cut off by fire or smoke.
- All staircases should be enclosed by doors which automatically close behind users so that they can be sealed off from fire or smoke.
- Ideally, no one should have to walk more then 10 metres to a staircase or emergency exit, reducing the likelihood of their being trapped by fire or smoke.
- 'Dead end' corridors should be avoided to reduce the risk of people wasting valuable potential escape time.
- Fire escape routes should be clearly marked, and there should be no obstructions along corridors or on staircases which could impede someone's escape in the dark or in dense smoke.
- No exits to the outside should be kept locked.
- Every bedroom should have a notice explaining what to do in the event of fire, with a plan indicating the nearest escape route.
- Fire extinguishers or hoses should be well-maintained and clearly visible. Ideally, there should be a smoke detector or sprinkler system too.
- Fire alarm call buttons should be clearly visible. A system which depends on the use of telephones to raise the alarm should be unacceptable.

Swimming pool safety precautions

- The deep end should always be clearly indicated and there should be no sudden changes in depth.
- The bottom of the pool should be clearly visible.
- Ideally, there should be a separate children's pool, well away from the deep end.

Balcony safety

- Balustrades should be at least one metre high, making it difficult for anyone to fall over the edge.
- Gaps between rails should be less than 150 mm wide, so that children can't slip between them.
- There should be no steps or anything that could be used as steps, on the balcony.

Lift safety

- No lift should be open on one side.
- A notice outside the lift should warn against using it during a fire.

This is what Cosmos had to say about 'safety and local standards' in its 1993 'Tourama' brochure:

> The safety standards and regulations in operation overseas are those of the country visited and often, regrettably, do not aspire to the same levels as the UK. Because of this, the general standards of safety, hygiene, fire precautions, etc., will be lower than those we have come to expect in the UK and the monitoring and enforcement of these local

Camels & The Imaginative Traveller

The camel has been the friend and trusted companion of travellers since ancient times and seems to us an appropriate 'symbol' for the style of holidays we offer. To help you identify the right kind of holiday for you, you will find one of these symbols beside every tour description.

Standards of accommodation and general facilities can vary greatly from one country to another, so you will find a more specific description of what to expect in the introduction to each country. As a guideline, though, our symbols can be explained as follows:

Ideal for the young at heart, these holidays use a variety of accommodation: tourist class hotels, mountain lodges, kibbutz guest houses and small pensions. The transport used tends to be more varied and more active, eg: donkeys, camels, jeeps and feluccas.

This symbol identifies tours that offer a superior style of accommodation, generally 4/5 star hotels, and a more luxurious method of travel; first class, air-conditioned cruise boats with private facilities, and comfortable coaches for sightseeing.

For those with a love of the great outdoors. A typical camping itinerary will include a mixture of established campsites and specially chosen 'wild' camps. Occasionally, we also use small pensions, mountain lodges or other special stops that will enhance the tour. Transport is by private coach.

Regardless of which style of holiday meets your needs best, you will enjoy the same high standards of service and personal attention that only long experience makes possible.

(a)

KEY

Expeditions *(includes all backpacking trips)*
Regular mountain walking/wilderness experience advisable

Tough treks
Regular hill walking background advisable

Steady treks
Hill walking and camping background useful

Fairly easy treks and walks
For all recreational walkers

Mountain bike trips

(b)

Fig. 3.7 (a) The Imaginative Traveller grading system and (b) the High Places key to expeditions and treks
(a) Courtesy: The Imaginative Traveller
(b) Courtesy: High Places

> regulations is a matter for the authorities of the country and the overseas supplier of the services concerned.
>
> (Courtesy: Cosmos)

However, as a result of the EC Package Travel Regulations it is at least arguable that a client who lost property as a result of a fire in a hotel in an EU country would be able to sue the operator for damages on the grounds that they had failed to perform the contract when the problem could have been foreseen.

Standard of beaches

The standard of beaches in resorts is another problem for operators who are clearly not directly responsible for the dumping of raw sewage or chemical waste at sea. Few, however, comment on the standard of seawater cleanliness in their brochures, preferring to use vague generalities like 'clean', 'clear' or 'translucent'. This is what Cosmos had to say, again in the 1993 'Tourama' brochure:

> Our brochure descriptions give a fair indication of the type of beach at the resorts and the availability of any watersports or other beach-related activities. Although many holidaymakers prefer swimming pools and surrounding terraces to the beach, as a responsible company we feel it only right to point out that the EC publishes a report annually which lists the beaches throughout Europe which do not meet the Commission's minimum requirements on cleanliness.
>
> (Courtesy: Cosmos)

QUESTIONS AND DISCUSSION POINTS

1 Discuss the different factors a tour operator with a programme of ski holidays to Austria and Italy for next season might need to consider before starting to plan the programme.

2 What advantages do you think a tour operator might obtain by buying hotels outright?

3 Make a list of points a contractor might want to discuss with a) an airline, and b) a hotelier before committing itself to a contract.

ASSIGNMENTS

1 You are working for a small operator with a programme of holidays to Greece, Spain, Turkey and Tunisia. You would like to develop one new short-haul destination. Select **three** possible destinations and write a report summarising the pros and cons of choosing each of them. Make sure your conclusion indicates which you think might be best and why.

2 For **one** of the destinations you have chosen, write notes discussing what would be the best method of contracting beds and seats, explaining your decisions.

3 'Quality' is a rather nebulous concept. Draw up a chart with columns for 'flight', 'hotel' and 'service', and then list all those items you would need to consider when deciding whether 'quality' was being offered to the client in each area. Discuss your conclusions as a class, before talking about how you would measure the standard being reached in each area.

4 If possible, visit a large local hotel used by holidaymakers as well as business travellers. Draw up a chart to record the ways in which it fulfils the fire and general safety requirements highlighted on pages 73–75.

CHAPTER 4

The tour operators' products

LEARNING OBJECTIVES

After studying this chapter you should be able to:

- **explain the difference between a short-haul and long-haul product**
- **list the main types of product created by tour operators**
- **describe the particular features of the different types of product**
- **assess which products are the big sellers and which are more specialist**
- **recognise which markets are expanding and which are contracting**

INTRODUCTION

Tour operators began by offering one and two week short-haul holidays to cultural destinations, the ski resorts and the Mediterranean. However, as the total holiday market grew in the 1980s, long-haul destinations began to grow in popularity too. The market was also divided into all sorts of niche sectors, as operators tried to identify every possible holidaymaker's need and then design a product to match it.

Figure 4.1 shows the most popular destinations for inclusive tour holidays in 1991 and 1992. The figures in brackets show the destination's ranking in 1991.

			1991	*1992*
			(figs in millions)	
1	(1)	Spain	2.66	3.08
2	(2)	France	1.87	2.42
3	(3)	Greece	1.37	1.58
4	(7)	Cyprus	0.40	0.74
5	(4)	Portugal	0.59	0.68
6	(5)	USA	0.50	0.59
7	(6)	Italy	0.44	0.51
8	(8)	Austria	0.39	0.42
9	(9)	Netherlands	0.35	0.39
10	(14)	Turkey	0.10	0.22

Fig. 4.1 Top ten inclusive tour destinations, 1991 and 1992

Source: International Passenger Survey

Perhaps the most striking aspect of these figures is that despite the apparent growth in popularity of long-haul destinations (*see* below), only the USA actually made it into the top 10, mainly as a result of Florida's popularity.

THE SHORT-HAUL PRODUCT

Short-haul destinations are those less than five hours' flying time away from the UK. Included within this definition are all the European countries west of the Urals including the Canaries, Madeira and the Azores, and Iceland. Morocco and Tunisia are regarded as short-haul destinations as well. Traditionally, Egypt is treated as a long-haul destination (*see* Fig. 4.2), although it now appears in some primarily short-haul summer sun brochures too.

Although the summer sun product is by far the most important component of this market, short-haul overseas holidays actually take many forms. They can be:

- flights with hotels
- flights with self-catering accommodation
- single centre (i.e. based in one resort or town)
- multi-centre (i.e. moving round more than one town or resort)
- coach trips with hotels
- coach trips with self-catering accommodation

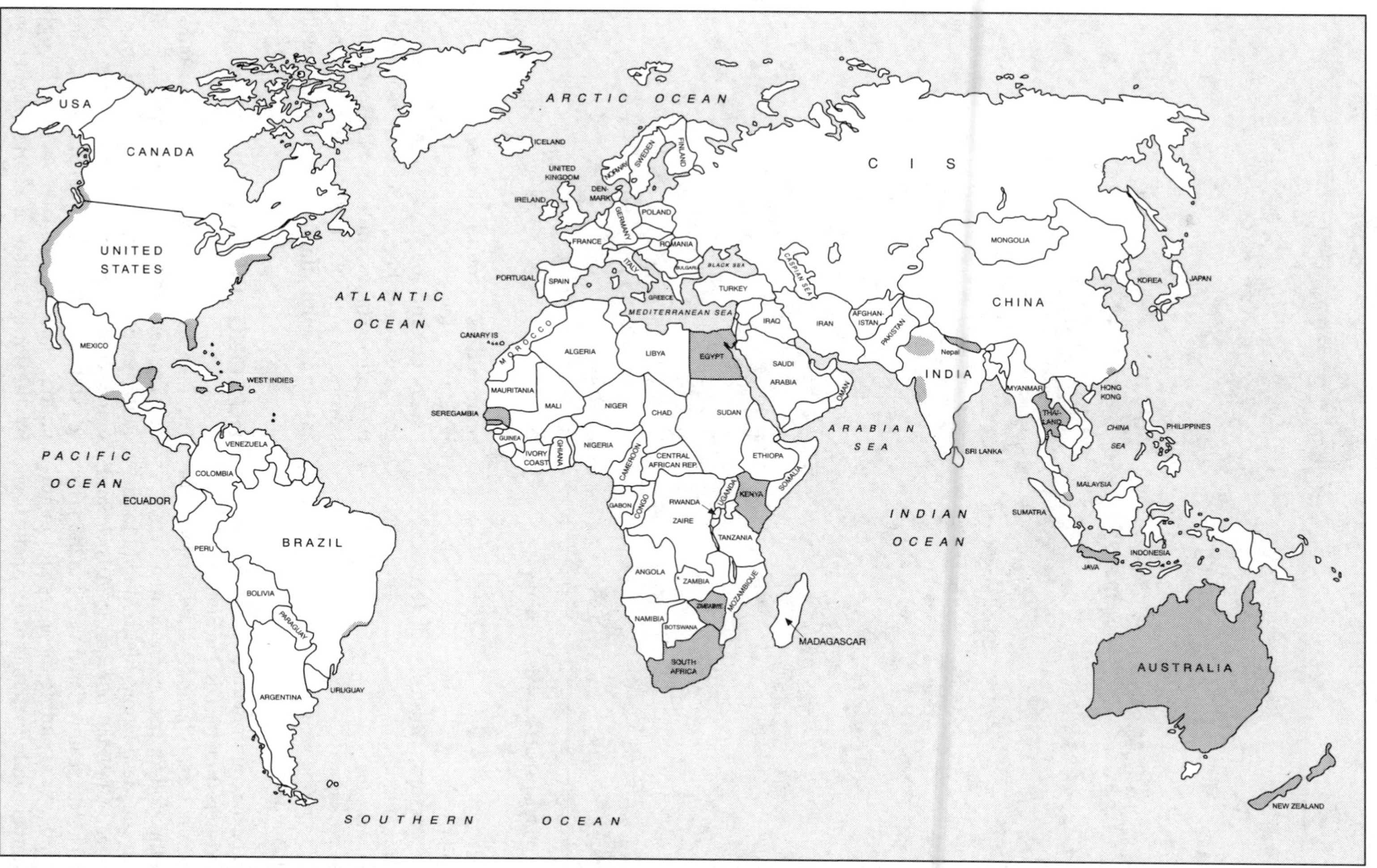

Fig. 4.2 (a) Popular long-haul holiday destinations

Fig. 4.2 (b) popular short-haul destinations

- coach tours
- luxury rail trips
- self-drive packages, inclusive of ferry crossing and accommodation
- fly-drive packages
- fly-cruise packages
- minibreaks or long weekends, often in cities
- campsite holidays

France may be the country which receives the largest number of visitors from the UK, but Spain (including the Balearic and Canary Islands) is by far the most popular destination for package holidaymakers.

Inevitably, the destinations featured tend to dictate the types of holiday offered. So Austria and Switzerland are normally offered as destinations for skiing in winter or exploring the lakes and mountains in summer, while Spain has traditionally been promoted as a country to visit for sun and sand holidays. However, as the holiday market has expanded and become more sophisticated, so companies have become more imaginative in what they offer. For example, by 1993 operators were starting to promote the Spanish hinterland as well as simply selling the over-developed coastline.

THE LONG-HAUL PRODUCT

The long-haul package holiday is a more recent development than the short-haul one. Before it could really take off, planes had to be developed which could fly long distances without needing to stop for fuel. The explosion of long-haul holidaymaking in the late 1980s was brought about by the introduction of charter flights on routes which had previously been accessible only by more expensive scheduled flights, thus bringing the price within reach of the mass market. By the early 1990s charter flights were available to the Caribbean, Florida, Goa (India) and Australia. Indeed, some charter operators were using large, modern jet aircraft capable of flying great distances without the need to refuel, thus offering the prospect of opening up new markets to holidaymakers who were reluctant to undertake journeys involving connecting flights. In the late 1980s Mexico's failure to take off as a mass-market holiday destination from the UK was in part because there were no direct flights to Cancun or Acapulco, forcing holidaymakers to change planes in Houston and/or Mexico City.

Long-haul tour operators offer most of the same types of holidays as short-haul operators. However, because of the distances involved and the number of borders to be crossed, people usually fly to a long-haul destination, even if they then join a coach or rail tour or a cruise. The types of holidays offered will also depend on the destinations featured. For example, the majority of holidays to India (with the exception of Goa) concentrate on exploring its cultural heritage and wildlife, while those to Nepal concentrate on trekking in the Himalayas. However, diversification is also taking place in the long-haul market, so that countries which were once associated with one specific type of product now offer a much wider range of holidays: brochures featuring Kenya are now as likely to offer beach holidays as safaris; those featuring Thailand will offer hill treks as well as beach breaks; Goa is now a popular winter sun destination.

Table 4.1 Kuoni's Top Ten best-selling long-haul destinations in 1993

1993			*1994 forecast*
1	(1)	Hong Kong	1
2	(2)	Thailand	2
3	(4)	Singapore	3
4	(5)	USA	7
5	(7)	Bali	4
6	(3)	Egypt	13
7	(8)	St. Lucia	9
8	(12)	Maldives	5
9	(10)	Barbados	10
10	(9)	Malaysia	8

(figures in brackets show 1992 ranking)

Long-haul holidays are usually promoted in slimmer, glossier brochures, and the programme will usually cover an entire calendar year rather than being split between summer and winter like short-haul programmes. Long-haul holidays are also more likely to make use of scheduled flights than short-haul ones.

Because holidays to remote places were originally the preserve of the rich they tended to be hotel-based. However, alongside the growth of charter flights has come a boom in self-catering in resort areas like Florida and the Caribbean, which has helped to keep prices down in the same way that it has in Europe.

TYPES OF HOLIDAY PRODUCT

In the past there were clear distinctions between the types of product available in short-haul and long-haul destinations, with long-haul customers more interested in experiencing the culture and/or wildlife of exotic destinations and short-haul customers usually more interested in sun, sand and nightlife. However, as the long-haul market has expanded, so this differentiation has diminished: summer sunseekers can now be found in Thailand and Kenya as well as along the Mediterranean; winter sunseekers head for Gambia and the Caribbean as well as the Canary Islands; there are coach tours round India as well as Italy; and there are fly-cruise packages to the Mediterranean as well as the Caribbean. Nevertheless some products like safaris remain more or less specific to long-haul rather than short-haul destinations.

The following were some of the main types of holiday product available in the early 1990s.

Summer sun holidays

The biggest, fattest brochures are those offering the stereotypical 'sun, sea and sand' summer holidays, designed to suit everyone but especially families with young children, and young couples and singles. In 1993 summer sun holidays made up 78 per cent of the total holiday market, down from a high of 82 per cent in 1986 but slightly up on the 76 per cent of 1991 and 1992.

Summer sun holidays are usually taken in hotels or self-catering apartments and last for one or two weeks, although there are also some more unusual holiday durations like five, ten or eleven nights, particularly at the start (April) and end (October) of the season, when airlines change their flight patterns from winter to summer configurations and vice versa. Many operators offer special deals to cover these periods to try and reduce the cost of flying 'empty leg' sectors (*see* page 181). Most people still fly to their destination, but it's sometimes possible to travel by rail or coach instead. Summer sun holidays are mainly concentrated around the Mediterranean coast, although Gambia also appears in some summer sun brochures. These holidays are all about relaxing, swimming, sunbathing, eating well and taking the odd excursion to a 'packaged' attraction. There's little emphasis on exploration or education.

Summer sun brochures are filled with special deals for families, including discounts or free places for children, and information about children's holiday clubs. This is by far the biggest chunk of the holiday market.

Since summer sun holidays are the bedrock of the tour operating market, they are also the main focus of this textbook. This chapter therefore looks primarily at subsections of and variations from the summer sun product.

Minibreak, or short break, holidays

In the late 1980s the combination of increased prosperity for those in work and longer holidays from work led to a boom in minibreak holidays, usually long weekends of between two and four nights. Minibreak packages usually include transport by

Fig. 4.3 The most popular summer sun destinations for UK holidaymakers

A Different Perspective

Green-hearted Luxembourg, just beyond Belgium's southern tip, is one of the leafiest cities you can imagine. Either side of a sliver of river it lies, or rather perches, for the River Pétrusse meanders through a wide gorge that divides the dreamy spires of ancient Luxembourg, encrusted upon its rock, from a second city south of the river. There is a third Luxembourg, where cigarette-lighter skyscrapers soar but, like Brussels, the city's appeal is not so much in its modern trappings as in its period dress: the friendly *haute ville* with its own Notre Dame, its elegant houses, its Ruritanian Grand Duke's Palace, pedestrian shopping streets and pretty squares where café tables sprawl under trees festooned with lights.

Luxembourg is a city to enjoy for its own sake and not to be approached with preconceived ideas. Life there is undeniably civilised and as refreshing as a glass of its own wonderful Moselle wine.

Anne Gregg

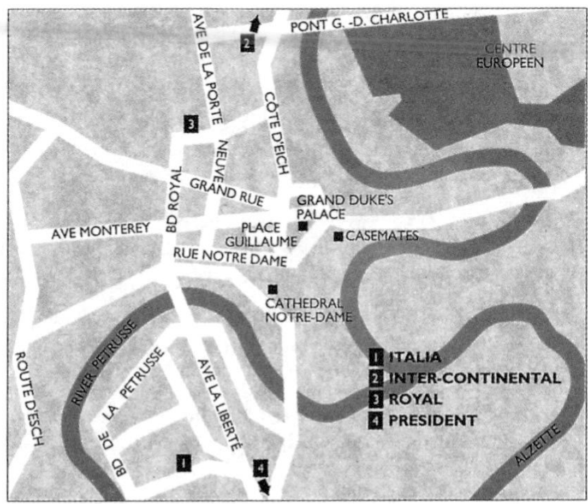

ACCOMMODATION

Most of the hotels are within easy walking distance of the old town (except Hotel Inter•Continental – see description below). Bedrooms have private bathrooms with bath and/or shower & wc. The star grading is based mainly on price and on our assessment of standards. A brief description of the hotels is given below.

> *Some hotels may carry additional supplements or reductions — these are shown under the individual hotel descriptions and are per person per night (pppn). Also some hotels give a reduction when three persons share a room. Reductions on request.*

Italia 2★

Small, well-run hotel with an outstanding Italian restaurant. Conveniently situated between the station and the old town. Lounge. All bedrooms have TV and direct-dial telephone. No lift.

> *Supplement pppn for larger superior room: £4 (double or twin only).*

President 4★

Elegant hotel, near the station and shops. Pleasant lounge and attractive restaurant. Tastefully decorated bedrooms with TV, minibar and direct-dial telephone. Prices are based on weekend stays (Fri, Sat & Sun nights). *(Not illustrated)*

> *Supplement pppn for midweek stays (Mon–Thurs nights): £15 (double or twin), £20 (single).*

Luxembourg Public Holidays
1992 April 20. May 1, 28. June 8, 23. August 15. November 2. December 25, 26.
1993 January 1, February 22.

Inter•Continental 4★+

***Excellent value** — special low weekend & summer prices*

Modern 5-star hotel, situated in the Europa Park, ten minutes by courtesy bus from the city centre. The hotel has a health centre and heated swimming pool. All bedrooms are air-conditioned with direct-dial telephone, minibar and TV. Buffet breakfast is included. Free car park. Prices apply to weekend stays (Fri, Sat & Sun nights) or any night during July and August.

Royal **Luxury**

Luxurious modern hotel, situated by the park in the city centre. Spacious lobby and lounge, restaurant with terrace, piano bar, swimming pool and fitness centre. Fully air-conditioned. Buffet breakfast is included. All bedrooms have TV, minibar and direct-dial telephone.
Prices apply to weekend stays (Fri, Sat & Sun nights) or any night from 15 July to 31 Aug.

Fig. 4.4 Time Off in Luxembourg – the minibreak in practice
Courtesy: Time Off

plane, rail or coach, and accommodation in a chain hotel on a half-board basis. Most minibreak packages are to European cities with a strong cultural appeal (e.g. Paris, Amsterdam, Rome, Vienna, Prague), although others will be to event attractions like the Dutch bulbfields in bloom or the Munich Beer Festival. Countries specialising in minibreaks include Time Off, Travelscene, Kirker and the Bridge Group (Paris Travel Service, Amsterdam Travel Service, etc.). Increasingly mainstream operators like Thomson and Sovereign also feature dedicated short break programmes.

Time Off started out offering minibreaks to Paris in 1967. By 1992 it was offering breaks to 24 cities from New York to Istanbul. This is how they explain their own success:

> We pioneered the development of city breaks . . . when Time Off started, Paris was the only one on offer . . . but we did them a little differently and we did them well. We offered our clients flexibility in choosing how to get there and where to stay. We packed them off with helpful guides, maps and a feeling they were travelling independently, although Time Off had put it all together. And if things ever went wrong, even through no fault of ours, we sorted out the problem swiftly and efficiently, proving we really cared about our customers.
>
> We have always put people before profit, because we feel this is a principle worth preserving. People count within the company, too. Each player has his or her part, and the sum of these parts plus the valuable supporting role of our many colleagues in the industry have contributed not only to Time Off's survival but also to its continuing success.
>
> We have promoted Time Off with a sense of style and we have managed to expand without overreaching ourselves. But, above all, we believe it is our attention to detail that has ensured a standard of service second to none.
>
> (Courtesy: Time Off)

1.	Paris	(1)
2.	Amsterdam	(2)
3.	Bruges	(3)
4.	Rome	(5)
5.	Vienna	(4)
6.	Venice	(6)
7.	Florence	(7)
8.	Gibraltar	(11)
9.	Madrid	(8)
10.	Brussels	(10)

Fig. 4.5 Travelscene's top ten city-break destinations, 1993

However, after the boom of the late 1980s, the market for short breaks declined slightly in the early 1990s, partly because the recession made second holidays an expendible luxury. Traditional destinations like Paris and Amsterdam also began to lose some business to the novelty destinations of Eastern Europe, like Prague and Budapest, and to more exotic cities, most conspicuously Istanbul. Travelscene's top 20 city-break destinations for 1993 also featured Reykjavik, New York and Copenhagen.

The minibreaks market has become increasingly important to domestic tour operators as British holidaymakers have abandoned the traditional two week seaside holiday in favour of short breaks in the country, in the cities or in upmarket holiday camps like the CenterParcs complexes. Unfortunately from the operator's point of view they often organise these for themselves or buy packages put together by hoteliers rather than tour operators.

Two-centre or multi-centre holidays

Two-centre or multi-centre packages allow people to holiday in more than one place without being part of a coach tour. Often they are made up of one week touring cultural sites with a second week on a beach, or of three days in one town followed by four in another. Transfers between the different centres may be by coach, rail or plane. Italy is a popular destination for multi-centre holidays which may feature two days in Florence, two in Venice and three in Rome or other similar combinations.

As the long-haul market became increasingly sophisticated, so some operators began to develop two-centre packages in the United States; for example, a week in Orlando (for Disneyworld) could be followed with a week relaxing on Miami Beach or the Florida Keys. From this it was a short step to developing more complex packages, perhaps combining Florida with Jamaica, the Bahamas or Mexico; California with Hawaii, Alaska or South America; or Bermuda with New York or Boston. The American Dream even offers combined ski-and-sun holidays to Colorado and Florida.

To succeed, such packages need to offer easy transport connections between the two centres, contrasting attractions in the two different areas and the perception on the client's part that they are being offered value for money. From the tour operator's point of view, such two-centre holidays can also open up new potential markets. For example, the Caribbean is traditionally thought of as a destination for couples. However, when a family-oriented company like Airtours packages it with Florida it is more likely that some families will consider trying it. Having done so once, they may then do so again in the future. It has been estimated that up to 25 per cent of British holidaymakers in Cancun (Mexico) travel there on two-centre packages.

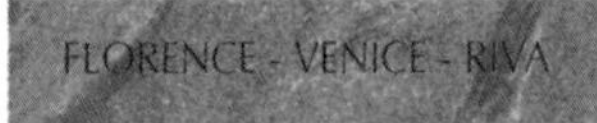

YOUR ITINERARY
14 Nights

Saturday departure from Heathrow on an Alitalia scheduled flight to Pisa. Rail and minibus or coach transfer to Florence hotel or nearest point (approx 1hr 30mins).
4 nights in Florence.
Wednesday departure from Florence to Venice by First Class rail (approx 4hrs 30 mins).
3 nights in Venice.
Saturday departure by boat and coach to Riva (approx 3hrs 30 mins).
7 nights in Riva.
Saturday departure from Riva by coach to Venice airport (approx. 3 hrs) for return flight to Heathrow.

HOW YOU TRAVEL	
FROM	RETURN
HEATHROW TO PISA	VENICE TO HEATHROW
Flight Details: See Page 126	

Malcesine.

Rialto Bridge Venice.

YOUR ITINERARY
14 Nights

Saturday departure from Heathrow on an Alitalia scheduled flight to Venice.
Boat transfer to hotel or nearest point (approx. 1hr 30mins).
7 nights in Venice.
Saturday departure from Venice by boat and coach to Malcesine or Riva (approx. 3hrs 30mins).
7 nights in Malcesine or Riva.
Saturday departure by coach to Venice airport from Malcesine or Riva (approx 3hrs) return flight to Heathrow.

HOW YOU TRAVEL	
FROM	RETURN
HEATHROW TO VENICE	VENICE TO HEATHROW
Flight Details: See Page 126	

Riva, Lake Garda.

The Duomo, Florence.

HOTELS

The combination of hotels shown are only a selection of those available. For alternative hotels or reverse itineraries please call 081 686 5533 for an instant holiday price.

DEPARTURES					01MAY-28 MAY	29 MAY-25 JUNE	26 JUNE-16 JULY	17 JULY-06 AUG	07 AUG-20 AUG	21 AUG-3 SEPT	4 SEPT-17 SEPT
HOL. NO.	ACCOMMODATION			NIGHTS	14	14	14	14	14	14	14
	VENICE	MALCESINE		BOARD							
2L14	ALA	V.SMERALDA		BB/HB	689	729	799	809	849	859	779
2L15	DO POZZI	MERIDIANA		BB/BB	559	569	579	589	599	605	605
2L16	PANADA	B.S.LORENZO		BB/HB	839	849	889	899	979	999	929
	VENICE	RIVA									
2L07	PANADA	V.NICOLLI		BB/HB	769	809	829	839	919	909	899
2L06	DO POZZI	EUROPA		BB/HB	759	799	809	829	919	929	869
2L05	ALA	SOLE		BB/HB	809	869	959	969	1009	1029	899
2L08	GABRIELLI	LIDO PALACE		BB/HB	1079	1149	1169	1179	1199	1219	1229
	FLORENCE	VENICE	RIVA								
3C43	ALBA	ALA	SOLE	BB/BB/HB	799	849	899	909	979	989	909
3C45	RIVOLI	PANADA	EUROPA	BB/BB/HB	819	869	899	919	925	939	889
3C47	P.LUCCHESI	CAVALLETTO	DU-LAC	BB/BB/HB	1139	1159	1189	1199	1229	1239	1219

Prices in pounds per person sharing a twin room or per person sharing an apartment with minimum occupancy.
For what is included in the holiday price please see page 127. For Citalia Insurance see page 129.

Fig. 4.6 Typical multi-centre holiday in Italy
Courtesy: Citalia

Safari holidays are increasingly offered as part of two-centre packages, encompassing the East African coast and some of its game parks. The client is given the opportunity to rest after what can be the strenuous experience of a safari, while also having a chance to see as much as possible of a faraway country to justify the lengthy journey required to reach it.

The Far East is particularly popular for multi-centre holidays, perhaps because many people want to see Hong Kong, Singapore and Bangkok but don't want to stay too long in any of them. Easy transport connections have enabled companies like Kuoni to package the cities with, for example, a beach holiday in Bali or southern Thailand, to give the customer a taste of many different aspects of the Orient. The Caribbean also lends itself to island-hopping two- or multi-centre holidays. For example, Thomson has paired Barbados with St. Lucia, Antigua, Tobago or Grenada, while British Airways Holidays has teamed Jamaica with Cuba, and Grenada with Mustique.

By 1993, 75 per cent of long-haul market leader Kuoni's packages involved multi-centre arrangements.

Self-drive packages

As more households acquired cars in the 1970s, so the idea of taking them abroad gained popularity,

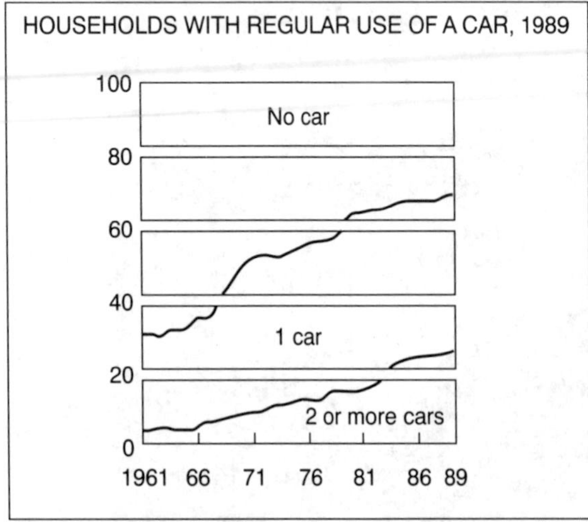

Fig. 4.7 Growth of private car ownership in the UK
Courtesy: Department of Transport

since it offered greater flexibility over where to go and allowed for taking almost limitless luggage. While some people are happy to book their own ferry crossings and hotels and to arrange their own insurance, tour operators have been quick to offer to make the arrangements for them. Several companies, including the ferry operators, now offer 'packages' consisting of ferry tickets, hotel vouchers and motor insurance policies (like AA Five Star or Europ Assistance) to help motorists make their own way around the Continent. France remains one of the most popular destinations with self-drive tourists and in 1992 this popularity received a boost when the arrival of the Single Market increased the amount of alcohol visitors to the Continent could bring back to the UK. When the Channel Tunnel opens in 1995 this, too, should boost France's popularity by making it even easier for people to get their cars across the Channel. A new company, Le Shuttle Holidays, will market a range of breaks, including ski-drive holidays, using the Channel Tunnel.

Company name	Type of product
Keycamp	Camping, villas and *gîtes*
Haven	Camping and mobile homes
Sunsites	Camping
Travelscene	Hotel-based and touring holidays
Cresta Holidays	Hotel-based holidays and short breaks
Just France	*Gîte* and villa holidays
French Life	Hotels, *gîtes*, holiday homes, camping
Eurosites	Camping and mobile homes
Unicorn Holidays	Upmarket hotel holidays in France, Spain and Portugal
AA Motoring Holidays	Self-catering and Motorail in France
Mundi Color	Self-drive Spanish holidays
Moswin Tours	Stays in private German houses

Fig. 4.8 Some companies offering self-drive packages from the UK, 1993

Lakes and mountains holidays

A popular subsection of the summer holiday market is the lakes and mountains market, which suits people who prefer to spend their one or two weeks amid beautiful mountainous scenery.

Lakes and mountains holidays are usually to France, Austria, Switzerland, Italy, Norway, Hungary, Romania or Slovenia and are particularly popular with middle-aged and elderly couples. Lakes and mountains operators include Inghams, Med Choice and Airtours. This market has proved relatively recession-proof; in 1992 Inghams even saw sales rise by more than 30 per cent.

Coach tours

Coach tours are another important subsection of the market, mainly for people with an interest in cultural sightseeing. In 1994 the UK had 150 registered coach tour operators. A typical coach tour might consist of 7, 10 or 14 nights touring European cities. Some tours concentrate on one country but others pack in as many countries as there are days in the tour (the 'if-it's-Tuesday-it-must-be-Brussels' syndrome). Some companies, like Wallace Arnold, specialise in coach tours while others, like Cosmos, offer coach tours as one product alongside more conventional summer sun holidays. Coach tours tend to be most popular with older clients, mainly in the 45 to 65 age bracket, perhaps because they offer the benefits of local pick-up points, couriers at hand to help with any problems and transportation of luggage right to the hotel door.

A few companies also offer long-haul coach tours, particularly of the USA where the excellent road and motel network, low fuel prices and variety of scenery lend themselves to this type of holiday. Clients opting for long-haul coach tours also tend to be older but are usually more affluent than those choosing to tour closer to home. Apart from the USA, Canada, Australia, New Zealand, South

Fig. 4.9 Favourite lakes and mountains destinations for UK holidaymakers

8 days from £255

Bonus Highlights

- **THE HAGUE** orientation drive
- **AMSTERDAM** diamond factory
- **VOLENDAM** visit
- **BONN** orientation drive
- **RHINELAND** cruise & Lorelei Rock
- **MOSELLE VALLEY** scenic drive
- **EPERNAY** champagne cellars
- **PARIS** city sightseeing

Visiting the Rhineland with river cruise, Brussels, The Hague, Amsterdam, Bonn, Luxembourg and Paris

Day 1 U.K. - Channel Crossing - Brussels. You can join your tour by travelling on our complimentary Feeder Services from London or any of our **Freelink** pick up points across the U.K. You will travel to the Channel port for your short ferry crossing and join your tour on the Continent where you will be met by your Cosmos escort. From here your comfortable coach sets off to Brussels. **pf**

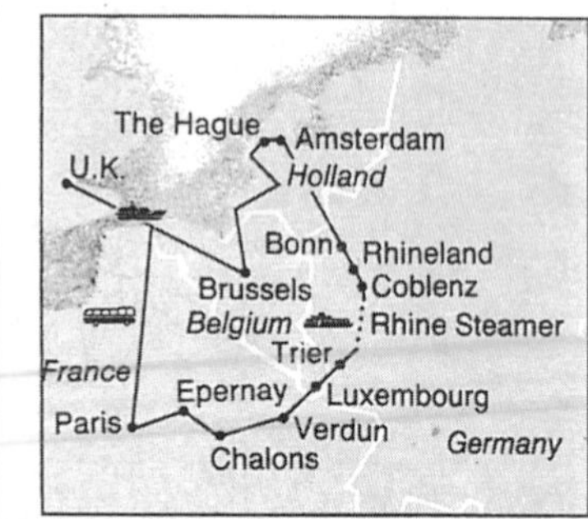

Day 2 Morning in Brussels - Visit The Hague - Amsterdam. Brussels (more fully described on page 12/13), the modern centre of the EEC, still has its old world charm and you'll have time for optional sightseeing. In the early afternoon drive through the flat Dutch dike country to visit The Hague and then on to Amsterdam. **B,D,pf**

Day 3 A whole day in Amsterdam. Amsterdam, delightful city of 1,000 bridges, is more fully described on page 12/13. Take an optional sightseeing tour and canal cruise and enjoy the included visit to a diamond cutter's workshop and the excursion to picturesque Volendam. **B,D,pf**

Day 4 Amsterdam - Afternoon in Bonn - Rhineland. You stop first at Cologne set on the Rhine and famous among other things for its magnificent Gothic Cathedral which survived the wartime bombing. Then on to Bonn. This was the birthplace of Beethoven - the house is now a museum. The "Alter Zoll", a mighty bastion overlooking the Rhine, the old Town Hall and romanesque cathedral make this an interesting visit before the short drive to the romantic Rhine Valley for your night stop. **B,D,pf**

Day 5 Rhineland - Coblenz - Rhine Steamer cruise - Trier. Mountain fringed Coblenz, at the confluence of the Rhine and Moselle is your first visit. Today's highlight is the legendary Rhine with its narrow gorge, castles, half-timbered wine villages, terraced vineyards and the famous Lorelei Rock. Enjoy the included steamer cruise and the scenic drive on the way to lovely Trier in the Moselle Valley. **B,D,pf**

Day 6 Trier - Luxembourg - Verdun - Chalons - Paris. Through the Duchy of Luxembourg into lovely French countryside passing the sombre battlefields of the First World War at Verdun. Past Chalons, on the River Marne, its vineyard country and Epernay where you will visit a Champagne cellar. By evening you'll be in Paris in time to enjoy an optional Parisian cabaret show. **B,pf**

Day 7 A day at leisure in Paris. A day to explore this exciting city (more fully described on page 12/13). Your included guided sightseeing starts with an inside visit of the Notre Dame cathedral, then many of the best-known Parisian sights; La Sorbonne, Boulevard St. Germain, the Eiffel Tower, the Opera, the Champs Elysées and the Rue de Rivoli. In the afternoon you'll have the option of visiting the great Palace of Versailles. In the evening make the most of the optional visit to Montmartre and then a farewell dinner. **B,pf**

Day 8 Paris - Channel Crossing - U.K. A last look at Paris as you drive north to the Channel port where your tour ends. After the short Channel crossing join the appropriate Feeder Service to your home destination. **B**

Fig. 4.10 Cosmos coach trip covering five European capitals
Courtesy: Cosmos

Africa, India, Mexico and the Far East also feature in coach tour brochures. Long-haul coach tour operators either offer deals inclusive of air fare and accommodation (Kuoni, Cosmos, Jetsave, etc.), or they sell only the ground arrangements put together by overseas coach tour operators (Travel 2, Jetset, etc.), sometimes to clients who have already booked a flight and accommodation elsewhere.

Coach tours are quite distinct from coach-accommodation arrangements offered by operators like Cosmos, Sunrider, Travel Europe and Club Cantabrica which simply offer coach transport as a cheaper way of getting clients to a stay-put resort. However, Cosmos in particular offers some holidays which combine the advantages of both types of holidays, with a one-week coach tour followed by a one-week stay-put in the resort break, travelling to and from the UK by coach. For the client, a definite bonus of such holidays is that coach companies usually offer a range of local pick-up points, whereas flights out of regional airports or connecting flights to London can be pricey; Cosmos, for example, boasts more than 200 local pick-up points. However, from the coach company's point of view, setting up an extensive feeder network when there may be only one or two people requiring each point greatly increases operating costs.

Coach tours are one of the few parts of the UK domestic holiday market to be fully packaged and retailed through agents. Market leaders, sharing about 25 per cent of the market, are Wallace Arnold and Shearings, with a cluster of smaller regional operators like Excelsior, Bowens, Robinsons and Grand UK with lots of local pick-up points behind them. Most of the other operators are very small and sell direct to the public rather than through agents. In line with a general trend towards shorter domestic holidays, most British coach tours nowadays are for up to five days, often leaving midweek and travelling to coastal resorts. However, Scotland remains by far the most popular destination. Centred holidays, with day trips out from a fixed base, have also become more popular than conventional touring holidays. Unlike most overseas operators, Wallace Arnold has invested in hotels in popular destinations in order to have more control over its prices. Prices can also be made to look lower than they actually are by charging for excursions separately.

The coaches used for touring holidays are usually smart and modern, with air-conditioning, videos, and toilets (certainly on longer continental tours). Often there is a no-smoking policy on the bus, but there will be frequent stops on longer stretches of road for people to stretch their legs and have a cigarette. Coach tour companies sometimes allow people to select their preferred seats in advance on a first come, first served basis; others rotate passengers so everyone gets a chance to sit in the best seats. Where seats are prebookable a seating plan will usually be included on the booking form (*see* Fig 4.11).

Some tour operators include the following note about seat allocations in their brochures:

> Requests for particular seats can be made on most holidays when booking, but allocations are made strictly on a first come, first served basis. Whilst we do everything possible to conform to the seating plans shown and to provide the seat numbers booked by clients we have to reserve the right to change these should conditions necessitate and we cannot therefore accept bookings which are conditional on the provision of specific seats. We do not allocate specific seats on coaches which operate 'feeder' services between the joining point and the main holiday departure point or on coaches which carry out transfers to or from air and seaports.

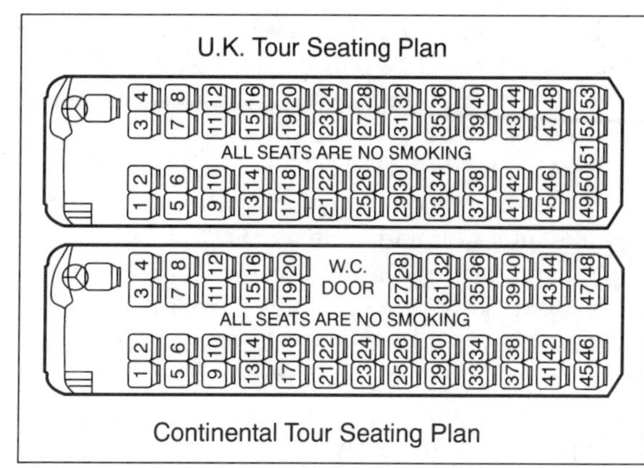

Fig. 4.11 Seating plans for Bakers Dolphin Ziptrips round the UK and the Continent

Courtesy: Bakers Dolphin

Wallace Arnold is one of the industry's old-timers, originally set up in 1912. During the 1980s it expanded by buying up ILG's Overland and Golden Circle products and by absorbing the Scottish coach company, Cotters. It now operates holidays to the Continent, the United States, Canada and New Zealand as well as round the UK. By 1992 it was carrying about 350,000 holidaymakers a year from 700 pick-up points around the country.

European campsite holidays

Several operators offer the possibility of staying at fixed-tent campsites on the Continent. The biggest such operator, with about 40 per cent of the market, is Eurocamp, while Airtours' EuroSites has another 25 per cent. Other significant operators are Keycamp, Haven and Canvas.

Campsite holidays have traditionally been popular with families with cars, who want to drive to their resort. However, some companies also offer coach transport to the camp sites. The tents themselves are often quite luxurious and equipped with things like fridges. Increasingly the sites also offer many of the 'extras' (like children's clubs) of conventional hotel holidays. Often the site will also encompass a swimming pool and other sports facilities like mini-golf and table tennis.

Until the late 1980s these campsites were relatively upmarket. However, the EuroSites product (launched in 1989) started to take prices downmarket in an attempt to increase its share in a stagnant market, a strategy compared to that pursued by air-tour operators in the early 1980s.

Campsite holidays are mainly sold direct to the public; of sales made through agencies, Haven scoops 25 per cent, EuroSites 20 per cent and Eurocamp, the market leader, only 18 per cent (retailed as Sunsites). In 1993 Cosmos launched the first camping 'square deals', offering reduced prices to people prepared to book their coach seats but wait until two weeks before the departure date to learn which campsite they had been assigned to.

Square deals/superdeals, etc.

Square deals are flight and accommodation packages where, in return for a lower than normal price, the clients don't know precisely where in a resort they will be staying. Such arrangements suit operators because they help them to offload surplus flight seats, although they may sometimes result in last minute efforts to find suitable accommodation. With some square deals the clients are not told which particular hotel they will be staying in but will be told which price category it is in and that it is one of the hotels featured in the brochures. Sometimes, however, the hotel is not featured in the brochure. Such packages can cause problems, because the client will have very little information to go on and the hotel may have been omitted from the brochure because it hadn't met the operator's original standards. Most 'square deals' are offered in the summer although increasingly there are similar offers in the winter, even at some ski resorts.

WINTER HOLIDAYS

During the 1970s increased prosperity and leisure time led to the evolution of a winter holiday market which tour operators were quick to develop because it enabled them to spread their fixed costs over the whole year and therefore reduce their average costs. At first winter holidays were priced to cover the operator's variable costs and make a small contribution to fixed costs; these low prices were mainly aimed at senior citizens for whom special 'long-stay' breaks were developed, and at mini-breakers. By the late 1980s, however, the winter holiday market had become far more sophisticated and could be priced in the same way as other parts of the market. Just as the first summer sun holidays offered were to Europe, gradually widening out to encompass other parts of the world, so the first winter holidays were short-haul products. Now, of course, there are almost as many long-haul winter holidays, particularly because few parts of even southern Europe have winter temperatures to compete with the Caribbean or Africa.

In the recession of the late 1980s and early 1990s, winter vacations were particularly badly hit. Although all holidays are discretionary purchases, winter ones are even more so. Families may feel they cannot do without their summer break, but can postpone a winter one. From 1986, when winter departures made up only 18 per cent of the market, until 1992 when they made up 24 per cent, the trend had been one of steady growth. Then in 1993 winter departures fell back slightly, to just 22 per cent of the market.

The winter holiday market divides into the following two distinct categories.

1. Winter sun

With the Canary Islands by far the most popular destination, the winter sun market also focuses on:

- Southern Spain and Majorca
- The Algarve
- Madeira
- Malta
- Cyprus
- Crete and Rhodes
- Southern Italy
- Florida
- Morocco and Tunisia
- Egypt
- Israel
- The Gambia and Senegal
- The Caribbean
- Kenya
- Goa in India

Peak season for the winter sun market coincides with Christmas and the New Year and, to a lesser

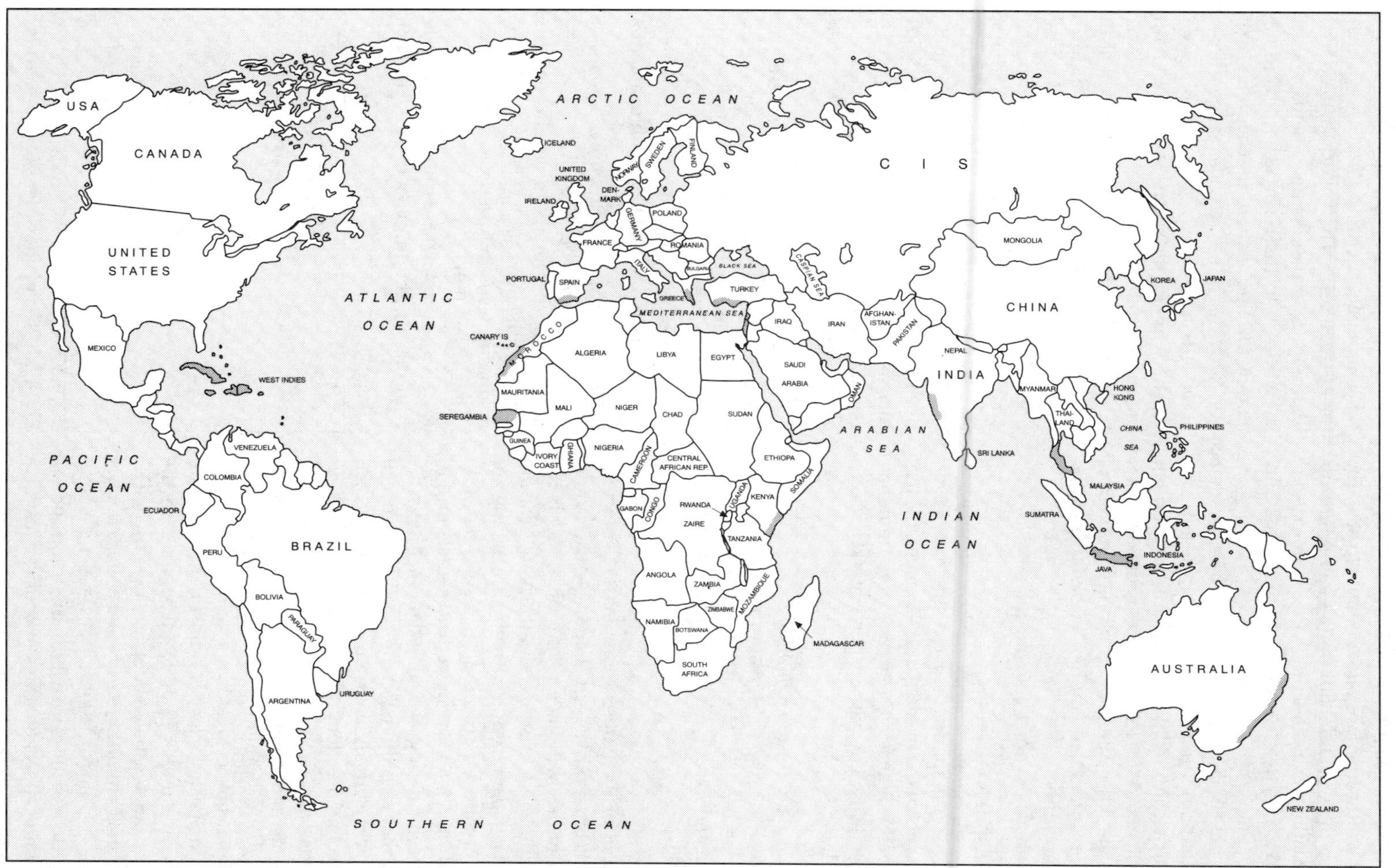

Fig. 4.12 The most popular winter sun destinations for UK holidaymakers

extent, with school half-term holidays in February. Long-stay winter holidays allow people to stay, for example on the Costa del Sol or in Tenerife, for up to three months at very low prices (sometimes as little as £2.95 a day), while saving on winter fuel bills at home.

Winter sun brochures are slimmer than summer sun ones, although in other ways their design and the range of accommodation on offer is very similar. In the static market of the early 1990s they increasingly contained the same sort of promotional offers (like free or discounted children's holidays) as the summer brochures.

2. Winter sports

The winter sports market is one of the most packaged segments of the market; in 1993, even of skiers visiting nearby France, 78 per cent were travelling on package deals. The winter sports market is centred on:

- France
- Austria
- Switzerland
- Bulgaria and Romania
- Norway
- Andorra
- Italian Alps
- United States and Canada

Peak season for the winter sports market coincides with the February half-term holidays when most European resorts will have plenty of snow on the ground, although Christmas and the New Year are also popular. Operators increasingly offer a range of transport options for reaching the resorts (air, rail, coach, self-drive), and a choice between staying in hotels or self-catering accommodation. More distinctively, they also offer accommodation in special chalets where staff, often trained in cordon bleu cookery techniques, look after clients. These holidays are best suited to groups and families since living rooms and sometimes bathrooms must be shared. Chalet holiday arrangements usually include a big cooked breakfast, afternoon tea and a large evening meal. Unless a family books the entire chalet, children under 12 or 16 (depending on the company) cannot usually book to stay in chalets. Most operators provide crockery and cutlery but not all include bed linen or local taxes. Clients sometimes have to pay for electricity in the resort too.

With winter sports holidays operators must also offer a wide range of 'extras', like ski and boot hire, ski school packages and lift passes, which push up the average price. They may also need to make provision for transporting clients' skis and/or snowboards to the resort (charter airlines usually charge for this, although scheduled airlines may not, provided the overall baggage allowance isn't exceeded).

The winter sports market suffered badly during the recession, partly because ski holidays are often taken as second holidays and partly because all the 'extras' can make them expensive and therefore expendable when times are hard. Many of the most popular European ski destinations (Austria, Switzerland, France) were also made more expensive by the devaluation of the pound in 1992. Nor did it help that the market for school ski trips declined dramatically during the early 1990s. Increased popularity also brought overcrowding to popular resorts, leading to queues for lifts, congested *pistes* and greater danger of collisions on the slopes. The crowds also detracted from skiing's rather elite image. In 1993 there were even suggestions that the ski boom had been a feature of the 1980s economic 'bubble' and that, as a product, it had already passed its peak. Operators responded to a 15 per cent fall in the market between winter 1991/2 and winter 1992/3 with different strategies:

- Bringing out new brochures sooner to try and catch the early bookers.
- Targeting beginners in an effort to increase the size of the market.
- Finding ways to bring prices down, e.g. by offering more Italian than French resorts while the Italian currency was the weaker of the two; increasing the number of ski-drive packages; or

THOMSON
CRYSTAL
NEILSON
INGHAMS
ENTERPRISE
BLADON LINES

Fig. 4.13 The main winter sports operators

Fig. 4.14 The most popular winter sports holiday destinations in Europe

adding more self-catering properties to brochures.

- Expanding programmes to cheaper ex-Eastern bloc resorts in Bulgaria, Romania and Slovenia.
- Special offers, e.g. in 1993/4 Ski Falcon and Sally Holidays offered to refund the difference in price if clients could find an identical holiday on sale more cheaply elsewhere.
- Taking out 'extras' which had been included in the price. In 1993 Ski Partners took lift passes and insurance out of its brochure prices, to reduce them by an average £100. This also freed travel agents to switch-sell to their own insurance, perhaps making them more enthusiastic about selling the product.
- Raising the upper age for eligibility for child discounts from eleven to nineteen.

Skiing is a complex product to sell because it assumes a knowledge of the actual sport: for example, which resorts are suitable for beginners, which for intermediate and which for advanced skiers. The jargon associated with skiing also makes it harder for those who haven't actually experienced it. The following are some of the most important terms to understand:

Après-ski Evening entertainment in the resorts – important both to skiers and their non-skiing companions. Typical *après-ski* activities include barbecues, fondue parties, sleigh rides, bowling, mountain picnics and fancy dress parties. The cost of *après-ski* activities can make a difference to the resort chosen.

Glacier skiing In some resorts it is possible to ski on glaciers even in summer.

Heliskiing Experienced skiers are helicoptered up to virgin snow and then picked up again at the bottom of the run.

Langlauf or cross country skiing Skiing on the flat instead of downhill slopes.

Lift pass Document complete with photograph that gives access to ski lift. A bit like an expensive bus pass.

Off-piste Areas of virgin snow outside the recognised pistes.

Piste Laid-out ski runs.

Ski leader/escort/guide An experienced skier who doesn't teach skiing but leads groups round the slopes to enable them to make the most of them. An idea pioneered by Neilson in 1983.

Ski lift Method of reaching the ski slopes. Can be a chair lift, drag lift or gondola. Vital that there should be adequate lifts if long queues are not to form at peak periods.

Ski pack Ski packs consist of hired skis, sticks and boots, sometimes with ski school admission and lift pass thrown in. Sometimes they can be booked and paid for in the UK, sometimes booked in the UK and paid for in the resort. Hiring equipment in the resort rather than in the UK eliminates the need to pay a flight supplement to carry the skis (perhaps £12–15) and ending up with boots that don't fit properly.

Ski school Classes where people are taught to ski on nursery slopes.

Snowboarding A sport described as a mixture of surfing, skateboarding and windsurfing, using boards to ride down the mountain instead of skis.

Snow cannons Some resorts use snow cannons to pump artificial snow onto the pistes when there's too little natural snow.

Snow guarantee Agreement to take clients to a resort with snow if the booked resort is snowless (*see* Fig. 4.15). Can be costly for operators in bad years.

Operators try to make life easier for agents by using colour-coding schemes in their brochures to indicate the level of difficulty of the different ski slopes (*see* Fig 4.16). They also use grading schemes (Neilson has 'peaks', Inghams has stars, Crystal has diamonds) to identify resorts which are, in general, suitable for beginners, intermediate or advanced skiers. However, there is little substitute for personal experience and so several operators take agents to the ski resorts on educational visits as well as providing home-based training packages, sometimes incorporating experience on dry ski slopes in the UK.

Although it is possible to put together a group to buy any product, skiing has always been associated with group bookings, hence the popularity of chalets where a group can have the accommodation to themselves. To encourage group bookings, ski operators offer discounts depending on the number who book and when they want to travel, ranging from

NEILSON

SNOW GUARANTEE

Free transport to a skiable area when snow conditions make skiing in your resort area impracticable.

When you book a Neilson holiday you will automatically be covered for transport to a skiable area if you are unable to ski in the resort in which you are staying.

This Guarantee takes effect if, owing to a lack of snow or adverse weather:

(i) 20% or less of the lifts and/or runs shown on the resort's official piste map are open;

(ii) The local ski-school director considers it is unsuitable to teach.

Transport will be arranged on a daily basis to the nearest area where skiing is possible. Where lift passes have been pre-booked, these will be rearranged at no extra cost.

The Neilson Snow Guarantee applies to downhill skiing only and does not cover cross-country skiing. However it does apply if lifts or ski schools are not operating as a result of too much snow, high winds or other adverse weather conditions.

When you book Neilson insurance, as detailed above, you will be able to claim from Neilson on your return to the UK, a payment of £25 per person for each day for which it was not possible to arrange transport to another area. Please address any such claims to Customer Services Department, Neilson, 71 Houghside Road, Pudsey, Leeds, LS28 9BR

Fig. 4.15 Neilson's snow guarantee
Courtesy: Neilson

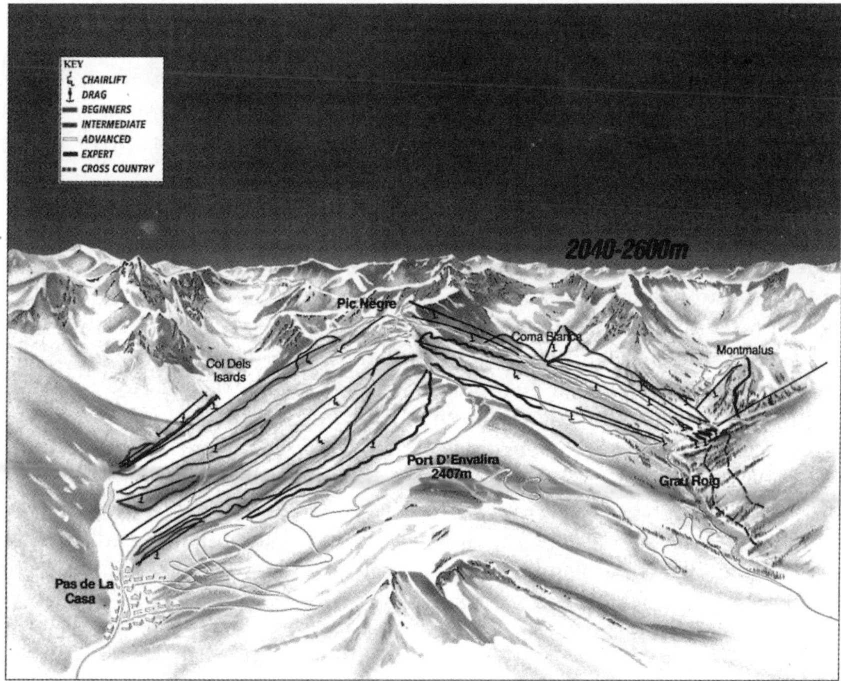

Fig. 4.16 How a ski resort is depicted in a Neilson brochure
Courtesy: Neilson

perhaps 20 per cent off one place for a group of eight travelling over Christmas, to five free places for a group of 36 travelling in the first half of December. Usually they are only available on holidays using charter flights. To prevent the idea of a 'group' being exploited, discounts only apply to people travelling on the same departure date, using the same type of transport, staying in the same accommodation and staying for the same length of time. Sometimes however, group members are allowed to depart from different places. Group discounts normally only apply to the basic holiday price and not to insurance, room supplements, ski hire, etc.

In 1993 most operators struggled to attract beginners because the decline in the school ski market threatened to deprive them of a source of newly-addicted skiers.

It is possible that skiers are becoming more fickle. Whereas in the past they happily returned to the same resorts year after year, some may now be looking for 'novelty', putting pressure on operators to come up with new destinations for skiing in the same way that summer and winter sun companies have had to in the past.

Fly-drive holidays

In the 1980s, fly-drive packages became increasingly popular as they enabled people with limited time to reach a faraway destination and then explore it under their own steam. Fly-drive packages tend to use scheduled flights and enable the client to pick up a hired car at their destination, often from the airport. The basic brochure price usually covers hire of the smallest, cheapest car with third party insurance, local taxes and an unlimited mileage allowance thrown in; there is usually a supplement to hire larger cars. Sometimes hotel vouchers are also included in the price. Fly-drive packages to the United States and Canada often include hire of a motorhome which is pricier than a normal car but removes the need for separate accommodation.

'Seat-only' holidays

In the early days of tour operating, complex rules made it impossible for tour operators to sell flight seats without accommodation. However, during the

1980s these rules were gradually relaxed and operators began to sell off surplus flight seats as 'seat-only' deals. This suited the needs both of some independent travellers and of the increasing number of people who owned properties (including timeshare apartments) on the Continent and wanted to be able to get to them cheaply. In theory operators were still supposed to provide accommodation but increasingly this amounted to little more than a voucher for a hostel which it was assumed the client would not actually use. In 1992 when the Single European Market came into effect, it became illegal for EU member states to insist that 'seat-only' packages be sold with minimal accommodation vouchers. Outside the EU, however, such regulations remained legal; so, for example, Cyprus continues to refuse to admit passengers without booked accommodation. In 1991 when 10.5 million overseas 'packages' were sold, it was estimated that as many as 2.5 million might in fact have been 'seat-only' arrangements. In 1993 the three bestselling seat-only destinations were Malaga, Alicante and Faro.

Like most parts of the package holiday market, the 'seat-only' sector was hit by the recession in 1991-2, causing several companies, including Airbreak, Flights Delight and Flight Seekers, to collapse. However, the situation was not as bad as it might have been, probably in part because accommodation-free deals look cheap in comparison with conventional packages. By 1993 all the big tour operators were producing flight-only brochures, usually for the summer and winter seasons and sometimes covering long-haul destinations as well as those closer to home. There was a danger that too many seats chasing too few customers would lead to cut-throat discounting. Certainly in 1992 when operators overestimated the overall size of the package holiday market, their reaction was to offload some of the surplus capacity as bargain-priced 'seat-only' deals, thereby cutting into the profits of the specialists.

'Seat-only' deals are particularly price sensitive, with clients often prepared to accept inconveniently-timed departures in return for a few pounds off the price. Much of the trade is also from late bookers which makes it particularly hard for the operators to know how much of their capacity they will be able to sell. It also means sales are, more than usually, likely to be influenced by external factors like favourable exchange rates and dismal weather at home. Most departures are from Gatwick and Manchester, although by 1993 there was an increased willingness to offer flights from regional airports, particularly Glasgow, Birmingham and Cardiff.

The big operators have different attitudes to 'seat-only' deals. Thomson and Airtours still tend to see them as a tactical way of shifting surplus seats whereas Owners Abroad viewed Falcon Flights as a product in its own right. Nevertheless the market leaders are big volume operators; in 1993 Avro was licensed to sell 750,000 seats.

Traditionally 'seat-only' packaging has been about using up surplus seats on charter aircraft. However, by 1993 as scheduled air fares began to come down even in Europe, it was thought that charter flights might eventually vanish from some routes, like those to Germany, forcing consumers to return to scheduled airlines. This is also an area of the business where new companies quickly emerge from failed ones: Bluebird Express is a successor to failed Euro Express; Flight Company emerged from Flights Delight; and Skybus is a descendant of Pegasus.

'Adventure' and overland holidays

Since the early 1970s when young people flocked overland through Iran, Pakistan and Afghanistan to India and Nepal, a number of companies have packaged the overland holiday experience as well; Hann Overland (now Hinterland Travel), for example, was founded in 1972. Their brochures tend to feature long-stay trips (up to six months in some cases), but aimed at those who want to travel long distances rather than at sun worshippers. Most such expeditions are aimed at younger people (primarily the under-40s), but because this is a dwindling segment of the market, some of the companies have diversified to offer shorter safaris and short mountain treks as well as the longer packages. Typically, such holidays involve travelling in large trucks capable of negotiating tricky terrain and often mean camping as well; more imaginatively, Top Deck uses converted two-decker buses as 'Deckerhomes' (*see* Fig. 4.17). The 'adventure' lies in the nature of the countries visited, although increasingly such packages may include opportunities for climbing, trekking, white-water rafting and other activities. Although the first overland companies concentrated on the trans-Asia route, most of them now cover most parts of the developing world as well as the wilder parts of the developed world.

Most overland holiday companies concentrate on long-haul destinations, although some also include unusual European holidays, like trekking in Corsica, as well. Because these holidays are mainly aimed at the young, the companies sometimes have upper and lower age limits for participants. Because of their length, some of these holidays also seem expensive, although on a week-by-week basis they can represent particularly good value for money; for

TOP DECK'S UNIQUE DECKERHOME

A. Permanent bunks for sleeping.
B. Ample seats (all seats are cloth covered).
C. All seats face a dining table.
D. Sink with running water from 120 litres (approx) water tank.
E. Oven/Grill – great for roasts and cakes.
F. 4 gas burners for cooking.
G. Sightseeing Deck for unparalleled views.
H. Personal storage locker (1 per person).
I. Food and storage space.
J. Bench area for preparing food.
K. Unobstructed views from all seats.
L. Stereo and microphone.
M. Fully equiped kitchen with pots, pans, cutlery, etc.
N. Storage locker for tools, spares, oil, anti-freeze.
O. Spare gas bottles.
P. Diesel jerry can racks.
Q. Modified ground clearance.
R. Special radiator with oil cooler.

Q. How does the food fund work?
A. The food fund will cover 3 meals per day whilst on the Deckerhome. The courier looks after this fund during the trip. He/she ensures that ample supplies are bought, usually from the local markets. Your food fund may also subsidise the occasional restaurant meal. But please note there will be times when you may be required to pay for meals in restaurants when not eating on the Deckerhome. This will depend mainly upon the financial position of the food fund.

Q. What are the sleeping arrangements?
A. The Deckerhome sleeps up to 21 passengers but our group limit is 20. Sleeping space is provided by permanent bunks upstairs (that can be used during the day whilst travelling) and when necessary, the table and seats on the upper and the lower decks convert into beds by adding 100mm thick foam mattresses. This makes the Deckerhome comfortable and self-contained. Don't forget to bring your sleeping bag.

Q. Are special diets catered for?
A. Yes, where possible. Please advise your travel agent when booking your trip and advise us on your booking form. Also inform your Tour Leader once on board so that he/she can make the necessary arrangements.

Q. Will I have to help cook, clean, wash-up etc?
A. Yes. Everyone is involved in the cooking and cleaning. We would like you to think of the Deckerhome as your home for the duration of the trip. Can't cook? No problem, your fellow travellers will always teach you.

Q. What about hygiene?
A. Your Deckerhome carries purified water, and there is also a basic first aid kit. Most importantly there will be strict guidelines set out by your crew to ensure that group hygiene is kept at a high standard.

Q. How much luggage am I allowed?
A. It is important that you keep your personal luggage to a minimum. Refer to the pre-departure information for a clothing list guide. NO suitcases are allowed. Frameless back-packs and soft carry bags are the best way to carry your belongings. Try to bring easily washable and durable clothes. Remember clothes are cheap to buy in Asia and also make great souvenirs.

Q. Are there showers/toilets on the Deckerhome?
A. No. You use the facilities at the campsites. If we're travelling, then we stop at the most convenient places.

Fig. 4.17 The 'Deckerhome'
Courtesy: Top Deck

Our expedition trucks

The essence of Overlanding is contact with the country and with your fellow travellers, and we believe that an expedition vehicle should be capable of being as 'open-air' as possible, and that members of the group should be able to see and talk to each other. So (unless it is cold for extended periods, as happens in South America) there is little point in having an enclosed body which isolates you from the countryside you are passing through and prevents the contact that is part of your reason for going. Forward facing seats (especially coach seats) are fine in theory, but in practice restrict your vision to one side of the truck plus a good view of the back of someone else's head, which can get dull after a few months.
Most of our trucks have inward facing bench seats which provide very good all round vision; our Mercedes trucks in Asia and South America have a mixture of forward, backward and inward facing seats arranged in three sections, which again give an excellent all round view.
Having the right vehicle to suit the road conditions on a particular expedition is important, and we go to a lot of trouble to build our trucks accordingly - there is no standard Exodus truck. Some are Bedfords; an increasing number are Mercedes, which are rather more powerful and spacious. In Asia and South America, where roads are generally good, faster two wheel drive trucks are appropriate, but in Africa, four wheel drive is essential if you want to get really off the beaten track.
All the trucks have individual luggage lockers, accessible at any time. Food, cooking equipment, spares etc. are stored in other lockers, some inside and some outside the truck. There are overhead nets or shelves to take bulky, light items like sleeping bags, and space behind the seats for cameras and hand bags etc. In the interests of safety, manoeuvrability and ease of access to baggage, we do NOT tow trailers.
The seats are well upholstered, and there is good head and leg room. Large fuel and water tanks allow a very long range without our having to pick up additional supplies, so that we can be completely self-contained for quite long periods if necessary. There is a waterproof canopy with clear windows, but the sides are rolled up most of the time to allow all-round visibility. When we do hit cold weather in Asia and South America, there are heaters in the passenger compartment which work independently from the engine; additionally, our South America trucks have a full insulated body to keep the worst of the cold out at all times. More information about our trucks can be found in our expedition dossiers.

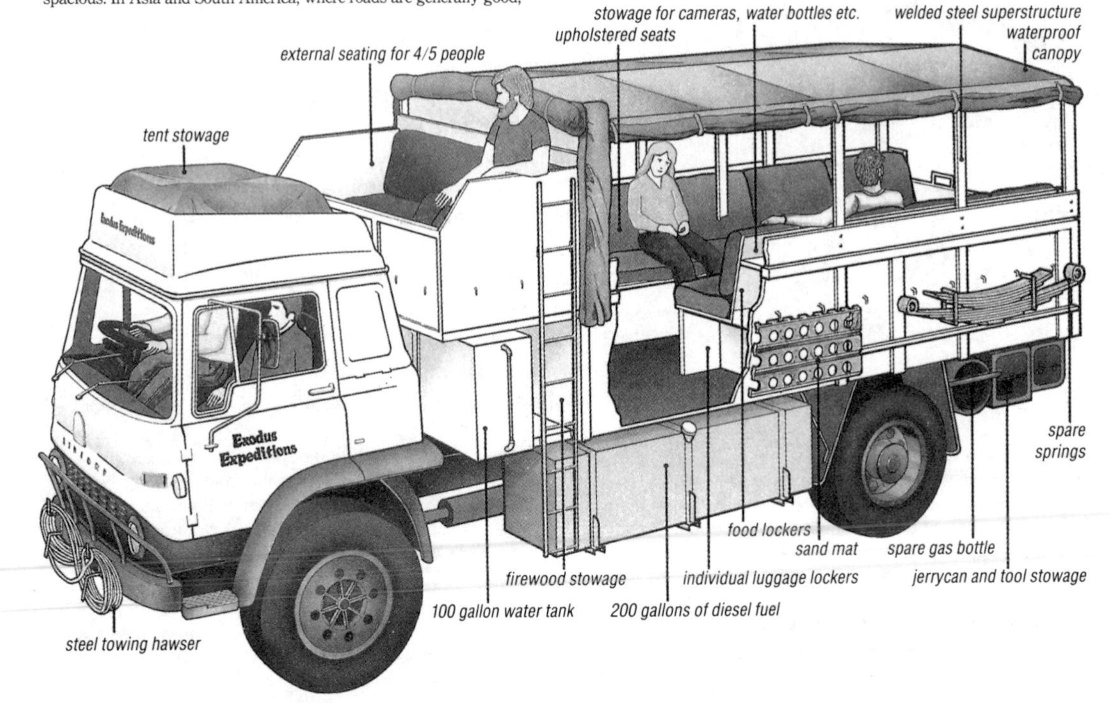

Fig. 4.18 The Exodus Expedition truck

Courtesy: Exodus Expeditions

example, in 1994 a 24 week Encounter Overland expedition from Tangiers to Kathmandu cost £3,565, which works out at £148.50 a week. Some overland companies also ask group members to pay into a kitty for buying food and other necessities *en route*.

Inevitably, these tours tend to visit parts of the world which are politically unstable. This is what Exodus Expeditions says about the likely problems:

Overlanding, by its very nature, is always subject to political upheavals. Since we ran our first expedition in 1974 we have seen and coped with numerous coups, wars and revolutions in all three continents, and our leaders have proved themselves to be pretty good at finding their way round the problems that politics can place in their way. But if all their best efforts should fail to solve the problem on the ground, our considerable resources as a broad-based adventure operator put us in an excellent position to get our expeditions through.

This is what they say about the general nature of overlanding:

> The journeys described in this brochure are expeditionary in nature, and cannot be classified as tours or holidays in the normally accepted sense. The whole philosophy of this type of travel is one which allows alternatives and a substantial degree of flexibility. The outline itineraries given for each expedition must therefore be taken as an indication of what each group should accomplish . . . Changes in itinerary may be caused by local conditions, flight cancellations, mechanical breakdown, weather, border restrictions, sickness or other unforeseeable circumstances . . . It is a fundamental condition of joining any of the expeditions described in this brochure that you accept this flexibility, and acknowledge that we cannot be responsible for delays and alterations and their results, such as inconvenience, discomfort, or disappointment.
>
> (Courtesy: Exodus Expeditions)

Few of the overland adventure companies are members of ABTA, although some belong to AITO.

Contiki	Europe, Great Britain, Russia, Scandinavia
Encounter Overland	Asia, Africa, South America
Exodus Expeditions	Europe, Africa, Asia, South America
Explore	Europe, Asia, Africa, the Middle East, North, South and Central America, New Zealand
Guerba	Africa
Hinterland Travel	Africa, Asia, the CIS
Imaginative Traveller	Egypt, Turkey, Jordan, Israel
Journey Latin America	South and Central America
Top Deck	Europe, Russia, Egypt, Central America, Middle East, Asia, South America, Africa, Australia, USA, Canada, Mexico.
Tracks	Africa
Trek America	USA, Canada, Mexico

Fig. 4.19 The big overland tour operators

Safaris

On safari holidays, clients are taken to watch wildlife from a safari vehicle, usually a Land-Rover or minibus, often painted with zebra stripes for 'camouflage'. Because visibility is such a crucial part of a safari, many companies boast that their holidays offer guaranteed window seats. Figure 4.20 shows how Hayes and Jarvis describe a safari.

Traditionally, safari holidays were an African product, mainly focused on the game parks of Kenya, Tanzania (*see* Fig. 4.23) and South Africa. Nowadays, however, there are safari holidays to India, Zambia, Zimbabwe, Botswana and other countries with plentiful indigenous wildlife. A distinctive type of safari takes small groups of people on foot into the rainforests of Zaire or Uganda to watch silverback gorillas in the wild; similar, if fewer, safaris offer the chance to view wild chimpanzees in Zaire or western Tanzania. Two or three day safaris can sometimes be booked as excursions attached to African beach holidays, and companies like Kuoni can also put together tailor-made safaris. Safaris can also be combined with other types of holiday, perhaps as a two-centre package: many operators now offer one week beach holidays on the Kenyan coast at Mombasa or Malindi with a one week safari package; a few combine a Kenyan safari with a week's more conventional sightseeing in Egypt. Holidays combining a Kenyan safari with a beach holiday in Mauritius or the Seychelles are also possible. Safaris to Zimbabwe usually include the chance to visit Victoria Falls as well, while those to Tanzania sometimes include a trip to Zanzibar too.

Alongside the conventional safaris, there are an increasing number of 'novelty' trips. Some companies, for example, offer people the chance to travel across the Masai Mara game park in a hot-air balloon; these excursions, which sometimes end with a 'sparkling wine' breakfast, are expensive and depend on weather conditions being right for the balloon to be launched. There are also a few pricy safaris where clients travel on camels instead of in normal vans. Foot safaris are occasionally possible, depending on the type of wildlife in the area and how dangerous it is. Safari itineraries are usually fairly flexible to enable groups to follow up

SAFARIS

A safari is an exciting journey, leaving the cities and towns far behind and travelling into the African bush, full of wild animals living proud and free in their natural habitat, as they have done for centuries past. The legendary days of porters, gun bearers, sun helmets, and long weary treks in search of tusks and trophies have now gone. Today you stay at comfortable lodges and travel in specially converted mini-buses. Your experienced English speaking driver/guide will position you perfectly to capture on film some of the most memorable moments in your life.

Fig. 4.20 The safari experience
Courtesy: Hayes and Jarvis

On Safari

Just a few points you should know:

*Accommodation on Safari can vary and some may be fairly basic. All the lodges we use on Safari, except the Tree Lodges and Olkurruk in the Mara have swimming pools. Food is good and plentiful but don't expect a la carte dining or a very elaborate wine list.

*Whilst you are staying in the parks you will be taken on game drives. This is the most exciting part of the safari when you go out in your vehicle to search for the animals. These normally take place early in the morning and late in the afternoon when the animals are most active.

*Changes in safari routings or game viewing drives may be necessary – despite the fact we have some of the best vehicles available the occasional flat tyre, bad road conditions, shortage of lodge accommodation may temporarily re-route the Safari.

*Single accommodation in Safari Lodges can be a problem and in peak times sharing is often the only solution. If you book and pay for single accommodation and this should happen, you will be refunded the difference.

*We recommend families with children under 12 have their own safari vehicle – it's very good value and ensures you don't need to worry about your children disturbing others' game viewing! Children under 7 years are not accepted on Safaris that include Treetops, the Ark and Mountain Lodge. Please see individual price boxes for full details.

*Individual luggage should be kept to a minimum. On most Safaris you can store your main luggage in your Nairobi or Mombasa hotel and collect it on your return from Safari.

*Above all remember this is Africa, roads are bumpy and dusty. The best time to see the game is at dawn and dusk, so early morning game drives are an exciting part of your safari.

Fig. 4.21 Kuoni's advice to safari holidaymakers
Courtesy: Kuoni

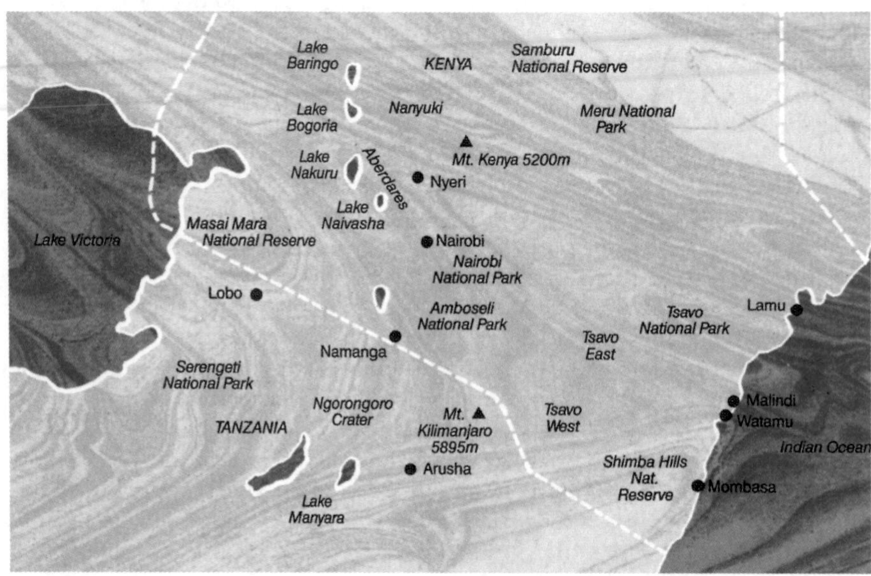

Fig. 4.22 The Kenyan and Tanzanian game parks
Courtesy: Kuoni

WHO JOINS A GUERBA TOUR

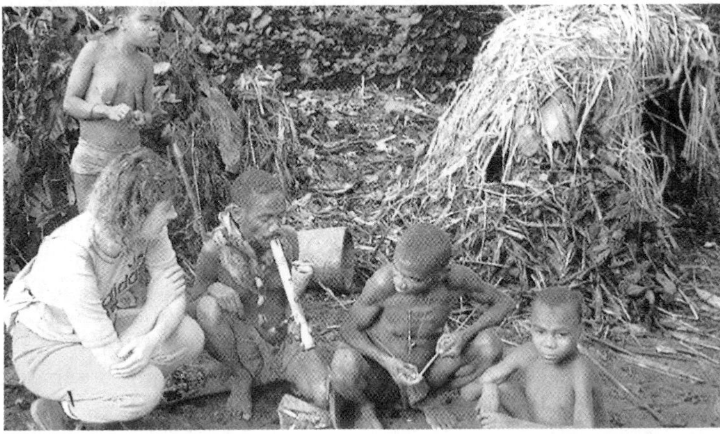

An African Safari or Overland Expedition is not for everyone. By the very nature of travelling in remote regions there are unforeseen challenges to overcome. Contributing to an expedition gives a real sense of involvement and achievement. As long as you are reasonably fit and young at heart, with a taste for adventure and willing to put up with the occasional but inevitable hardship – Africa awaits.

Everyone gets involved with the daily chores, gathering firewood, helping the Guerba cook, shopping for food in the local markets and repairing roads and bridges if the need arises. Very few of those who join our tours have experienced this type of travel before but everyone soon gets into the safari lifestyle.

The majority of our passengers are aged between 20 and 50 although a restricted number below and above this range do sometimes participate in, and enjoy, our tours. Guerba tours are sold worldwide and most have four or more nationalities in the group but all with one uniting factor – a desire to see and experience the 'real Africa'. This can only be achieved by escaping from the constraints of a standard package holiday, and a willingness to take the rough with the smooth for the rewards involved. Don't worry about coming on your own, many people do. You will be joining a group of people who will be as keen as you are to see Africa and make the most of the adventure. We can promise you that the experience will at the very least be exhilarating, and may cause you to take a fresh look at the world we live in.

LIFE EN ROUTE

When you arrive in Africa you will meet the Guerba crew and your fellow travellers. Each tour begins with a predeparture meeting when you will be shown around the vehicle and briefed on what life en route is all about, and how everyone gets involved and contributes equally to the running of the tour. Getting involved can be collecting firewood, filling water containers, helping the cook/campmaster or whatever jobs need doing.

Once on the road everyone quickly settles into the daily routine. An early breakfast, as we need to make the most of the daylight hours, pack up camp and we are on the move. Itineraries are flexible to allow for photography and the unexpected or unusual events we meet en route. We stop to browse around areas and places of interest, call at village markets for fresh food and seek out interesting handicrafts to buy or just spend time chatting to the local people.

Towards late afternoon we look for a campsite. Everyone swings into action, campfire lit and kettles on, tents set up, the smells of cooking, camp stool out and it is time to sit down and enjoy the silence of the desert, the night calls of the bush or voices and music from a nearby village. Now we can sit round the fire to discuss the events of the day, and be briefed on tomorrow. Evenings are a relaxing time, listening to music, writing diaries or playing a friendly card or board game in the back of the vehicle.

When in towns we may enjoy the local restaurants and the nightlife and occasionally indulge in an hotel.

Fig. 4.23 A Guerba tour
Courtesy: Guerba

Kenya Game Parks

Amboseli: In Masailand in the shadow of Africa's highest mountain – Mt. Kilimanjaro, buffalo, elephant, and occasionally lion and leopard can be seen. Good bird life depending on seasons.
Safaris visiting the area – Leopard, Serengeti.

Tsavo National Park: halfway between Nairobi and Mombasa, it is one of the world's largest parks. Tsavo West adjoins Amboseli and is the site of the now famous Mzima Springs where you can often observe hippo underwater from a viewing tank.
Safaris visiting the area – Leopard, Safari Experience.

Mount Kenya and the Aberdares: the location of the best known Treehouses in the world. Mountain Lodge is probably the best tree lodge (all rooms have private facilities and overlook the water hole). Treetops the most famous and the Ark the most originally designed. All have a floodlit waterhole and salt lick and game can be viewed well into the night. The area is generally very scenic and rich in wildlife – elephants, buffalo, giant forest hog, a varied species of antelope, monkeys and birds.
Safaris visiting the area – Cheetah, Leopard, Lion, Equatorial and Safari Club.

Samburu (Buffalo Springs): the wide Uaso Nyiro River runs through the park and attracts a large variety of game. Unique are long-necked gerenuk, Grevy's zebra and reticulated giraffe. Leopard are regularly seen around the lodges, lion can also be viewed and the river is home to crocodile and hippopotamus.
Safaris visiting the area – Cheetah, Leopard, Lion, Equatorial, Dick Hedges Camping.

Lake Baringo, Lake Nakuru and Lake Naivasha: bird life in abundance at all the Great Rift Valley Lakes with Nakuru being most famous for its large numbers of flamingo. Near Baringo is Lake Bogoria famous for its hot springs and home to the rare greater kudu. Lake Naivasha boasts 340 species of bird life including the fish eagle.
Safaris visiting the area – Cheetah, Leopard, Equatorial, Out of Africa, Dick Hedges Camping.

Masai Mara: on Kenya's southern border at the northern end of the Serengeti, the Mara is Kenya's leading game reserve. It is rich in grassland therefore attracting vast herds of wildebeeste, zebra, antelope and a countless variety of other plains game which in turn attracts predators one of the most exciting of all the game parks we offer.
Safaris visiting the area – Cheetah, Leopard, Equatorial, Out of Africa, Safari Club, Dick Hedges Camping.

Fig. 4.24 How Kuoni describes the main game parks

particularly interesting sightings. More adventurous versions offered by the overland companies often allow time for clients to climb either Mount Kenya or Mount Kilimanjaro as well.

Safari accommodation varies considerably. Most of the big African game parks now have lodges which match the standards of the best hotels and have sometimes been built in positions which make game-watching possible even without leaving the premises: for example, lodges near saltlicks may attract elephants, buffaloes, bushbucks and rhinos. 'Treetops' in the Aberdares is a giant tree-house on stilts above a waterhole and within view of several saltlicks. Some of these hotels are sufficiently formal to insist men wear jackets and ties for dinner. Bales includes a Kenyan safari in its programme of 'Topmarket Tours', with stays at The Ark in the Aberdare Country Club, Mount Kenya Safari Club on Mount Kenya, the Lake Baringo Club beside Lake Baringo and Lake Naivasha Hotel by Lake Naivasha. At the opposite end of the spectrum, there are also some tented safaris which vary considerably in the degree of comfort on offer but suit those prepared to forego hot baths and haute cuisine in favour of a hardier outdoor experience. Tents are mosquito-proofed and usually have their own wash-basins and gas lighting, while the campsites normally have separate shower and toilet cubicles; sometimes these are even built into individual tents.

Although the accommodation and food on some safaris can be luxurious, the experience can nevertheless be a tough one since many African roads are poorly made, and horribly dusty and potholed in the dry season, or muddy and slippery in the wet.

All-inclusive holidays

There are some places in the world to which tour operators offer all-inclusive holidays, with the brochure price covering all meals, drinks, entertainment, sports and tips. The first destinations so featured were in the Caribbean where two groups in particular, Sandals Resorts and Superclubs, offer all-inclusive deals, but it is now possible to take an all-inclusive holiday in places as far afield as Thailand, the Maldives and Mexico as well as in Antigua, Barbados, Bermuda, the Cayman Islands, Cuba, the Grenadines, Jamaica, St Kitts and St Lucia. All-inclusive holidays make it possible for tourists to spend their entire stay in their hotel complex without ever venturing outside, perfect for those who are wary of getting to grips with a different culture. Arguably, such holidays also do least damage to indigenous cultures by putting an effective *cordon sanitaire* around the tourists to keep them apart from local people. Conversely, since they are booked and paid for in the tourist generating country, the host country may see little return

Tanzania
Wildlife Safari

17 or 24 days Hotel/Mountain Hut/Camping - World's Most Spectacular Wildlife

Only in Africa can you find the spectacle of wildlife in its rawest exuberance, amid an incredible diversity of landscapes. We use a special 4-wheel-drive 'go-anywhere' Unimog to explore some of the best gamelands on earth.

3-day Foot Safari

Our first few days are spent exploring the great diversity of flora and fauna in Arusha National Park. Numerous forest animals are spotted as we climb the game trails up to the Meru Crater, accompanied by an armed Park ranger. From here we can appreciate the spectacular ash cone and sheer cliffs rising to the summit of Mt Meru (15,000').

Lake Manyara

Following our descent, we drive to Tarangire National Park where a wide variety of animals roam among a forest of primeval baobabs. We'll also spend some time game viewing in Lake Manyara Park, famed for its tree-climbing lions. We travel to the Rift Valley and relax at Lake Natron, the home of millions of flamingoes.

Great Serengeti Plains

Then we enter the great Serengeti, famed for its huge lion population, and are at once among the vast herds of wildebeest, zebras and Grant's gazelles. Other wildlife includes hyenas, jackals, topi and cheetah, and large numbers of giraffe are usually seen near Lobo Lodge. We'll also visit the archaeological site of the Olduvai Gorge, where Doctor Leakey found the fossil of *Zinjanthropus boisei*, the so-called 'Nutcracker Man'.

Ngorongoro Crater

Descending a steep and narrow track into Ngorongoro we arrive at the heart of this beautiful crater, which some believe to have been the proverbial Garden of Eden. The 100 square mile sunken floor is a natural wonder, the world's largest intact caldera, containing the biggest permanent concentration of wildlife in Africa. It offers year-round game viewing. Our safari ends in Arusha. *A 'Kilimanjaro Hike' can also be added to this trip (see below).*

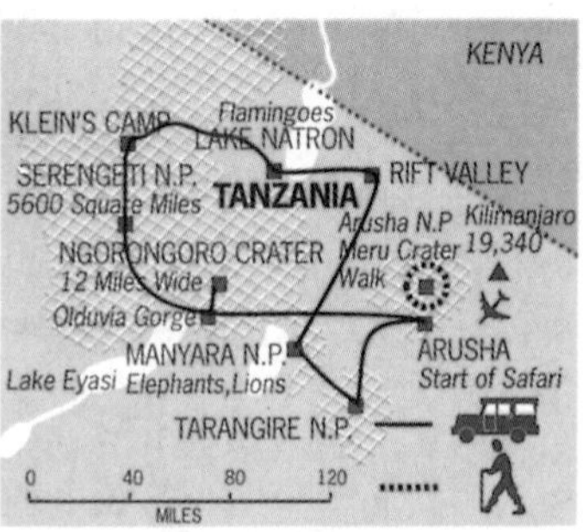

Tour Ref.TZ: Itinerary: Day 1 Fly London/Arusha. **2** Arrive Arusha (4600'). **3** Short drive to Arusha N.P., walk from Momella Gate (4950') to Miriakamba Hut (3hrs). **4** Explore Meru Crater rim (4-5hrs), overnight at Miriakamba Hut. **5** Walk back to Momella, drive to Tarangire N.P.; game drive. **6** Drive to Manyara N.P.; game drive. **7** Continue into Rift Valley. **8** Drive to Lake Natron. **9** At Lake Natron; birdwatching. **10** Drive to Klein's Camp. **11** To Serengeti. **12 & 13** In Serengeti, game drives. **14** To Ngorongoro Crater (7500') via Olduvai Gorge. **15** In Ngorongoro Crater, game viewing. **16** Drive to Arusha. **17** Fly London.

Ref.TZK: 'Kilimanjaro' extension Day 1 to 16 Same as above. **17** Bus to Moshi. **18** Trek to Mandara Hut (9000'). **19** Continue to Horombo Hut (12,300'). **20** Day to acclimatise at Horombo. **21** Trek to Kibo Hut (15,500'). **22** Pre-dawn summit ascent; return to Horombo Hut. **23** Final descent to Moshi. **24** Fly London.

Accommodation & Meals: Bed/breakfast at hotel (2nts); all meals at Miriakamba mountain hut in Arusha N.P. (2nts); elsewhere, camping and camp meals (11nts). *'Kilimanjaro ' extension—As above plus full board at hotel (2nts) and mountain huts (5nts).*

Mode of Travel: 4WD Unimog/3 day Foot Safari to Meru Crater.

Comment: Our high-sided, purpose-built *Unimog* is an ideal vehicle for rugged off-track travel and game viewing. The trip includes 2-person tents, camp equipment and game park fees. Bring a sleeping bag, mat and daysac. Walking boots or stout shoes are advised for the hike up to Meru Crater rim.

Group Size: Approx. 9 to 11 (min. 6).

Driver/Leader: Also a cook. Armed Park guide on Meru Crater Foot Safari.

Trip Dossier Ref.TZ: On request.

on such holidays unless they take place in locally-owned hotels.

In 1993 30 per cent of Kuoni's Caribbean holidays were all-inclusive deals.

An entirely different kind of all-inclusive product is offered within Europe by Thomson's HCI Club holidays. While long-haul all-inclusive holidays are mainly aimed at couples, the HCI Club is a product developed specifically for families. The Club makes it possible for parents to relax knowing that the grounds are safe; most even have a private beach. Unlike on other holidays, parents find most sports and entertainment are free; even wine and soft drinks with meals are included in the price.

The French company *Club Mediterranee* (Club Med) offers nothing but all-inclusive holidays at over 100 purpose-built beach villages around the world. There are Club Med villages in France, Spain, Israel, Turkey, Morocco, Tunisia, Ivory Coast, St Lucia, Guadeloupe, Martinique, the Bahamas, Turks and Caicos islands, Dominican Republic, Haiti, the USA, Mexico, Brazil, Mauritius, Thailand, Malaysia, Indonesia, Bora Bora, Moorea, New Caledonia and Australia. In addition it also offers all-inclusive ski holidays in 19 villages in the French Alps, the Pyrenees, Switzerland, Austria, Italy and Japan. This is what the Club Med brochure says about the villages:

> . . . your Club Med 'village' is more than just another holiday hotel. It is a self-sufficient community with all your holiday needs 'on-site', including: accommodation, restaurant(s), bar(s), a boutique, medical care, a bank, sports facilities, children's clubs and entertainment.

Fig. 4.25 The Overland Experience – an Explore safari

Courtesy: Explore

CARIBBEAN CONNECTION
THOMSON FARAWAY SHORES
COSMOS DISTANT DREAMS
AIRTOURS
HAYES AND JARVIS
SILK CUT TRAVEL
KUONI
BRITISH AIRWAYS HOLIDAYS
CARIBTOURS
HARLEQUIN HOLIDAYS
UNIJET
VIRGIN HOLIDAYS

Fig. 4.26 Some of the operators featuring all-inclusive holidays

However, while drinks are included in the price of some all-inclusive holidays, only wine with meals is included in Club Med prices. Clients must buy plastic 'bar beads' or 'carnets bar' booklets of tickets with which to get drinks at the bar.

Club Med puts a lot of emphasis on sports and excellent food. The average client is 38 years old, although there are clubs to cater for children as young as four months. French is the first language in many Club Med villages.

CRUISES

Cruises are a form of all-inclusive holiday, with the cost of food, accommodation, entertainment and port taxes rolled up in the overall price; only the cost of alcoholic drinks, shore excursions and tips usually has to be added on. In 1993, roughly 250,000 British holidaymakers opted to take a cruise, and this is a market which is continuing to grow. On a cruise holiday the client travels from port to port in a ship which is really a floating hotel and usually very luxurious. The cruise market concentrates on:

- the Mediterranean
- the Black Sea
- Scandinavia, the Baltic and the North Sea
- the Caribbean
- West Coast USA and the Pacific Coast
- south-east Asia and Australasia
- the Atlantic islands
- the Arctic and Alaska
- the Indian Ocean
- Antarctica

In addition, river cruises operate along the European rivers and waterways including the Danube and Elbe, along the Nile (200 boats), along North American rivers, along the Yangtse in China, along the Amazon and along some Asian and Australasian rivers.

Some cruises last for just a few days (around the Galapagos islands off Ecuador, for example), while round-the-world cruises may last for up to three months. Some can be joined in the UK (at Southampton, Tilbury, Liverpool or Bristol), but more often the passenger flies to the port and then joins the ship (the 'fly-cruise'). In general, cruises are perceived as expensive holidays. However, the prices can be brought down by choice of cabin; outside cabins with portholes will be more expensive than inside cabins without windows. The entry of Airtours into the market in 1995 also heralded a new era of cheaper products, with a lead-in price of £399 for a seven-night Western Mediterranean cruise.

Cruising is like a coach tour holiday in the sense that it enables clients to move around and see an assortment of different places. However, whereas all the packing and unpacking associated with coach touring can be tiring, on a cruise the hotel goes with the guests, making for a more restful experience. Most ships organise a programme of shore excursions, but these are never obligatory. As with conventional excursions, prices vary considerably. Intense competition has made the basic price of many Caribbean cruises look very attractive. However, the cost of each shore excursion can be between £50 and £70 compared with perhaps £20 to £30 in the Mediterranean.

Cruises mainly attract an older clientele, many of them over 55. However, this is a destination-led market; the Caribbean is seen as a slightly more youthful destination and is popular with first-time cruisers, while children are a rare sight on cruises round the Norwegian fjords. In the USA, the market is large enough for some segmentation to have taken place; Costa now has a programme of American Family Cruises, while Carnival has launched FiestaMarina Cruises aimed at the Latin

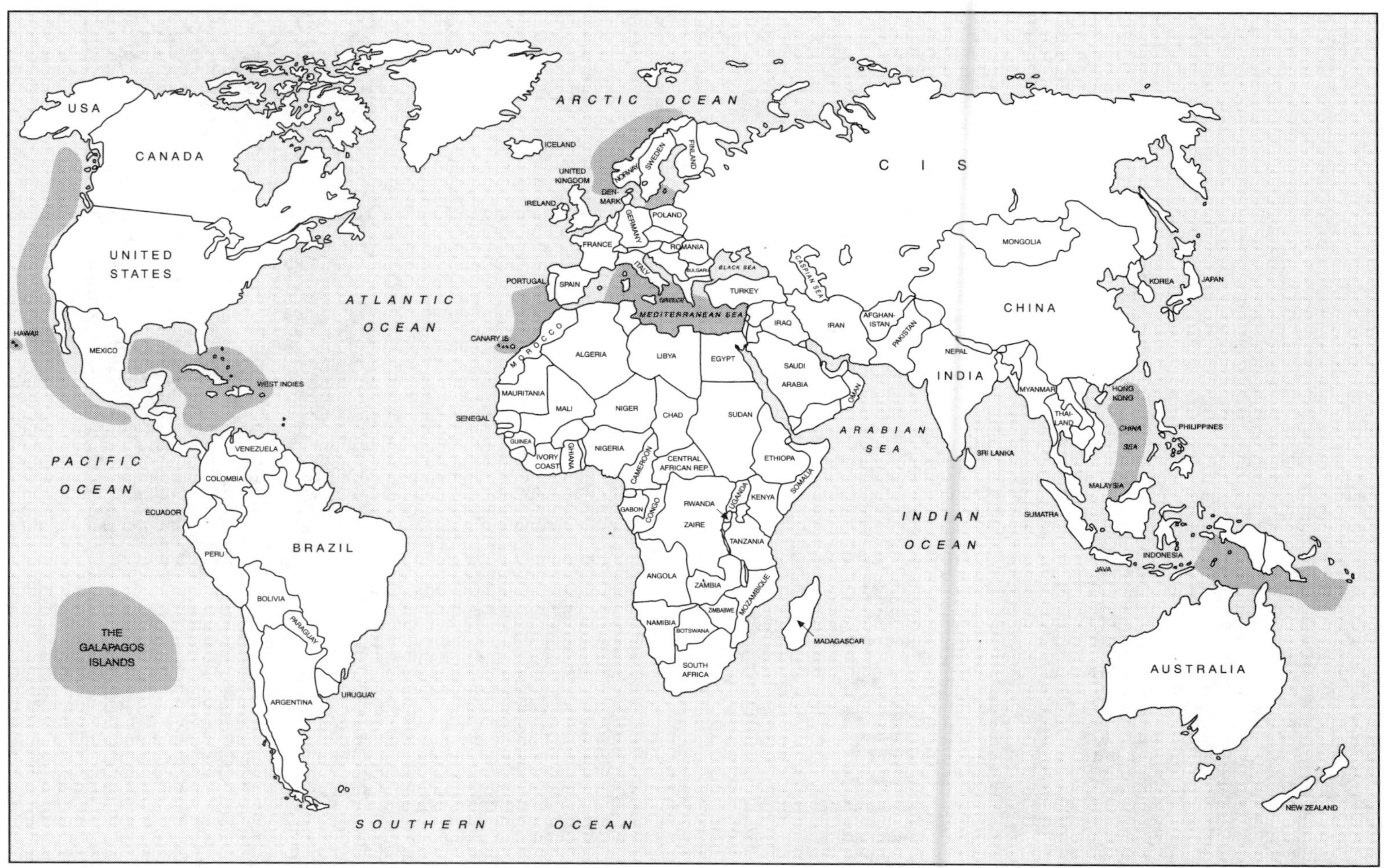

Fig. 4.27 Popular cruising areas of the world

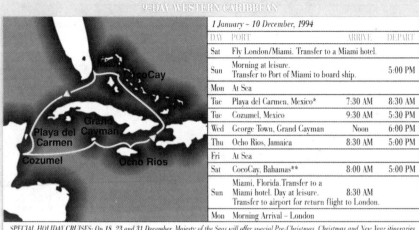

9-DAY WESTERN CARIBBEAN

Miami
CocoCay
Grand Cayman
Playa del Carmen
Cozumel
Ocho Rios

1 January – 10 December, 1994

DAY	PORT	ARRIVE	DEPART
Sat	Fly London/Miami. Transfer to a Miami hotel.		
Sun	Morning at leisure. Transfer to Port of Miami to board ship.		5:00 PM
Mon	At Sea		
Tue	Playa del Carmen, Mexico*	7:30 AM	8:30 AM
Tue	Cozumel, Mexico	9:30 AM	5:30 PM
Wed	George Town, Grand Cayman	Noon	6:00 PM
Thu	Ocho Rios, Jamaica	8:30 AM	5:00 PM
Fri	At Sea		
Sat	CocoCay, Bahamas**	8:00 AM	5:00 PM
Sun	Miami, Florida. Transfer to a Miami hotel. Day at leisure. Transfer to airport for return flight to London.	8:30 AM	
Mon	Morning Arrival – London		

SPECIAL HOLIDAY CRUISES: On 18, 23 and 31 December, Majesty of the Seas will offer special Pre-Christmas, Christmas and New Year itineraries. For full details, see your travel agent.

Fig. 4.28 Typical itinerary for a Western Caribbean fly-cruise
Courtesy: Western Caribbean Cruise Holidays

SELLING TIPS

HERE are some tips to help agents sell more cruises:

• 'Many clients still prefer not to fly – and an increasing number of cruises are leaving from and returning to UK ports. The range of ports is increasing, too, with Bristol, Harwich and Liverpool among the new and revived departure points.

• Clients who like to see as many places as possible, if only to impress friends/relatives/neighbours, should be advised that cruises score over coaches on comfort, things to do, food and, most of all, packing and repacking – not needed on a voyage!

• Hell may be other people, but cruise ships have now become so large and spacious that the shy and retiring need never worry about having to make friends unless they want to. Even meal-times can be private affairs, as most ships offer tables for two as well as more traditional larger tables.

• Clients worried about seasickness can be directed to most cruises with confidence. Only the 'adventure' or 'expedition' itineraries occasionally ignore the industry doctrine of warm, calm-weather destinations for ships – sometimes to the extent of moving them between continents from season to season.

All ships have stabilisers and, failing all that, there are several popular panaceas (or placebos) for mal de mer that can be prescribed.

• A PSARA sticker in the window does not guarantee you all the cruise business going, particularly in these days of discounting, but it certainly helps. Make sure there is always a PSARA staff member available and that other staff have at least an awareness of the cruise product's benefits.

• Finally, cruise prices only seem expensive. They are the most inclusive of all holiday prices as they cover transport, transfers, accommodation, meals throughout the day (and sometimes night, too) and most entertainment.

The only significant extras are drinks, tips, shore excursions and gambling debts and, on some of the more expensive ships, all but the latter are included in the brochure price. This means added value and more commission.

Zenith ... a Chandris cruiser in the Caribbean

Fig. 4.29 The benefits of cruising
Courtesy: *Travel Weekly*

Company	Destinations	Ship names
American Hawaii	Hawaii	
Carnival Corporation	Caribbean, Bahamas, Gulf of Mexico	*Sensation, Olympic, Fantasy, Ecstasy, Fascination*
Celebrity Cruises	Caribbean, Scandinavia, Bermuda	*Horizon, Meridian, Zenith, Amerikanis, Britanis*
Costa–OCL Cruise Lines	Mediterranean, Scandinavia, South America, Far East, world cruises	*Mermoz, Ocean Pearl, Costa Romantica, Enrico Costa, Daphne, Costa Allegra, Costa Classica*
Crystal Cruises	Panama Canal, Far East	*Crystal Harmony*
CTC Cruise Line	Africa, Caribbean, Norwegian Fjords, Arctic Circle, Baltic and Russia, Scandinavia, Canaries, Mediterranean, Israel, Egypt, Black Sea, Australia, New Zealand, Far East, Pacific, Canada, Antarctica, Amazon, Galapagos	*Kareliya, Azerbaydzhan, Gruziya, Belorussiya, Columbus Caravelle*
Cunard	Caribbean, Mediterranean, Baltic, Alaska, Panama Canal, New Zealand, world cruises	*Crown Jewel, Crown Dynasty, Crown Monarch, Cunard Princess, Cunard Countess, Sagafjord, Sea Goddess I & II, Vistafjord, QEII*
Diamond Cruises	Mediterranean	*Radisson Diamond*
Discovery Cruises	Mediterranean	*Odysseus*
Epirotiki	Mediterranean	*Neptune, Odysseus, Pallas Athena, Triton, Jason*
Festival Cruises	Mediterranean	*Azur*
Fred Olsen	Mediterranean, Nile, Rhine and Moselle, Scandinavia	*Black Prince*
Holland America Line/ Windstar	Caribbean, Mediterranean, Alaska, Far East, Pacific islands, world cruises	*Statendam, Maasdam, Ryndam, Rotterdam, Wind Spirit, Wind Song*
Kloster Cruise	Caribbean	
Norwegian Cruise Line	Caribbean	*Windward, Dreamward, Norway*
Ocean Cruise Lines	Far East	*Pearl*
Orient Lines	South-east Asia, China, Japan, New Zealand, South America	*Marco Polo*
P&O/Princess Cruises	Mediterranean, Norway, Russia, Atlantic Isles, USA, Canada, Alaska, Panama Canal, Caribbean, Baltic, Red Sea, Far East, Australia, world cruises	*Canberra, Oriana, Crown Princess, Golden Princess, Pacific Princess, Island Princess, Sea Princess, Royal Princess, Regal Princess, Sky Princess*
Regency Cruises	Caribbean, Mediterranean	*Regent Rainbow, Regent Spirit, Regent Jewel, Regent Sky, Regent Sea, Regent Sun, Regency Star*
Royal Cruise Line (RCL)	Mediterranean, Scandinavia, Alaska, Panama Canal, Mexico, West Coast USA, Canada, Far East, Australia, New Zealand	*Star Odyssey, Crown Odyssey, Royal Odyssey*
Royal Caribbean Cruise Line (RCCL)	Caribbean, Bahamas, Bermuda, Panama Canal, Mexico, Alaska, Mediterranean, Greece, Scandinavia, Russia, Canary Islands	*Nordic Prince, Nordic Empress, Majesty of the Seas, Sovereign of the Seas, Monarch of the Seas, Sun Viking, Song of Norway*
Royal Viking Line	Mediterranean, Baltic, Panama Canal, South America, world cruises	*Royal Viking Sun, Royal Viking Queen*
Seabourn	Mediterranean, Baltic, Panama Canal, Canada, South America	*Seabourn Pride, Seabourn Spirit*
Silversea Cruises	Caribbean, Mediterranean, Baltic, Scandinavia, Panama Canal, South America, East Africa, Seychelles	*Silver Cloud, Silver Wind*
Starline Cruises	Africa, Far East	*Royal Star*
Swan Hellenic	Mediterranean, Nile, Main	*Orpheus*

Fig. 4.30 The main cruise operators

American market. Some cruise companies, like Discovery Cruises, also operate educational cruises for schools. There are also some smaller cruise ships adapted for adventurous cruising (for example, into Antarctica) where conditions on board are more spartan. In launching its own cruise product on MS Seawing, Airtours emphasised the ship's suitability for family holidays. Among other features, it highlighted:

- a nightlife for the parents without leaving their 'hotel'
- babysitters within easy reach
- special children's meals
- all-inclusive prices
- children's clubs for two different age groups
- a minidisco and children's karaoke show

Cruise ships carry anything from 180 to 1,900 passengers, but increasingly it is possible to 'cruise' in smaller boats too. For example, flotilla holidays (off the Greek and Turkish coasts) involve clusters of small boats with a representative in overall charge of them, each individual boat carrying between 4 and 8 people. More experienced sailors can charter a crewless 'bareboat' which can accommodate between 4 and 12 people, while those who want to take it easy can charter a boat for 20 or more people, complete with a crew.

Because cruising is generally a luxurious experience, staff-passenger ratios can be particularly high; Fred Olsen's *Black Prince*, for example, carries 450 passengers but has a staff of about 200.

Traditionally travel agents have seen cruising as a difficult product to sell and most bookings have been made direct with the operator. Direct selling has also seemed natural in a market attracting a lot of repeat business: sometimes as much as 30 to 40 per cent on one sailing. However, since the mid-1980s, as part of an effort to expand the potential market for cruising, PSARA (the Passenger Shipping Association Retail Agents scheme) has tried to make it easier for agents to sell cruises by organising visits to inspect ships in port and running training sessions.

By 1994, cruise operators were becoming more interested in the ex-UK market, mainly because heavy discounting of cruises out of Miami was eroding the profitability essential if they are to cover the high fixed running costs of maintaining their ships. Much of a cruise ship's profit comes from selling 'extras' (drink, merchandise, excursions) and from the proceeds of gambling in their casinos. Discounting doesn't just eat into their profits but also tends to attract bookings from poorer passengers who are less likely to spend large sums on board the ship.

Weddings and honeymoons

Increasingly long-haul tour operators like Kuoni arrange packages which enable couples to get married abroad; in 1993 around 8,000 couples booked overseas wedding packages. Popular destinations include Barbados, Antigua, Jamaica, St Lucia, Grenada, Bahamas, Florida, Kenya, the Seychelles, Mauritius, Bali, Penang and Phuket. Where a company is offering wedding packages it needs to provide information about the legal requirements (for example, how many days you may need to have been resident in the country to be allowed to get married, what paperwork you need to take with you, etc.). The extra cost of a wedding package may cover:

- a wedding cake
- a bottle of sparkling wine
- flowers for the bride and groom
- the wedding ceremony
- the minister's fees, the marriage licence and certificate, the religious ceremony and transport to the wedding venue
- services of a 'best man', 'maid of honour' and witness
- video and photographer

Thomson's 'Weddings in Paradise' product is probably the market leader, but other companies in this market include Kuoni, Cosmos, Airtours, Caribtours, Airwaves, Unijet and Hayes and Jarvis.

Where a company offers specific honeymoon packages, they will usually be to destinations which can be reached on Sunday flights. Normally arrangements would be made for flowers and wine to be placed in the couple's hotel room as well.

'Singles' holidays

There are two distinctly different types of 'singles' holiday market. One (usually the more youthful) consists of single people who are not necessarily travelling alone but who probably count the opportunity to meet members of the opposite sex high

Legal requirements for your wedding in Kenya, the Indian Ocean and Far East	Kenya	Seychelles	Mauritius	Bali	Penang	Phuket
Minimum residency required prior to marriage (*working days)	5	3	3*	7	7*	3*
Passports: the first six pages of both parties	✓	✓	✓	✓		✓
Birth certificates of both parties	✓	✓	✓	✓	✓	✓
If divorced, Decree Absolute	✓	✓	✓	✓	✓	✓
If widowed, death certificate	✓	✓	✓		✓	✓
If name changed by deed poll, legal proof	✓	✓	✓			
Minimum age 18	✓	✓	✓			
Details of full names, addresses, professions and religions of both parties	✓	✓	✓			
Details of full names and addresses of parents of both parties	✓					
Details of professions of fathers of both parties	✓					
Letters signed by UK Minister of the Church stating neither party has been married before	✓					
Copy of baptism and confirmation papers				✓		✓
Affidavit to prove status: ie. single/bachelor/spinster					✓	✓
Permission from Catholic Priest (if applicable) and proof from the Priest of couple's single status					✓	✓

Fig. 4.31 Legal requirements for weddings in Kenya, the Indian Ocean and the Far East

Courtesy: Kuoni

among their reasons for going on holiday. The other consists of genuinely solo travellers: those who live alone because they are unmarried, widowed or divorced.

The first of the two markets is the easier to cater for since it doesn't necessarily involve the problem of finding single hotel rooms. In the early days of package holidaymaking, young people's needs were assumed to be the same as those of their elders. However, shrewd operators soon realised the potential for designing holidays specifically for the young, sending them to hotels where they wouldn't need to mix with families and older people and picking resort reps who were expert at creating a party atmosphere. In 1961 when Horizon had signed a contract with British United Airways that left it with difficult-to-shift midweek night flights, the idea for the first Club 18-30 holidays to take up the slack chimed very well with the growing affluence of young people and the developing 'youth' cult. Club 18-30 remained part of Horizon until it was bought out by David Heard, whose original concept it had been, in 1972. Heard ran it independently until 1978, when he sold it to former rival company, Buddies. Ultimately Club 18-30 became part of the ILG stable and acquired a reputation for attracting a rowdy, drunken clientele. Thomson's 'Freestyle' programme, launched in 1984, aimed at a similar market as did several other products. Following the demise of ILG in 1991, Club 18-30 was resurrected as The Club which is so far doing well. In 1993 Thomson relaunched Club Freestyle, only to pull out again, claiming the youth market was a difficult one because it represented a transitory lifestyle and didn't result in repeat custom. Thomson also contested how many people really wanted such special treatment. Nevertheless, in 1995 Airtours launched a new *Escapades* brochure aimed at the 18 to 30 market. Twenties, founded in 1977, and The Club are now the market leaders.

The youth 'singles' market has very distinctive traits:

- it is highly cost sensitive
- it is particularly concerned with 'image' and 'in' places
- it is more interested in partying than cultural sightseeing
- it is especially responsive to word of mouth recommendations

As a result, it is concentrated on relatively few resorts, particularly those with good discos and nightlife. For many years, Ibiza has been the most favoured destination, but also popular are Corfu, Rhodes, Crete, Mykonos, Zante, Kos, Benidorm, Majorca, the Canary Islands and Bodrum in Turkey.

From the tour operator's point of view, it is

particularly important that they employ the right representatives to work in the resorts. Even more than usual, they will need to be people able to work long hours and good at helping to create the right atmosphere. It is also vital to be able to attract enough bookings to all the hotels for partying to be possible.

Since the late 1970s, the 18–30 age group has been declining. Faced with a static or falling market, operators have attempted to diversify. For example, The Club has tried to launch long-haul products but with only limited success, perhaps because the sort of client who is happy to buy a two week £400 package to Corfu isn't necessarily able to take a three week holiday to Australia costing considerably more. Companies like Contiki and Top Deck, which offer adventure holidays with a partying atmosphere to younger people, have found it easier to tap into a wider market represented by overseas visitors to the UK (mainly from Australia, New Zealand and the USA) who want to tour mainland Europe as a short part of a longer visit to Britain.

The true 'solos' present operators with particular problems, primarily in finding single rooms to accommodate them. In 1993 it was estimated that 98 per cent of holidaymakers wanted twin or double rooms, and many Mediterranean hotels were built without any single rooms at all. The traditional solution has been to slap single occupancy supplements on rooms let to one person; often these supplements can turn relatively cheap holidays into expensive ones, so, not surprisingly, they are very unpopular. However, the number of adults living without partners is rising; the 1991 census suggested that 26 per cent of English and Welsh households contained only one adult, and the Henley Centre for Forecasting believes the number will have risen by 20 per cent by the year 2000. In such circumstances, some operators are showing greater interest in catering for single travellers. For example, Sovereign's 'Small World' product is aimed at solo travellers, sometimes putting together small house parties in *gîtes* or *châteaux*.

Although this is generally thought of as uneconomically time-consuming, some companies will try and match up solo travellers so they can share rooms and avoid supplements. Coach tour companies in particular, with their older client profile, will often do this; on Cosmos 'Tourama' programmes not only can room-shares be arranged but the coach seat planning is rotated so people get the chance to get to know each other. An increasing number of (particularly long-haul) brochures feature 'no single supplement' offers on certain dates, usually away from the high season.

Single parents also tend to be viewed as 'problems' by operators who usually cost their discounts on the basis of two full-fare-paying adults sharing a room with a child. However, with the rise in the number of single parents, some are now agreeing to give discounts to single parents sharing with their children. Sometimes these offers are restricted to specified dates.

Senior citizen holidays

As people are living and staying healthier longer, some operators are also interested in offering products aimed at 'senior citizens', variously thought of as over-55s, over-60s or even over-65s. The biggest company in this market is direct sell Saga Holidays, but all the big operators now have products designed for the older client.

A particular feature of such brochures is the long-stay holiday, lasting up to three months and enabling people to stay away all winter, saving on their UK heating bills while paying from as little as £2.95 a day for a holiday in somewhere like the Costa del Sol. But most operators feature a mix of sun and sand resorts and touring holidays with plenty of chance to walk and sightsee.

In the early 1990s, this market was adversely affected by the fall in interest rates which cut into income generated by invested savings.

Company name	Product name
Thomson	Young at Heart
Airtours	Golden Years
Enterprise	Leisurely Days
Cosmos	Golden Times
Sunworld	Golden Circle

Fig. 4.32 Programmes designed for senior citizens

Sports holidays

Although there are some specialist sports holiday tour operators, many mainstream operators also offer some specific sports holidays, particularly golf and/or diving trips.

1. Golf

About 50,000 British golfers buy packaged golf holidays every year. Particularly popular destination countries are France, Ireland, Portugal (the Algarve), Spain (Costa del Sol) and the USA (Florida and South Carolina), with Thailand, Madeira, Kenya, Tunisia and South Africa also gaining favour. However, the golfing market fared badly in 1992 and Kuoni's attempt to break into the market with holidays to the Caribbean and the Far East ended in failure.

LONGSHOT GOLF
BRITISH AIRWAYS HOLIDAYS
SOVEREIGN
PANORAMA
TAP AIR PORTUGAL
CRESTA
CADOGAN

Fig. 4.33 Tour operators offering golf holiday programmes

2. Diving

Particularly popular destinations for diving holidays include the Red Sea/Sharm el Sheikh (Egypt), Kenya, the Comores, Mauritius, the Maldives, Thailand, Malaysia, Australia/the Great Barrier Reef, Cozumel (Mexico) and the Cayman Islands. Where a tour operator features diving holidays, it will usually negotiate a special insurance policy that does not exclude diving from its cover.

3. Trekking and mountaineering

Many overland tour companies offer trekking holidays within their broader programmes. Indeed on some of the longer trips, trekking may be an optional part of a journey which is not primarily about walking at all; for example, when African overlanders are taken to see the gorillas of Uganda or Zaire, or Asian overlanders take part in a trek in Nepal or amongst the hill tribes of Thailand. In the same way, such packages may include optional mountain-climbing; perhaps of Mounts Kenya or Kilimanjaro in Africa, or Mount Kinabalu in Eastern Malaysia. Because some overland holidays do involve such strenuous activities they sometimes specify how fit participants need to be. Holidays which are likely to be more arduous are sometimes described as 'expeditions' to make that fact clear; so Journey Latin America features a series of 'environmental expeditions' in its brochure.

Other companies specialise in the sort of treks that cross over into mountaineering, and in real mountain expeditions. Among them are the appropriately named Himalayan Kingdoms, and High Places which also organises cycling safaris in Kenya, and bike, hike and boat rides through Southern India.

Stopover packages

As the market for long-haul flights to Australia and New Zealand expanded in the late 1980s, an increasing number of people were able to buy fares that let them break the long journey somewhere *en route* at little if any extra cost. Originally possible stopovers were restricted to the eastbound routes. However, by the early 1990s it was also possible to break journeys heading westwards too. Operators, sometimes linked to the airlines, were not slow to develop packaged stopover arrangements to fit clients' needs. In 1993 a survey carried out by the Australian Tourist Commission showed the following preferences for stopover destinations:

Country	*Percentage of visitors choosing it*
Singapore	53
Hong Kong	36
New Zealand	23
Thailand	22
USA	20
Hawaii	17
Fiji	15
Malaysia	11
Caribbean	7
No stopover	4

Stopover packages are usually short, perhaps lasting three or four nights, and usually include transfers to and from the airport, hotel accommodation and perhaps a sightseeing trip. Some countries in the world have little package holiday traffic other than people on stopovers; Dubai, with its excellent duty-free shopping and ideal position *en route* to India and the Far East, is one such country which is only slowly breaking into brochures as a stay-put destination.

'Tailor-made' packages

In a sense the 'tailor-made', or bespoke, package is a contradiction in terms, since the original concept of a package holiday grew out of the idea of selling items in bulk rather than to suit individuals. However, as the public has grown more used to travelling and generally more sophisticated in its outlook, it has become clear that a sizeable number of holidaymakers don't want the 'herding' that they associate with packages. On the other hand they still want the cheaper prices that operators can obtain by buying in bulk and are also grateful to have someone experienced to organise their holiday. As a result many operators, including Kuoni and Cox & Kings, now have 'tailor-made' departments where they can put together 'packages' to suit individual clients' requirements. These are particularly helpful when the client wants a complex multi-centre holiday as is often the case with travellers to the USA or the Far East.

In pre-computerisation days, creating tailor-made packages was uneconomically time-consuming for most operators. However, nowadays they are particularly helped by transparent links (*see* page 147) with airline reservation systems like Galileo which enable them to see at a glance what is available. Because this is so quick it helps to keep costs down so that tailor-made packages don't become prohibitively expensive.

The degree to which tailor-made holidays had taken off was exemplified in 1993 when Intourist, the state-owned Soviet tour company set up in 1938 and once a byword for herding people around in groups, launched a package of tailor-made holidays to Russia and beyond, called 'Independent Traveller'.

QUESTIONS AND DISCUSSION POINTS

1 The 'death of the package holiday' is frequently predicted. How are tour operators reacting to this? What evidence is there in existing products that they will succeed in outliving the move towards independent travel?

2 Why do you think Morocco and Tunisia are treated as short-haul products while Egypt is generally regarded as long-haul? What difference would it make if Tunisia and Morocco were treated as long-haul, or if Egypt was treated as short-haul?

3 Which product areas have most long-term potential and why? Which product areas are having problems? Do you think these problems can be overcome?

4 Can you think of any product areas/types that operators are not already providing but which might find a market?

5 Look at Kuoni's top ten selling destinations for 1992/3 and their forecasts for 1994 (page 79). Discuss why you think these are most popular and why their relative ranking had either already changed between 1992 and 1993, or was forecast to change in 1994.

ASSIGNMENTS

1 You are product development manager for a 'second-tier' operator with a small programme of winter sun holidays. At the moment they are all to Mediterranean destinations with the exception of Gambia which you have featured successfully for three years. Currently, none of your holidays could be said to be at all 'specialist'. You wish to offer one new long-haul programme next winter and are looking round at your competitors' products for ideas.

Collect some winter sun brochures to examine. They can be those of the bigger operators, which should have a wide range of options, or of other second-tier operators who may, like yourself, be offering just one non-Mediterranean destination but not necessarily Gambia.

Analyse what is being offered and then write a report weighing up the pros and cons of **three** possible new destinations (conceivably you may want to suggest a destination that no one else seems to be featuring at the moment although take care that there are not good reasons for this). Make sure you include information about how easy they are to get to, what temperatures they have in winter, what people could do in these resorts, how safe they are and so on. Finally, decide which one you would recommend and explain the reasons for your decision.

2 Each member of the class should choose **one** different product area. They should then prepare a presentation to be made to the rest of the class outlining the features of the product, and its strengths and weaknesses in terms of sales.

3 Working in pairs, students should design and carry out a survey to find out which holiday products are selling best. To be representative they *must* interview people other than college students. Only those who have taken a holiday involving at least one night away should be included in the survey. The number of people to be interviewed by each pair should be agreed with their lecturer in advance.

When all surveys have been carried out, the class as a whole should analyse the overall results and decide how best to present them to the college.

CHAPTER 5

Preparing the brochure

LEARNING OBJECTIVES

After reading this chapter you should be able to:
- **understand the importance of the brochure as a selling tool for tour operators**
- **explain the stages in production of the brochure**
- **list the different components of a brochure**
- **understand the trend towards smaller, specialist brochures instead of one all-inclusive edition**

INTRODUCTION

According to ABTA, brochures are 'publications which specify the contents of a tour, holiday or travel arrangement offered by a tour operator'. The unusual intangible nature of the tour operator's product means that the brochure is of crucial importance to the selling process. The brochure has to be able to:

a) invite people to buy the holidays it advertises
b) provide the information necessary to persuade the client to purchase a holiday
c) create and reinforce the company's image with its clients

It must, therefore, contain detailed information on all the hotels and resorts on offer, together with information about flights, how to book, what insurance is available, what special offers are being made and so on. In presenting all this information the brochure must abide by the requirements of all existing legislation, including the Trades Description Act and the EC Package Travel Regulations.

Because of the brochure's crucial role in selling holidays ABTA has drawn up standards for brochure production which form a part of the Tour Operators' Code of Conduct.

Brochure size

Most brochures are designed to an A4 format because this:

a) fits most agency brochure racks
b) fits standard envelopes and matches standard letter size

Until 1992 city-break specialist Time Off used a smaller leaflet-sized brochure which could be stacked in brochure carousels or counter holders but which didn't fit the standard A4 rack space. Although this made it stand out as different, in 1992 it switched to the more familiar A4 format, believing it would lose shelf space and therefore sales if it didn't do so.

Paper quality

Most brochures are printed on glossy coloured paper. The bigger the brochure, the flimsier the paper it is printed on tends to be, both to keep down production costs and to stop it becoming unmanageably heavy. Long-haul brochures (and slimmer short-haul ones) are usually printed on thick, high-gloss paper. Pull-out price pages are more normally printed on cheap, two-colour paper. Some companies will also have slightly thicker, glossier front covers to protect the brochures in transit and on the shelves, and to create a better image.

Paper colour

Although the large tour operators produce brochures in full colour, it is cheaper to choose

LOCH LOMOND & THE TROSSACHS

5 DAYS from £119

See some of the best Scotland has to offer on this value for money tour. We have some lovely inclusive excursions in our programme and an optional excursion to Edinburgh as well all guided by our fully experienced tour drivers.

Our choice of hotels include the Cobbler Hotel in pretty Arrochar and the Arrochar Hotel itself overlooking Loch Long. Both hotels are set amongst spectacular scenery and have rooms with private facilities, tea/coffee making facilities and both have comfortable lounges, television rooms and a bar providing a warm Scottish welcome. You can be sure of a warm Scottish welcome whichever you choose.

Our planned excursions

- A tour of the famous Glenturret distillery and the highland towns of Crieff, Killin and the Dochart Falls.
- A spectacular scenic tour of Glen Lochy, Oban, Inverary on Loch Fyne with a short stop at the 'Rest and be Thankful'.
- Our optional (extra) day tour to the Scottish capital Edinburgh will ensure that you have a really memorable day out.

ZIP 214A	ZIP 214B
ARROCHAR HOTEL	COBBLER HOTEL
4 & 25 OCTOBER 8 NOVEMBER £129	22 FEBRUARY £119 8 & 22 MARCH 19 & 26 APRIL £129
No single room supplement	Single room supplement £11

Fig. 5.1 Bakers Dolphin – keeping it simple
Courtesy: Bakers Dolphin

fewer colours. Many smaller companies therefore opt for two or four colour reproduction. Regent Holidays, for example, produces most of its brochures in two colours (with different colours to distinguish different destinations at a glance). Bristol-based Bakers Dolphin has a programme of 'Ziptrips', mini-breaks in the UK and to the Continent, which are publicised in a four-colour brochure, with a full-colour front cover.

Even where a company produces a full-colour brochure, it may opt for two- or four-colour pages for details of prices, conditions of carriage and other details, particularly where these are produced on a pull-out centrefold for easy alteration. Companies may also produce two- or four-colour preview brochures to pull in a few advance bookings while the main brochure is still being produced. For example, by August 1993 Royal Cruise Line had an eight page, black and white 'Preview Cruise Collection' brochure outlining its 1994 cruise programme and offering a five per cent discount to early bookers; this would have been perfectly adequate for repeat customers who would already be familiar with the ship layouts, etc.

Sometimes operators use different coloured pages to help distinguish between different destinations within one brochure. The page colours can then be keyed with the destinations listed on the contents page at the front.

What the brochure must contain

ABTA standards for tour operators specify that every brochure should contain 'clear, legible, comprehensive and accurate information to enable the client to exercise an informed judgement in making his choice'. As far as ABTA is concerned, the minimum information contained must include:

1 **Governmental/statutory licensing authority:** all information necessary to comply with the regulations for the time being of the Civil

Aviation Authority and any other governmental or statutory licensing authority.

2 **Legal identity:** the legal identity of the tour operator responsible for publishing the brochure containing the tour, holiday or travel arrangement offered, including its ABTA and ATOL number where applicable.
3 **Means of travel:** The means of travel (e.g. ship, train, coach, motor vehicle, charter or scheduled airline).
4 **Destination and/or itinerary:** The destination and/or itinerary as appropriate.
5 **Date, place and time of departure and return:** The date, place and approximate time of departure and return. Where any or all of these items are subject to alteration by a regulatory body (e.g. Airport Scheduling Committee) reference must be made to same.
6 **Nature of accommodation and the meal facilities:** The nature of accommodation and the meal facilities included in the price.
7 **Additional facilities:** Any additional facilities or special arrangements included in the price.
8 **Booking conditions:** (*see* below).
9 **Insurance details:** If a tour operator offers holiday insurance, an accurate and sufficiently detailed summary of the cover provided and the premiums associated therewith must be shown in the brochure. Furthermore it is necessary for the tour operator to indicate close to the basic price the location of such summary and premiums in the brochure.
10 **Price policy:** (*see* below).
11 **Health matters:** The brochure must contain adequate information pertaining to health requirements of countries featured or a reference to the Dept of Health leaflet *Protect your Health Abroad*, available from any ABTA travel agent or the Department of Health. Clients should also be advised to check with their own doctor before their departure as to which inoculations are available and necessary for specific areas.
12 **Arbitration:** (*see* Chapter Ten).
13 **Noise:** Brochures which feature resort-based holidays must contain adequate information relating to all known sources of noise which exist or might be expected to exist at resorts and which may reasonably be considered to cause offence to clients. Such sources of noise include, but are not limited to, night clubs, bars, discos, amusement parks and airports.
14 **Building works:** Where it is known, or can reasonably be expected, that building works which are likely to adversely affect the enjoyment of a holiday will take place during the period covered by the brochure, all specific information must be published on the relevant page in the brochure.
15 **Publication date:** The month and year of publication must be printed in the brochure.
16 **Delays at point of departure:** Brochures must state clearly and unambiguously the tour operator's policy on the handling of clients who are delayed at the outward and/or homeward points of departure. Tour operators are encouraged, but not obliged, to provide refreshments/meals appropriate to the time of day and overnight accommodation dependent upon the length of delay and nature of holiday. Furthermore, the brochure must state what action will be taken in the event that circumstances prevent the policy referred to above being carried out.

In 1993 the EC Package Travel Regulations turned many of these ABTA guidelines into legally-enforcable requirements (*see* Chapter Ten).

THE FRONT COVER

The **front cover** is particularly important since it is what the client will see first of all. The cover must therefore be designed to be eye-catching but must simultaneously convey certain crucial messages. First and foremost it must show the company name, normally at the top of the page, together with any company logo. Then it must show the period of validity of the brochure; for summer sun products this will normally be April to October, for winter sun from November to March and for worldwide products from January to December. Nowadays brochures are often reissued with price adjustments which means the front cover may also need to state whether it is a first, second or third edition.

In addition to these three essential features, the front cover may also highlight a 'lead-in price' (i.e. the cheapest price in the brochure), any no surcharge guarantee (*see* page 178) or any other outstanding features: for example, departures from regional airports, discounted child places and so on. Some brochures will also list the resorts covered so clients can see at a glance whether the one they are interested in is featured.

The front cover must also be designed to convey other important messages about the company. The choice of picture can, for example, make it plain what sort of product is on offer: pictures of sand and sea for summer sun products, of palm-fringed beaches for Caribbean products, of famous tourist attractions for city breaks, etc. It can also indicate the type of person the product has been designed for: a brochure for The Club will therefore have pictures of young people enjoying themselves emblazoned on the cover (*see* Fig. 5.2), while a Thomson summer sun brochure will show families on a beach. The more expensive and exotic the product on offer, the less likely it is to show clients on the cover at all, preferring to concentrate on what they will see at their chosen destination.

The front cover may also give a clue to the sort of price bracket the brochure is aimed at. Before its demise in 1991, Intasun was essentially a downmarket, budget end of the market company; its front covers habitually featured a sketched female holidaymaker in a bikini rather than a classier photograph. In the early days, Airtours, too, had a rather downmarket image reflected in its choice of front covers. However, by 1993 the company was moving upmarket and its covers reflected this, becoming increasingly stylish and eradicating human beings altogether from some products. For example, Airtours Greece featured a beautifully bronzed and tastefully photographed female sitting on the sand, while Airtours Ski showed the swirl left in the snow by a passing skier. Even the quality of paper used can indicate something about the holidays inside: so upmarket, long-haul companies may use much glossier paper than those anticipating a more budget-conscious clientele.

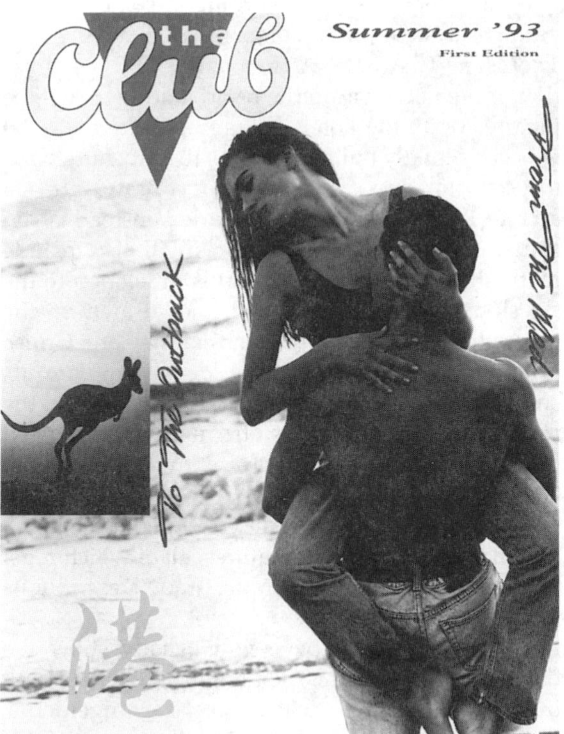

Fig. 5.2 Front cover of a brochure for The Club
Courtesy: Stewart Williams

Unfortunately, after the operator has put all this effort into designing an eye-catching front cover which will convey a particular message, the effect can be completely spoilt by travel agents slapping stickers haphazardly onto it. In the early 1980s these stickers were reasonably discreet, mainly giving information about the agent's address and telephone number to encourage readers to book with them. However, by the 1990s they were often enormous, including information about all sorts of discounts and special offers. It was suggested that operators could resolve this problem by building a space for stickers into the design brief.

The opening pages of the brochure

The first few pages are vitally important since they will contain general information relating to all the holidays described later on. There will usually be an introductory page or paragraph highlighting the most saleable features of the products on offer, followed by a contents page which will list the resorts covered by geographical area and page number.

The first few pages of the brochure will also contain a statement about the company's policy on prices, explaining whether it offers an absolute no surcharge guarantee or reserves the right to pass on some price rises and, if so, in what circumstances. The following are two examples of statements on prices taken from 1993 brochures:

The price of your holiday is fully guaranteed and

will not be subject to any surcharges. Once you have made your booking and paid your deposit, then the cost of your holiday cannot be increased.

The price and all other details of your holiday will be confirmed to you or to your travel agent by us at the time of booking. Once your holiday has been confirmed by us with confirmation and final invoice your holiday price is guaranteed at that figure and whatever happens to the cost of aircraft fuel, airport taxes or exchange rates, there will be **absolutely no surcharges**.

The front pages will also contain information on miscellaneous topics, which may include:

- how to interpret symbols used in the brochure
- child discounts and free places
- group bookings
- other discounts, e.g. spring and autumn savers, dates when single supplements don't apply, dates when three weeks for the price of two are offered, etc.
- information about particular hotels, e.g. the Spanish Sol chain
- details about long-stay holidays
- information about the airline used

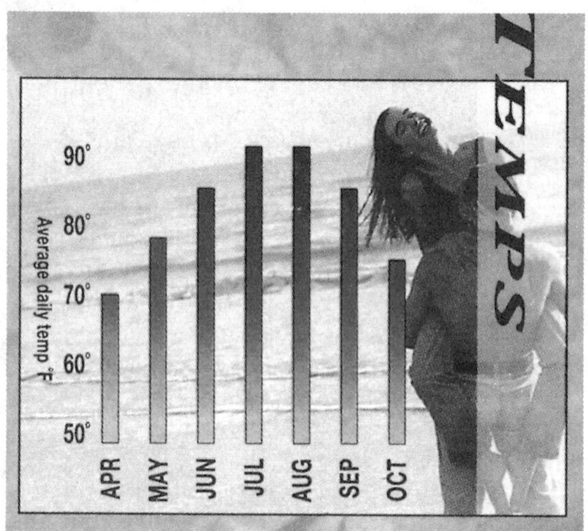

Fig. 5.3 How The Club represents temperature in a resort

Courtesy: Stewart Williams

The body of the brochure

The bulk of the brochure will consist of pages detailing the holidays on offer, arranged in some sort of geographical order. Each new region will usually be preceded with a page or so of general description of the country, together with, perhaps, a map. In the case of a country like Spain which has innumerable resorts, each resort area will be treated like a separate country, with a first page describing the resort area, again with a map. This introductory page will also include details about weather at the resort (often comparing it with temperatures at home), usually presented in terms of average temperatures (*see* Fig. 5.3). There may also be information about optional excursions out of the resort. The way in which this information is presented varies little from company to company, although The Club has tried to liven up the information charts with background imagery.

A typical page in the main part of the brochure will feature one or more hotels. The name of the hotel(s) will be shown together with its/their grading which may be according to some external grading system or a company system, e.g. the Thomson 'T' system. A map may show the situation of the hotel within the resort, and there will be pictures of all the hotels featured. Where the hotel was not actually built at the time the brochure went to print, an artist's impression or a drawing of an architect's model may be included instead of an actual photograph. Ski brochures will also include maps showing where the resort is in relation to the ski slopes, with colour-coded lines drawn on the slopes to indicate how demanding they are. Cruise brochures will also include deck-plan layouts showing where different cabins are in relation to the rest of the ship. Operators offering tours will need to include the outline itinerary, with perhaps a map showing the route as well.

There will be a written description of each hotel, together with a list of its features, all of which must be accurate to comply with the Trade Descriptions Act.

A panel on each page will usually show the dates of departure for each holiday, together with information about costs, meal arrangements, flights, etc. Sometimes, however, all or some of this information may appear at the back of the brochure or in a pull-out section in the centre. A pull-out

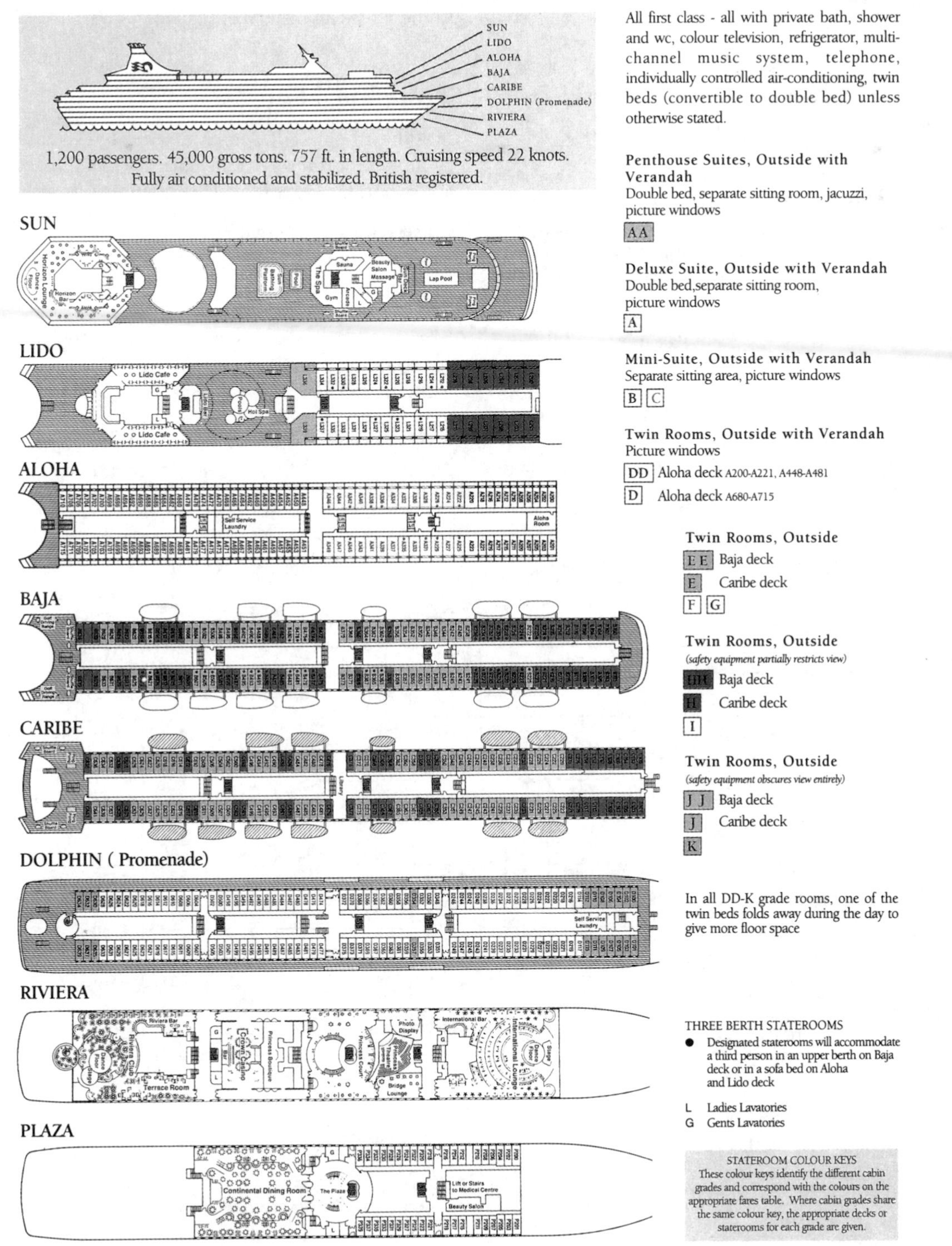

Fig. 5.4 Layout of the P&O Royal Princess cruise ship

Courtesy: P&O Cruises

section makes it easy to revise price and flight details without having to reprint the entire brochure.

Page design

In most brochures the actual page design is not particularly striking. Sometimes an effort is made to give them a linking theme, with borders designed to look like baggage tags, for example, or the background gently marbled. However, it is mainly the companies aimed at the style-conscious young who make the most effort to make their designs interesting. Most stylish of all is The Club brochure which used striking monotone photographs and the linking theme of camera film to make its 1994 brochure stand out. On each page, the usual pictures of hotels and people enjoying themselves, the text and price charts were superimposed on two-tone 'ghost' background images.

A surprisingly small number of companies have created an 'image' that they can reproduce throughout their brochure. So The Imaginative Traveller (the reincarnation of Transglobal) uses cartoon camels not just for grading its holidays but to liven up the pages as well (*see* Fig. 5.6).

The back of the brochure

Like the front of the brochure, the back will also contain important general information relating to all the holidays featured. This may include:

a) a step by step guide to making a booking
b) information about what's included in the prices and what's excluded
c) data about the types of aircraft used
d) information about when the exchange rate used for pricing holidays was fixed
e) details of the insurance policy offered and of its premiums
g) a 'Fair Trading Agreement' statement, setting out clients' rights and those of the tour operator. Since these are effectively the details of the

APARTMENTS	CLUBE PRAIA DA ROCHA Self Catering				APT. CHILD PRICES	CLUBE PRAIA DA ROCHA Half Board				
HOLIDAY CODE	DDPTA					DDPSA				
PRICES BASED ON	4 ADULTS IN A 1 BEDROOM APARTMENT					PB WC BALCONY				
NO. OF NIGHTS	7 Adult	10 Adult	11 Adult	14 Adult	7/10/11/14 1st Child	7 Adult	10 Adult	11 Adult	14 Adult	7/10/11/14 1st Child
Basic prices in £ per person at the time of going to press for departures on or between										
8 APR – 16 APR	—	—	—	—	—	324	—	—	364	198
17 APR – 30 APR	—	—	—	—		259	—	—	339	98
1 MAY – 9 MAY	209	224	227	229	59	304	379	389	419	59
10 MAY – 17 MAY	219	234	237	239		314	389	398	429	
18 MAY – 24 MAY	229	247	249	254	98	324	419	419	459	129
25 MAY – 29 MAY	289	289	294	298		379	439	449	469	
30 MAY – 8 JUN	239	279	284	289		334	389	409	449	
9 JUN – 22 JUN	249	289	304	309		344	414	429	479	
23 JUN – 6 JUL	289	334	337	339		389	484	494	559	
7 JUL – 13 JUL	314	365	369	375	139	409	519	539	594	159
14 JUL – 20 JUL	324	385	389	395		429	529	549	598	
21 JUL – 7 AUG	339	434	437	439	179	459	539	559	619	198
8 AUG – 14 AUG	339	434	437	. 429		459	529	554	614	
15 AUG – 22 AUG	339	424	427	419		449	514	539	594	
23 AUG – 31 AUG	339	389	389	398	129	429	479	498	534	159
1 SEP – 13 SEP	289	334	337	339		364	419	434	469	
14 SEP – 25 SEP	269	294	297	298	89	349	398	398	449	98
26 SEP – 31 OCT*	229	243	245	249		304	379	394	429	
SUPPLEMENTS PER PERSON PER NIGHT	May/Oct For 3 £1.49, 2 £3.98	Jun/Sep £2.79, £6.98	Jul/Aug £4.59, £11.98		—	—				

*For 7,10 or 11 night departures on or between 17 Oct - 22 Oct add £40.
For flight details, codes and supplements see pages 394-403. See page 411 for Insurance. Please read the Cosmos Consumer Protection Plan on pages 404 and 405.

Fig. 5.5 Typical price and departure date panel

Courtesy: Cosmos

Fig. 5.6 The Imaginative Traveller's camel takes a photograph

Courtesy: The Imaginative Traveller

contract between the tour operator and the client, this page is vitally important and has become even more so since the EC Package Travel Regulations obliged operators to provide details of the contract to all clients. Increasingly the booking conditions and holiday information are spread out over two pages. Both Nielson and Sunworld have tried to make the details clearer by dividing them up to answer questions clients might have, like 'Do I need holiday insurance?' and 'Is my money safe?'

h) a booking form
i) details of car hire schemes
j) information about visa and health requirements. This will be particularly important in worldwide brochures.

The ABTA Tour Operators' Code of Conduct lays down details of what information about making a booking should be included in the brochure and says that this information should not be printed on the front or back of the booking form unless they are also provided separately to the person who will be signing the booking form. In other words, the client must be able to keep a copy of the contract. The code stipulates that information must be given about:

(i) payment of the deposit and the balance due date
(ii) confirmation of the booking
(iii) the price policy
(iv) what happens when alterations to confirmed bookings are made by the client
(v) what happens when alterations to confirmed bookings are made by the tour operator
(vi) what happens when the client cancels a confirmed booking
(vii) what happens when the tour operator cancels a confirmed booking
(viii) the procedures for handling complaints
(ix) the tour operator's liability towards the client
(x) the existence of conditions of carriage by the carrier

Once again, the EC Package Travel Regulations effectively turned ABTA's guidelines into law in 1993.

THE BOOKING FORM

Although some companies like Airtours have dispensed with traditional booking forms, most still include them at the back of the brochure. To make brochures reusable and eliminate waste some smaller operators use loose-leaf booking forms. Booking forms must bear the company's address, telephone number and ABTA and ATOL numbers.

The booking form will usually have space for all the following:

- The names and titles of the occupants of up to three rooms, with space for the age and date of birth of anyone under 18 or over 60 on the date of departure.
- A booking reference and the date the option or confirmed booking was made.
- Indication of the meal arrangements booked.
- Details of any special requests (usually with a note that these cannot be guaranteed).
- Details of any car hire arrangements – driver's name, the pick-up point, the group of car, the length and dates of rental.
- Information about insurance. Often there is an opt-out clause whereby all clients will be assumed to want the operator's insurance unless they indicate otherwise and provide details of alternative cover they have already taken out.
- Indication of the amount of deposit, balance and/or insurance premiums enclosed.
- The client's signature (or that of the parent or guardian if under 18) indicating that the booking conditions have been read and agreed to, with space for any alternative address for correspondence.

The bottom of the booking form usually has a cut-off slip for the agent to send with their remittance. This will ask for:

- the booking reference number
- the agent's ABTA number
- the client's departure date
- the flight code
- the client's lead name (i.e. the name in which the booking is held)
- the value of the remittance

There will also be a box for the agency to endorse the remittance slip with its office stamp incorporating their trading name and ABTA number.

Now that so many bookings are made and confirmed through viewdata systems, booking forms often have 'to be retained by agent' stamped across them. This is so that the client can still give written confirmation of the booking which can be stored with their details in case it should be needed later.

Pricing policy

The ABTA Tour Operators' Code of Conduct also insists that information about the company's pricing policy must appear in the brochure. Some of this information may appear at the front of the brochure, some at the back, or it may be all together in one place. The brochure must show:

a) how the total price should be calculated, together with a precise statement of the services included. Where an operator offers a variety of prices to give the client a choice, it must be made clear what the basic price is and what it includes. The prices shown must include VAT and any non-optional additional charges of fixed amounts (except taxes payable locally overseas). Information about non-optional additional charges of variable amounts and optional additional charges should be printed near to the information about the basic price. Alternatively a note near the basic price should indicate whereabouts in the brochure details can be found. Information about charges for optional extras like car hire can appear anywhere appropriate in the brochure.

b) the base date used for calculating prices and the relevant exchange rates, published in the *Financial Times* 'Guide to World Currencies', on that date.

c) a statement about surcharges where the operator reserves the right to levy them. This must appear close to the information about the basic price, with an indication of whereabouts in the brochure further details can be found.

THE TEXT

The purpose of the brochure text is to present the operator's products in a way that will make them appealing to potential customers. Depending on the product, different aspects of the holiday will need to be emphasised. So summer sun brochures tend to emphasise freedom, good food, good company (and a sense of belonging), the chance to relax, instant gratification of a variety of needs and value-for-money buys. In contrast, overland company brochures (and to a lesser extent many long-haul brochures) emphasise the exotic, the prospect of adventure, remoteness, the 'otherness' of the destination, sometimes even the sheer difficulty of the journey.

Most brochures are written in a distinctive type of purple prose, disparagingly called 'brochurese', in which nothing is ever *quite* nice or *rather* pleasant, but instead is always expressed in superlatives. Skies are always bright blue, azure or turquoise, seas are always crystal clear. Sand is always white or yellow, the beaches palm-fringed, the local people always smiling and welcoming. The landscape is always spectacular or breathtaking, the food mouth-watering, the buildings exotic. In brochure language, places continue to be 'fishing villages' long after the last fisherman pulled in his nets and retired. Where something cannot be expressed in such positive terms without falling foul of the Trade Descriptions Act the temptation is often to miss it out altogether. So few brochures, even those covering developing countries, dwell on the dirt and poverty commonplace in such destinations.

The effect of this style of language is to remove any differentiation between places. The following introductory descriptions are taken at random from recent brochures, and describe resorts in countries as diverse as Turkey, Greece and Gambia. However, as they have been described, it would be hard to tell which was which.

> . . . perfect for sun-lovers, with palm-studded beaches, friendly people and hours of sunshine.

COSMOS SUMMER SUN 1993 BOOKING FORM

Once your holiday reservation has been made with us, your local travel agent will ask you to complete this booking form and pay the appropriate deposit amount. You should receive your confirmation of booking (which is also an account) within two weeks or so. Payment of the balance due for your holiday must be made not less than six weeks before departure. For bookings made within six weeks of departure full payment must be made at the time of booking. You should therefore ensure that you pay the agent in sufficient time to allow payment to reach Cosmos by the due date. (See Cosmos Consumer Protection Plan)

Please use block capitals. Do not write in shaded areas. **2nd Edition**

BOOKING REFERENCE	DEPARTURE DATE	TRAVEL OR TOUR CODE	HOLIDAY CODE	No. of Nights	No. in party excl. infants	AIRPORT OF DEPARTURE	NAME OF HOTEL(S), APARTMENT OR TOUR

BOARD TYPE (e.g. S/C, B&B, Half/Full)		Emergency Contact Telephone No. for out of office hours, when your Travel Agent may be closed →	

	TYPE OF ACCOMMODATION	Mr Mrs Mst Miss Inft	Initial	SURNAME (Note: Person signing the booking form must appear first)	AGE if under 20 on departure
ROOM 1					
ROOM 2					
ROOM 3					

TO BE RETAINED BY TRAVEL AGENT

SPECIAL REQUESTS (not guaranteed and subject to availability)

CRUISE HOLIDAYS For Cruise state cabin type as confirmed	CABIN 1	CABIN 2

INSURANCE: If the party is not taking Cosmos arranged insurance delete. YES

All persons named on this booking form will be automatically covered by our holiday Insurance unless you delete "YES". If Insurance has been requested, payment of the deposit ensures immediate cover. The premium will be included on your account. If you are not taking Cosmos arranged insurance, you must enter below the name of your Insurers providing comparable or greater cover.

My Insurers are:

On behalf of the above persons I confirm I have read and accept the Cosmos Consumer Protection Plan, holiday information, and other information set out in the Summer Sun 1993 brochure and this Price & Flight Guide and any late offers information and conditions relevant to my holiday. I authorise my Travel Agent to make this booking on my behalf and I enclose cheque/P.O. to the value of £ as a deposit of £60 per person (or £75 for Egypt and Caribbean destinations) payable to Cosmos and instruct them to deal with this booking form in accordance with Cosmos' requirements.

Signature:

Persons under 18 years must also have signature of parent or guardian.

Date:

1993

March					
Mon	1	8	15	22	29
Tue	2	9	16	23	30
Wed	3	10	17	24	31
Thu	4	11	18	25	
Fri	5	12	19	26	
Sat	6	13	20	27	
Sun	7	14	21	28	

April					
Mon		5	12	19	26
Tue		6	13	20	27
Wed		7	14	21	28
Thu	1	8	15	22	29
Fri	2	9	16	23	30
Sat	3	10	17	24	
Sun	4	11	18	25	

May						
Mon		3	10	17	24	31
Tue		4	11	18	25	
Wed		5	12	19	26	
Thu		6	13	20	27	
Fri		7	14	21	28	
Sat	1	8	15	22	29	
Sun	2	9	16	23	30	

June					
Mon		7	14	21	28
Tue	1	8	15	22	29
Wed	2	9	16	23	30
Thu	3	10	17	24	
Fri	4	11	18	25	
Sat	5	12	19	26	
Sun	6	13	20	27	

July					
Mon		5	12	19	26
Tue		6	13	20	27
Wed		7	14	21	28
Thu	1	8	15	22	29
Fri	2	9	16	23	30
Sat	3	10	17	24	31
Sun	4	11	18	25	

August					
Mon		2	9	16	23	30
Tue		3	10	17	24	31
Wed		4	11	18	25	
Thu		5	12	19	26	
Fri		6	13	20	27	
Sat		7	14	21	28	
Sun	1	8	15	22	29	

September					
Mon		6	13	20	27
Tue		7	14	21	28
Wed	1	8	15	22	29
Thu	2	9	16	23	30
Fri	3	10	17	24	
Sat	4	11	18	25	
Sun	5	12	19	26	

October					
Mon		4	11	18	25
Tue		5	12	19	26
Wed		6	13	20	27
Thu		7	14	21	28
Fri	1	8	15	22	29
Sat	2	9	16	23	30
Sun	3	10	17	24	31

ATOL CAA COSMOSAIR PLC

ABTA No. 23318 (COSMOSAIR PLC) & 24043 (COSMOS COACH TOURS LTD)

ATOL CAA COSMOS COACH TOURS LTD

COSMOS PAYMENT SLIP - SUMMER SUN 1993 - 2nd Edition

Send to Cosmosair PLC, Tourama House, 17 Homesdale Road, Bromley, Kent BR2 9LX

TRAVEL AGENTS

Please retain booking form. If you wish to make an individual remittance, please send this slip attached to the payment.

AGENT'S STAMP OR CLIENT'S ADDRESS

BOOKING REF. ____

ABTA NO. ____

AMOUNT ENCLOSED £ ____

LEAD NAME ____

DEPARTURE DATE ____

Fig. 5.7 Typical tour operator's booking form

Courtesy: Cosmos

> An extremely attractive town, a wide variety of nightlife and good balance between sunworshipping and sightseeing.
>
> . . . lovely beaches in secluded coves, a super mix of peace and activity, and a warm welcome from the friendly people.
>
> A charming, fishing town with a relaxed care-free atmosphere, ideal for sunworshippers.
>
> . . . it also boasts some of the friendliest and most hospitable people you'll ever meet and an atmosphere that's refreshingly carefree and unspoilt.
>
> . . . Gin, clear waters, near endless sunshine, fast 'n' furious nightlife . . .

A few companies have tried to make brochure prose less breathless. Time Off, for example, employs professional travel writers to prepare its introductory descriptions, and some of the long-haul overland companies make more effort to portray destinations realistically; indeed Voyage Jules Verne have pioneered a type of brochure which comes closer to a magazine format, complete with articles on places and people, than the standard brochure (*see* Fig. 5.8). Another possibility is to incorporate prose descriptions of destinations by famous authors or historical travellers in the brochure: so High Places, a mountain travel company, includes quotations from modern explorer Robin Hanbury-Tenison and the seventeenth-century traveller Richard Boothby. However, the brochure remains essentially a selling tool which makes it hard even for those companies that want to be realistic to do other than emphasise the positive aspects of a destination and those features of it they believe the likely purchaser is looking for.

Another feature of much brochure text, regardless of the product on offer, is the frequent use of the words 'you', 'we' and 'our' to emphasise the central role of the clients and their needs, and how 'at home' they will feel, even when abroad. Often statements are phrased to bring out the benefits that clients will draw from specific features of their holiday; for example, from the hotel facilities. The following examples are taken at random from assorted 1993 and 1994 brochures:

> You will learn the true meaning of the Austrian phrase 'gemutlichkeit', as locals give you the warmest of welcomes and make you feel that little bit special.
>
> There is always something going on . . . so you will be kept as busy as you want to be during your stay . . . you can play tennis or squash . . .
>
> Our Rajasthan itineraries concentrate on overland road journeys to enable us to cover the many highlights along the route . . . thus allowing flexibility and time to appreciate the marvels of these dramatic and historic lands.
>
> You'll only be 700 metres from the beach, and just over a kilometre from the centre of the cocktail world . . . Whichever hotel you choose, you'll have use of the facilities in both Club units . . . have a beer from the bar, shoot some pool, watch the ol' box . . . or bronze that body on the sun terrace poolside.

The photographs

Photographs, too, play an important role in the selling job, arguably a more important role than the written descriptions since pictures probably have more immediate impact. Just as the words used in the text are chosen to present the destination in the best possible light, so the images are chosen to fulfil the same task. It would be an unusual brochure that included pictures of hotels taken on overcast days, even though sun can't be guaranteed every day even in Greece.

Two common ruses make it possible to present 'problem' hotels in a good light. Where a hotel is surrounded by other buildings or has a main road running in front of it, a close-up photo will often crop out such unappealing features. Conversely where it stands in acres of space there may even be an aerial shot to highlight this fact.

Of course, it goes without saying that all photos used for brochure production must be high-quality originals. Companies may also prefer to include pictures of their prettiest accommodation even when it offers limited capacity, for the sake of the picture. However, if this results in lots of requests that have to be turned down it can be a counterproductive strategy.

Most photos in summer and winter sun brochures are of hotels. However, there will also be some pictures to illustrate 'local colour'. Long-haul brochures are more likely to include pictures of the

Voyages Jules Verne

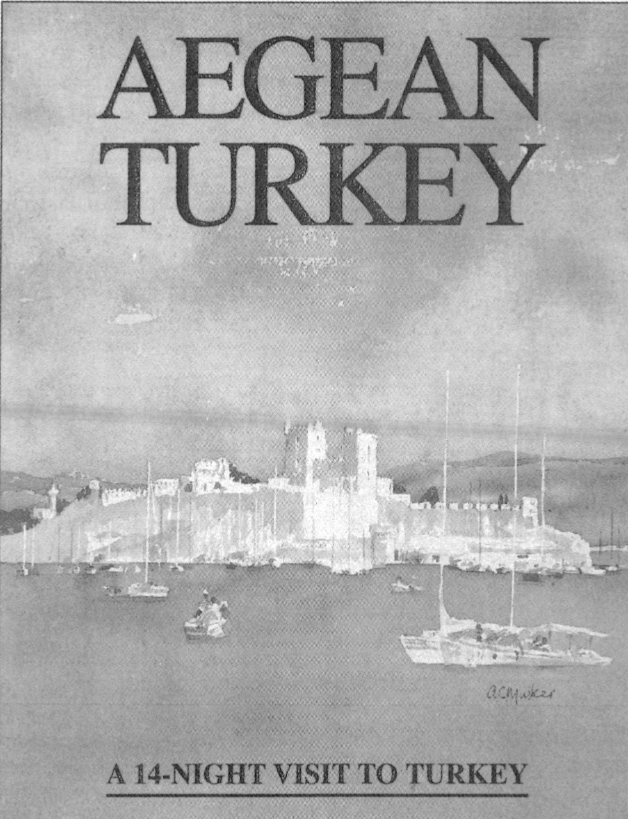

including 7 nights' cruising, 3 nights in Istanbul and 4 nights in Antalya or Kusadasi from £899.00

Here is a marvellous opportunity to explore Turkey's idyllic and unspoilt coastline from the comfort of the MV *Tura*, a delightful, large, private yacht accommodating 40 passengers. Sailing from Antalya, we will journey along the wild and beautiful coastline of Lycia and in addition to visiting the better known ancient sites, we go to some romantic places which travellers hardly ever see. Being ship-borne enables us to visit the most attractive and remote harbours and move slowly through the scenes of half-sunken buildings east of Kas.

Nature, ruins and relaxation form the central part of this tour. However, three days in Istanbul, that most endlessly captivating of cities will be busy and absorbing, taking in the incomparable sights from the exquisite architecture of Haghia Sophia to the splendours of Topkapi Palace.

The MV Tura

The vessel, built in 1984, flies under the Turkish flag, is registered in Istanbul and is the only Turkish registered cruise vessel sailing in the Aegean. The tonnage is 394.65 and the vessel carries the most modern and sophisticated navigation equipment and safety features and accommodates up to 40 passengers. The MV *Tura* is ideal for smaller gatherings and lends a delightful ambience of a house-party to the holiday. A crew of 26, under the expert hands of the captain, offers a splendid and friendly service with excellent food. The vessel is air-conditioned throughout and all cabins have two lower beds and a shower, washbasin and wc.

This will not, however, be a 'luxury' cruise: there will be no formal dressing for dinner, none of those blush-making jollifications that one dreads for days beforehand and, we absolutely promise, no deck games. Our aim is to provide you with a comfortable base for a leisurely journey to some of the most historical sites and areas of natural beauty.

Itinerary

Day 1 London/Istanbul - fly from London Heathrow in the afternoon with Turkish Airlines to Istanbul. Transfer to the Sokhollu Pasha, a character hotel located in the Sultanahmet district of the old town. The hotel occupies a building originally constructed as a residence for the royal Chief Physician in the late 18th century. It has been well restored, maintaining many of the original features. There are 37 rooms, a restaurant, bar and walled garden. Stay for three nights.

Day 2 Istanbul - morning free. In the afternoon a city tour has been arranged to include the main sights of Istanbul such as Haghia Sofia, the Blue Mosque and the Hippodrome.

Day 3 Istanbul - the day is free to spend at leisure, to explore independently in Istanbul's bustling streets and markets, or perhaps to visit the magnificent Topkapi Museum in the fabled palace of the Ottoman sultans.

Day 4 Istanbul/Antalya - depart for Istanbul airport after breakfast and take the flight to Antalya on Turkey's south coast. Arrive and embark on the MV *Tura*, sailing in the late evening.

Day 5 Myra/Kekova - arrive in the morning and drive to Myra with its well-preserved Roman theatre. Sail at lunchtime to the island of Kekova and view the castle and sunken city from motorboats. Time free for swimming before returning to the MV *Tura*. Sail in the evening for Kalkan arriving after dinner.

Main: Bodrum harbour (watercolour by Alison Musker).
Left: Yivli Minareli, Antalya.
Right: the MV Tura.

Day 6 Kalkan/Gemili Island/Fethiye - drive to the pretty fishing village of Kas at the foot of the Taurus Mountains, encircling a crescent bay. Narrow streets radiate from the harbour with its brightly painted fishing boats and here you will find traditionally built, white-washed houses with intricately carved fretwork balconies and terracotta-tiled roofs, vivid bougainvillaea and great pots of hydrangeas perched on wooden balconies. Kas is built on the site of Lycian Antiphellus and has a well-preserved Hellenistic theatre. Return to the MV *Tura* for lunch and sail to Gemili island, a relaxing and beautiful place to swim and relax. Set sail for Fethiye arriving in the early evening.

Day 7 Fethiye (Telmessos) - visit the fascinating Lycian rock tombs and 'Death Sea' (picnic lunch). Return to the vessel mid-afternoon and sail around the beautiful bay of Fethiye.

Day 8 Dalyan/Marmaris - shore excursion by motorboat to Kaunos and visit the ruins of this ancient town. Return to the MV *Tura* for lunch and sail to the resort of Marmaris. Shore excursion by motorboat to Turunc, Kumlubuku area, phosphorus cave and aquarium. Sail at midnight.

Day 9 Datca/Knidos/Bodrum - arrive Datca. Morning at leisure before sailing at lunchtime to Knidos. Free time to explore the site of Knidos, settled since 1000 BC, particularly renowned for the temple and statue of Aphrodite. Sail for Bodrum, arriving in the evening.

Day 10 Bodrum - Bodrum is a colourful and lively resort. Morning excursion to St Peter's Castle, the tomb of King Mausollus and the Marine Museum. Afternoon free in Bodrum. Sail at midnight.

Day 11 Kusadasi - disembark and drive to nearby Ephesus visiting its major sights. Return to Kusadasi for four nights' stay in a comfortable hotel.

Days 12 - 14 Kusadasi - at leisure.

Day 15 Izmir/London - in the morning drive to Izmir and fly from Izmir airport with Turkish Airlines to London Heathrow, via Istanbul.

Departure Schedule & Prices

Thursdays 1994
per person in twin-bedded cabin

April 14, 21, 28
May 5, 12, 19, 26
June 2, 9, 16, 23, 30
July 7, 14, 21, 28
August 4, 11, 18, 25
September 1, 8, 15, 22, 29
October 6

Lower (inside) £899.00
Main (outside) £985.00
Upper (outside) £1085.00

Single cabin supplement on request

Prices include: return flights, transfers, accommodation, full board on ship, half board Kusadasi/Antalya, breakfast only Istanbul, shore excursions, services of a national guide. **Not included**: travel insurance, airport tax, visa £5, tips to ship's staff. **All prices are subject to change.**

NB On alternate weeks, the cruise itinerary operates from Kusadasi to Antalya, thus giving 4 nights in Antalya instead of Kusadasi.

5-Star Accommodation

If you wish to be upgraded to 5-star accommodation (the Ramada, Istanbul - the Falez, Antalya - and the Fantasia, Kusadasi according to the itinerary), the inclusive supplement is £135.00 per person in a twin (£65.00 single room supplement).

How to Book

For reservations please telephone Voyages Jules Verne on 071-723 5066 to take out an option on the departure of your choice. Our offices are open weekdays from 9.00am to 5.30pm and at weekends for telephone reservations only from 9.00am to 5.00pm.

VOYAGES JULES VERNE
21 Dorset Square,
London NW1 6QG
ABTA 68215 ATOL 883B

Fig. 5.8 A page from the Voyages Jules Verne brochure
Courtesy: Voyages Jules Verne

actual destination, and generally feature very few pictures of the accommodation, since the companies are confident that their clients are more interested in what they will see at their destination than in where they will stay. All sorts of brochures include pictures of previous clients enjoying themselves, inviting would-be buyers to imagine themselves in their place. Clearly, therefore, those pictures must be chosen to depict the type of customer for whom the product has been designed: families in summer sun brochures, couples in Caribbean brochures, older people for cruise and coach tours, younger people in overland brochures and emphatically young people in The Club brochures. (This job can be done in text instead; for example, Himalayan Kingdoms actually gives the age and gender make-up of its trekking and expedition groups.)

While it remains true that pictures never lie, critics of tourism point to the way that local people rarely appear in brochures except in servile positions (waiting on tourists, driving them around, etc.) or as exotic parts of the landscape, in some cases presented alongside and with very little differentiation from the country's native flora and fauna. This is no doubt because tourists to long-haul destinations are often in search of the 'other' and are most interested in those aspects of a country that set it apart from their own. However, by showing only exotic aspects of a country it is possible to lie by omission. So some visitors to India have been shocked by the poverty which is sometimes briefly alluded to in brochure copy but certainly never represented in the images – more usually of the Taj Mahal, exotically beturbanned Rajasthani tribesmen and Bengal tigers. Conversely, by homing in on the fairy-tale architecture of Kuala Lumpur station, most brochures fail to make it clear that the city is really the fast-modernising capital of Malaysia, a fast-modernising Far Eastern country.

It could be argued, therefore, that most brochures use pictures to present cliched images of destinations in the same way that their prose does. Indeed, looking through a batch of long-haul brochures it isn't hard to find the exact same pictures reproduced time and again, hired from the same pictures agency.

Advertising

By 1993, some operators were using surplus space in the brochure (for example, the back cover) for advertising purposes. Sometimes they simply advertised other parts of their own programmes. However, the back of the 1993 Airtours Ski brochure featured three pages of adverts for ski clothing, equipment and videos. More surprisingly, the back of the 1993 Cosmos Summer Sun brochure featured an advert from Ibatur advertising the steps it was taking to ensure the Balearics remained what it called 'protected islands'.

BROCHURES: THE LEGAL POSITION

In addition to providing all the information already discussed, tour operators' brochures must also fulfil certain legal requirements. In particular, they must conform to the terms of the Trade Descriptions Act, the Unfair Contract Terms Act and the EC Package Travel Regulations (*see* Chapter Ten).

According to the Trade Descriptions Act, it is an offence to 'recklessly' publish something inaccurate. However, because tour operators' brochures must be printed so far before the holidays they describe are actually taken, it is almost inevitable that some inaccuracies will creep in. Provided the operator can prove they had taken all reasonable care to ensure that what they said was true, they should be safe from prosecution under the Act. This is how Sovereign explains its brochure descriptions:

> The descriptions of resorts, hotels, apartments, etc., in this brochure have been compiled as a result of inspection by our staff and checked and rechecked to ensure that they are correct. However, there may be occasions . . . especially in low season . . . when accommodation owners, proprietors of resort facilities, etc., may decide to withdraw some of their facilities. A pool may need cleaning, a disco closes for redecoration for example, and these facilities will then be temporarily unavailable. After we have printed the brochure, a hotelier may decide to alter his meals system to buffet or back again to waiter service. Similarly, air conditioning or heated swimming pools, wherever mentioned in the hotel description, may, at the hotelier's discretion, be available only at certain times of the year. These are

regrettably beyond our control. However, when we are told of such changes we will inform you at the time of booking or, if you've already booked, you will be contacted before your departure if there is time.

Public holidays and religious festivals may also affect the availability of resort and hotel facilities. The relevant National Tourist Office can provide details of such events and further information regarding your chosen holiday resort.

(Courtesy: First Choice)

BROCHURES: THE MORAL POSITION

During the late 1980s concern began to be expressed about the ways in which brochures presented holiday destinations. In part this was a response to the increase in the number of long-haul packages being sold. As long as Europeans holiday within Europe, they travel to cultures which differ from theirs only in detail. With the exception of Yugoslavia, most popular European holiday resort areas have also been relatively stable politically since 1945, and when changes have happened (as when the Greek colonels staged their *coup d'état* in 1967, or when the Spanish dictator, General Franco, died in 1975), they have been widely publicised. There can have been few would-be holidaymakers in 1993 who didn't realise that a visit to 'Yugoslavia' was no longer on the cards. Further afield, however, and the situation is very different. In the first place tourists can be travelling to places with very different cultures from their own (e.g. Morocco, India), where there may be an enormous gulf between their own standard of living and that of the local population (e.g. Kenya, the Gambia, India) and where there may also be considerable political instability (e.g. Sri Lanka, South Africa). Because these countries are so far away most of the newspapers either pay them little attention or relegate stories about them to inside pages, ensuring that most tourists know very little about some of the countries they choose to visit. This was highlighted in 1992 when a British holidaymaker died in Egypt after Islamic fundamentalists, who had already declared their intention to target tourists, shot at the coach in which she was travelling. Even faraway countries with cultures like our own can offer risks to the unwary, particularly where there is a dispossessed underclass who may see tourists as walking cash registers; in 1993 several tourists were shot and killed in New Orleans, Washington and Miami, making the United States as risky a holiday destination as some of those with more exotic images.

There has been considerable debate over whose responsibility it is to alert tourists to potential risks in their holiday destinations. Some would argue that it is up to the Foreign Office to keep travellers informed or that it is up to travellers themselves to make enquiries about their planned destination. Even more would see this as the job of the travel agent. Arguably, however, tour operators have a responsibility to ensure that in attempting to 'sell' a destination they do not misrepresent it in their brochures. (*See* Fig. 5.9.)

However, even if tour operators were more scrupulously honest in how they represented holiday destinations, there would still be a problem in that the brochures are printed months before the holidays they describe actually take place. Events like *coup d'états* can happen out of the blue which means there will always be a role for the travel agent to play in keeping the public informed. For example, in 1992 there was an attempted *coup* in Thailand, usually thought of as a relatively safe and stable Far Eastern destination, which it would not have been realistic to expect tour operators to anticipate. Nor, since the disturbances settled down fairly quickly, would it necessarily be reasonable to expect them to mention it in future brochures. However, travel agents should probably have drawn it to would-be visitors' attention for some months after it happened, when the outcome was still uncertain.

If some of the voiced concern centred on the safety of tourists in far-flung parts of the world, some of it was more about the indigenous populations of the tourist-receiving countries. Since ill-considered tourist development and inappropriate behaviour by visitors can have damaging consequences for the host communities (*see* Chapter Eleven), it was argued that tour operators have a responsibility to provide their clients with enough information to make sensible decisions about where to go and what to do when they're there. In particular, operators were criticised for presenting the inhabitants of some developing countries as 'exotic' and glossing over the harsh reality of their living conditions. At a conference on 'Marketing Tourism –

MOMBASA

Telephone IDD code from UK: 010 254 11
General Description: The city of Mombasa on the Indian Ocean is second only to Nairobi in importance and size. It has long been a major trading post with oriental contacts which have led to the city's middle eastern feel, its Arabic 'old town' and the traditional Arabic sailing boats, dhows, in its harbour. It occupies an island linked to the coast by causeways and, for points south, the Likoni ferry. The tourist hotels are north and south of the city, for some 20 miles in either direction, spaced out in a long, flat line along the beaches that stretch almost continuously.

In most cases the hotels are quite separate from each other with nothing much in their immediate vicinities. The most developed resort areas, with shops, banks, travel agencies, restaurants, bars – and even a disco or two – are BAMBURI on the north coast and DIANI on the south coast. Generally speaking the hotels are self contained and visitors tend to stay at the one they have chosen without wandering far afield. At night, especially, it is wise to take taxis rather than walk anywhere. A common complaint among visitors is the constant pestering from hawkers on the beaches and in practice few visitors seem to lie out on the sands, preferring instead the hotels' pool areas. The exception is at Diani where sunbathing on the beach is more popular. At weekends hotels may be invaded by wealthier residents of Mombasa and Nairobi though their main market is package tour business from Europe.

Accommodation: There is some seasonal variation in hotel rates. The winter months December–March is traditionally Mombasa's busiest time and a supplement is charged over the Christmas period. The summer months used to be low season but in recent years July/August have been busier with charter flights from Europe. Quoted hotel rates usually include taxes, government training levy and 10% service charge.

Entertainments: Land sports are mainly restricted to what the hotels offer – many have tennis and squash courts – and there is a golf course in the Nyali area, a few miles north of Mombasa, where guests can arrange to play. WATERSPORTS – nearly all hotels or concessions based at them provide a range of sports. Offshore coral reefs fringe the whole coast, between half a mile and a mile out to sea. There are several designated marine parks and numerous diving schools, often operating from hotels. Deep sea fishing trips are offered, too, all along the coast. The beaches are uniformly sandy and wide, extremely wide at low tide, but prone to weed (especially during rainy seasons) which some, but not all, hotels try to clear away on a regular basis. The sea can sometimes be churned up and murky looking. Because of the sharp coral it is sensible to wear shoes for swimming or walking on the beaches.

Public transport: Taxis are the usual means of getting around, agree fares before setting off, they are quite expensive. Car hire is available but expensive and the road conditions are poor, so for anyone who only wants to do limited sightseeing taxis or organised excursions are probably better options. A British driving licence is needed and driving is on the left, hirers must be at least 23 years old. Many hotels provide transport into town. Trains and buses (7 hour journey) go to Nairobi. The Likoni ferry links Mombasa to the coast south of it, carrying cars and foot passengers; there are frequently queues for it.

Local excursions: Organised tours pick up at hotels. Mombasa City tour – by bus incl visits to the old city, harbour and bazaar. Sometimes incl a dhow ride. Half day. Bush tours – by bus, inland to a village with folk dancing and handicraft displays. The aquarium and snake farm is sometimes visited, too. Half day. Shimba Hills – by bus to the game reserve, the nearest one to Mombasa, south and inland. Good coastal views from here and wildlife incl elephants and buffalo. Half day. Dhow Safari – these depart from different points north and south of Mombasa, usually incl some sailing along the coast, lunch on board or at an offshore island. Full day. Wasini Island – picnic lunch, snorkelling at island off the south coast. Full day. Malindi and Gedi ruins – by bus 75 miles north of Mombasa to Malindi for glass bottom boat trips (the quality of these boats is not the best, however) over the coral reefs of the Marine National Park. Stops en route at the ruins of the 14th century city of Gedi and, often, to see a tribal dance troupe. Full day. Lamu island – by air then boat to the Swahili town of Lamu, visits to the Lamu museum and a beach. Full day. It is possible to extend one's stay on Lamu for a few days; watersports are particularly good there. Tsavo East National Park – by bus/jeep, an early start for a 60 mile drive from Mombasa towards Nairobi to this game park which has much wildlife incl giraffes, rhinos, gazelles, elephants and a waterhole for night viewing. Overnight at a lodge. Longer stays here can be arranged as can safaris further afield to Amboseli National Park with Mount Kilimanjaro as its backdrop or, by air transfer to Nairobi then road, to the Masai Mara. A day trip by air to Amboseli is offered by some ground operators, enabling a taste of safari life without an overnight stay.

Fig. 5.9 Greater objectivity . . . How the ABC Long-Haul Gazetteer represents Mombasa
Courtesy: Agents' Long-Haul Gazettee, Reed Travel Group, 1994

THE INDIAN SUBCONTINENT: TRAVELLERS ADVICE

At Cox and Kings we believe that a good holiday is not luck but judgement. We have therefore compiled the following travellers advice to outline the nature of travel in the subcontinent and to help you prepare for your holiday. Our unrivalled experience has shown that sometimes minor problems can occur. While our ground staff are always on hand to rectify such occurrences we do request that you have a patient and broad approach to travelling in the subcontinent.

● MONEY

We advise you to take the majority of your money in UK Sterling travellers cheques for security purposes. These are easily exchanged in the major hotels and banks. Please note that it is imperative that you retain evidence of your transaction as this is required when changing your rupees back. The import and export of the Indian Rupee is prohibited and you will not be able to obtain them prior to your departure. On departure you will need to change this into an international currency.

Most hotels, restaurants and some shops accept major credit cards such as American Express Diners Club, Visa and Mastercharge.

● AIRPORT DEPARTURE TAX

The cost of our tours does not include airport departure taxes. It is therefore necessary for you to pay these locally. Your tour manager or guide will advise you of the current rate upon your arrival in India.

● ACCOMMODATION – see hotel guide

● FOOD

In the main city hotels this can incorporate European as well as Indian and Oriental cuisine. In the more remote areas and smaller hotels and palaces, food is quite basic and principally Indian. We suggest that in these areas you request vegetarian food since this tends to reduce the risk of stomach upsets. The hotels are keenly aware of Europeans reaction to Indian food and they take great care in areas of hygiene. While health problems can occur, these are usually minor and often result from the change in diet or over consumption of food.

● SHOPPING

There are many wonderful handicrafts that can be purchased in India, but we strongly recommend that you take note of the following precautions. Always check on the levels of import duty levied for the items that you wish to purchase. In Delhi and Bombay and some smaller cities, there are state run emporiums where a wide range of Indian handicrafts can be purchased. Here the prices are fixed and quality is quite good. Elsewhere, there are bazaars in every city, but be prepared to haggle – it is the way business is done! Please beware of 'authentic' or valuable objects which may not be all they are claimed to be. Please also note that Cox & Kings cannot be responsible for any purchases that you make. Neither can we take up any correspondence on your behalf if you return from India dissatisfied with your purchases or if delays occur with delivery.

● POVERTY/BEGGARS

It is an inescapable fact that the Indian subcontinent has areas of extreme poverty. Where possible, we try to avoid such areas, but in order to visit some of the temples and monuments it is impossible to escape sights which are shocking from a Western viewpoint. India does have a large number of beggars, in part because many Indians give money or 'alms' to them for religious reasons. Those found by the hotels and tourist sites are usually professionals and please be aware that not all are genuine. We ask that you try to accept that poverty and beggars are not seen as at all unusual in the Indian culture and we recommend that you do not give money to any beggars. Also do not be afraid to return 'gifts' for which you are then expected to pay. If you feel the need to help India, there are many worthy charities.

● ROAD TRAVEL

Most cars are of Indian construction. These may appear antique but are comfortable and ideally suited to the Indian roads. Coaches are also principally Indian made, and while not of a European standard they are comfortable and maintained to a high standard. In the south of India there is shortage of air-conditioned coaches due to the high taxes that are levied on such vehicles in this area. Please note therefore that it may not be possible to arrange an air-conditioned coach for the tours travelling in the south of India, however in the north of India Cox & Kings will use air-conditioned coaches.

● TRAIN TRAVEL

In most cases the trains in India are basic but comfortable. Where possible, we will always try and reserve first class or air-conditioned carriages. but these cannot always be reserved and do not exist on all routes. Please contact our tour consultants to discuss the facilities that are available on the route that you would like to take and they will advise you accordingly.

● AIR TRAVEL

Travel in India is by the major internal airline, Indian Airlines whose fleet of aircraft is principally Boeing 737's and Airbuses. The airline has acquired a reputation for unpunctuality which it lives up to on occasion. In flight catering is basic and normally consists of sandwiches and Indian snacks served with tea or coffee. The impatient traveller will find this aspect of travel trying from time to time, but it does need to be borne with patience and humour.

India is not an Oriental version of Europe and much of its charm derives from its unpredictability and its very different approach to day to day affairs. The Indian subcontinent is not always what you expect it to be but it is always what you make of it.

Fig. 5.10 How Cox and Kings prepares travellers to India for culture shock

Courtesy: Cox and Kings

EXPLORE

small group exploratory holidays You'll see more

Egypt

Nile Valley Cruise & Treasures

Issued October 1992. Valid from 01 Jan 1993 to 31 Dec 1993

CONNECTING TRAVEL FROM LONDON

15 days/14 nights Tour including Connecting Group Flights London-Cairo-London

Depart Monday from London Heathrow Airport to join tour in Cairo (day 1 of itinerary). Transfer to hotel.

Return Monday from Cairo (day 15 of itinerary) and arrive London Heathrow the same day.

JOINING TOUR ABROAD

15 days/14 nights Tour Only Cairo back to Cairo

Join Cairo on Monday (day 1)
End Cairo on Monday (day 15)

Clients booked on **'Tour Only'** arrangements should make their own way to the joining point in Cairo. Please refer to separate **'Joining Instructions'** for name and address of hotel and time of rendezvous with tour leader.

The famous antiquities of the Nile Valley go back to the beginning of civilization, the oldest and most remarkable monuments in the world. In this ancient land, whose patient fellahin are the direct descendants of the pyramid builders of 5000 years ago, we plan to explore one of the Great Oases of the Western Desert, see the archaeological and temple sites of Beni Hasan, Tell el-Amarna, Abydos and Dendera, and spend two days at Luxor

pharaonic antiquities in the world, and its scope and interest is inexhaustible. We also visit Giza to see the celebrated Pyramids, among the most famous man-made spectacles in the world. The Great Pyramid of Cheops is the largest of the group (originally 475' high with a square base of 760'). Second is the Pyramid of Khepren (445' high, width 690'), and third, Mykerinos, the smallest. The complex includes the Sphinx, a crouching lion with a human head carved from solid rock and the Granite Temple. The pharaohs of the Old Kingdom began planning their pyramids (tombs) as soon as they assumed power. The Great Pyramid was built in 20-odd years in about 2600 BC, with only the simplest implements and without draught animals or even the wheel. Other places of interest in the Old City include the Citadel of Saladin (from where marvellous views overlooking Cairo and the Pyramids can be enjoyed), and mosques like the Sultan Hussan and the El Azhar. The Papyrus Institute is also an interesting place to visit.

Day 4. Drive via El Fayyum to El Minya
Today we begin our drive up the Nile Valley stopping at Lake Qarun. The lake is the remains of an inland sea, and irrigation has made the soil around so rich that the place is considered the garden of Egypt. Peaches, oranges, mandarins, olives, prickly pears, grapes and pomegranates all grow here in abundance. Lining the roads are palm, tamarisks, acacia and eucalyptus. The lake is full of fish, and the pharaohs used to hunt crocodiles and wild duck here. Fayyum is also known for its pigeon-houses and old 'saqiyas' or water-wheels to which clay pots are tied with string. Take plenty of film with you. Continuing to Beni Suef, we follow the Nile's ribbon of green via Maghagha and Beni Mazar to El Minya, where we stay the night. ***Overnight hotel and breakfast.***

Day 5. To Assyut, visiting Beni Hassan
In the morning we explore some of the famous rock-cut tombs of Beni Hassan, which depict in paint the daily life of Egyptians of the Middle Kingdom - crafts, sports, games and dancing. With an aspect overlooking the Nile, from here it is easy to see the precious band of fertile land against the

Fig. 5.11 Sample trip dossier for a holiday in Egypt, produced by Explore
Courtesy: Explore

the Power of Images' in 1992, Tina Bryant of the University of Hertfordshire produced clippings from assorted long-haul brochures showing how pictures of different tribal people from Kenya were indiscriminately labelled 'Masais', presumably because the Masai are the best known of the tribes. Arguably, it is difficult for tourists to make informed decisions about the countries they are visiting when the 'facts' served up to them by those in a position to get them right are treated as if accuracy were an optional extra.

Even more serious criticism has arisen over the portrayal of local women in brochures. While most British tour operators have taken a lower-key approach to sex tourism than their Far Eastern counterparts, there was a particular scandal in 1989 when Redwing produced a Sunmed Go Places brochure for holidays in Thailand in which it suggested that 'when you see a girl in a bar with strategically torn slits in her shorts dancing suggestively with a live snake, then instead of thinking of her as a harlot, picture instead a little girl trying to shock an adult out of pure devilment'. This was at a time when some organisations were already worried about the growth of child prostitution in Bangkok and Pattaya. In the ensuing furore Redwing was forced to reprint 100,000 brochures. For a while it even looked as if it would have to pull out of Thailand altogether. At the time British Airways had a 50 per cent stake in Redwing and so shared in the ignominy.

Tour operators might reasonably protest that it is difficult to provide more information without the brochures becoming unmanageably large and expensive to produce. Specialist companies are obviously in a better position to find space for the 'warts and all' picture. Cox and Kings have been arranging travel to India since 1758; at a quick glance their images and descriptions of the subcontinent differ little from those in other operators' brochures; read the small print at the back, however, and you will find the issues of poverty, beggars and inefficiency at least mentioned (*see* Fig. 5.11). Some of the overland tour companies get round the space-in-the-brochure problem by producing separate 'trip dossiers' of more detailed information which they provide when people make a definite booking (*see* Fig. 5.11). Sometimes potential clients can also ask to be sent up to three trip dossiers in advance to help them make their choice.

BROCHURE PRODUCTION

The brochure is produced according to a 'creative brief' which sets out:

a) the number of copies required
b) the number of pages (which will always be in multiples of four i.e. of an A4 double-page spread)
c) the number of hotels/tours to be included on each page
d) what general information should be included
e) the type and size of paper to be used
f) any special design features to be included

The creative brief should also indicate the maximum cost budgeted for each brochure, which is usually between 50p and £2. The biggest operators may budget to produce more than a million copies of their brochure, the medium-sized ones about 500,000.

The creative brief will be drawn up early in the year, and the designers will then start work, in constant contact with the operator, aiming to have the brochure format ready by spring. Large operators have facilities to design and produce their own brochures, sometimes under the remit of the sales and marketing department. Smaller ones traditionally put the work out to designers and printers, in which case the design studio comes up with ideas for the cover as well.

Photographs for the brochure can come from:

- a commercial picture library, e.g. Spectrum Colour Library
- the hoteliers
- national tourist offices
- professional photographers
- tour leaders or guest lecturers

While designers are working on the creative brief, the contractors must be working out the holiday costings so that they will be ready to coincide with the brochure going to print. Final costings are held back as long as possible in the hope of undercutting competitors and to take into account as many unexpected circumstances as possible.

The designers produce a 'pagination' sheet which lists the contents of the brochure and highlights the most important hotels, usually those for which contractors have made a commitment (*see* page 61). Then they produce a mock-up of the brochure on thick boards. At this point there is still scope for the operator to suggest alterations or improvements. When the layout has been finalised, the text goes to the typesetters. If required, ABTA can check through the proofs to ensure everything contained in the text is legally accurate.

The typesetters produce the first, or 'galley', proofs from the boards and these are sent to the tour operator for checking. When they have been approved, the printers produce metal print plates from the proofs. Once this has been done it becomes expensive to make further alterations. From these metal plates the printers produce another set of proofs, or 'ozalids', which are again sent to the operator for checking. Finally a set of full colour proofs is produced and checked.

At this stage the brochures are ready to be printed and bound. The pages are run off and then trimmed and bound by a finisher who may work for the printer. The finisher will also put any last touches, like lacquering, gloss finishes to the cover and foil backing, to more upmarket brochures.

Finally, the brochures are sent out for distribution.

Nowadays, some smaller operators may opt to forego using outside printers and instead produce the brochure themselves on a desk-top publishing computer. One company that does this successfully is Panorama Holiday Group. Everything, from typing up the text to checking the proofs and colour mark-ups, can then be done in-house, at a considerable saving not just in cost but also in time for different bits of the brochure to travel backwards and forwards to the printer's.

1. The creative brief is drawn up.
2. The designer produces a layout to an agreed format.
3. The copy is written and photographs are assembled.
4. Booking and insurance details are drafted.
5. The front cover is designed.
6. Mock-ups of the brochure pages are created.
7. The mock-ups are transferred to the typesetter and galley proofs produced.
8. The proofs are corrected and approved.
9. Colour proofs are produced and checked.
10. The price panels are added in.
11. The final proofs and colours are agreed.
12. The brochures are printed and finished.
13. The brochures are distributed.

Fig. 5.12 The brochure production process

One brochure or more?

In the 1970s and early 1980s, the big tour operators produced one comprehensive brochure detailing all their holidays. However, by the late 1980s they were offering so many holidays of so many different types and to so many different destinations that this approach no longer made much sense. Nowadays they are more likely to produce one main summer sun brochure, supplemented with a number of more specialised brochures. It is cheaper to produce and distribute the smaller brochures. What's more, it is less wasteful and allows better targeting of markets, since people can home in on a smaller brochure offering holidays tailored to their own needs rather than taking a larger, more expensive brochure, when only two or three pages are relevant to their needs. However, agencies have limited rack space and may be reluctant to rack multiple brochures from one tour operator.

Conversion ratios

The 'conversion ratio' is the phrase used to describe how many brochures will have been given out to achieve one booking. Ideally operators hope to get six or seven confirmed bookings for every 50 brochures produced but this may not always be possible. The conversion ratio is to a large extent controlled by travel agents rather than the operators themselves. In 1993 it was estimated that the average brochure cost 72p to produce but that conversion rates were so low that holidaymakers were sometimes paying as much as £20 for brochure wastage, concealed within the overall price of the trip. Some operators were said to have conversion ratios as poor as 32 brochures for every one booking. But a BP Travel Trade Services survey in 1993 suggested that only 44 per cent of travel agents (31 per cent of independents) even kept records of the brochures they ordered. Without such information they were unlikely to be aware of how poorly they were performing.

The cost of producing the brochures is passed on to the customer via the overall holiday price. So if a brochure has cost £2 to produce and 8 of them are needed to generate one booking, then £16 of the holiday price may be attributed to providing the brochure.

BROCHURE DISTRIBUTION

Once the brochures have been printed the tour operators will want to get copies to travel agents as quickly as possible. Some copies will also be mailed direct to clients who have indicated that they want to book directly with the company. Big operators like Thomson organise their own brochure distribution network, but smaller companies may depend on specialist companies like BP Travel Trade Services to do it for them.

Bulk supplies of brochures will need to be mailed to travel agents who sell the operator's product. This must be done as quickly as possible, but, to ensure agents have something to work from until bulk supplies reach them, operators may send out promotional packs with an office copy of the brochure and a letter from the sales and marketing manager, highlighting the main features. The promotional pack may also contain posters to go in the window indicating that the product is now on sale and some looseleaf booking forms.

By 1994 there were 7010 ABTA travel agencies. It would be too expensive for most operators to send bulk brochure supplies to all of them, so only the biggest have an **intensive distribution system**, covering most outlets. Others prefer a **selective distribution system** which prioritises some agencies above others. For example, priority may go to agencies in towns with airports used by the operator; so bulk supplies may be sent to Manchester before Bradford if the operator uses Manchester airport but not Leeds/Bradford. This policy means agencies in the south tend to get priority since people often opt for southern airports in preference to those in the north because the airport supplements are lower.

Tour operators grade travel agencies according to their sales record, although it may take two or three years for a pattern to emerge. The agencies with the best sales record will be sent the most brochures. An agency with a good sales record may receive 500 copies, whereas one with a poor sales record will only receive 20. Where a distribution company is being used they will have to be sent details of what to send where.

Agencies usually receive about 30 per cent of their total brochure allocation at the start of the booking season, perhaps five or six days after the office copy arrives. Another 30 per cent will be delivered within the next six weeks. After that there will be two more deliveries of about 15 per cent each. The agency can ask to be sent the other 10 per

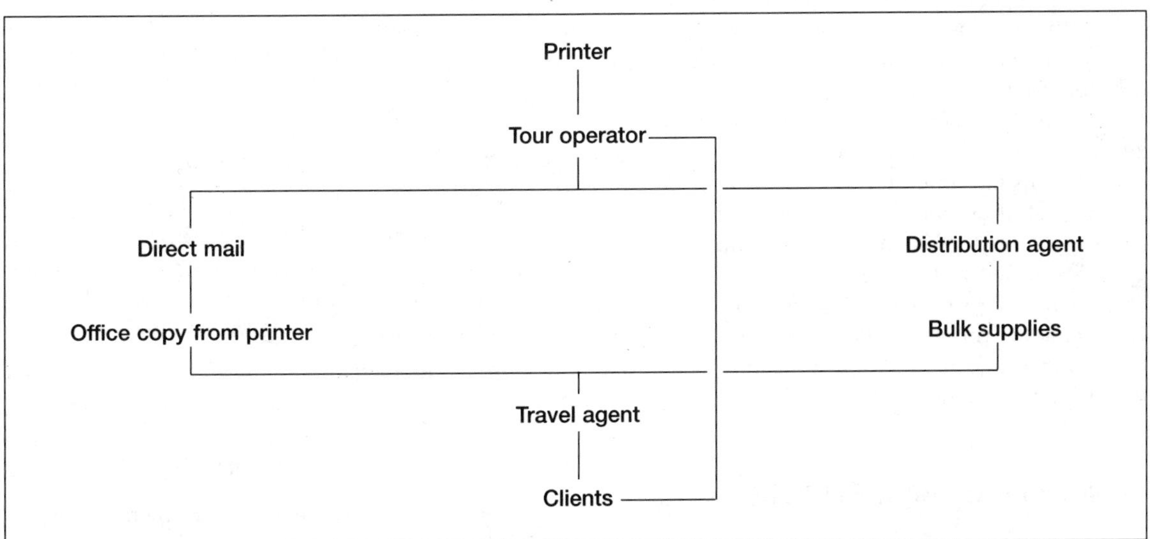

Fig. 5.13 How brochures reach the client

cent at any time. All in all, an agency with a good sales record may receive five or six brochure deliveries over the season.

How brochures reach travel agencies

There are three main ways in which tour operators get their brochures to the agencies:

1. By parcel carrier

The quickest method is to use a specialist postal carrier like the Royal Mail's Parcelforce. Brochures can be collected daily and delivered overnight via mechanised local sorting offices. Heavy lorries are not required which makes delivery to busy shopping centres with parking problems easier.

2. By haulier

Alternatively, operators may use a haulier (a company specialising in transporting goods by road) for bulk brochure delivery. However, this is slower than using a normal parcel delivery service.

3. Consolidated delivery

The cheapest method of delivery is for an operator to have its brochures delivered together with those of other operators, either in one large parcel, or in a bundle of separate parcels strapped together. However, although this is a way for small companies to keep delivery costs down, consolidated deliveries take longest to reach their destination. What's more, the arrival of a mixed bag of brochures does not usually make such an impact on a travel agent as the arrival of a single operator's.

The cost of distribution will have to be added to that of printing the brochures in working out which agencies get what. If there are about 7000 agencies and each were to receive just 50 brochures, that would mean printing 350,000 brochures. If it cost £1 to deliver each bale that would mean £7,000 in distribution costs alone.

A closer look at BP Travel Trade Services

Based in Ashford, Kent, BP Travel Trade Services has been working with the travel industry since 1972. Its 2.4 million cubic feet of warehouse space store packaging, assembly and shrink-wrap facilities. BP packs up brochures for operators and sends them to Tufnells Parcels Express in Northampton for delivery. Each parcel has a unique number to identify it, so it can be tracked if necessary. BP also provides the following services to more than 500 clients:

1. **Brochurebank** – an on-line brochure ordering service accessible via Fastrak, Istel or New Prestel. Travel agents are not charged for using it to encourage them to do so. By signing up for Brochurebank, operators ensure their names will be seen regularly by agency users. The service is used by Haven, First Choice and Hayes and Jarvis, among others.
2. **Brochure despatch** – Standard Service despatches brochures to ABTA agencies around the UK every three working days. Exclusive Service offers a daily delivery tailored to an individual operator's needs.
3. **Masterfile** – a constantly updated list of travel agencies which tour operators can grade according to their sales records to determine who gets what.
4. **Brochure Manager System** – supplies statistics and makes it possible to calculate conversion ratios and plan deliveries.
5. **Mailbag** – a twice weekly mailing to High Street travel agencies which can be tailored to deliver only to, for example, multiples or agencies with IATA licences. Mailbag Coach World mails 3,700 coach operators.
6. **Faxmail** – enables operators to fax 3,900 travel agencies, or a selection of them.
7. **Brochureline** – a 12-hour a day, 7-day a week telephone answering service for agents to order brochures. An operator can choose to have its own private line or to share a communal one.
8. **Holidayfinder/Flightfinder** – a viewdata system to show late availability for an 8-week period. Operators can opt for 'preferred' status in which case their name is highlighted in gold.
9. **Merchandising service** – to get merchandise to 7,000 agencies.
10. **Briefing service** – a member of BP's uniformed

field sales staff will visit agents and brief them on the operator's new product, highlighting its unique selling points, leaving a file copy and checking that brochures are being displayed.

Other mailings

Tour operators also need to circulate leaflets and posters to travel agencies. Some of these will be sent out through the normal mail services. However, once again, operators can have their mailings consolidated with those of other companies for economy. BP Travel Trade Services offer a consolidated mail service to do this and will also design and print leaflets; typical cost would be about £92 to design and print 1,000 two-colour, one-sided A4 leaflets, with each additional thousand run off costing another £32.

Distributing companies tend to get particularly busy when holiday sales are slow and when operators may be sending out lots of details of late availability or special offers. However, increasingly this sort of information is relayed to agents via computerised information systems like Istel. Some companies have their own pages in the system, in which case they can update them directly. Others buy pages through 'umbrella' information providers, or make use of 'digest' pages like those of Holidayfinder 2900 which show tour operators' availability on a daily basis.

Even with the most efficient distribution system, travel agents still run out of brochures, especially towards the end of the season. Most will keep at least a company file of each brochure they use so that they can refer to it, although nowadays, with computerised systems, some are happy just to work through screens of information with would-be customers. AT & T Istel had also been working on the Eurotop project, which would have made it possible for agents to call up pictures of hotels and descriptions of restaurants, etc. from operator's brochures onto their screens. It was hoped this would enable operators to reduce print and supply costs. However, in 1993 the project came to a halt as investment funds dried up.

Alternatives to the brochure

Even the best brochures suffer from the fact that they have to represent three-dimensional products in a flat, two-dimensional way. As home ownership of videos became commonplace in Britain in the 1980s, some tour operators began to produce VHS videos to depict their most popular destinations. Although these still cannot transmit the entire reality of any particular holiday, they are more vivid than picture representations and are therefore likely to become more popular; in particular they are good at giving a better idea of more exotic destinations. The main deterrent is that whereas brochures are currently free, videos must usually be purchased for normal video prices of around £12 a time. However, some agents hire out videos at a more reasonable price and deduct the rental fee from the price of any ensuing firm booking.

In 1994, Thomas Cook pioneered a 'Travel Kiosk', offering an interactive holiday brochure which enabled clients to browse through pages of their City Breaks and Euro Disney brochures on screen, pressing buttons to see more details of anything interesting. Then they could use a video phone to contact the Peterborough head office to book and pay by credit card, getting a printed confirmation of booking from the machine. If successful, similar kiosks could be installed in supermarkets and banks.

CD-Rom technology uses compact discs to store vast quantities of pictures and data which can then be called up on screen at will. This, too, has obvious potential for use in place of the traditional brochure.

QUESTIONS AND DISCUSSION POINTS

1 The more brochures are picked up without bookings being made from them, the higher holiday costs have to be to pay for them. Discuss ways in which brochure conversion rates can be improved and who is able to influence them.

2 Make a list of all the risks a holidaymaker runs when travelling abroad. Which of these do you think they should be specifically warned about in advance? Whose responsibility is it to see that the client understands all the risks – the tour operator's or the travel agent's? Is a brochure the best way to pass the information to the client?

3 At the moment the brochure is a vital selling tool for tour operators. How else can they publicise their holidays? Is the prospect of travel agencies without brochures a likely one? If not, why not?

ASSIGNMENTS

1 You work for a design company which hopes to win a contract to produce the brochures for a medium-sized tour operator. This is a new field of business for you so you need to carry out some background research to prepare yourself.

Collect six brochures from a local travel agency and analyse their design, paying attention to:

a) the company logo (*see* pages 196–7)
b) the front cover design
c) the contents page
d) one resort introduction page
e) one main page with information about a hotel and picture(s) of it
f) a typical price panel (this may appear on the same page as (e) above)
g) the flight information panel

Your analysis should include looking at why certain images have been chosen, the colours used, how clearly information is presented, etc. Make sure you know what market the brochure was designed to appeal to.

Summarise your findings and present them in report format with a conclusion explaining which design you found best and why. Not all your winning designs need to come from the same brochure.

2 You have been given the task of checking the proofs of a brochure before they are set at the printers. Read through the text and mark the corrections that need to be made with the symbols shown on the chart of proof corrections on page 137.

DISCOVER
BODRUM

Bodrum . . . all the excitement and buzz of a sophisticated resort, a truly magnificent castle and colourful yacht marina within a beautiful setting, make this the holiday capital of the Aegean coast.

The easy combination of East and west thriving side by side has attracted visitors from all over the world and made it a lively, cosmopoltan resort, like no other. Yet much of the magic of Bodum lies in the beauty of the place. against a backdrop of rolling hills, whitewashed villas and palm-lined streets, the two adjoining bays of Bodrum are guarded by the strikig Crusader castle of St. Peter. By night, Bodrum really comes into its own. It's dazzling variety of bars, lokantas and restaurants on the waterfront and in the winding streets buzz with activity Don't miss Bodrum's famous Halikarnas Disco and laser show built close by the sea in the form of an amphitheatre.

- The perfect place for lively, fun-filled nights and enjoyable, sunfilled days
- Western sophistication with a distinctive turkish flavour
- easy access to the beachs of Gumbet and Turgutreis

From Adnan Menderes or Dalaman Airport to Bodrum: 3hrs 10 mins – 4 hours by coach.

FLIGHT DETAILS

GATWICK	Friday, Wednesday
* STANSTED	Wednesday
BRISTOL	Wedneday
* CARDIFF	Wednesday
* EAST MIDLANDS	Wednesday
BIRMINGHAM	Wednesday
MANCHETSER	Friday, Wednesday
* NEWCASTLE	Wednesday
GLASGOW	Wednesday

RESORT FACT FILE

- **General Character:** Very lively, cosmopolitan resort with an intriguing mix of East and West in a setting.
- **Highlights:** Spectacular castle exciting nightlife and colourful yacht harbour. Good base for exploring classical Turkey.
- **Negatives:** Never completely quiet.
- **Beach:** Ten minutes by°dolmus to Gumbet's sandy beach. Also dolmus to nearby beaches of Bitez and Turgutreis.
- **Watersports:** It possible to hire boats for water-skiing and paragliding.
- **Discos:** A choice, including the excellent Haliarnas disco.
- **Bars/Restaurants:** Plenty to choose from. From fast food and European to the many fish and traditional restaurats.
- **General Facilities:** Supermarkets, banks, chemists, doctor and post office.
- **Transport:** Frequent dolmus services to villages all around the peninsular. Also, daily ferries across to Greek island of Kos.
- **Suits:** Those looking for plenty to do!

HOTEL MAYA

The Maya offers comfortable accommodation in a very peaceful location, yet within a few minutes' walk of the resortcentre and about 150 metres from the harbour. The hotel offers a fine range of facilities including a small gym, suna and table tennis the swimming pool has a large terrace area and bar and there is also a childrens pool.

- Cpmfortable accommodation
- Swimming pool and children's pool
- Restaurant and leafy open-air terrace
- Good facilities
- Map reference B3

Prices are per person for bed and breakfast in a room with to or three beds, shower and w.c.

HOTEL ALIZE

this charming and attractive hotel is set right in the hart of Bodrum, and is ideal for those who want to be within a stone's throw of the centre. The Alice offers clean and simple accomodation, a cosy lounge and an attractive swimming pool area. For those of you who choose to stir from the poolside, Gumbet beach is easily accessable by dolmus, and in the evening, there are bars and restaurants nearby.

- Lovely swimming pool area
- A pleasant and charming hotel
- Located right in the heart of Bodrum
- Map ref C/D5

Prices are per person for bed and breakfast in a room with two beds, shower and w.c. Some double beds are available.

PANSIYON MANDALIN

The freindly Mandalin is owned and run with the Hotel Maya and shares its gardens, swimming pool, gymnasium and sauna, bars and restaurant. Breakfast is taken at the hotel. The accommodation, although simple, is clean and comfortable. Its situation is exsellent with the harbour and promenade less than two minutes' stroll away.

- Simple, comfortable, clean accommodation
- Full use of Hotel Mayas' facilities
- Very close to harbour and town centre
- Warm welcome
- Map reference B3

Prices are per person for bed and breakfast in a room wuth two beds, shower and w.c. Some double beds are avaliable.

Proofreading correction conventions

When correcting proofs, you should use the following marks which are familiar to printers:

Margin mark / Meaning

An invitation to meet ABTOF!

Margin mark / Meaning

On Wednesday 1st December 1993 ABTOF will be introducing itself to the Press at the New Connaught Rooms, Great Queens Street, London WC2. We are delighted to take this opprtunity to invite you to meet our members and other important figures in the French Tourism Industry over a buffet luncheon from 1pm to 3.30pm. To join us, simply fill in the enclosed registartion form and return it to us by fax or post before November 24th.

Change letter o/

Transpose letters

Here are three good reasons to attend:

1. Get to know ABTOF!

Delete letter and close space

The Association of British Tour Operators to France respresents the majority the of British travel Trade specialising in France. Over 100 Tour Operators make up the membership of ABTOF, ranging in size from the smallest one-man concern to the very largest operators. **The unifying factor is their interest in France as a holiday destination.**

Change to capital letter ≡/

Transpose words

The majority of ABTOF member companies will be attending the luncheon – mostly represented by their key decision makers – an virtually all of them will have their new brochures out for 1994, making this an ideal opportunity for you to find out how the trade views the coming year

Wrong typeface ⓧ

Insert 'd' d⅄

Insert full stop ⊙⅄

2. Collect your copy of the brand-new ABTOF Handbook and register for regular ABTOF PRESS Releases.

Change to lower case ≠

As a holiday destination, France offers a host of possibilities!

Run on

Keeping track of all of the ~~the~~ new product developments is extremely time-consuming. ABTOF has, therefore, developed a handbook which will prove to be invaluable to you – not only does it list companies by holiday types offered, but also by region and, of course, alphabetically. At our December Press Luncheon you will be able to collect a copy of the Handbook AND at the same time we shall ensure that you are registered to receive regular ABTOF Press Releases that will updateyou with all the latest developments in travel to France.

Delete word

Insert space

3. Exclusive Statements from ABTOF Sponsors

M. Patrick Goyet, Director of the French Government Tourist Office, will address the luncheon on the French view of tourism trends in France. Other ABTOF sponsors, including Eurotunnel, National Breakdown, Europcar and Travellog Systems, will also be present. All of these companies have a major influence on the shape of travel to France and all of them are keen to issue statements and comments at the ABTOF Press Luncheon that will be exclusive to those journalists and travel writers attending the function.

Start new paragraph

Reduce space between words

Cancel indent

The occasion will also provide an excellent opportunity for you to 'corner' key decision makers from these companies to put your own questions to them.

3 You are a writer who wants to find work preparing brochure copy for a local tour operator. Visit a local hotel and write a short description of it, using the text in assignment 2 as an example of what to include. If possible, take a photograph to go with your description. Write a brief description of your town/village to accompany the hotel text. Finally, write a covering letter to the operator, explaining who you are and what you would like to do. Attach the two pieces of text and the photograph to your letter.

4 Read through the descriptions of India and Sri Lanka below which appeared in tour operators' brochures.

Visit the library and see what you can find out about these two countries. Good books to consult might include: the *ABTA/ANTOR World Travel Guide,* Lonely Planet's guidebooks to India and Sri Lanka and the *Amnesty International Handbook.*

Decide whether or not the brochure descriptions provide an accurate and full enough picture of these countries to prepare visitors for what they will find in them. Choose one or other of the two countries and write another introduction which, in your opinion, would be better than the ones given. Your rewrite need not take the same format as the originals.

INDIA

1. For the serious traveller, the Indian sub-continent is a magnet of vivid spectacle and excitement . . . it leads from one unforgettable scene to another, from one unforgettable memory to the next. The picture is an ever-changing one of scene, dress, language and food, where mere words fail to do justice to these splendid sights. Tours to India will constantly provide the visitor with an almost unbelievable variety of sights and monuments, all of which testify to the past of this cradle of culture and history. Then there is Goa, a unique blend of Portuguese and Indian ancestry where golden beaches stretch for mile after mile, where the pace of life is languid and the climate superb. All of this is India . . . a vast panorama which dazzles the eye and stimulates the mind.

   Our Opinion
   The Indian sub-continent is like no other with its great variety of scenery, sightseeing, food and mind-boggling array of castles and religious sects. As the second most populated country in the world, the sheer numbers of people are impressive while the bureaucracy for which India is famous means that two essential prerequisites for the traveller here are patience and a sense of humour, particularly at airports!

2. A visit to India is a unique experience . . . the extraordinary blend of races, religions and cultures offers such a feast of exotic sight and sensation that one single visit could never be enough. Each province or state of India is almost a world in itself, with contrasts that range from the hustle and bustle of Delhi through the sun-baked deserts of Rajasthan and down to the enticing palm-fringed beaches of Goa on the Arabian sea . . . At first, some of the contrasts are almost bewildering in their magnitude, but it's these which make a visit to India so rich and varied, the very essence of the country's magical charm.

   Our Opinion
   To see India's fascinating sights means covering long distances often in extreme heat. Travelling is made easier by the good hotels we have chosen throughout and by early starts in the cool of the morning (though transport is good, flights within India are often subject to delays and overbookings). Indian people are courteous and welcoming, making you feel an honoured guest in their country, but you will experience a culture shock and a slow pace of life. Indian food is superb . . . but be cautious initially.

SRI LANKA

1. Sri Lanka, the Resplendent Isle, known to the Arabs as Serendib, is well named. For few countries have such an exotic combination of beauty, serenity, mystery and excitement as this captivating island set like a green, pear-shaped gem at the foot of India. With its fabulous beaches it's hard to imagine a more seductive place for just lazing in the sun. For the curious Sri Lanka offers a wealth of dramatic sights and beautiful scenery, and a breathtaking confection of rugged mountains, lakes, high plains, lush jungles and cool rolling uplands where the green carpet of tea plantations is splashed with the vivid colours of the pickers' saris. You can explore the vast ruins of 'lost' cities, elaborate temples and shrines dating back over 2500 years, as well as churches and forts left by the Portuguese, Dutch and British. Little wonder that Ceylon has caught the imagination of travellers for centuries.

Our Opinion
Sri Lanka is often called the Garden of Eden and despite its past troubles it would be hard not to succumb to the island's quite extraordinary beauty. Entertainments and resort facilities can be limited, but the often slow service comes with a smile, the beaches are lovely and the scenery and sights superb.

2. Sri Lanka, the tropical teardrop island at the toe of India, never fails to weave its spell over even the most practised of travellers. Mystical ancient cities, thick jungles, cool hill stations and of course miles of palm-fringed sandy beach are hard to resist. And as if all that were not enough to lull the senses, the people themselves, with traditions that are steeped in the gentle faith of Buddhism, always have a ready smile and a warm welcome for the foreign visitor.

Our Opinion
One of the most beautiful and scenically interesting islands in the world. Costs are incredibly low and the people very hospitable indeed. There's something to suit all tastes here with superb beaches, plenty of cultural attractions and a host of interesting sights. Entertainment though is limited here and simple cuisine is the norm. Some of the resthouses on the tour and the lower grade beach hotels are simple and beach swimming on the west coast can be dangerous during the rainy season from May to October.

5. Take one summer sun and one long-haul brochure and use them to compile a list of all the descriptive words and phrases that appear over and over again regardless of the destination, creating the effect known as 'purple prose'. Take one destination and write a new description of it using as few of these cliched words and phrases as possible. In groups compare your efforts with the original descriptions. Do you think it would still be possible to sell holidays on the basis of your (hopefully more moderate) descriptions?

CHAPTER 6

Reservations and administration

LEARNING OBJECTIVES

After reading this chapter you should be able to:

- **describe the work of the main administrative departments of a medium-sized UK tour operator**
- **explain the different ways in which holiday reservations are made, and weigh up the pros and cons of computerised *vis-à-vis* manual systems**
- **describe the role of the sales representative**
- **list the paperwork and administration required to back up each booking**

INTRODUCTION

All UK tour operators have head offices where their products are designed and put together and from where the sales effort is directed. In a medium-sized company, reservations and administration are usually handled by discrete reservations and administration departments, and there may also be a special late bookings department and a section to deal with clients' queries after making their bookings. Some operators will also have their own retail division handling any direct sales to the public and perhaps some specialist functions like conference and incentive bookings.

By the time the brochure has been printed the tour operator must have employed enough sales reservations staff to be able to handle any direct bookings from the public or travel agents and any queries from agents with access to the operator's own computer. Until the early 1980s all holiday reservations had to be made manually, by means of complex charts. Computerisation has now revolutionised the tour operations business and only small, specialist companies continue to use chart systems for making reservations. All tour operators receive a small number of direct bookings from the public, especially from repeat bookers. However, some companies prefer to do all their selling direct with the public, thereby cutting out the travel agent's middleman role. Home computer and teletext technology hold out the prospect that eventually all bookings will be made direct with the operator from the client's home.

The typical tour operator's year might look something like this:

January–March – traditional peak booking season. Most administration staff dealing with phone enquiries, and processing booking forms and deposits.
Late February/early March – sending out invoices for April/May departures. By the end of March operators like to have sold about 60 per cent of their summer capacity.
Late March/early April – sending out tickets, vouchers, baggage labels and travel details.
May – launch of winter sun/winter ski brochures and burst of promotional activity.
Mid-May/early June – dealing with late summer bookings.
Late June – sending out documentation for peak season travellers (very busy time).
July – preparations start for the next season.
Mid-August – launch of new summer sun brochures, followed by burst of promotional activity.
Late August – staff holidays once peak season has passed.

Traditionally, January and February were the peak booking months for summer sun operators. However, by the 1990s more and more clients, particularly those without children who could be more flexible over dates, were leaving their holiday decisions until later in the year. There may also be a burst of late booking in July and August if the weather in the UK has been poor and people are hoping to squeeze in a week in the sun to make up for it. However, January and February remain very important to direct-sell operators who focus much of their mailing and advertising on this period.

THE UK RESERVATIONS AND ADMINISTRATION DEPARTMENTS

In the smallest companies all members of staff may share the administrative functions. Where the company sells several different products, individual staff members may look after all the administrative functions for one particular product or geographical area. In larger companies, however, there will be separate reservations and administrative departments.

1. Reservations

The reservations department employs staff to handle bookings from travel agents and the public. Most such departments are fully computerised and staff will usually wear telephone headsets to talk to customers, freeing their hands to operate the computer keyboard. Reservations staff need to be able to advise on suitable holidays in just the same way as travel agents, although obviously they only handle their own company's products and so should have a more detailed knowledge of them. Ski operators may have a special subsection of reservations specifically to deal with group bookings which, because they involve large numbers of people, can become very complicated, with frequent name changes and alterations; they also tend to generate more queries than standard bookings.

2. Operations administration

This department may have four separate sections:

(i) Staff in processing will check bookings and make sure confirmation invoices are sent out.
(ii) Staff in ticketing have responsibility for issuing the tickets and passing them to documentation.
(iii) Staff in documentation will send out itineraries, tickets, luggage labels, vouchers, information booklets, etc. once the holiday has been paid for in full.
(iv) Staff in manifests produce passenger lists (manifests) for each holiday and despatch them to the airlines, hoteliers, ground handling agents and resort reps.

3. Client services

In small operations any enquiries clients have after their booking is made will be handled by the same staff who made the booking. However, in medium-sized companies there may be special staff to handle any questions that arise before, after and during the holiday.

4. Late bookings

Again, in small companies late bookings will be handled by the main reservations staff. However, in medium-sized companies there may be a special section to handle these time-consuming bookings and to make the necessary phone calls to resorts to find extra beds and to airlines/air brokers to find extra seats. Obviously, increased computerisation is making their task far easier.

5. Retail operations

Some companies have one or two retail offices as well as their head office. These may be open to the public to handle direct bookings, and may also handle specialist business which might be related to:

- conference and incentive travel
- business travel

MANUAL RESERVATION SYSTEMS

Originally all holiday bookings had to be made manually. Once the programme had been agreed, all the holidays were listed either on card index cards or on a wall chart. Aircraft seats and hotel rooms would be listed on a week-by-week basis and each room and seat would be given a code which could be combined with the holiday date and duration to create a unique booking reference. For example, 2010T5202114 might indicate a 20 October departure, using twin room number 5 and flight seats 20 and 21, for a stay of 14 days.

Whenever an enquiry was received, staff would check the seats and rooms available. The system for marking the booking then varied. With some systems, if the client wanted to take out an option rather than a definite booking, reservations staff would mark the number of seats and beds in some way: for example, with a red dot. When the booking form was received and the option became a firm booking, the marked symbol would be altered: for example a red dot might become a blue triangle. Other colours and symbols would be used to indicate group bookings, balances paid, special requests, tickets despatched, etc.

With other systems the wall charts would have pegs beside each flight and hotel with coloured discs hanging from them. When a booking was made discs would be removed from the appropriate pegs and put into a booking envelope marked with the booking details. When all the coloured discs had been removed from a particular peg, that holiday was sold out.

Manual systems required meticulous care on the part of reservations staff, and the larger an operation grew, the more scope there was for error. Below are listed some of the drawbacks of manual booking systems.

1 Manual systems had physical limitations, given that there was finite space for wall charts to be displayed; although Cosmos used to have a Bristol office, under the manual booking system limited wall space meant it could only handle flight departures from Bristol, Cardiff and Exeter airports.
2 Late bookings usually required separate boards, to which data from the normal boards had to be transposed when it got to within six weeks of the departure date. With limited space, several reservations staff might find themselves jostling each other to read these boards.
3 Manual systems also required laborious price calculations for every booking, leaving scope for error.
4 Once programmes got past a certain size it was easy to misread the chart columns, especially when reading them from a distance while on the phone.
5 If reservations staff failed to notice an unconfirmed option, a room might be left unsold (automated systems usually clear unconfirmed bookings out of the system automatically after a fixed period of time).
6 If a member of the sales team removed an accommodation card from a peg temporarily, to give more details to an agent, in the meantime no one else could see it. What's more, it was easy to put a card back in the wrong place after use.
7 It was possible for two members of the sales team to be dealing with enquiries about the same holiday at the same time without realising there were only two seats left. Whoever got to the board first to remove the pegs would then secure the booking, leaving the other clerk to tell the client they had been double-booked.
8 It was relatively easy to misplace a filed optional booking, making it difficult to retrieve when the client wanted to confirm it.
9 Even dependence on the writing on envelopes could be tricky, because some people's writing is hard to read and because, where options had been taken out and then released, details might have been crossed out and rewritten several times.
10 Making one straightforward booking through a manual system could take 15 minutes (longer in the case of a late booking) which was very hard on the agency's phone bill. Afterwards, the operator still had to spend more time on back-up paperwork.

A few small tour operators continue to use manual reservations systems because the scale of their business neither necessitates nor justifies installing an expensive computer system. However, computer reservations systems sales teams increasingly offer such favourable terms to encourage operators to sign up that the number sticking with old manual systems is rapidly diminishing. However, large operators may still use a manual system to handle new products or resorts while they assess how well they will sell.

COMPUTERISED RESERVATIONS SYSTEMS

In 1976 Thomson Holidays introduced its TRACS computer system, which later became accessible to travel agents via the viewdata TOP system, to replace the old manual system. During the 1980s, improvements in computer technology led most other large tour operators to replace their manual systems with computerised ones. Computers are now widely used for front-office functions (reservations) and back-office functions (administration, ticketing, etc.), with mid-office software often used to link up what could be two entirely separate areas of work.

When a computer system is first installed there can be problems. Not all staff will be familiar with the typewriter keyboard. Nor will they all know the necessary airport codes. Some people may also be apprehensive about the very idea of a computer. However, provided the right system has been chosen, such problems can usually be overcome with appropriate training. Once the system is up and running people usually find they can't imagine how they managed before.

Choosing the system

Because computerisation is so expensive, it is vital that the right system for the task is chosen, and this can be a time-consuming business. Before choosing a system the person in charge of selection should ensure they can answer all the following questions:

a) Why is a computer system needed? What tasks must it be able to fulfil? Are there are any other tasks it would also be able to fulfil ideally?
b) Will a particular system meet all the business's needs?
c) How much business must it be able to handle?
d) Will it be possible to upgrade the system as the business grows and changes?
e) What budget has been set aside for the project? Is it realistic?
f) What potential suppliers exist? Do you know anyone who is using a system like the one you want who can recommend a supplier?

When all these questions have been answered, the operator can draw up an ITT, or invitation to tender, asking potential suppliers to present their particular product. When all the presentations have been assessed, the operator should ask for quotations on those which look suitable. These quotes should cover the immediate cost of delivery and installation, and the ongoing costs of staff training and maintenance.

Even when a final decision has been made on which system to buy, it's essential to allow time to install the system, programme it with the requisite data, iron out any initial hiccoughs and train all the staff to use it.

Setting up the system

When the operator is using its own computerised system, data processors or reservations staff must load all the information about the holiday programme into the system at the start of each booking season.

First a **main accommodation file** will have to be set up. This will include the following information for each property used in the programme:

- accommodation type – hotel/villa/campsite/ship, etc.
- accommodation name
- address, telephone, fax and telex number
- the facilities offered
- details of acceptance of vouchers, etc.

Then, within the main accommodation file, **accommodation unit files** will need to be set up for each unit of accommodation. These will indicate:

- the unit description – room/tent/cabin, etc.
- the unit type – twin with private bath, single, twin with sea-view, etc.
- the number of beds/extra beds

Information about the availability of each unit of accommodation (whether it's on request, committed, on option, etc.) must also be fed in.

Secondly, a **main flight file** will need to be set up. This will show:

- the transport type – flight/coach/ferry, etc.
- the routeing – e.g. LGW to ATH
- the flight/transport code
- aircraft types

Transport codes will then need to be matched to departure dates, and for each departure date information will also need to be fed in about availability: whether the transport is freely available, on option, on request, committed, etc. Local departure and arrival times must also be fed in for each flight/destination.

Where the operator also sells touring holidays, files containing skeleton itineraries and information about relevant accommodation and transport will need to be set up.

The basic price of every holiday combination for every departure date will have to be programmed in, together with details of all the discounts and supplements possible. The system can also be programmed to calculate commissions on every holiday, and to work out surcharges when they are required.

Finally, files may also have to be set up with details of things like car hire which can be bought and paid for in the UK.

Choosing the right system is crucial. Ideally, it should allow for quick updating of details like new VAT rates. It should also be able to offer alternatives if a client's particular requirements are full, making it easier for the reservations clerk to switch-sell to another product. Additionally, it should enable searches to be made, based on as many variables as possible: date, accommodation type, departure airport, length of stay, etc.

Using the computer to make reservations

Most computer booking systems are programmed to process information fed in in a specific sequence. The information needed will be:

a) the destination
b) the preferred date of travel
c) the holiday duration
d) the departure point
e) the number of passengers
f) what accommodation is required
g) the passengers' names

The computer should also be able to throw up displays to answer such general enquiries as 'Where can I go on this date?', 'When can I go to . . .?', 'If I take this flight, where could I stay?' and 'When is this particular hotel available?'

Once all the information has been fed in and all questions answered, the computer will indicate whether space is available and will generate an option number. It can be programmed to release all options back into the pool of availability if they are not confirmed within a specified time. At the start of the season this may be between five and seven days after the option was taken out, although as the departure date gets closer it may be for only 24 hours, just long enough for the client to sort out payment. When the client wishes to confirm the booking, the clerk will be able to pull it up on screen by using the option number (booking locator/reference number); alternatively if the number is unavailable, the booking can be recalled using the client's lead name (the name in which the booking was made) or the departure date. The booking can then be confirmed by feeding in information about the method of payment. Once the booking has been confirmed the computer will generate a booking number in place of the option number.

If a booking is to be cancelled, it can be called up on screen and the cancellation details fed in. The computer will then calculate the cancellation costs and release the holiday units back to the availability pool, before storing the dead booking in case of future need. Similarly the booking can always be called up on screen to be amended.

In the 1990s, many operators started using a matrix grid to obtain basic information about a possible booking. With a matrix layout, the date of travel and type of holiday will be fed into the top and side of a grid and the system will flash up the cheapest applicable price. This is particularly helpful with late bookings, enabling the reservations clerk to determine at a glance whether the holiday fits within the client's budget.

Computerised booking systems have many advantages over manual ones:

1 They are faster to use and therefore cheaper.
2 Provided the information has been fed in correctly there should be less scope for error than in the old systems.
3 The computer will be able to generate a price for each individual holiday about which an enquiry is being made.
4 Computer systems have also taken the pain out of late bookings, which used to be something dreaded by operator and agent alike. In that sense it could be argued that technology has actually helped create the trend towards late bookings by making them more practical.

Computerised systems do much more than just make the reservation and cost it. They also generate confirmation ('balance due') invoices (usually with the same number as the booking reference), tickets, flight manifests, hotel rooming lists and statistics which make it easier for the company to keep track of sales. They can also be used for such mundane tasks as running off labels with the names of travel agencies on for mailings.

The confirmation invoice will normally show:

- the invoice number and whether it is a confirmation/final/revised or cancellation invoice
- the client's name and address, or the agent's address
- number of passengers and all names
- departure date
- transport details
- accommodation details and resort name
- number of nights
- car hire details, if applicable
- basic holiday price
- supplements and/or discounts
- cost of insurance
- any surcharges applicable
- cost of car hire if applicable
- note of any special requests (which may not be guaranteed)
- deposit paid
- balance due date

When bookings are made through travel agents, their copy of the invoice will have the remittance advice showing how much commission is due on the booking.

However, installing a computer is enormously expensive so a company needs to be doing enough business to justify the cost. What's more, so long as a company is very small there remains something to be said for the old wall chart system which allows an at-a-glance overview of the current situation, something which is not so easy with a computerised system.

Whichever system is chosen, it's essential that it is reliable. Just as operators lost potential clients in the past because travel agents couldn't get through on perpetually engaged phone lines, so they can still be lost if, for example, the system crashes and agents are unable to access it; with so many competing operators, chances are that the agent will try another company rather than spend time redialling their first choice. When Airtours lost out to Thomson in the frantic September 1993 bookings race, it blamed this in part on problems experienced with its reservation system which agents had sometimes been unable to access.

After the collapse of ILG in 1991, several companies computerised rapidly to enable them to take on extra windfall business (Iberotel even bought the LTS system from the ILG receivers). However, many operators really need assistance to help them arrive at the right decision. To help them, in 1991 ABTA set up a technology advisory service, Abtech, now run by the Link Initiative, an independent travel consultancy, which aims to give free and unbiased advice. Abtech now also advises AITO members.

Company name	Computer system name
Thomson	TOP
First Choice	TOFS
Airtours	SPACE
Kuoni	KUDOS
British Airways Holidays	PAL/BA-Link
Sunworld	LTS
Crystal Holidays	JFA

Fig. 6.1 Names of some tour operators' computer booking systems

Few tour operators actually want to manage their own computer systems, although most wish to retain control of the databases used. So in 1992 even Thomson put management of the TOP system out to tender; the contract was won by Midland Network Services (MNS), now renamed Imminus. Thomson hoped this arrangement would save them money on the cost of maintaining their network, especially because the 10-year-old system was becoming more costly to maintain as it aged. Dial-up travel agents (*see* below) now use Imminus/Fastrak to access TOP, although many independent agents already had direct links via AT&T Istel to TOP.

A few computer companies, including Autofile, Astrologic and FSS, specialise in supplying purpose-designed systems for tour operators.

Travel agency access to computerised systems

Thomson was the first operator to make its computer system (TOP – Thomson Open-Line Programme) accessible to agents via viewdata, and it now accepts nothing but computerised reservations from its agents. But increasingly agents now have 'real time' access to other operators' computers too, and can therefore make a booking in just the same way as if the client had phoned the operator him or herself. This has helped them in a number of ways:

1 The time spent waiting for the operator to answer the phone has been reduced.
2 The cost of phone calls to the operator has been reduced. Since the computers are accessed via telephone lines, an agent in, say, Edinburgh, might run up large phone bills for using the computer. However, most large operators offer link lines which enable big agents to access their computers for the cost of a local call.
3 The fact that the computer can work out the cost of each individual enquiry has been a particular benefit for travel agents who have to work with the products of lots of different operators, often with different methods for calculating their prices.
4 The advantage of 'real time' access is that the agent is looking at the actual availability and not just a snapshot summary of what was available at the start of the day. This avoids the frustration of the situation in which the client sees just what they'd like, only to find it's sold out when the agent gets through to the operator.
5 Paperwork has also been reduced since, in most cases, travel agents need only send a remittance slip and not an entire booking form to the operator.

Unlike airline computer systems, most tour operator computer systems have been designed to be user-friendly, making it possible for agents to use them without elaborate training and discouraging them from reverting to using the phones. From the client's point of view the main problem is that each system is unique to one operator, so, although when an agent feeds in a suggested date the system will search through all that operator's products for something suitable, it cannot cross-check availability with other companies simultaneously; to do this the agent must leave one system and clock into another which can be offputtingly slow. In 1994, AT&T Istel reintroduced a centralised database for late bookings. It was intended that small and medium-sized operators would send details of their late availability to this one focal point which could then be accessed by travel agents, a cheaper and more efficient means of reaching them than faxing or mailing them individually.

Most retail travel agents still use viewdata/videotext systems, rather than more powerful personal computers which can carry out ticketing, invoicing, accounting and other administrative functions as well as simply booking package holidays. The chief advantage of viewdata from their point of view is that it uses simple commands which mean staff need little training to be able to use it. The three most important suppliers of viewdata systems for travel agencies in 1993 were:

AT&T Istel
Imminus – Fastrak
New Prestel

Direct-connect services enable agents to pay a single annual fee for access to the system regardless of how often they actually use it. In contrast, with dial-up services agents must pay a local call charge every time they use the system.

From the tour operator's point of view, giving more agents access to their computer systems frees their own reservations staff to handle queries from non-computerised agents and members of the public more quickly. For example, in 1993 Unijet was still receiving 6,000 phone calls a day to its reservations department, despite all its programmes being accessible on viewdata. As long as this was the case it needed to retain an unnecessarily large reservations force of its own, so one of its main objectives for 1993/4 was to familiarise agents with the system and persuade them to use it to sell all their products instead of phoning. British Airways Holidays reckoned that it lost about 20 per cent of its phone calls because only 20 per cent of their bookings came in through the PAL system, leaving reservations staff too busy to answer all the phone calls. Before Seasun Tentrek went into liquidation in 1993, it also complained that it had had trouble persuading agents to use its system instead of phoning.

However, not all operators find that viewdata works for them. In 1993 Cadogan withdrew its viewdata service to agents, concluding that only seven per cent of their business was coming through viewdata at an annual cost of £20,000. Their average holiday sold for £680 a head (as compared to an industry average of £346), and people paying as much as that were often booking something either tailor-made or needing a lot of discussion, necessitating a phone call to the operator. It is also arguable that increased computerisation has had the effect of distancing the operator from its agents in a way which wasn't the case when individual agents would be phoning up regularly.

Whatever system is being used, it's vital that it should be reliable. At the start of the 1994 summer booking period, Airtours was believed to have lost a lot of reservations when its system crashed. Even Thomson had some problems with its system in 1994.

The way ahead for computerised booking systems

Increasingly tour operators have been exploring ways of integrating their reservations systems with the airlines' computer reservations systems (or CRSs). Since 1989 when Redwing linked up with the British Airways BABS computer, about 10 per cent of operators have started to use 'transparencies' which enable them to access airline reservation systems through their own computers and without having to use complex CRS language, giving them immediate access to fares and availability. Most operators have transparent links with Galileo or Worldspan. Such links are most useful to operators offering tailor-made long-haul holidays on scheduled flights and to seat-only specialists wholesaling discounted scheduled air tickets. They are of relatively little use to short-haul operators using charter services.

Enabling operators to use transparent links to make hotel bookings has proved harder than enabling them to book flights, partly because many hotels are unenthusiastic about putting new rates for tour operators on CRSs and partly because most operators prefer to continue to contract their own rates with the hotels rather than use industry-wide rates available through a computerised system. Many small independent hotels don't store their rates on CRSs anyway. Some companies like Crystal Holidays and Ultimate Leisure already offer agents the possibility of tailor-making holidays through their viewdata systems; they do this by using transparent links to CRSs for flight availability and then providing information about hotels from their contracted allocations through their own computers.

At present travel agents usually invest in CRSs to handle their business travel accounts but not their leisure requirements. It would only be worth their while extending CRSs to leisure if the systems could handle package holidays as well as airline, hotel and car hire reservations. With this in mind American Airlines CRS operator Sabre is currently examining the possibilities.

Until mid-1993, Thomson was working with Galileo and AT&T Istel to develop a personal computer- (or PC-) based technological system which would combine CRS (computer reservation system) and viewdata functions through a single terminal. This project was called GTI and involved replacing slow viewdata messaging with quicker electronic data interchanging, or EDI. Airtours and Owners Abroad had also expressed interest in the new system which would have cut operators' networking costs to agencies and enabled agents to make bookings more quickly, freeing them to handle more enquiries. However, in May 1993 Lunn Poly decided it wouldn't be interested in using the system, effectively signing the project's death warrant since it would have needed retailer support to make it commercially viable. As the multiple chains increasingly focused on promoting the products of their owner-operators, they had less reason to be interested in a non-company specific system, especially if it would involve expensive updating of their existing computer equipment. Vertically-integrated multiple agencies also wanted to be able to control how their owner-operators' products appeared on the front screen which would not have been possible with GTI.

Despite the collapse of the GTI project, the Travel Technology Initiative (TTI), which also aimed to harness electronic data interchange to enable operators' and agents' computers to talk to each other, remained in action, with 80 operators (including Airtours and Owners Abroad), agents and technology companies working together to develop common booking procedures and improved administrative systems.

The future?

In theory, user-friendly technological developments have made it even easier for holidaymakers to bypass travel agents. For example, an increasing number of homes now have access to Ceefax which shows holiday availability. In 1993 a company called Chauntry was also working on a new computer system which could be installed in supermarkets and which would search for holidays to match a customer's individual requirements. To do this, it would need direct access to tour operators' databases but in a more flexible manner than is currently the case, when travel agents must laboriously comb through each individual operator's system to find something suitable for their client. If Chauntry succeeds in creating such a system, holidaymakers would be able to use it to make their booking directly with the appropriate operator. Apart from being installed in supermarkets, such a system could also be accessed via cable television services.

Although few travel agents made much use of personal computers in the early 1990s, it seemed likely that this situation would change very rapidly.

BOOKING FORMS

When a booking is made via a manual system, the agent has to send the operator a booking form signed by the client which will form the basis of the contract between the operator and the client. When a computerised system is used, the operator no longer requires the agent to send in a booking form (although some may still opt to keep a signed copy on their files in case of any later query). Instead the agent will only need to send a remittance slip with the payment. This remittance slip may form part of a traditional booking form, in which case they can cut it off the bottom (*see* Fig. 5.7, page 121). Some computerised companies, including Thomson, no longer include a booking form in their brochures.

DIRECT SELL TOUR OPERATIONS

Direct sell tour operators use the same systems to make their bookings. For example, Portland Holidays' PACE (Portland's Advanced Computer Environment) system contains exactly the same information as the main Thomson TRACS system. However, all their clients contact them directly rather then going through a travel agency.

THE BOOKING SEASON

Traditionally the peak booking season for package holidays was from January to March. It was assumed that as soon as Christmas was out of the way and the dreary English winter had set in, people's minds would turn to the thought of two weeks in the sun and they would flock to the travel agencies. Consequently much travel advertising was concentrated into this period. Direct sell operators still attract most of their business in this period.

However, summer sun brochures are actually produced much earlier than this and the date has been slowly creeping forward, from September 10 years ago to mid-August by 1993. The first booking period therefore takes place from mid-August to December, and this period has become increasingly important, particularly with tour operators keen to increase their market share. In the late 1980s and early 1990s there had been an increasing trend towards late booking (*see* below), partly because, in a time of recession and high unemployment, many would-be holidaymakers were afraid to commit themselves too far in advance. Even the long-haul and cruise markets were following the late-booking trend, which was perhaps surprising given the amount of money some such holidays cost. This was very unsatisfactory for tour operators in two ways: it meant they got hold of customers' money much later in the day and so could earn less interest on investing it; and, more importantly, it was almost impossible for them to know how much of a programme was actually going to sell and so decide whether to consolidate flights and drop hotel allocations. Left with surplus holidays on their books, they were often forced to discount prices to sell them, thereby making nonsense of their forecast profits. What's more, a vicious circle was created: the more they discounted late bookings to sell them, the more holidaymakers delayed booking in the hope of getting a better deal.

By summer 1993, therefore, the emphasis had shifted to trying to sell as many holidays as possible as soon as the brochures were launched. To do this both operators and agents offered early booking discounts and other incentives, the operators justifying this by saying it was better to sell as much as possible, as early as possible, so they could tell what would be left over and make adjustments during the January to March period. Others, however, argued that in bringing forward bookings they would probably have obtained anyway, they were simply giving away money they would almost certainly have made. In 1993 such tactics proved highly successful in getting people to book early, especially for long-haul and cruise holidays where a 10 per cent discount meant the most; for example, Royal Caribbean Cruise Lines offered discounts of up to £250 to early bookers and persuaded 61 per cent to take them up. When the figures were analysed, Thomson had taken 46 per cent of the summer bookings made in September 1993, compared with 19 per cent for Airtours, 9 per cent for Owners Abroad and 6 per cent each for Cosmos and Iberotel; total sales for September 1993 were twice those for September 1992.

Regardless of these efforts to bring forward people's bookings, operators still found it hard going in the flat trading conditions of 1992 and 1993. Indeed, in 1993 it was difficult to sell May holidays without discounting which unfortunately tended to persuade the public that all they had to do was hold on and summer 1993 prices would also come tumbling down.

Similar booking patterns also apply to winter programmes, and ski operators too have started to produce their brochures (or at least preview brochures) earlier to try and persuade people to book early. In 1993 Crystal Holidays also offered £30 discounts to anyone booking from the preview brochure before the main one was produced in June in another effort to encourage early bookers.

In general it should be easy to sell the first 60 per cent of a well-designed product, but the next 30 per cent and then the crucial last 10 per cent, which often means the difference between break-even and profit, can be much harder to move.

Late bookings

Late bookings are usually defined as those made less than 56 days/8 weeks before the departure date, although some companies define anything booked up to 12 weeks before departure as a 'late' booking. They are some of the trickiest for operators to handle because they will usually have released surplus flight seats and hotel rooms held through an allocation system back to the principals to avoid being left with them unsold. This means they may need to make *ad hoc* arrangements with the airlines and hoteliers, involving faxes and/or telexes. Sometimes they will need to make arrangements with hotels not featured in their brochures. If the booking is made less than a week before the departure date the operator may need to organise 'Ticket on Departure (TOD)' facilities to enable clients to collect their tickets and documentation at the airport. Long-haul late bookings where visas need to be obtained can be particularly tricky; some companies make provision to use their contacts to get visas issued speedily, usually making a charge (perhaps £10) for the service. It can also be difficult for operators to arrange ski packs or to organise the normal range of special requests for late bookers.

Despite these difficulties, late bookings are still worth having since they offer the chance of selling flight seats right up to the date of departure, together with hotel rooms to which operators are committed. Sometimes operators will produce special leaflets or posters to publicise unsold availability. In the late 1980s and early 1990s they also resorted to discounting late bookings in order to sell them, although this tended to have the unwanted side effect of encouraging holidaymakers to book later and later in the hope of getting a better deal. Big companies review their unsold peak season prices on a daily, perhaps even hourly, basis to see if they need adjusting.

When a reservation is made within eight weeks of the departure date, operators will require the client to pay in full at the time of booking, using cash, a credit card or a guaranteed cheque issued by a bank or building society.

Late bookings take place throughout the year, but particularly in the early and late summer periods. Flight-only and ski holidays are particularly likely to be booked at the last minute.

PROCESSING THE BOOKING

Reservations can be seen as one administrative function of a tour operating business. However, there are lots of other administrative requirements too, many of them associated with processing bookings, collecting payments and ensuring all the correct documentation is despatched to agencies and direct clients in time for their departures.

When a booking form is received, the reservations department will check details of the reservation for accuracy and sort out any mistakes. It will then be passed to the accounts department for the costing to be checked and a confirmation produced. Accounts department staff will key details of the deposit required and any insurance premiums to be collected into the system; with a manual system the details will be typed up. They will also raise an invoice showing the balance to be collected and the date by which it must be paid. The company keeps one copy of the confirmation invoice. The travel agent keeps a second that will show the amount which must be forwarded to the operator after deduction of the agent's commission and the insurance premiums. A third copy will be given to the client. Once this confirmation invoice has been produced the travel agent will become liable for the holiday costs and should therefore have collected enough money from the client to cover what is owed.

Data processing staff are often in charge of running off confirmation invoices, a task which may have to be done outside normal sales hours to avoid overloading the computer. They will match the invoices with the booking forms and pass them to reservations who then forward them to the travel agent, filing the operator's copy according to departure date and destination.

Every time the booking is altered, a new invoice will have to be generated. If the booking is cancelled, a cancellation invoice showing the costs incurred will be generated and sent to the client to enable him/her to make a claim against any insurance policy he/she may have taken out. In the event that the client has already paid more than the costs incurred by cancelling, the overpayment will also have to be refunded.

Approximately ten weeks before the departure date a final balance invoice will be run off. The travel agent will then have to collect the outstanding balance and send it to the operator with a remittance slip detailing the amount.

Direct sales tour operators will have to pursue a slightly different procedure. Credit control staff and the accounts department will play a crucial role in making sure balances are not allowed to overrun because, without the intermediary of the travel agent, the tour operator will have to settle all debts to hoteliers and airlines resulting from non-payment by clients.

HOLIDAY DOCUMENTATION

General administrative staff or reservations staff will have responsibility for packing the documentation for each holiday into a cardboard wallet. This will include some or all of the following:

- joining instructions
- tickets
- accommodation vouchers
- itinerary
- baggage labels
- insurance certificate
- information on vaccinations and health precautions
- information on visa requirements
- promotional leaflets e.g. for airport car parking

Tickets

Scheduled airlines will release tickets to operators when they have been paid for them. With charter airline tickets, especially for airlines owned by the operator, the company may print its own tickets or hand-write details onto preprinted tickets. Where the operator has its own ticket stock, these must be stored safely since they can have real value.

When the operator is using a computer system, this may generate tickets automatically once information about the balance payment has been fed in. Sometimes they will be generated automatically depending on the date, in which case tickets for which final payment has not been received must be held back pending payment. Most systems will have a manual override system for ticket production as well.

Tickets must then be posted to travel agents. Redwing tried to introduce a satellite ticket printer which would have let agents print the tickets themselves, but this was not very successful, partly because of the cost to the operator of developing it and partly because agents were reluctant to invest in new printers. MNS has also developed a system called Fasticket, which operators have been similarly slow to exploit, probably because they are waiting to see what happens with ATB – the automated ticket and boarding pass system being developed by the airlines which incorporates an electronic record of the booking, aimed at increasing security, and may eventually speed up checking-in procedures. P&O European Ferries and TTI are also developing an ATB Mark Two, while car hire companies are working towards a common voucher system. Ideally, agents will want to wait until there is one system for all these tickets before investing in new printers.

Accommodation vouchers

The operator may print its own vouchers too. Some act as the actual means of payment, whereas others are simply proof that payment has been made.

Itineraries

Again, the operators will produce their own itinerary documents which will be most important in the case of tailor-made or multi-centre holidays where there is greater scope for misunderstanding or something going wrong. Details of the itinerary may come from the overseas department and may be produced by the in-house computer or printed elsewhere.

Baggage labels

As well as being used to identify whose baggage is whose, baggage labels are simultaneously used to promote the tour operator.

Joining instructions

These explain to the client when they should check-in where, and what arrangements will be made for meeting and escorting them to their resort.

Information on health requirements and visas

Although these details may not be sent out until the tickets are despatched, this is really too late. Clients need this information well in advance of their travel date in order to make arrangements for getting the vaccinations, starting the malaria tablets and organising their visas. The EC Package Travel Regulations make it obligatory for operators to provide their clients with information about visas and health requirements.

Promotional leaflets

Tour operators may send clients details of special car parking deals at departure airports, of discounts at airport hotels, and of travel merchandise like electrical adaptors, etc. In some cases, they may be paid commission if clients take up these offers, in which case they will have needed to ensure a code identifying the source appears on the documents.

INTERNAL DOCUMENTATION

Apart from the paperwork needed to process bookings and payments, and the documentation needed for each booking, the administration department will have to look after the paperwork required by the hotels and airlines.

Passenger manifests

The airline will need a **passenger manifest** listing all the clients and showing the age of any children. The reservations staff may run this off the computer together with any special requests (e.g. for kosher food or wheelchair assistance) clients may have made. They will check the names against the tickets before they are sent out. Then one copy of the manifest will be sent to the UK airport handling agent and another to the overseas representative or ground handling agent. A third copy will be kept at head office.

Similar passenger manifests, or arrivals lists, are produced for coach tours. Since these may have to be shown at borders, passenger passport numbers may have to be added to them.

Sometimes the manifests, like other documentation, will be run off outside selling hours to avoid overloading the computer. Some computers can interface with fax/telex machines, in which case copies of the manifest may be sent straight to the resort fax/telex to cut down on time and postage.

Rooming lists

One month before each departure date, reservations staff will also run off a rooming list for the hotel, indicating which types of rooms (singles, twins, etc.,) are required and what board arrangements have been booked. A copy of this list will be sent to the hotelier and to the resort representative. From these lists the hoteliers decide which rooms to set aside for which clients.

Pick-up lists

These lists show all a company's passengers on a particular flight but grouped according to tour or hotel for the convenience of the representative meeting the flight.

If any other details need to be confirmed, the operator will either mail these out to the resort representative with the rooming list or arrange a subsidiary mailing.

FORMS OF PAYMENT TO THE TOUR OPERATOR

Most operators will receive the majority of their payments in bulk by cheque from travel agencies. Direct sell operators, however, will receive payments by cheque, credit/charge card or bank/building society cheque. Occasionally, they may receive cash payment. In the case of late bookings they will want cash or credit card payment rather than personal cheques.

1. Cash payment

When an operator receives cash they will need to count it carefully, preferably in front of the client. If a particularly large sum is involved they may get someone else to check it too. Notes must be inspected to make sure they are not forgeries. Whoever receives the money should check the sum taken against the invoice to make sure it's the right amount. They should then prepare a receipt and either give it to the client or post it immediately. All cash received must be put in the till or safe immediately.

2. Cheque payment

When accepting a cheque the operator must ensure:

a) that the amounts in words and figures agree
b) that it's correctly dated
c) that it's signed
d) that it's made out to the correct company name

In addition, it's important to check against the invoice that the cheque is for the correct sum.

In general, most banks only guarantee personal cheques for up to £50 if the cheque card number has been written on the reverse by the person accepting the cheque. Banks now issue cards guaranteeing

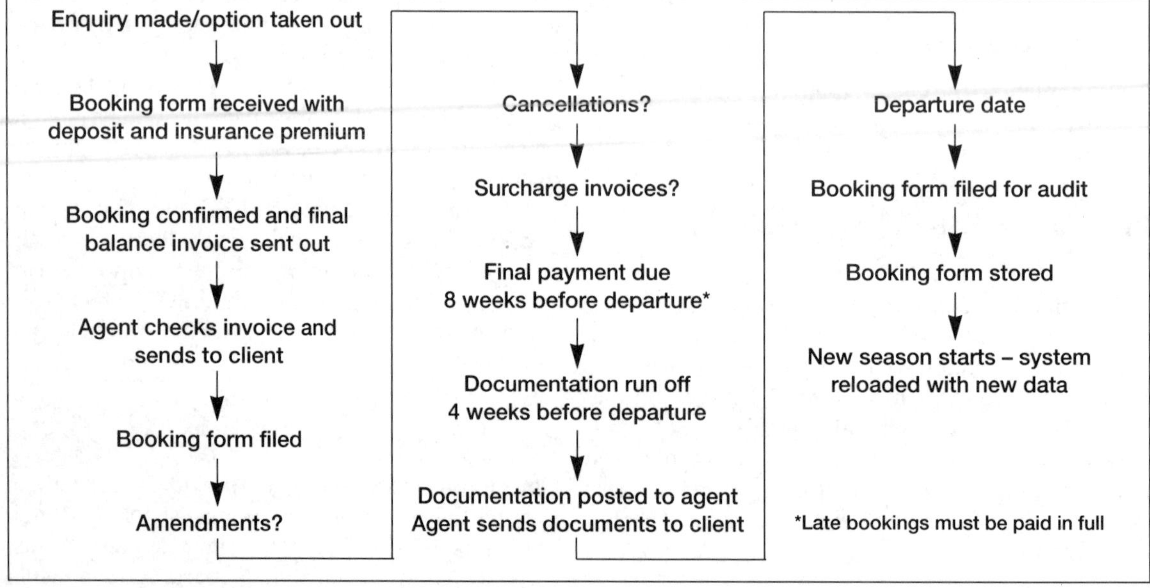

Fig. 6.2 The paper chase

£100 cheques to selected customers. It is not acceptable to write out several cheques, each of them for under £50 to cover a larger sum. Nor does the £50 guarantee apply when a cheque is issued for a larger sum; not even the first £50 will be guaranteed. Where a cheque is accepted for more than £50, enough time must be allowed for the cheque to be presented through the banking system and rejected if funds are not available to cover it. However, cheques issued by banks or building societies are guaranteed for whatever sum is written on them since they would not be issued unless the bank or building society had first checked that the client had enough funds to cover them.

3. Credit/charge card

The large tour operators now accept Visa, Access, American Express and Diner's Club cards in payment for holidays. Before accepting a card, however, they will want to get authorisation from the issuing company. The authorisation number must be recorded on the credit card form.

Credit cards are particularly useful for late bookings where immediate payment is required. The client can even arrange payment over the phone, in which case tickets can only be despatched to the address at which the card owner is registered as living.

Since the card companies charge commission for use of their cards, tour operators may be choosy about which ones they accept. In theory they can charge someone paying by credit card more than someone paying by cash or cheque, to cover the card commission.

4. Credit payment by travel agent

Most travel agents will settle their accounts with tour operators once a month with a single cheque. When this cheque is received the operator will need to check that the amount agrees with the invoices submitted and will then allocate different amounts to different bookings. In 1993, a row erupted when British Airways Holidays said in future it would only deal with independent travel agents who signed a direct debit mandate (*see* below) to let them collect their payments on a weekly basis.

5. Direct debit payment

Direct debits are a way of paying bills through the banks on a monthly basis; the person or company to whom they are being paid can apply to the bank to adjust the sum involved without first consulting the person paying, although they must be notified immediately afterwards. They are a common way of paying council tax or utility bills.

In 1993, ABTA approved a scheme for some tour operators to use direct debits as a way of collecting payment from travel agents. The Travel Agents Fund will in future reimburse operators if an ABTA agent ceases trading before a payment has been made. Airtours, Balkan Holidays, British Airways Holidays, Globespan, Hamilton Travel, Iberotravel, Inspirations, Kuoni, Leisureline, First Choice, Sunset Holidays, Thomson, Unijet and Virgin Holidays have all launched direct debit payment schemes, and computer systems specialist Autofile is expected to develop a system suitable for other operators.

OTHER ADMINISTRATIVE FUNCTIONS

Computer systems usually allow operators to set up agency files which will need to include the following information:

- name, address, telephone, fax and telex number
- ABTA/ATOL numbers
- contact name and that person's position
- description of agency
- area and nearest departure points
- category – according to volume of business

These files can then be used to keep a record of:

a) when brochures were despatched
b) what options are taken out
c) how many options become confirmed bookings
d) the agency's turnover of the operator's products

They can also be used for printing out name and address labels for the agencies. Sometimes operators will also keep separate files on non-ABTA agents as well; with the demise of Stabiliser in 1993, this is likely to be a more regular occurrence.

Producing reports

Computerisation has greatly facilitated the production of all kinds of reports summarising information on, for example, sales of the operator's own insurance policy, car hire arrangements, pre-booked excursions, ski packs, etc. Other reports can be produced to show booking patterns by week or month, and tour or holiday profitability. Year-on-year statistics can also be generated for quick comparison. All of this is enormously helpful in planning the next year's programme.

THE ROLE OF THE SALES REPRESENTATIVE

Traditionally, the biggest tour operators employed sales representatives whose job it was to visit travel agents and help them with any problems. How frequently they visited depended on the agency's sales record; the best agencies might receive visits once every six weeks, while others might receive no visits at all. However, in 1993 Airtours and Thomson axed their sales teams, leaving only Owners Abroad of the Big Three still routinely visiting agents.

Sales reps are not normally in the business of the hard sell. Instead they are supposed to help productive agents do even better by answering their queries and sorting out any difficulties they may be having, for example with brochure distribution. They may also help with window displays, ordering brochures, etc., and may even attend promotional events organised by agencies. Some will arrange training sessions for favoured agents. They also help select which individuals should be sent on company 'educational' visits to the resorts, which are often seen as a sort of 'thank you' for business already secured. Sales representatives may also escort these trips.

Where a company can't afford its own sales force, it can buy in the professional services of a company like BP Travel Trade Services which has a uniformed sales force to carry out some of the functions of a sales rep for a variety of clients; for example, checking to see that the company's brochures are being racked on delivery.

Customer relations

Inevitably, when tour operators are handling so many customers every year there will be some complaints. Many of these will be handled in resort by the company's representative. However, others will have to be dealt with by the customer relations or customer service department when the client returns home.

Operators usually describe the procedure for making a complaint in the back of their brochure. Clients are advised to raise the matter with the resort rep as soon as possible. If the problem can't be resolved, they should fill out a report form, detailing the complaint. The rep will keep a copy of this form. The client should also report his/her complaint to any third party involved (e.g. a tour bus driver, waiter, etc.). On returning home, the client should write to the customer service department explaining what happened and quoting his/her holiday booking number and report form number. Normally they are given only 28 days from the date of their return to the UK to do this.

The ABTA Tour Operators' Code of Conduct lays down guidelines for how long operators should take to react to complaints. They say that an acknowledgement should be sent within 14 days and a full reply (or an explanation for why one is not forthcoming) within 28 days. The entire matter should be resolved within 56 days (two months) of receipt of correspondence from the client.

In the event that amicable settlement still cannot be reached, the client or tour operator can refer to an arbitration scheme devised by the Chartered Institute of Arbitrators. The scheme provides 'a simple and inexpensive method of arbitration on documents along with restricted liability of the client in respect of costs', but doesn't apply to claims worth more than £1,500 a head or £7,000 in total or to claims which are mainly about physical injury, illness or the consequences of these.

ENVIRONMENTAL CONSIDERATIONS

The paperfree office seems to be as far away from tour operating as any other business. However, in the 1990s more operators were at least conscious of the possibility of running an office less wastefully. With roughly 120 million of them produced every year, brochures are one obvious area offering scope for improvement. Several companies now claim that their brochures are produced on paper from environmentally-considered sources; Thomson, for example, claims that 'the paper used in the production of this brochure . . . is made from trees grown as a commercial, renewable resource: for every tree felled at least two are planted to replace it'. Airtours notes that it does not 'use any paper material derived from the world's tropical rain forests in the production of its brochures. All paper used is manufactured from sustainable sources where a minimum of two trees replace every one used'.

However, when it comes to recycling there is still a long way to go. Asked how they disposed of surplus brochures, 67 per cent of those responding to a 1993 AFD Associates questionnaire said they sent them to the council skip and 18 per cent either didn't know or wouldn't say; only 17 per cent sent the brochures to a recycling company. Despite talk of a centralised recycling scheme for travel agencies to dispose of brochures nothing has, at yet, come of it.

In theory, technology holds out the prospect of eliminating brochures altogether, and Abtech has suggested that agencies could operate without them, using computerised pages of information instead, by 1997/8. However, people often pick up brochures to look over with their partner at home, so this is probably a more theoretical than realistic scenario.

RECRUITMENT AND TRAINING

Recruitment

Tour operators mainly recruit their staff by advertising in the travel press (*TTG*, *Travel Weekly*), although jobs in travel are so popular that they will also receive a lot of speculative enquiries about work from school and college students. Often they prefer to employ staff who have taken college courses in travel and tourism or who have had Saturday jobs in travel agencies which have given them experience of working with the public and of the travel business in general.

Training

Unlike most other types of business, tour operators must train not just their own staff but also their effective sales force – the network of travel agents scattered around the country. Normally two different groups of staff will look after the training of UK-based staff and travel agents, and the overseas staff.

1. Training the operator's own staff

Depending on the size of the company, most operators will run an induction day or week for new staff when they will be introduced to company policies and the work of the different departments. The induction process usually happens early in a new member of staff's employment, although it may not take place immediately because it makes more sense economically to wait until there are several people who can be trained together. During induction the new member of staff will learn about the company's product and be introduced to its technology. There may also be some kind of educational trip to experience some part of the programme.

Large and medium-sized companies will employ their own trainers who run courses in selling skills, telephone techniques, letter-writing and customer care skills for new staff. Individual departments may well have responsibility for job-specific training and for teaching new employees how to use the reservations system. In addition, throughout the year there may be training sessions run by representatives of the airlines, hotels and national tourist offices.

Some companies take part in the government's 18-month Youth Training programme, although openings in tour operating are far rarer than in travel agencies; Thomson for example, takes only 15 YT trainees a year. When companies do employ YT trainees they often let them work in several different departments and guarantee them a job at the end of their course if they pass all the necessary qualifications.

A few companies run graduate training schemes as well. For example, Thomson recruits ten graduates a year to work in marketing and information technology, putting them through an intensive four-month training scheme.

2. Training overseas staff

UK-based staff will also have responsibility for training staff who are going to work in the resorts. This is particularly important since the company's representatives will act as the company's public face to its customers. While the way that they treat customers is not the only factor that will determine whether people enjoy their holiday, they nevertheless play an important role in suggesting how much the company values its customers and their business. With most companies keen to encourage customer loyalty and repeat bookings, the well-trained representative's attitudes and behaviour can make a vital difference.

3. Training travel agents

Thomson has a product promotions manager who organises training days around the UK; roughly 1,000 agents a year will attend organised half-day seminars on how to sell Ski Thomson alone.

The scale of the training effort would be beyond the budgets of most smaller operators (for example, Neilson trains about 2,500 agents a year), who therefore rely on promotional events and educational trips to do most of the work for them (*see* page 217). Bigger operators will use these training methods too, but may also run formal seminars either in their own head office or by going out to the agents; frequently the latter type of training is undertaken by the operator's sales force as they travel around agencies. However, now that Thomson and Airtours have dispensed with their mobile sales forces, formal training sessions like this are likely to become much rarer. With most operators based in and around London, London travel agents may well become the recipients of most training in future.

Much of the training effort is centred on the launch of a new brochure. When this happens Thomson sends every agent a Launch Training pack which highlights new features and changes from the previous year and gives tips for selling the new product. But operators also circulate more detailed information about their products to particularly productive agents via 'fact files' on specific destinations; for example Thomson's Grecofile which provides further information about all the resorts and hotels the company features in Greece, in looseleaf format for easy updating. There is also a Ski Thomson file and a series of videos to help agents familiarise themselves with different products.

The ABTA National Training Board

Some training for tour operators is also provided by the ABTA National Training Board in Woking which is the managing agent for the government Youth Training (YT) programme for tour operators. This puts post-16-year-olds through a training programme consisting of formal teaching sessions in a local college and self-teach manuals which aim to help them achieve National Vocational Qualifications (NVQs) in tour operating practice. Since this is a government-subsidised scheme, operators can employ a YT trainee for just £35 a week while they are training. In 1994, new NVQs in field operations and guiding operations (suitable for resort reps and couriers) were launched.

The ABTA National Training Board's self-teach manuals are also available to full-time operator employees to enable them to study in their own time. Some companies will pay some of their staff's costs to study privately.

In 1994, it looked as if the National Training Board would be privatised.

Careers in tour operating

Staff who work for Thomson, Airtours, First Choice or Cosmos can look forward to conventional careers within the one company. However, those employed by smaller operators may find career openings relatively hard to come by unless they are prepared to move company and sometimes geographical location. This is not because the smaller companies don't want to promote internally, but that when they employ very few staff the opportunities for specialisation and therefore for a career ladder just aren't there.

For someone starting out in reservations, promotion might involve moving to another department, perhaps working on tailor-made holidays or putting together travel agents' educational trips. Alternatively it might mean going out to work in one of the resorts as a rep or as a tour leader.

QUESTIONS AND DISCUSSION POINTS

1 How do you think tour operators could become 'greener' businesses? Is the paperfree, brochureless office a realistic goal or a pipe dream?

2 Discuss the pros and cons of computerisation for even the smallest tour operators.

3 At the moment the big outgoing operators receive the vast majority of their business through travel agents, Do you think this situation is likely to continue? If not, why not and how would it affect the operators?

ASSIGNMENTS

1 Working in pairs, students should take **one** page for one resort of a big tour operator's brochure and try to create the paperwork for a manual booking system to sell it. Before starting, they should discuss how they are going to go about the task and what materials they will need. Afterwards they should write their lecturer a memo of no more than one side, highlighting any difficulties they had and how long it took to write up the paperwork.

2 If the college has a training office or agency and access to a dummy computer booking system, a role-playing exercise can be undertaken. Students should be grouped into threes, one person representing the client, the second the travel agent in a non-computerised agency and the third the tour operator. If the students have been on work placements in travel agencies they should be asked to devise the scenarios themselves; otherwise, the lecturer can do this. In two stages the students can then role-play the client talking to the agent about a possible holiday and then the agent passing the details onto the operator (tasks which happen simultaneously in real life). By the end of the exercise it should be clear what information the travel agent needs to have obtained from the client, and in what order, to pass it on efficiently and economically to the operator.

3 Provided the college has access to a dummy computer booking system, the students should take turns at using it to make bookings, ideally with other students phoning details through to them. If this is not possible, other students can select holidays from brochures for their own families or friends, record the details in writing and pass them to the student making the booking.

4 You work in the Customer Complaints Department of a major tour operator which has received a letter (*see* page 158) from a dissatisfied client.

Construct a chart itemising precisely what complaints the client is making, with columns to indicate whose fault each problem was. When you have done that, write a reply, setting out what action your company proposes to take to resolve the situation. Remember that the tone of your letter may make a lot of difference to how it is received, and also that you should be very careful about admitting liability and committing the company to large compensation payments.

Afterwards the class as a whole should discuss how individuals thought a complaint like this should be handled.

The Henge
Woodlands Rd
Bristol
BS1 2BD

24 November 1993

Dear Sir/Madam

My husband and I have just returned from a holiday in the Seychelles booked with your company. It was our silver wedding anniversary and we had looked forward to a really enjoyable trip for which we thought we were paying good money. What we actually got was not just disappointing but, we think, completely inadequate and we were astonished that a reputable company like yours could have let us down so badly.

We arrived at the airport in plenty of time to check in, only to find the flight was delayed. The rep didn't seem to have any information, and although the flight actually took off eight hours late, she kept telling us we wouldn't be waiting much longer. Of course, by the time we did actually get on our way, we were extremely tired and very hungry, not at all in the right frame of mind to arrive to find two of our bags had been left behind at Heathrow!

The rep on the island was better than the one at the airport and did at least sort out enough money for us to buy a few bits and bobs until the bags showed up two days later. But when we checked into our room, there was yet more disappointment. Not only was there no sea-view (which we had booked and paid for), but the flowers and champagne we had requested were missing too. So our first morning had to be spent sorting out compensation for the lost bags, swapping rooms and generally complaining. Not a good start, I hope you'll agree.

In the brochure the Paradise Hotel looks wonderful and is said to have a good-sized swimming pool. In fact the pool was closed for repairs. Even if it had been open I'd hardly have described it as 'good-sized' – more like a children's paddling pool actually! My husband is a fussy eater so we'd specifically picked a hotel that offered English cuisine but even this was a let-down. You hardly expect tepid, soggy chips when you're paying to stay in a 'luxury' hotel, do you? The brochure talked about 'laid-back island attitudes'. Turns out what they meant was half-hour waits for service at dinner without a smile in the evening. We talked to the rep again but I think she was getting tired of fending off complaints and got a bit snappy with us.

The last straw was when we turned up at the airport for an excursion to another local island only to find the flight had been cancelled and all the others during our stay were full. To cap it all, my husband went down with gastro-entiritis and had to spend the next three days in bed.

We feel that we are owed compensation for a holiday that in no way lived up to the promise of the brochure. We had forked out £2,880 between us and feel at least £500 of this should be refunded to make up for the disappointment.

We look forward to hearing from you in the near future.

Yours faithfully
Margaret Smith

CHAPTER 7

Overseas operations

LEARNING OBJECTIVES

After reading this chapter you should be able to:
- **describe the work of the overseas department**
- **explain the role of the resort representative**
- **list the other staff that operators employ overseas and their functions**
- **explain the procedures to be undertaken during an 'emergency'**

INTRODUCTION

Although much of a tour operating company's work takes place in the tourist generating country, operators of overseas holidays obviously have to conduct a large part of their business abroad. Large companies have an extensive workforce in the UK, but also have their own employees overseas to handle the day-to-day running of their holidays. The most conspicuous of the overseas staff are the resort representatives who are effectively the public face of the company. They are usually supervised in part by resort managers and in part by the home-based overseas department. Smaller companies may not have their own representatives, making use of intermediaries instead.

On coach tours, the couriers are even more prominent than hotel representatives on stay-put holidays. In the ski resorts, the usual representatives will be supplemented with ski leaders (whose job it is to guide skiers in groups) and chalet staff (who cater and clean up for guests as well as escorting them to and from their accommodation).

In general, overseas work for tour operating companies has two main characteristics: it is seasonal and it isn't usually very well paid. Although some good staff manage to find winter season work to follow on from a summer season and may eventually become employed full-time, perhaps in a home-based job, the number of such people is small in relation to the total overseas workforce.

THE OVERSEAS DEPARTMENT

The overseas department must recruit, train and then look after the resort representatives while they're in resort. For countries not in the EU it must arrange work permits for all staff working overseas which can be a time-consuming task since some countries would prefer companies to employ local people; Turkey, for example, requires that there must be a Turkish courier escorting all coach tours although the UK-based company may insist that one of their employees goes along too.

An important function of the overseas department is to train overseas staff before they reach the resort.

THE OVERSEAS STAFF

Big companies usually have an office based in major resorts areas to look after the day-to-day administration of their holidays. Staff employed in these offices have much less contact with clients than the reps. Instead they will be responsible for co-ordinating transport and accommodation arrangements and booking excursions. Usual office skills are required for these jobs (i.e. basic numeracy, typing and organisational skills, and ability to operate telex and fax machines). Because clients may telephone or call into the office, they also need good communication skills. Administration staff and their managers may also be required to speak the local language to enable them to communicate easily with local hoteliers, ground handling agents, etc.

1. Resort representatives

Resort reps who are going to work on the summer programme will usually be recruited between late autumn of the year before and January of the year in which they will start work. Advertisements will be placed between November and January, in the travel press (*TTG*, *Travel Weekly*, etc.) and sometimes in national newspapers as well. The first selection of candidates is usually made between December and February, with final selections in March. Extra reps may well be recruited from the reserve list to handle the peak July/August rush.

Training takes place at the start of April, with some of it in the UK and some overseas in the relevant resort. Training of reps will cover some or all of the following areas:

- the history of the company and an introduction to its policies
- a description of the job and what it entails
- conditions of employment
- advice about how to handle customers
- introduction to administrative procedures and paperwork
- information about the resort:
  - airports
  - transfer procedures
  - accommodation
  - fire procedures
  - excursions
  - merchandise
  - holiday insurance conditions
  - what to do in an emergency

The ABTA Tour Operator's Code of Conduct requires operators to ensure that all their reps are familiar with their company policies so that they can 'comprehend and perform within written procedures'.

Not all tour operating companies use resort representatives. This may be because they are too small and have too few clients in any one place at any one time to justify the cost. However, as the travel market became increasingly sophisticated in the 1990s, with many more experienced travellers than before, even some mainstream companies began to question the need for reps at all resorts. In summer 1993, Thomson decided to change its arrangements in Corfu, Tenerife and Ibiza, all of them long-established mass-market destinations. In these resorts, service centres, open from 8a.m. to 8p.m. every day, were set up to replace personal visits to all the hotels by the resort reps. It was hoped that this would enable Thomson to reduce the number of reps needed and so cut costs, although there was some uncertainty over whether the end result might not be a drop in revenue from the lucrative sale of excursions in the hotels.

The reps need to be settled in their resorts by the start of the season and will be returned to the UK gradually as it draws to a close. The area and resort managers will stay in the resort until the end of the season.

The role of the resort rep

The resort rep is the public face of the tour operator in the resort and, as such, is vitally important. Their function is to ensure that the client's holiday runs smoothly and to sort out any problems that might arise. A large tour operator may employ more than 600 reps and 60 assistants to cover their programmes.

The rep's work starts before the first guests arrive, when they will need to visit all the hotels featured in the programme to familiarise themselves with the layout, meet the owners and ensure their noticeboards are prominently positioned.

Once the season is underway, the rep will meet each flight as it arrives and direct passengers from the arrivals hall onto their transfer coach. They are provided with uniforms so it will be easy for clients to identify them. On the way to the resort they will usually give an introductory talk about the hotels, the resort, their job or anything else that seems appropriate. On arrival at each hotel they will see that the client is taken care of at reception. Usually, where they have a lot of clients at any hotel, they will organise a welcome party where clients will be given a drink while details of their holiday are explained. This is often when excursions are sold to clients.

In larger hotels in big resorts the tour operators usually have a desk for their reps where they will be available at specified times each day to help with any problems that come up. Reps will also maintain a noticeboard which may simply list the available excursions or give all sorts of information about the resort. They may also prepare a file of local information which must be kept constantly up to date and which clients will be able to consult to find out about things like excursions, local restaurants, entertainment, where the post office is, etc.

Unless there are separate entertainment reps, the same reps will also organise some of the entertainment in the hotel. Some will be on call 24 hours a day for five days a week, while others work shifts. The important thing is that there must always be someone available in case of an emergency.

At the end of the holiday, the rep has to go through the arrival procedure in reverse, travelling with the transfer coach to each hotel to collect the clients, accompanying them to the airport and then ensuring that everybody manages to check in without problems.

Reps are crucial when things go wrong, such as when someone loses a passport or air ticket, or is robbed. They will also have to sort out problems arising from faults by the company, the airlines, the ground handling agents or the hoteliers. In the early 1970s, as tourism really took off, overbooking was a frequent problem which had to be sorted out. However, by the 1990s this was fortunately rare, even in peak season. When it did happen, as in Cyprus in summer 1992, it was the reps who had to calm down irate customers left without rooms and liaise with the head office to find alternative accommodation for them. In fact the resort reps are the first port of call for most client complaints, particularly those that are likely to lead to continued dispute. Ideally, the rep will sort out the problem on the spot, or at least prevent it from getting worse, so that if compensation does have to be paid, it can be kept to a minimum and the company will attract as little bad publicity as possible.

In between carrying out these duties, reps must deal with the paperwork involved and keep accounts, for example of excursions they have sold.

Because they are working in the resorts, it helps if reps can speak the local language. This will be particularly important in the event of a serious problem (theft, death, etc.). However, since their clients are from the home country this is not as absolute a requirement as might have been expected. Indeed in the Tour Operator's Code of Conduct, ABTA states only that operators should

Age: Applicants should be aged approximately between 20 and 30

Qualifications: Applicants must be fluent in English and a working knowledge of at least one relevant foreign language is desirable. Previous knowledge of working with the general public is considered a great advantage, as is some experience of travel abroad.

The personal qualities we look for are, above all, a sensible and responsible outlook combined with a friendly and outgoing manner. You will have to be tactful and patient in your dealings with clients at all times, and we expect our representatives to be of a neat and pleasant appearance. To cope with the long and difficult working hours you will have to be in good general health, with a great deal of stamina and adaptability.

Duties: The work of a representative involves meeting the clients at the overseas airport and accompanying them to their hotels by coach. You will conduct informal drinks parties for all new arrivals to welcome the clients and give them information on the hotel and resort, and describe the optional excursions available. At set times you will be available to the clients in your hotels to help them with any queries they may have.

The job involves regular and detailed paperwork plus accounting, and you will be expected to liaise between your area office and the hotel management. There are no set working hours and representatives are expected to be on call at all times to deal with any problems which may arise.

Conditions: Work is seasonal (usually April/May to October), and you are employed on a full time, temporary basis. A limited amount of winter work is available, especially to those representatives who have completed more than one season with our company. We cannot guarantee that you will be allocated to the resort of your choice, and it is sometimes necessary to move representatives from one resort to another during the season.

The representative will be provided with food on a half board basis and accommodation whilst in resort. At times it may be necessary for you to share accommodation.

A uniform will be provided which you must wear at all times on company duty.

Fig. 7.1 General outline of duties and conditions for a Cosmos representative

Courtesy: Cosmos

The alarm goes off all too soon at 7 a.m. on a Friday morning, ready for you to start desk duties at 8.30 a.m. After a midnight airport transfer the previous night, that certainly is not music to your ears! A quick check on work needed for that day is made, as well as a routine check for uniform, immaculate grooming, etc., before leaving for work.

A quick breakfast and the first P.R. appearance of the day is made in the dining room at about 8.15 a.m. Then it's up to the desk for 8.30 a.m. sharp.

At 8.35, it's time for the day's excursions to depart. If you're not guiding this particular one, you're certainly around to check numbers, liaise with the guide, reassure guests about procedures and wave them off for an enjoyable day.

By 8.40 the trip has left, and until 10.00 there is a mountain of paperwork, accounts and customer queries to deal with. At 10.00 the previous day's arrivals start filtering into the lounge, ready to be given a Welcome Party. Then it's up on stage, microphone in hand, ready to part with a lot of the information you've gleaned over the season, and also to use your art in selling days and nights out. Drinks are served, booking forms are collected, then tickets are written and trips booked in. (Woe betide you if you forget to do the latter!)

Before finishing desk duty at 10.30 a.m., a brief meeting with reception is needed to check on the day's arrivals and departures and also to follow up any 'no shows' at the welcome party. As well as this, of course, the representative is the local expert, the guide, the mine of information on the resort and surrounding areas and is constantly offering advice and reassurance, issuing bus times and advising on local customs.

After morning duty, time for a change of uniform to shorts and polo shirt, ready for refereeing the morning's water polo match. A few laughs with the guests, and a dunking in the pool after being accused of being biased ensure excellent customer care and public relations.

At 1.30 p.m. it's time for some lunch and a couple of hours to relax. After an hour's sleep, it's time to iron a shirt and get ready for evening duties.

At 6 p.m. it's back to the hotel where guests are waiting to pay for excursions booked earlier that day. A number of problems have also arisen. One guest has had to go into hospital, another is unhappy with her room and a third thinks the hotel's food leaves something to be desired. Suddenly the 'diplomat' becomes the 'ambassador' and 'arbitrator' between guest and hotel. The 'secretary' also makes himself present to write a report. Above all the representative is always a friend.

Throughout evening duties, transfer coaches are constantly dropping off guests to the hotel, introductions are being made and vital first impressions created.

A quick dinner at 8.30 p.m. ensures that you are outside on the terrace to hob-nob with guests prior to the evening's entertainment, which this evening is the Reps' Show. At 9.30 p.m. it's the X Team in the hotel, hotfooting it around on stage, eager to entertain guests.

After packing away all the sound and light equipment, it's gone midnight, and all you're thinking about is your bed.

Whoops, that's not *all* you're thinking of . . . planning has to be made for the next day, rotas must be checked and a mental record made of, 'Where have I got to be and at what time tomorrow?' With a groan, you remember that tomorrow is 'liquidation day', when all money taken for trips must be declared at the office, and all paperwork recorded and signed . . .

Although very busy, a rep's life is certainly never boring . . .

Fig. 7.2 Reality – a day in the life of a resort rep

ensure that all representatives can communicate clearly in *English*. Most operators will only employ people over 21 as reps. This is both to avoid problems with different ages of majority in different countries and because it takes maturity to deal with some of the problems that occur. How hard they have to work may depend on where they are based; in busy resort areas like Majorca where flights may be arriving on five days a week, reps will be very much busier than on smaller Greek islands where there may flights on just one day a week.

By the early 1990s, many holidaymakers had been abroad before and the role of the resort rep was becoming less important; in some cases it was even thought that some customers were put off booking a package by the thought of being jollied along by the rep on the way from the airport and then herded together with other tourists at the hotel. In 1993 Thomson experimentally removed its reps from hotels in Corfu and Ibiza, handing out an office address and telephone number where they could be contacted if necessary instead.

Although representatives are not well paid and sometimes work very long hours, they are expected to be cheerful at all times, and most big operators issue clients with questionnaires which, among other things, ask about the helpfulness, cheerfulness and approachability of their rep. The results of these surveys are taken very seriously; those who achieve high scores are more likely to land winter jobs and eventual promotion than those who don't.

The large tour operators may have a lot of reps in a popular area like the Costa del Sol. There will, therefore, be a hierarchy of command; the resort reps are supervised by resort managers who are, in turn, supervised by an area manager.

At the close of each season a debriefing session will be held so the company can learn from what has taken place.

2. Children's representatives

Most of the large tour operators cater primarily for families and their children, and increasingly they employ representatives specifically to look after the children, thereby freeing the parents to enjoy at least parts of their holiday alone.

Children's representatives must normally be at least 19 and no more than 30, and operators often prefer to employ people with NNEB (National Nursery Examination Board), nursing or childcare qualifications or previous experience in working with groups of children. As usual personality will be an important consideration, with employers looking for friendly, caring individuals who will be able to get on well not just with children but with their parents too.

Children's representatives will run the company's children's clubs, and provide other services like babysitting and special children's excursions. Reps may also supervise separate mealtimes for children, read bedtime stories, take them for walks, etc. At all times the children's safety will be the paramount consideration.

In addition to these specific functions, children's reps may also be expected to help with airport transfers and attend welcome parties to explain their role to guests.

3. Entertainment representatives

Sometimes resort representatives are expected to provide part of the entertainment for guests themselves. However, companies may employ their own professional entertainers too. Thomson recruits people with experience of stage management, compèring, sound and lighting equipment, sports and leisure activities and warns that they must be expected to work very unsociable hours, probably why they are also expected to be between 21 and 35 and single.

4. Young people's representatives

Companies offering special programmes for young people usually employ representatives carefully picked for their ability to relate to the 18 to 30 age group. Usually they still need to be 21 themselves. However, these are very demanding jobs which often require the rep to live in the same accommodation as the guests and to be in constant contact with them, organising and joining in with an intensive programme of entertainment. Consequently even more than for ordinary repping jobs, applicants have to be bubbly, fun-loving extroverts.

5. '*Gentils organisateurs*'

Club Med calls its representatives '*gentils organisateurs*' and its clients '*gentils membres*'. The GOs don't wear uniforms and are forbidden to accept tips. Not only do they carry out all the normal functions of a resort rep but they also take an active part in organising sports activities and teaching clients new activities like scuba diving. They may join guests at the dinner table as well.

COURIERS

Instead of resort representatives, coach tour operators recruit couriers who are rather like mobile resort reps, travelling with their clients on the same coach and providing a commentary as they travel from place to place. Sometimes the courier will also escort guests round tourist attractions, providing a commentary, although some countries insist this work is carried out by local guides. Larger operators usually want couriers to be fluent in at least one foreign language and to have previous guiding experience. The work is not usually very well paid because the courier is receiving free accommodation and will usually be given tips by satisfied clients and commission from restaurants and souvenir shops to which they take their groups.

SKI RESORT STAFF

1. Wintersports representatives

Operators of skiing programmes also employ resort representatives, but usually expect them to double up as ski escorts or ski leaders as well which means they must usually be able to ski to an advanced standard. Normally they must be aged between 21 and 35 and be able to speak French, German or Italian as well as English. Ski reps will be in charge of organising a programme of *après-ski* entertainment. Usually they will be employed from December through to April.

Although wintersports representatives are no better paid than ordinary reps, they usually qualify for considerable perks apart from bed and board. They usually get, for example, free ski hire and a season's free lift pass which can be worth a lot of money.

2. Chalet representatives

As more and more operators include chalet parties in their brochures, so there are more openings for chalet representatives. People as young as 18 will sometimes be taken on to do this job which involves looking after the chalet as well as its guests. Chalet reps usually need to have some previous experience of catering, preferably for big groups of people; sometimes they must be able to cook to cordon bleu standards (would-be chalet staff are sometimes expected to cook a trial meal as part of their interview). However, they will also need to be competent housekeepers and are usually expected to be able to ski too. Chalet reps usually get one day off a week, when they provide a help-yourself breakfast and afternoon tea only.

3. Ski chalet nannies

Since chalets are often let to families, some companies also employ nannies to look after children aged six months to five years. Usually they will need to have NNEB or equivalent qualifications and will be expected to offer a childminding service from 9.30a.m. to 4.30p.m., five days a week. Chalet nannies will create a crèche in the lounge or dining-room of a chalet, arranging cushions, rugs and stairgates to ensure the children in their care can play safely, If the weather is good, they will also organise outdoor play activities. They may also act as babysitters for the family, either free or for a fixed hourly rate. Nannies are usually employed on a one nanny to three or four children basis, depending on the children's ages.

4. Ski instructors

A few companies employ their own ski instructors, although usually ski schools are staffed by local people. Obviously, only experienced skiers are acquired for these posts which can be demanding (especially when you have to teach children) and stressful (you also have to be able to cope with mountain emergencies when, for example, someone injured has to be airlifted to safety). Ski instructors are usually expected to teach for about two to six hours a day and to help with organising evening entertainment.

Companies employing instructors usually want people who have gained the British Association of Ski Instructors (BASI) Grade I or II qualification. The minimum grade possible is III which is achieved after undergoing two weeks training, five days assessment and 60 hours teaching.

CAMPSITE ORGANISERS

The companies offering holidays in European fixed-tent campsites employ staff who are sometimes called 'campsite couriers', although their job is actually very different from that of the traditional courier. Campsite staff are needed to welcome clients, to clean tents and caravans between visitors and to deal with the general day-to-day sorting out of problems like car breakdowns. Sometimes, like conventional resort reps, they also help to organise a programme of evening entertainment. Some campsite couriers also take responsibility for looking after children.

At the start and end of the season (March/April and September/October), the fixed tents must be set up and taken down again. Sometimes the same staff undertake this work; at other sites the operator uses a second set of temporary employees for this.

Eurocamp alone employs about 1,000 seasonal campsite staff and has traditionally recruited most of them from the ranks of college and university students. However, increasingly they are also employing retired couples and older people as well. Most staff are recruited by the end of January each year and may be employed for the whole season, or from April to mid-July or from mid-July to the end of September. Jobs are advertised in newspapers like the *Sunday Times* or in the *Directory of Jobs Abroad*. Circulars are also sent to colleges.

As usual pay is not wonderful, although tented accommodation will be provided. However, this sort of work does enable someone to get to know an area well and perhaps improve their language skills (although being bilingual is not normally a requirement for employment as a campsite courier).

ADVENTURE TOUR LEADERS

The overland and adventure holiday companies employ couriers of a rather different kind to guide their trips. Their couriers often have to be prepared to spend lengthy periods of time (sometimes three to six months) with a group of mainly young people. They will be expected to provide the usual commentaries on what is being visited, and guiding services at specific destinations, but as well as this they have a vital role to play in making the group cohere, ensuring that setting up camp, shopping and cooking meals goes smoothly and handling difficulties at borders, etc. Some companies still expect their tour leaders to wear uniforms; others take a more relaxed view of dress. Employees are usually young because this can be very demanding work.

Jobs are usually advertised in the quality newspapers. The tour companies interview staff for these posts and then put them through a six-week training course that they must normally pay for themselves (although the cost is usually reimbursed on employment).

This is what Journey Latin America has to say about its leaders:

> Leadership is most important, because in many cases it is the leader's enthusiasm and commitment that makes the trip. He or she is not a conventional 'courier' but actually leads the trip. Certain qualities are essential: all our leaders speak Spanish and/or Portugese and they all know the ground. And to each leader, the leading of a trip is a 24-hour-a-day job, not a holiday. But each leader is different: some are highly organised, some prefer to think on their feet, some have an unusually sympathetic ear, others a special interest in archaeology or ornithology, or can hold forth on the Peruvian economy. By the same token, they're not all experts on everything, though of course they are happy to share their local knowledge with you. It's a job they enjoy doing, but we demand much of our leaders.
>
> In addition most of our leaders work in the sales and reservations office when they are not 'on the ground' in South America . . . and prospective clients may speak to the person who most recently led the trip they are considering.
>
> (Courtesy: Journey Latin America)

Some of the overland tour companies employ staff whose main task is to take responsibility for the cooking, shopping and camping chores.

DRIVERS

Coach tour companies employ their own drivers, as do the overland tour companies. For such jobs you need a Passenger Service Vehicle (PSV) licence which costs roughly £400 to obtain. The overland companies also want drivers to have mechanical skills since often they will be driving across terrain which makes breakdown likely and where help may not always be available. Some of the overland companies employ dual-skilled driver-couriers who share the driving and other tasks between them. Guerba runs trips with a main driver and a second driver who, although fully licensed, may be a trainee either going along on his/her first trip to get general experience for leading a trip to Africa or learning about a new route.

CRUISE COMPANY EMPLOYEES

The big cruise ships require an enormous number of people to run them; the *Queen Elizabeth II*, for example, has a staff of almost 1,000 people. The staff divide into two main groups: those who look after the safe sailing of the ship and those who look after its functions as a floating hotel. Since those looking after the sailing of the ship have little directly to do with the clients, this section looks only at the work of those looking after the 'hotel' side of cruising.

Cruise ships do not normally have facilities for

training staff and instead recruit people who have previously worked in hotels. The luxurious nature of most cruise ships means that preference goes to people who have worked in four and five star hotels.

Because cruising is associated with eating well, ships normally have a large complement of chefs, sous-chefs and commis-chefs, as well as plenty of silver service waiters and waitresses, and separate wine waiters. Stewards and stewardesses are also employed to look after the ship's public areas, including the bar and decks, and to take care of the cabins. Some will have jobs rather like entertainment reps in the resorts, taking charge of organising deck games and nightlife. Because cruises tend to attract an older clientele, only a few cruise companies put childcare experts at the top of their recruiting list.

Like other large enterprises, ships require administrators to make sure everything runs smoothly. The purser's department looks after such administrative functions as directing clients to their cabins and answering their questions, running the foreign exchange desk, organising excursions (which can mean sorting out port taxes and making sure everyone has the right documentation), looking after the ship's paperwork and deciding the crew's rotas. Large ships will have separate catering officers to take charge of the 'housekeeping'; on smaller ships, the pursers will look after the kitchens and cabins too. When recruiting pursers, shipping companies look for good secretarial skills and experience in reception work and handling cash. Preference tends to go to candidates with second languages, especially those that match the ship's client profile (i.e. Spanish on ships attracting Latin Americans, Italian on those attracting Italians, etc.).

Like other tour operators, shipping companies use client questionnaires to assess the competence and customer care skills of their staff; those who score highly are likely to be rewarded with promotion. Obviously working on a ship can entail months at a time away from home, but it is occasionally possible for people who have worked on the ships to transfer to work in the company's head office.

Cruise ships are a cross between floating hotels and floating villages, and the bigger the ship and the longer its voyages, the more facilities it needs to provide. Consequently vacancies sometimes arise for everyone from hairdressers to midwives, from shop assistants to entertainers, from printers to cinema projectionists. The *QE II* alone employs two female and two male masseurs, three bankers, seventeen croupiers, two doctors, one librarian, four photographers, four secretaries, ten dancers and two orchestras. Some companies also employ guest lecturers to entertain their guests: Swan Hellenic, for example, takes eminent historians and archaeologists on its art-historical cruises. Other ships may choose from a wide range of experts, including famous travel writers, naturalists and well-known television personalities.

It's important to remember that cruise companies increasingly recruit overseas in order to keep labour costs down. Jobs on ships are therefore very hard to come by.

WHAT HAPPENS IN EMERGENCIES

The resort rep's role is at its toughest when an emergency arises. Typical emergencies may include:

- the illness or death of a holidaymaker
- the illness or death of a holidaymaker's next of kin at home
- a major accident or incident in the resort
- international problems e.g. the outbreak of civil war in 'Yugoslavia'
- the collapse of the holiday company

ABTA has drawn up general guidelines for what should be done in an emergency but whatever the nature of the incident, records must be kept of everything that happens. In particular, all expenses incurred must be recorded for future insurance claims. No company employee should ever say or do anything that might amount to an admission that the company or its employees was at fault.

Bearing in mind the likelihood that some sort of emergency will eventually occur, there are steps companies can take to be prepared in advance. They can, for example, keep a current emergency contact list for key staff, with telephone numbers where they can be contacted outside office hours. Ideally, these numbers should be recorded on a small enough card to fit into staff wallets so they can be carried around at all times. ABTA recommends that contact numbers for the following should be included:

ABTA
airports
airlines
car hire companies
coach terminals
coach operators
cruise companies
ferry and shipping terminals
hotels used at home and abroad
insurance companies
rail contacts at home and abroad
resort contacts
taxi companies (to bring staff to work if public transport is not running)
other tour operators

Where possible, a crisis co-ordinator should be appointed, ready for when his or her services are needed. It makes sense to have found out in advance from the company's own insurers what can and cannot be done without getting specific authorisation.

1 Illness of holidaymaker

If a client is taken seriously ill the rep must ensure that he/she is seen by a doctor and hospitalised if necessary. The senior rep and head office must be advised of what is happening; in the event of an accident the police must also be kept informed. The client must be visited regularly. If a claim against his/her insurance is likely to be made, the insurance company must also be contacted. Sometimes the insurance company may agree to repatriate the client, after consultation with the doctors and the rep (and sometimes with the consul too).

2 Death of holidaymaker

If a client dies while on holiday, the rep will have to inform a senior rep who will then contact head office and inform the British consul in the country where the death occurred. A death certificate will have to be obtained, preferably with a translation. Head office will need to know:

- the client's full name (and those of others in his/her party)
- his/her arrival date and destination
- his/her home address
- his/her travel agent's details
- his/her insurance company's details
- which hospital the client was taken to
- the contact number of the overseas consul
- the client's passport details

Head office will notify the British police who will then contact the deceased's next of kin if necessary. The tour operator (or travel agent) will normally help with arrangements for the next of kin to travel to the resort. Unless they particularly want to look after arrangements, the consul will usually take charge of organising the repatriation of the body or ashes. Certain religions stipulate speedy burial, so there should be no delay in contacting relatives to find out what is required.

3 Major accident or international difficulties

Typical problems that might have to be dealt with include:

- transport incidents – crashes, hijacks
- problems with buildings – fire, collapse of structure
- political problems – civil war, riots, terrorist incidents
- industrial problems – strikes affecting holidaymakers
- medical problems – outbreaks of cholera, other widespread health hazards
- '*force majeure*' – earthquakes, floods, hurricanes, fires, other 'Acts of God'
- unnatural death or injury

In all these situations, it's vital that staff act quickly and efficiently and in a way that will minimise distress for everyone. They should never say anything in public which would concede the company's responsibility in advance of any inquiry.

Although companies may have their individual procedures, ABTA has drawn up general guidelines to help in these situations and may help co-ordinate links between the tour operator, the travel agent and official bodies. The ABTA Handbook contains sample paperwork for keeping track of emergency situations. Sometimes ABTA may also express general industry views to the media.

In general, this how ABTA suggests that a company should proceed:

1 The resort staff should report any emergency to the UK head office immediately.

2 The company's pre-appointed crisis co-ordinator should take charge. An incident control room should be set up; sometimes it will need to be staffed 24 hours a day. The crisis co-ordinator may need to appoint:

   a) an incident location team
   b) a public relations team
   c) a passenger information team
   d) a company information team

   Obviously only larger companies can divide up the work in this way. For smaller companies it is usually a matter of all hands to the pump.
3 The priority should be to list all the clients involved in the incident, with the names and contact addresses/telephone numbers of their next of kin (travel agents may be able to help here). As the situation develops, the incident location team should keep a detailed log of events and actions.
4 The company solicitor, public liability company and insurance underwriter should be kept informed about what is happening. Members of staff should be kept informed too, so that they can handle any enquiries.
5 Depending on what has happened, the crisis management directorate team may have to arrange for relatives and/or priests to fly to the resort.

Who does what in an emergency

The crisis co-ordinator and crisis management directorate

The crisis co-ordinator should set up a crisis management directorate to oversee the whole operation. He/she should also contact ABTA's corporate affairs department and the company's legal and insurance contacts. The crisis management directorate should make an early assessment of the resources which are likely to be needed to handle the incident. The public relations and passenger information teams will report to the crisis management directorate.

The incident location team

Unless someone is sent from head office to take charge, the senior rep will usually supervise the overseas incident location team and should ensure that an up-to-date list of all the clients affected is kept available. The incident location team will handle the nitty-gritty details: contacting the British consul, the local police and the insurance companies; visiting clients in hospital; obtaining death certificates, etc. If possible, the team should try and find out full details of the incident. As the people on the spot, they should certainly keep an ongoing record of everything that happens.

The public relations team

All press enquiries should be referred to a public relations team which will need to keep as up to date as possible with what is happening. Ideally, it should issue a statement very quickly, particularly in view of the sometimes aggressive tactics adopted by the press when anything newsworthy goes wrong. This statement should cover:

(i) what has happened
(ii) where and when it happened
(iii) the number of passengers involved and their condition
(iv) what is happening now
(v) what is expected to happen next
(vi) what relatives/friends should do
(vii) an emergency telephone number, where appropriate
(viii) an indication of when the next statement will be

Care should be taken that no information about the individuals involved is released until the next of kin have been informed. It goes without saying that anything announced should be verified fact rather than supposition. Any facts that show the operator in a good light should be highlighted.

The public relations team should work in close collaboration with ABTA's corporate affairs department, because many enquiries from the press are likely to be routed via ABTA. Records should be kept of all calls handled.

The public relations team may need to continue working for some time after the immediate crisis has passed. No other staff members should ever say anything to the press about the emergency.

The passenger information team

The passenger information team will need to take charge of the list of clients' names and addresses

CRISIS CO-ORDINATOR

- assumes central control and establishes crisis management directorate
- maintains contact with legal/insurance companies
- contacts ABTA corporate affairs department

INCIDENT LOCATION TEAM

- on-site emergency services liaison
- British consular liaison
- compilation of client details on site
- arranges hospital attendance
- detailed log of incident and action taken

PUBLIC RELATIONS TEAM

- media information
- prepares appropriate press statement
- maintains log of journalists spoken to and responses given
- staff advised of appropriate incident information

PASSENGER INFORMATION TEAM

- sets up passenger database
- receives calls from the public/relatives
- liaises with police in the UK regarding bereavements

Fig. 7.3 Who does what in an emergency
(Source: *ABTA Handbook*)

and make sure next of kin are contacted before anything about the people involved reaches the media. It may also have to deal with telephone enquiries and visits from clients' relatives. The sort of questions they are likely to have to answer include:

(i) what caused the incident?
(ii) what arrangements are being made to repatriate anyone injured or to take their relations to the place where the incident happened?
(iii) what will happen about insurance?
(iv) what will happen about compensation?
(v) who is liable?
(vi) has such an incident ever happened before?
(vii) what is the company doing to ensure there is no repetition of the incident?

Since they will not be able to answer all these questions, they should be provided with a brief containing suggested answers to avoid the danger of admitting liability, etc.

The passenger information team will have to contact all the travel agencies whose clients are involved. If there are too many of them, ABTA may be able to help by supplying pages on Abtel.

After the event

Once the immediate crisis is over the operator should contact all clients to apologise for disruption to their holiday. It is also good public relations procedure to contact any local authorities involved to thank them for their help. Ideally, the operator should stage a post-mortem to see what, if any, lessons can be learnt for the future. Finally, staff involved in the emergency may have been put in a very stressful situation and considerate employers should consider whether any of them may be in need of counselling.

QUESTIONS AND DISCUSSION POINTS

1 What do you think are the good and bad points about working as a resort rep?

2 Look out for instances where tour operators have to make statements through the media after an emergency or other major incident. What particular problems do you think you might face in having to deal with the press in these circumstances?

3 There are signs that resort reps are becoming an endangered species. Discuss the likely consequences of this both for the operator and the client. Do you think the resort rep is really expendable?

ASSIGNMENTS

1 You are working for a tour operator which wants to recruit some new representatives to work in Spain. The company is concerned that many applicants for the job seem to have an unrealistically glamorous vision of what the work involves. They ask you to prepare a ten-minute presentation to give at local colleges where they hope to find new recruits. It should highlight the drawbacks of the job, while also explaining the good points. Your audience will be young, so your presentation should be lively enough to appeal to them.

2 You are just finishing a Tourism and Leisure course at a college where this presentation has been given. Having listened to it, you still think you would like to be a rep. Opposite is an application form (Fig. 7.4) for work with a major tour operator, Cosmos. Fill it out carefully, paying particular attention to the section which asks why you think you are qualified for the job. Then write a covering letter to go with your application.

3 When recruiting resort reps, tour operators are usually more interested in personality than formal qualifications. Part of the interview process often involves standing up in front of the other applicants and talking about yourself for two minutes. You may also be asked to talk about a subject that interests you for five minutes. Prepare two speeches suitable to make on such an occasion and then make them to your class, bearing in mind that you will be expected to look as if you are speaking spontaneously.

4 You have been taken on to work as a resort rep in a popular Mediterranean holiday resort which your company has not featured before. On arrival you need to prepare a file of information for clients to look at, and a noticeboard with details of local excursions, etc. on it.

Decide what resort you are going to be working in and then prepare the necessary file and notices.

Note to lecturers:
This assignment is best carried out in the resort. Take a supply of paper, pens, scissors, felt tips, a file and adhesive with you. Before leaving, the group should decide on the topics to be covered. They should then divide into pairs and decide which pairs will be responsible for what information. Once in resort the pairs should collect the necessary information. If possible set aside two afternoons to complete the work in the resort. The end product can then be made available to college students and staff through your training agency. (If you intend to do this, it makes sense to collect information on local hotels and comparative costs in the resort and include that in the file too.)

COSMOSAIR PLC
REPRESENTATIVES DEPARTMENT
PERSONAL DATA SHEET

PLEASE ATTACH TWO PASSPORT SIZE PHOTOS

POSITION APPLIED FOR ______

FIRST NAMES ______
CURRENT ADDRESS ______
______
______ POSTCODE ______
TEL NO ______
CONTACT NAME AND ADDRESS OF PARENTS/
NEXT OF KIN ______
______
______
POSTCODE ______ TEL NO ______
RELATIONSHIP ______

SURNAME ______
DATE OF BIRTH ______ AGE ______
MARITAL STATUS ______
PASSPORT NO ______
PLACE AND DATE OF ISSUE ______
NATIONALITY ______
NATIONAL INSURANCE NO ______
DO YOU HOLD A DRIVING LICENCE? ______
WOULD YOU BE WILLING TO DRIVE
OVERSEAS? ______

EDUCATION (FROM AGE 11)

SCHOOL/COLLEGE	FROM/TO	SUBJECTS TAKEN AND EXAMINATIONS PASSED*

*PLEASE ATTACH PHOTOCOPIES OF ANY RELEVANT CERTIFICATES

OTHER RELEVANT QUALIFICATIONS OBTAINED OR COURSES ATTENDED (WE ARE PARTICULARLY INTERESTED IN CUSTOMER CARE, SALES, TYPING, ADMINISTRATION & MEDICAL TRAINING SKILLS)

EMPLOYMENT HISTORY
PLEASE GIVE DETAILS OF YOUR PRESENT EMPLOYMENT AND YOUR PREVIOUS TWO POSITIONS (OR THE TWO MOST RELATED TO THE POSITION BEING APPLIED FOR)

POSITION HELD ______
NAME & ADDRESS OF COMPANY ______
______
FROM/TO ______ SALARY ______
REASON FOR LEAVING ______

POSITION HELD ______
NAME & ADDRESS OF COMPANY ______
______
FROM/TO ______ SALARY ______
REASON FOR LEAVING ______

POSITION HELD ______
NAME & ADDRESS OF COMPANY ______
______
FROM/TO ______ SALARY ______
REASON FOR LEAVING ______

PLEASE GIVE THE NAMES, POSITIONS HELD AND FULL ADDRESSES OF TWO RECENT WORK REFEREES AND FROM WHEN APPROACHABLE

NAME ______
POSITION ______
ADDRESS ______
______
______
WHEN APPROACHABLE
______

NAME ______
POSITION ______
ADDRESS ______
______
______
WHEN APPROACHABLE
______

DATES YOU WOULD BE AVAILABLE TO WORK
FROM ______ TO ______ LENGTH OF NOTICE ______

Fig. 7.4 Cosmos application form
Courtesy: Cosmos

continues

LANGUAGES SPOKEN	DEGREE OF FLUENCY

COUNTRIES IN WHICH YOU HAVE SPENT EXTENDED PERIODS OR HAVE SPECIAL KNOWLEDGE

HOBBIES & INTERESTS

HEALTH

ARE YOU IN GOOD HEALTH? ______

PLEASE GIVE DETAILS OF ANY SERIOUS ILLNESS/DISABILITIES/RECENT OPERATIONS/MEDICATION TAKEN ON A REGULAR BASIS

HAVING READ CAREFULLY THROUGH THE ACCOMPANYING INFORMATION LEAFLET WHY DO YOU FEEL THAT YOU ARE QUALIFIED FOR THIS JOB?

HAVE YOU APPLIED TO COSMOS BEFORE? ______ IF SO WHEN? ______

FOR WHICH POSITION? ______

WHAT WAS THE RESULT OF YOUR APPLICATION? ______

MEASUREMENTS FOR UNIFORM

MALE COLLAR ______ WAIST ______ FEMALE BUST ______ HIPS ______

CHEST ______ HEIGHT ______ WAIST ______ HEIGHT ______

STOCK SIZE (eg 10, 12, 14) ______

PLEASE NOTE THAT MOST INTERVIEWS ARE HELD IN DECEMBER AND JANUARY. IS THERE ANY TIME WITHIN THIS PERIOD WHEN YOU WOULD BE UNAVAILABLE?

I CERTIFY THAT TO THE BEST OF MY KNOWLEDGE THE ABOVE INFORMATION IS CORRECT AND THAT I HAVE READ FULLY THE ACCOMPANYING LEAFLET AND WOULD BE HAPPY TO ACCEPT THE CONDITIONS SHOULD I BE SUCCESSFUL IN OBTAINING EMPLOYMENT.

N.B.

ANY FALSE STATEMENTS OR DELIBERATE OMISSIONS RENDERS THE APPLICANT LIABLE TO DISQUALIFICATION AND IMMEDIATE DISMISSAL.

APPLICANT'S SIGNATURE ______ DATE ______

FOR OFFICE USE ONLY

Fig. 7.4 ***Continued***

CHAPTER 8

Financial matters

LEARNING OBJECTIVES

After reading this chapter you should be able to:

- **list the different sources of finance available to tour operators**
- **explain the different price components of a holiday**
- **describe how a holiday cost is calculated**
- **understand the cost consequences of consolidations, amendments, surcharges, etc.**
- **discuss how costs can be kept down**

INTRODUCTION

Tour operators need to cost their holidays in such a way that they will be competitive with the prices charged by their rivals but will still enable them to make a profit. Unfortunately, during much of the 1980s the large tour operators engaged in price wars which forced prices down and reduced profits. Since much of the public was only looking for sun, sea and sand from their holiday, they were prepared to switch buy to whichever part of the world offered this combination for the lowest price. So Greece and Spain alternated in popularity, largely according to which had the keener prices. This policy culminated in the collapse of the International Leisure Group (ILG) in 1991 (*see* page 46).

The cost of the traditional Mediterranean 'sun and sand' package breaks down roughly as follows (*see* next column).

Where transport by scheduled airline is used, particularly to long-haul destinations, the transport element can rise to 75 per cent of the total cost. In contrast, in a package to a nearby destination which can be reached by means other than air, the transport element may make up a smaller part of the total cost than the accommodation.

By the late 1980s, the seven per cent gross profit was being pared down by intense competition.

Percentage of total cost	*Breakdown*
37	accommodation
37	transport
10	agency commission
7	profit
16	operators' costs
	lighting
	heating
	rent/rates
	UK salaries
	stationery
	telephone
	fax/telex
1.5	marketing/brochure
1.5	resort staff

FORECASTING

Tour operators have to forecast costs and sales for their programme and then check these forecasts against actual costs and income as bookings start to come in, a process made much easier by computerisation. This checking may be done on a monthly basis, and because the forecasting has to be done up to 18 months in advance of holiday departures, there is always likely to be some slippage from the expected pattern. Anticipated revenue from the sale of holidays must be set against the cost of salaries, heating, lighting, communications, advertisements, entertaining, contract payments and so on. So, for example, if the sale of holidays is expected to bring in £2,500,000, this might have to be set against overseas costs of £1,900,000 and other expenses of £520,000, leaving an anticipated profit of only £80,000.

When making their forecasts economists need to consider:

a) whether the market is expanding or contracting
b) the size of programme they want to produce
c) the size and cost of competitors' programmes
d) whether demand is likely to exceed the supply of holidays
e) whether prices should rise, stay much as they were in the previous season or be reduced. In deciding this they may need to take into account:
  - the inflation rate
  - the mortgage rate
  - net disposable incomes of the travelling public
  - the inflation rate in destination countries
  - fuel costs
  - whether exchange rates are stable or not
f) whether enough aircraft will be available
g) whether enough accommodation will be available
h) whether it will be possible to consolidate bookings if sales don't go well, or whether a 'no consolidation guarantee' will have to be offered

Once a forecast has been made, budgets must be drawn up to fit within it. A small company may have one overall budget, but a larger one will have innumerable different budgets – for advertising, salaries, entertaining, etc. – all of which must fit within the overall forecast.

Getting the forecast wrong can have serious consequences. For example, in 1992 most of the operators overestimated the size of the holiday market which meant that they were left with a glut of unsold holidays at the start of the peak summer season and had to offer discounts to get rid of them, thereby cutting into their own potential profitability. In 1993, the forecasters did better which meant few last-minute bargains for consumers but better prospects for the holiday companies.

COSTING A HOLIDAY

Once the forecasters have done their stuff, a skeleton price grid without actual prices can be produced. This will show:

- the name of the hotel
- the meal arrangements planned
- the departure airports
- the holiday durations
- the departure day
- the departure time
- the first and last departures for 7 and 14 night holidays
- the holiday reference number
- the sequence of departure dates

Once that has been done, it is necessary to highlight the peak periods when optimum prices can be charged. These will coincide with school holidays, bank holidays, factory closing times, etc. It is also important to identify dates which are likely to generate the smallest numbers of passengers: for example, the first week in December.

After that, different operators will have different methods of carrying out their actual costings. Most will allow for a quick recosting just before the brochure is finally launched.

An air holiday has to be costed on the assumption that not all the flight seats will be sold. However, a high 'load factor' is necessary to keep costs down. If the break-even point is close to capacity, prices can be kept lower than if more leeway for empty seats is built in. Most operators work on a 90 per cent load factor, meaning that they must sell 90 per cent of their seats to break even.

Working out the cost of a typical package holiday

1 An operator has paid £6,120 for 60 seats to Faro, in the Algarve. This works out at £102 per seat if all seats are sold.
2 The operator is working to a break-even point of 90 per cent. It therefore needs to sell 54 of the 60 seats to break even. If it is assumed that the £6,120 will have to be recovered from selling 54 seats, the cost per seat rises to £113.30 (£6,120 ÷ 54). As soon as the 55th seat is sold, the operator will start to make a profit.
3 The cost of airport taxes and other extras could add another £14 to the cost per seat, bringing it to £127.30
4 The operator has contracted rooms at a hotel for 6,765 escudos per twin per night on a half-board basis. This works out at 3,382.50 escudos per

person per night. So for a seven night holiday, the per person cost of the hotel would be 23,677.50 escudos.

5 The escudos must be converted into sterling at a pre-agreed rate. If the exchange rate was 225.50 escudos to the pound, 23,677.50 escudos would add another £105.00 to the holiday cost.

6 The cost of hiring a transfer coach to the hotel is 47,918.75 escudos one way, or 95,837.50 escudos return. Assuming there are 54 occupants, that works out at 1,774.75 escudos return per person (95,837.50 ÷ 54). Using the 225.50 escudos to the pound exchange rate, that works out at another £7.85 per person.

7 The holiday cost so far is therefore:

	£
seat	113.30
taxes	14.00
hotel	105.00
transfers	7.85
	240.15

8 The net price of the holiday is therefore £240.15 per person. But this just covers the cost of the package components. To this the operator will need to add a mark-up to cover other costs, the 10 per cent commission to the travel agency and a profit. If they added 35 per cent mark-up to this holiday, that would add £84.05 per head, making the total cost £324.20. This would be rounded up to £325.

If the tour operator sold all 60 holidays for £325 it would take £19,500. Of this, 10 per cent, or £1,950, would go to the travel agency as commission, leaving total revenue of £17,550.

From this £17,550, the operator would now have to pay out costs as follows:

	£
aircraft seats	6,120.00
airport charges	840.00
hotel rooms	6,300.00
transfers	471.00
	13,731.00

So, of revenue of £17,550, £13,731 would be paid out to principals for the components of the package holiday, leaving only £3,819.00 to cover the operator's own costs (salaries, etc.) and to make a profit. (Some operators will cost for printing the brochure, advertising, etc. as separate items.)

These complex calculations will have to be made for every combination of flights and hotels in the brochure. Nor can fourteen night holidays simply be costed at twice the price of seven nights, since the flight costs will be the same, no matter how long the client stays at the resort. Where multi-centre itineraries or longer holidays are involved, the calculations will become even more complicated. When a company offers more than one brochure, the same calculations will have to be done for each of them in turn.

Most cost calculations are based on the use of one of the London airports (Gatwick, Luton or Heathrow) and separate calculations will have to be made to arrive at supplements for departures from regional airports. There may also be supplements to travel at the most convenient times of the day or week.

Finally, the company must also come up with costs for all the extras like car hire, ski hire, etc.

How much mark-up is added to the basic holiday cost will vary depending on the departure date. The highest mark-ups will be loaded onto peak period departures (usually Easter, July/August and Christmas/New Year, and February half-term for winter holidays). Conversely, there may be a very small mark-up on departures at the lowest point of the low season; it is better to sell a seat at break-even cost than to let the plane take off with it empty.

Once all these calculations have been made the operator will be able to come up with a 'lead-in' price which can be used for promotions. This will be the cheapest price for the shortest holiday to a nearby resort from a southern airport in low season. 'Lead-in' prices work much like loss-leaders in supermarkets. Sometimes they will not actually cover the cost of the holidays involved. However, they may have considerable publicity value (as when Airtours announced £299 fortnight holidays to Cuba in 1993). What's more, if the would-be client finds the particular bargain holiday they were after is sold out, a skilful agent may manage to build on their expectations to sell them something else which will perhaps be worth more, to the operator.

Brochure prices are not usually finalised until about 10 weeks before the brochure is printed to allow maximum opportunity to make necessary changes. However, tour operating is such a cut-throat business that second and third editions of the brochure may be produced with different prices if it turns out that competitors have come up with significantly lower prices as a result of negotiating better deals with hoteliers, airlines, etc.

VAT on holidays

Under the Tour Operators' Margin Scheme for VAT payments, passenger travel is zero rated but VAT is charged at the standard rate (currently 17½ per cent) on accommodation. Operators offering packages involving transport and accommodation must work out a year in advance what percentage of their business is VATable. They can adjust for errors in subsequent payments.

In 1994, the EU was considering putting VAT on operators' profit margins on air transport. It is currently against EU law to levy VAT on air travel. However, if profit margins are treated as 'administrative costs', then it would be legal to charge VAT on them.

Deposits

Tour operators will normally make a booking in return for a deposit payment provided it is more than 8 to 10 weeks before the departure date. Deposits are not normally refundable and vary in amount, depending on the cost of the holiday, from about £65 to £250 per person. Sometimes the insurance premium is included in the deposit sum, but more usually it has to be paid as a separate amount. Once deposit payments start to reach the operators they can invest them and start accruing interest on them.

Occasionally tour operators offer 'low deposits' as incentives to encourage early booking; the full normal deposit usually becomes payable if the client cancels. 'Low deposit' offers are more usually made by travel agents, who still have to pay the full deposit as printed in the brochure to the tour operator.

When bookings are made within 10 weeks of the departure date, payment must usually be made in full before the operator will confirm the reservation.

Fixing the exchange rate

The pound sterling's exchange rate against foreign currencies tends to fluctuate, reflecting various economic and political considerations. Since this can make it difficult for traders to plan ahead, the 12 countries of the European Community eventually created the Exchange Rate Mechanism, or ERM, which offered fixed exchange rates between member states for long periods of time. Britain was slow to enter the ERM, only joining in October 1990. During 1991 and 1992, tour operators featuring EC countries knew what the exchange rates between member countries would be. It was the intention that eventually the EC countries would create a single monetary system with a single currency.

However, towards the end of 1992, as Europe moved into recession, the ERM came under increasing strain, and in September Britain and Italy were forced to leave it, while several other countries had to devalue their currencies within the system. This meant that operators were back to the lottery of floating exchange rates, not just with non-EC countries but within the EC too. By the summer of 1993 when France was also forced to pull out, the ERM had effectively collapsed.

Because exchange rates do change, it would be possible for two operators using the same aircraft and hotels to come up with different holiday prices just because they had based their costings on exchange rates at different times in the year. To stop this happening and ensure an even playing field, ABTA decides two dates in every year (in March for winter holidays and July for summer ones) which all ABTA operators use for their foreign exchange

French franc	9.60
Spanish peseta	182.50
Portugese escudo	242.00
Italian lira	2,160.75
Greek drachma	349.83
Cyprus pound	0.8265
Maltese pound	0.5825
Turkish lira	13,355.40
Swiss franc	2.52
Tunisian dinar	1.6215
Egyptian pound	6.50
US dollar	1.918

Fig. 8.1 Exchange rates on 20 July 1992

costings. Figure 8.1 shows the exchange rates of currencies in holiday destinations against the pound on 21 July 1992. They were taken from the *Financial Times*. These were the rates that were used to price 1993 summer sun holidays.

Buying currencies forward

Tour operators who are in a position to do so buy their annual currency requirements as soon as the dates for fixing the rates are agreed. In 1992 operators who bought their currencies in July would have avoided the problems created by Britain leaving the ERM and the pound's devaluation which made everything abroad more expensive from mid-September onwards. Those with absolute 'no surcharge agreements' could not pass these unanticipated extra costs on to their clients. The only other way to save themselves from the added expense was to renegotiate contracts to get the hoteliers to bear some of the loss. Inevitably, it is easier for large companies with bigger financial reserves to buy currency forward. When Riva Travel collapsed in 1993, one reason given for its failure was that it had trusted the ERM to keep the pound's exchange rate steady and had not therefore bought its currency forward; when the pound left the ERM and was devalued, the company incurred enormous losses on currency exchange rates.

Figure 8.3 shows how the TOSG exchange rates have fluctuated over the last four years and the forward buying rates for summer 1994. These looked encouraging for both the Spanish peseta and the Greek drachma, meaning that operators who bought forward should have been able to price their summer 1994 Mediterranean products competitively. In contrast, the forward buying rate for the dollar looked very poor, creating dilemmas for operators to Florida.

Because fluctuating exchange rates cause such difficulties, Malta introduced a fixed forward-buying rate (FBR) for tour operators in 1986. This was, in effect, a government subsidy for tourism to help keep prices down at a time when Maltese holidays were not selling well. The FBR has been steadily rising and, with the market once again stable, the government intends to phase it out altogether by 1995. The existence of the FBR has enabled operators to Malta to price their holidays, confident that surcharges as a result of currency changes would not be required, so this will be a blow.

Changes in the value of some currencies have knock-on effects for others too. For example, the value of the Cypriot pound is linked to that of the German mark and the value of the Tunisian dinar to that of the French franc. In particular, the pricing of holiday components is calculated in US dollars for many other countries than just the United States, so fluctuations in the value of the dollar can affect

Spanish peseta	173.90
Greek drachma	330.275
Portugese escudo	225.50
Italian lira	2,397.50
Cyprus pound	0.7342
Tunisian dinar	1.4940
Maltese pound	0.5273
Egyptian pound	4.9540
US dollar	1.4910
ECU (European currency unit)	1.2528

Fig. 8.2 Exchange rates on 30 March 1993

	TOSG rates					
Currency	*Summer 91*	*Summer 92*	*Summer 93*	*Summer 94*	*%+/– 93/94*	*12 month onward rates*
Dollar	1.82	1.68	1.91	1.50	–21.5	1.47
Peseta	181.45	184.20	182.50	199.90	+9.5	214.25
Lira	2,171.75	2,201.25	2,160.75	2,368.25	+9.6	2,452.50
Drachma	291.07	322.94	349.82	348.48	–0.4	415.75
Cyprus £	0.83	0.8070	0.8265	0.7569	-8.4	N/A

Fig. 8.3 Fluctuating exchange rates 1991 to 1994

prices of holidays as far apart as China and South America.

Between July 20 1992 and March 29 1993 (the dates used for fixing exchange rates for summer 1993 and winter 1993/4 holidays respectively), the pound fell by about 22 per cent against the dollar, 10.3 per cent against the Swiss franc, 15 per cent against the Austrian schilling, 13.5 per cent against the French franc and 3 per cent against the Spanish peseta.

Child discounts

Nowadays large tour operators usually offer discounted holidays for children (normally defined as aged from 2 to 11 or 12), and sometimes a few free places as well. From their point of view, offering these limited discounts can be a way of encouraging early bookings which helps with planning and allows them to invest deposits for the maximum length of time. Although the free places sell out very quickly, disappointed clients who've got as far as the agency may then agree to settle for a discounted place or a completely different holiday.

Discounts usually depend on:

a) the child's age – infants under two are normally carried free provided they sit on a parent's lap on the flight (a small fee is usually payable direct to the hotel for use of a cot, etc.), while those aged up to 11 or 12 are eligible for discounts. In 1993 there were even a few offers which defined youngsters as old as 18 as 'children' to encourage sales.

b) the number of adults travelling with each child. To qualify for a discount a child usually has to be sharing a room with two full fare-paying adults.

Companies hoping to attract lots of families with children will also feature hotels offering some or all of the following facilities:

- cots
- highchairs
- children's pool or area of pool
- playpens
- children's play areas
- early suppers and/or special meals for children
- babysitters
- a children's club supervised by a nurse, a teacher or a special children's representative, e.g. Thomson's Big T Club, Cosmos' OK Club, Falcon's Trouble and Wild Bunch Clubs, Airtours' Getaway Gang and Enterprise's Sunbeam Clubs
- a separate floor for families
- a baby patroller
- a shop stocking baby goods
- a teenagers' club e.g. Thomson's Teen Scene, Cosmos and Falcon's Teen Clubs, Enterprise's Club 12–15

SURCHARGES

ABTA defines a surcharge as:

> a supplementary amount requested from clients after the booking has been confirmed by the operator and which is levied in addition to the originally confirmed holiday price.

Because operators have to cost their packages so far in advance of the departure date, there is always scope for miscalculation. A lot can happen in 18 months to throw their calculations out. For example, the cost of aviation fuel can go up, foreign exchange rates may fluctuate unfavourably or hoteliers may decide to hike their rates. Sometimes government actions can make a difference. For example, towards the end of 1992 the Greek government introduced a £14 per head airport tax which those calculating prices for 1993 summer sun holidays could not have taken into account.

In the early 1980s, operators responded to such changes by levying surcharges on top of brochure prices. Sometimes these were notified at the time of booking but sometimes they were added afterwards and clients were not allowed to cancel because of the surcharge without having to pay cancellation fees. Not surprisingly this policy went down badly with holidaymakers who found themselves faced with extra costs for which they hadn't budgeted. Travel agents also disliked surcharges since they, rather than the operators who had levied them, were the ones who had to try and explain them to the public. What was more, although they had to collect the surcharges, the operators didn't usually pay commission on them.

Gradually operators started to offer 'no surcharge guarantees' to get round this problem. In return for not passing on price increases brought about by unfavourable currency fluctuations, they decided they would not pass on any gains made if exchange rates moved in their favour either. However, not all no surcharge guarantees were as cast iron as their wording suggested. In the small print of the brochure it sometimes said that the operator wouldn't pass on increases of more then 10 per cent of the cost, or £10, or any increases notified less than eight weeks before the departure date.

In 1988 ABTA introduced a set of *Standards on Surcharges* governing the levy of surcharges. These now form part of the Tour Operator's Code of Conduct. The operator must now absorb any increased costs that don't exceed two per cent of the entire holiday cost (excluding insurance premiums and amendment charges). If the surcharge then levied exceeds 10 per cent of the holiday cost the client must be allowed to cancel and receive a refund of all the money paid (except the insurance premium and any amendment fees).

They must also be allowed 14 days to make up their mind whether to cancel. Where a surcharge is levied, the operator must provide a written explanation of why it is necessary and what it covers. A more detailed explanation of the calculations involved must also be available, should a client wish to see it. No surcharges can be levied within 30 days of the departure date; in the case of a late booking, the price quoted to the client must be inclusive of any surcharges. Optional extras (car hire, ski hire, etc.) must be treated separately from the main holiday, and once again the first two per cent of any price increase must be absorbed by the operator. Operators are allowed to charge an administration fee of no more than 50p per person for levying a surcharge.

ABTA requires operators to notify it of their surcharge policy. They have three forms for this purpose. Form A (*Notification of Costing Basis*) must be sent to ABTA with a copy of the relevant brochure within seven days of its publication. It must show precisely what wording has been used in the brochure to cover the company's surcharge policy and, once it has been submitted, it will be binding on the company for that season.

If the operator decides to levy a surcharge they must send ABTA a copy of Form B (*Notification of Intention to Surcharge*) at least seven days before they intend to send the first surcharge invoice to a client. The form must be accompanied with information to explain the surcharge. For example, in the case of a surcharge arising from currency fluctuations it must be accompanied by the *Financial Times*' rate shown in the 'Guide to World Currencies' for the date used for the recalculation. Alternatively, ABTA needs a bank letter confirming the rate of exchange used to purchase currencies for the holidays concerned.

If the surcharge is levied for reasons other than currency fluctuation, the operator will need to send relevant justificatory letters, invoices, etc. with Form B.

Finally, if a surcharge is being levied, ABTA requires the operator to fill out Form C (*Surcharge Calculations*) showing the calculation of a specific surcharge. If there are any inconsistencies in the information provided, the matter can be referred to ABTA's Surcharge Monitoring Committee.

Even after receiving the correct paperwork, ABTA can still ask the operator to withdraw or modify the surcharge. If it is accepted, the operator will be added to the list of companies with permission to surcharge on New Prestel. Should an operator try to pass on a surcharge which has not been approved by ABTA, it can be referred to the code of conduct committee for disciplinary action.

The same regulations covering surcharges also apply to tailor-made foreign inclusive holidays and to seat-only arrangements on European charter flights where accommodation is theoretically available for the duration of the holiday.

In the Tour Operator's Code of Conduct ABTA lists the wording that should be used in brochures when discussing surcharges.

A Full Price Guarantee

> The price of your holiday is fully guaranteed and will not be subject to any surcharges.

This is the only situation in which an operator can splash 'No Surcharges', 'Guaranteed No Surcharges' or 'Full Price Guarantee' across its cover.

B Partial Price Guarantee

(i) We guarantee that the price of your holiday will not be subject to any surcharges except for those resulting from governmental action. Even in this case, we will absorb an amount equivalent to 2 per cent of the holiday price which excludes insurance premiums and any amendment charges. Only amounts in excess of this 2 per cent will be surcharged, but where a surcharge is payable there will be an administration charge of *p together with an amount to cover agents' commission.

If this means paying more than 10 per cent of the holiday price, you will be entitled to cancel your holiday with a full refund of all money paid except for any premium paid to us for holiday insurance and amendment charges.

Should you decide to cancel because of this, you must exercise your right to do so within 14 days from the issue date printed on the invoice.

This statement can be used when the price is guaranteed against anything except government action.

(ii) Whatever happens to the value of the pound, the price of your holiday will not be subject to any currency surcharges. The price of your holiday is, however, subject to surcharges on the following items: (a full list of surchargeable items must be included in this sentence, e.g. government action, aircraft fuel, overflying charges and airport charges).

Even in this case, we will absorb an amount equivalent to 2 per cent of the holiday price which excludes insurance premiums and any amendment charges. Only amounts in excess of the 2 per cent will be surcharged but where a surcharge is payable there will be an administration charge of *p together with an amount to cover agents' commission.

If this means paying more than 10 per cent on the holiday price, you will be entitled to cancel your holiday with a full refund of all money paid except for any premium paid to us for holiday insurance and amendment charges. Should you decide to cancel because of this, you must exercise your right to do so within 14 days from the issue date printed on the invoice.

This statement should be used where, although surcharges will not be levied for currency fluctuations, they are still possible for other reasons.

C No Price Guarantee

The price of your holiday is subject to surcharges on the following items: governmental action, currency, aircraft fuel, overflying charges, airport charges and increases in scheduled air fares. Even in this case, we will absorb an amount equivalent to 2 per cent of the holiday price which excludes insurance premiums and any amendment charges. Only amounts in excess of this 2 per cent will be surcharged but where a surcharge is payable there will be an administration charge of *p together with an amount to cover agents' commission.

If this means paying more than 10 per cent on the holiday price, you will be entitled to cancel your holiday with a full refund of all money paid except for any premium paid to us for holiday insurance and amendment charges. Should you decide to cancel because of this, you must exercise your right to do so within 14 days from the issue date printed on the invoice.

This paragraph should be used where any or all of the items listed may result in a surcharge.

Surcharging in practice

In 1992, as currency instability made the need to levy surcharges more likely, some long-haul companies, like Hayes and Jarvis, printed two-level price guarantees. An absolute no surcharge guarantee was offered to clients paying in full and requesting the guarantee at the time of booking; the amount they would be charged was to include any surcharges already due. Otherwise, the company only promised to absorb the first 2 per cent of any increases and to offer an opportunity to cancel if the surcharge rose to more than 10 per cent of the total holiday cost. Bales offered a similar fixed price guarantee to clients booking and paying in full before the end of December. These two-level guarantees had the added bonus of encouraging clients to book early, so operators could invest their money.

In 1993, ABTA gave 56, mainly long-haul, operators permission to levy surcharges. This was because the rate of exchange of the American dollar against other currencies had sunk far below that assumed by operators when calculating their prices. Most levied surcharges of 8 or 9 per cent, a crucial 1 or 2 per cent below the 10 per cent threshold which would enable clients to change their mind about travelling without penalty. Surcharges were levied on holidays in areas as far apart as the Far East, China, South America and the Caribbean.

KEEPING COSTS DOWN

In order to keep prices down, operators are under pressure to keep their costs as low as possible. The price of flight seats represents a high proportion of their outlay but there are several ways the cost can be minimised:

1 Where the operator actually owns the airline it will have greater control over it and better hope of controlling costs.
2 Whenever planes are on the ground, they accumulate airport charges, so it's important to ensure they stay in the air as much as possible. This means ensuring that embarcation/disembarcation, loading, cleaning and refuelling are completed as quickly as possible. Flights are also operated 'back to back', flying out with one group of passengers who are starting their holiday and then returning with another group who are coming home again.
3 To make the greatest use of them, aeroplanes are often scheduled to fly a 'W' pattern (*see* Fig. 8.4), rather than just back and forth between the same two points. So a flight leaving Luton at 8 a.m. might arrive in Mahon at 10.15 a.m. After spending one hour on the ground, it would leave Mahon at 11.15 a.m. to fly to Brussels, arriving at 2 p.m. After another hour on the ground, it would fly to Alicante, arriving at 5 p.m. Another hour on the ground, and it would fly back to Gatwick, arriving at 8 p.m, and so on.
4 Assuming a high break-even point when calculating costs will also allow for a lower overall price.
5 Night flights are cheaper than daytime ones because of lower airport charges.
6 Operators who only have summer programmes will have two expensive 'empty leg' flights, at the start of the season when they must fly out one group of passengers with none to bring back, and at the end when they must fly a plane out to bring a group home without being able to deliver another group to take their place. Running a year-round programme can reduce the risk of 'empty leg' flights, although summer and winter flight schedules may not always dovetail neatly. In that case, holidays of odd durations can be sold off as bargain-priced spring and autumn savers to avoid having empty seats.
7 Offering a 'seat-only' option makes it possible to offload surplus seats for at least their break-even cost.
8 Transferring holidays to different aircraft can sometimes lead to price reductions. So for winter 1993/4 Thomson transferred some holidays from 737s to larger 757s and 767s to reduce costs.

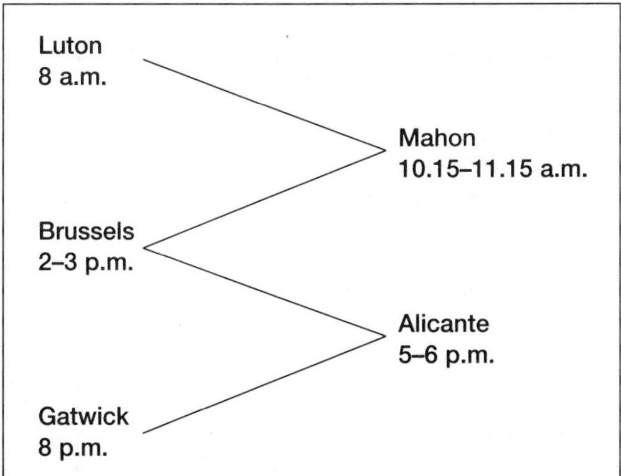

Fig. 8.4 'W' flight pattern

Consolidations

As bookings come in, the sales and reservations managers will have to assess whether destinations are selling at the rate which was forecast. If they're not, there are several things that can be done to try and improve the situation:

a) If there will be a second or third edition of the brochure, they can reduce prices to the region which is selling badly, or promote it with new special offers.
b) They can take out more advertising space in the media and use it to plug the destination.
c) They can organise a press trip which might get the resort highlighted on the travel pages of newspapers and magazines.

If, in spite of their efforts, sales are still slow they may be confronted with the risk of expensive unsold flight seats. Once again there are several possible ways round this problem:

a) They can try and sell the surplus seats on to another company.
b) They can try and persuade the airline to use a smaller plane.

c) They can consolidate flights i.e. cancel one and carry its passengers on another half-empty plane.

When operators negotiate their contracts with the airlines, they may build in the right to consolidate flights if they have not sold enough seats on individual ones. If the cancelled flight is a 'shadow' of another one (i.e. leaving within half an hour of it), then passengers may not be badly affected. However, some consolidations lead to major changes to holiday times and departure dates. These are obviously unpopular with the public, so it's important for the operator to try and keep them to a minimum. The ABTA Tour Operators' Code of Conduct requires operators to offer compensation where consolidation results in major changes to someone's holiday (*see* page 184).

If several flights are consolidated, the company will need fewer hotel beds, in which case, when deciding which rooms to drop, they will give priority to hotels to which they are committed and then to those at which they have an allocation.

The sales and reservations managers will decide when consolidation is necessary, basing their decision on the number of confirmed bookings already received. The ABTA Tour Operators' Code of Conduct states that operators shouldn't make 'material changes' to holidays less than 14 days before the departure date, and that written confirmation of the changes must be sent to the travel agent or client. It also says that clients must be given the opportunity to cancel the tour and receive a refund of the money they've paid and that compensation must be offered on a sliding scale.

TOUR OPERATORS' OTHER SOURCES OF INCOME

Apart from the profit mark-up on holiday prices, tour operators also earn money from some or all of the following sources:

a) **Interest** The longer a tour operator can hold onto clients' money, the more interest can be earned from investing it. When most people used to book their holidays between January and March this was an important source of income for operators. The late booking trend has inevitably reduced its importance.

If a tour operator sells 300,000 holidays by the end of February, taking a £60 deposit for each, then they will have £19,500,000 to play with. Some of this will need to be paid to the hoteliers and airlines to secure bookings. Some will go towards producing the next season's brochure and other day-to-day costs. But some will be left over and can be invested for perhaps five or six months.

Similarly, final balances are usually due two months before the departure date although the tour operator will not actually settle its bills with airlines and hotels until much closer to the date. Once again money is available for short-term investment.

b) **Cancellation costs** Operators usually charge clients more for a cancellation than they will have to pay to the principal.

c) **Amendment costs** The same is true of amendment costs.

d) **Car hire** Operators may earn more than 25 per cent commission on car hire bookings but will give the travel agent only their usual commission rate, normally 10 per cent, and bank the difference.

e) **Insurance** The commission on insurance sales may be as much as 100 per cent of which perhaps only 10 per cent will be passed to the travel agent.

f) **Advertisements** Some companies print advertisements for other products in their brochures and charge for doing so. For example, the 1993 Cosmos Summer Sun brochure carried an advert for Ibatur, the Balearics Tourist Board, on its back cover.

g) **Sale of ancillary products** Some operators sell ancillary travel products, including traveller's cheques, passport wallets, luggage and guidebooks, to supplement their takings.

h) **Excursion commission** Companies earn commission on excursions sold in the resorts by their reps.

i) **Foreign exchange deals** The largest tour operators can make money (or at least save it) by buying currencies they know they will need in advance when rates are good. For example, Greek drachmae and Spanish pesetas fetch premium rates in summer, so it will be cheaper to buy them in winter. To protect themselves against unexpected rate changes, operators sometimes buy on the understanding that they will only pay when the currency is actually required.

j) **Direct bookings** Operators save the average 10 per cent agency commission on the small number of direct bookings most receive.

k) **Miscellaneous 'extras'** Operators who own their own aircraft may be able to generate extra money by, for example, selling excess cargo space in the hold.

Cancellation charges

Operators apply cancellation charges on a sliding scale depending on how far in advance of the date of travel the cancellation is notified (*see* Fig. 8.5). Usually the charges apply to the basic holiday cost inclusive of flight and room supplements but exclusive of extras like car hire. Insurance premiums are never refundable since the cover came into force from the day it was taken out, and the client may be able to recover some of the cost of cancellation through the insurance company.

Where the booking was made through an agency, the operator will pay the agent commission on the cancellation fee. The operator will also hold the agent liable for the cancellation charges, so it is essential that the agents ensure they have always collected enough money from the clients to cover whatever cancellation charges would apply at any specific date. This is why late bookers must always pay in full at the time of booking.

Operators normally need to have received written confirmation of cancellation before they will act on it; a phone call is not enough.

Period before scheduled departure date within which written notification of cancellation is received by the operator	Amount of cancellation charge as a % of the total price inclusive of extras (but exclusive of insurance premiums)
More than 42 days	Deposit
29–42 days	40
15–28 days	60
1–14 days	80
Departure day or after	100

Fig. 8.5 Typical scale of cancellation charges on a package holiday

Amendment charges

Operators levy fixed charges (perhaps £10–25) for alterations made to a confirmed booking. These include:

- changing the booking into a different passenger name
- swapping the booking to a different resort
- moving the booking to a different hotel
- changing the type of room booked
- adding more passengers into a booking
- reducing the number of passengers booked. In this case the people cancelling will be charged cancellation charges, while those continuing with the booking may be charged amendment fees.

Changes made to a booking less than six weeks before the departure date are sometimes treated as cancellations for charging purposes.

OPERATORS' COSTS

1. Travel agency commission

Tour operators usually pay travel agencies 10 per cent commission on all sales. The agent will usually deduct this from the balance payment (rather than the deposit) before remitting it to the operator. Commission is sometimes paid on the entire holiday cost inclusive of supplements, insurance payments and any extras, but sometimes it is only payable on the basic holiday cost. Sometimes a different rate of commission will be paid on the insurance premiums.

Agencies who sell a lot of one particular operator's products often qualify for an **override commission**, of 12½ per cent or more. Usually, this too will be deducted from the balance payment, although sometimes the operator opts to pay the extra commission as a lump sum at the end of the season, allowing them to invest the money for longer. Override commission is sometimes only paid on the basic holiday cost, exclusive of insurance premiums, supplements and extras. It is obviously in operators' interests to avoid the expense of paying override commissions wherever possible; indeed Thomson prides itself on never making such payments. However, as the 'Big Three' tour operators tightened their grip on the multiple travel agencies in 1993 it became harder for small operators to find rack space for their brochures; in such circumstances they are sometimes forced to agree to pay override commission even though they are least able to bear the extra cost. In 1993, chalet specialists Bladon Lines complained that Lunn Poly asked them to pay 14 per cent commission on sales in return for rack space.

In 1993, the multiple agencies used their ability to negotiate override commissions to cut brochure prices to clients by 10 per cent. This led to a surge of early bookings so that in the end operators also stood to benefit.

In 1993, ABTA's tours committee wanted to produce a black-list of operators which paid agents unreasonably low commission rates. However, it found this difficult to do because some operators claimed to be paying the normal 10 per cent while actually omitting to pay commission on VAT and expecting agents to pay the VAT out of their commission.

2. Compensation payments

In the early 1980s, operators didn't pay compensation to clients when they altered their holidays. Alteration would usually happen because the company had decided to consolidate several holidays that weren't selling well into one. This would lead to some holidays being cancelled altogether, or to significant changes in flight departure times.

However, in the mid-1980s, there were particularly long delays at British airports and some people found themselves spending a whole day out of a seven-day holiday stranded in an airport terminal. This led to pressure for compensation to be introduced. To an extent this demand was fulfilled by insurance companies which started to offer compensation for delayed departures. But increasingly operators offer compensation on a sliding scale for 'major changes' made to bookings. The following might be regarded as 'major changes':

- change of departure airport
- change of departure date
- switch from a day flight (usually 5.30 a.m. to 6.30 p.m.) to a night flight (10.00 p.m. to 5.30 a.m.).
- reduction in the number of nights away
- change of resort for entire holiday
- change to lower graded accommodation for the whole holiday
- change to higher graded accommodation for the whole holiday
- flight time change of more than three hours

Where an operator makes any of these changes, it may offer clients the following options:

a) Accepting the new arrangements, sometimes with per head financial compensation on a sliding scale (*see* Fig 8.6); Thomson offers compensation on two scales depending on the seriousness of the disruption caused. This compensation will usually come in the form of a reduction in the holiday price rather than as straight cash. If several changes are made to the holiday, most companies will make only one compensation payment to cover them all.

Notification more than 42 days before departure	*Notification between*		
	29–42 days	*8–28 days*	*0–7 days*
Nil	£10	£20	£40

Fig. 8.6 Typical sliding scale of compensation for changes to package holidays

b) Changing to another holiday without amendment charges.

c) Cancelling without incurring cancellation charges. When the change has been made within six weeks of the departure date the company may issue credit notes for compensation as well as refunding whatever money has been paid.

Not surprisingly, operators are reluctant to make refunds and the whole area of compensation is hedged around with let-out clauses. For example, it may only be payable on holidays of six nights or more.

All operators reserve their right to refuse to pay compensation in situations which they regard as outside their control, or *force majeure*. This is usually defined as war or threat of war, riot, civil strife, industrial dispute, terrorism, accident, natural or nuclear disaster, epidemic or health risk, fire, airline failure, closure or congestion of airport or ports or prohibitive government action. Some operators even regard adverse weather conditions as *force majeure*.

The operator's financial year

Tour operating has a distinctly seasonal financial pattern. During the first half of the year, even the largest operators may dip into the red as they start to pay some of their summer season costs with only clients' deposits coming in. This was why the Gulf War in the first part of 1991 was so damaging to the ILG group which estimated that it lost 400,000 possible bookings or an estimated £24 million in £60 deposits at a time when it needed to start paying hoteliers to secure its summer accommodation.

Most operators ask for final holiday payments between 8 and 10 weeks before the departure date. Assuming that the peak season for summer holidays starts in the third week of July, they can expect final payments to start rolling in from mid-May onwards. Most late bookings will also be made between June and September; since these must be paid for in full at the time of booking, they give another boost to summer takings.

Those operators that run winter sun and winter sport programmes in addition to the summer sun one can keep receipts flowing in all year round, although the winter programmes are invariably on a smaller scale than the summer ones.

Profitability

The CAA collects data not just on the number of passengers carried by Air Tour Organiser Licence-holders but also on the finances and profitability of the companies it licenses. Table 8.1 shows the number of passengers carried by ATOL-holders, the revenue earned on air holidays between summer 1991 and winter 1994, and the average price of holidays over the same period.

Table 8.2 shows the profitability of the top 30 ATOL-holders between 1973 and 1993. These figures reveal the relatively low profitability of tour operating as a whole. Indeed, the 1992 figures show profitability falling even on a higher turnover. However, the figures for the early 1990s are a clear improvement on those for the late 1980s.

Table 8.1 Passengers carried and revenue earned under all ATOLs, 1991–4

	Return passengers (million)	*Change over last period (million)*	*%*	*Revenue earned £ billion*	*Change over last period £ billion*	*%*	*Average price £*	*Change over last period (£)*	*%*
Summer Season (April to September)									
1991	7.32	(0.8)	(9.3)	2.34	(0.1)	(4.1)	320	17	5.7
1992	9.22	1.9	26.0	3.02	0.7	29.1	328	8	2.5
1993	9.89	0.7	7.3	3.45	0.4	14.2	349	21	6.5
Winter Season (October to March)									
1991/92	3.69	0.6	20.6	1.08	0.2	24.1	293	8	2.9
1992/93	4.34	0.7	17.6	1.48	0.4	37.0	341	48	16.5
1993/94	5.15	0.8	18.7	1.84	0.4	24.3	357	16	4.8
Year to March									
1992	11.01	(0.1)	(1.0)	3.42	0.1	3.3	311	14	4.7
1993	13.56	2.6	23.2	4.50	1.1	31.6	332	21	6.8
1994	15.04	1.5	10.9	5.29	0.8	17.6	352	20	6.0

Notes

The Winter 1993/94 figures show an increase of 18.7% in traffic volume over the previous Winter season and an increase of 4.8% in the average price paid. For the full twelve months, traffic was 10.9% up compared with the previous year and the average price was higher by 6.0%. While this increase is significantly ahead of the rate of inflation, it does not necessarily indicate an improvement in margins: one contributory element is the increased popularity of long-haul holidays.

Source: ATOL Business Monitor CAA

Table 8.2 Profitability of top 30 ATOL holders, 1973–92

Year	*Turnover £ million*	*Total profits £ million*	*Total losses £ million*	*Net result £ million*	*% turnover*
1973	246	2.5	(2.9)	(0.4)	(0.2)
1974	227	1.8	(4.8)	(3.0)	(1.3)
1975	278	13.7	(0.8)	12.9	4.6
1976	326	12.8	(1.1)	11.7	3.6
1977	355	10.0	(2.1)	7.9	2.2
1978	531	35.1	(0.7)	34.4	6.5
1979	695	39.3	(2.6)	37.3	5.4
1980	907	47.2	(3.4)	43.8	4.8
1981	1,020	54.7	(2.5)	52.2	5.1
1982	1,300	37.6	(9.9)	27.7	2.1
1983	1,407	58.2	(2.9)	55.3	3.9
1984	1,799	64.0	(10.7)	53.3	3.0
1985	1,841	79.9	(19.0)	60.9	3.3
1986	2,132	49.7	(14.1)	35.6	1.7
1987	2,791	23.5	(48.3)	(24.8)	(0.9)
1988	3,005	44.8	(29.3)	15.5	0.5
1989	3,048	34.1	(34.2)	(0.1)	0.0
1990	2,731	41.9	(1.6)	40.3	1.5
1991	2,743	110.9	(6.1)	104.8	3.8
1992	3,621	102.2	(1.6)	100.6	2.8
1993	3,826	130.6	(31.6)	99.1	2.6

QUESTIONS AND DISCUSSION POINTS

1. The trend towards late bookings has made it harder for operators to assess how well destinations will sell and has also given them less opportunity to invest clients' deposits. What can operators do to encourage early booking?
2. The data in Table 8.2 shows that tour operating is not a highly profitable business. Discuss why that is and the factors that make it difficult to make it more profitable. Could the big operators do anything to improve profitability in general?
3. In 1993, some operators raised the age for child discounts to 16 or 19. What benefits do you think they hoped to gain from this?

ASSIGNMENTS

1. A tour operator books 80 seats to San Antonio on Ibiza at a cost of £95 per head. Airport charges amount to another £10 per head. It also books twin rooms in a hotel on a half-board basis for 5,217 pesetas per person per night. The transfer coach to the hotel costs 8,695 pesetas one way. The break-even point is 90 per cent. The rate of exchange is 173.90 pesetas to the pound.

   Calculate the per head components cost of a 14 night holiday.

   Add a 35 per cent mark-up to the price.

   If the operator sells all the holidays, how much will it pay out and what will its profits be?

2 Find the exchange rates used for costing the current season's holidays. Compare these with those for 20 July 1993 (shown below) and work out the percentage change up or down for each currency. Which destinations have become pricier as a result of exchange rate changes and which cheaper?

Spanish peseta	199.90
Greek drachma	348.475
Portugese escudo	248.00
Italian lire	2,368.25
Cyprus pound	0.7569
Tunisian dinar	1.5388
Maltese pound	0.5848
Egyptian pound	4.93
American dollar	1.4985
Moroccan dirham	14.007
Tunisian dinar	1.5388
Turkish lira	16,768.35
Austrian schilling	17.995

3 Using this season's brochures, check to see what surcharge guarantees are being offered by large and small operators. Draw up a chart and note on it which operators are offering which types of guarantee.

Then calculate the price per adult of a two week ski holiday travelling by air to Mayrhofen in mid-February. If a surcharge of 4 per cent was levied on this holiday, how much extra would it cost? What if the surcharge was 8 per cent?

Now work out the price per adult of a three week holiday in Barbados in early August. If a surcharge of 4 per cent was levied on this holiday, how much extra would the client pay? What if it was 8 per cent? (Obviously the precise price you get will vary depending on the date you choose and which company's brochure you are looking at. The idea is to enable you to see how much difference a surcharge can make to any brochure price.)

CHAPTER 9

Marketing for tour operators

LEARNING OBJECTIVES

After reading this chapter you should be able to:

- **explain the role of a marketing department**
- **carry out a SWOT analysis for a given tour operating business**
- **understand the relative importance of the different advertising media**
- **write a press release publicising a specific product development**
- **understand the limitations on advertising freedom**
- **plan a brochure launch or similar promotional event**

INTRODUCTION

As tourism has grown in scale and sophistication, marketing has become an increasingly vital role for tour operators. This is how the Institute of Marketing defines 'marketing' which can sometimes seem a nebulous concept:

> Marketing is the management function which organises and directs all those business activities involved in assessing customer needs and converting customer purchasing power into effective demand for a specific product or service, and in moving that product or service to the final consumer or user so as to achieve the profit target or other objective set by the company or other organisation.

More simply, Nigel Jenkins, marketing director of Unijet, has defined marketing as:

> establishing a need for a product or service, and then delivering it in an efficient manner in order to provide a profit on activity.

In *Marketing in Travel and Tourism*, Victor Middleton has drawn attention to the difference between companies with a marketing orientation and other more inward-looking companies with a product or sales orientation. Seeing marketing as being primarily about achieving voluntary exchanges between customers who buy and use products and producer organisations who supply and sell them, he sees four distinguishing characteristics of the market-orientated company. These are:

a) a positive, innovative and highly competitive attitude towards the conduct of exchange transactions;
b) a continuous recognition that the conduct of its business must revolve around the long-term interests of its customers;
c) an outward, responsive attitude to the external business environment;
d) an understanding of the need to balance the requirement to earn short-term profits from existing assets and the need to plan ahead in order to secure future profits as well.

Tour operators are normally market rather than product oriented, primarily because they rarely own the product or its component parts. However, it could be argued that some operators are being forced into more product- and sales-oriented attitudes by their ownership of charter airlines whose seats they must fill at whatever cost (*see* Chapter Three).

In the smallest companies marketing may be just one facet of everyone's role. In medium-sized companies it may be a function of the sales department, but the largest companies have a separate marketing department which is in charge of deciding what kind of holidays the operator should be selling to what types of client. It will then be in overall charge of promoting and selling those holidays. A company may have a sales director and manager or a marketing director and manager, or occasionally both.

The marketing department

The task of the marketing department is to identify and plan holidays to meet potential clients' needs, and to ensure the company offers the right holidays at the right price to the right clients at the right time. Ideally when doing this they should be working within the framework of the company's overall strategic plans which will have identified such long-term objectives as:

- increasing its market share by a set amount over a set period of time (in the case of a new product this would be establishing a set market share by a set date)
- increasing profitability by a set amount by a set time
- achieving a set growth target by a specific date
- developing new products to reduce dependency on specific markets or destinations

Marketing departments can be divided according to function, product or brand, or geographical area. When the department is divided according to **function**, each section will deal with one specific part of marketing for the whole of the company's programme: for example, market research or advertising (*see* Fig. 9.1). This type of division allows staff to build up expertise in particular areas of marketing which they can then readily apply to new products.

When departments are divided according to **product** or **brand**, individual sections may look after all the marketing functions for their particular product, although there will have to be one section to co-ordinate all their activities and another to put a single brochure together (*see* Fig. 9.2). This type of division allows staff to become experts on certain products but can be tricky if sudden switches of destination are called for.

Multinational tour operators may choose to divide their marketing department along geographical lines, with one part looking after the domestic holiday market and another looking after the needs of, for example, the British market.

The work of the marketing department

1. Diagnosis

The marketing department's work should start with a diagnostic look at the company's position which should consider:

a) sales and revenue trends, preferably over a five-year period. By using the CAA's figures for the total number of passengers flown and their

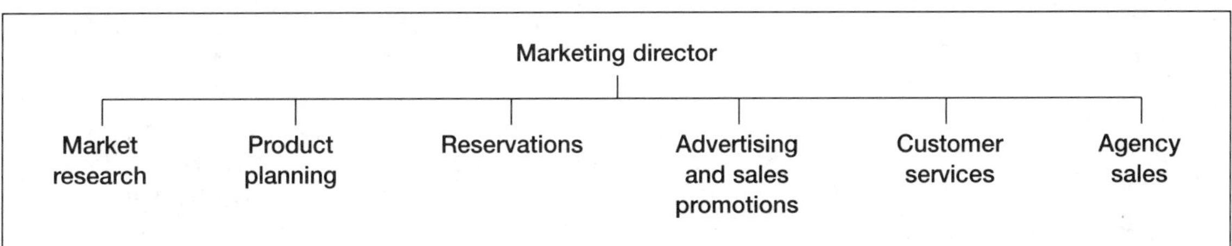

Fig. 9.1 Marketing department divided according to functions

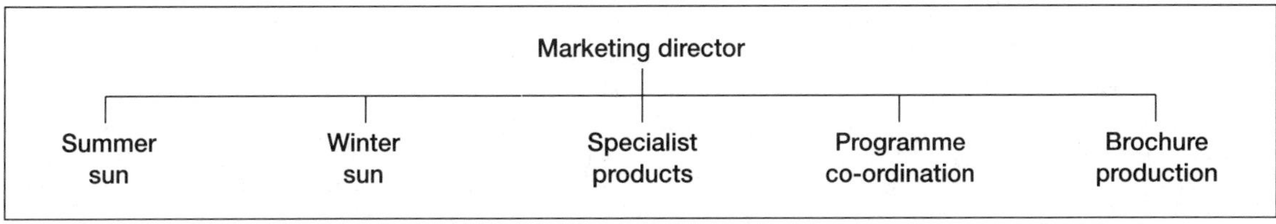

Fig. 9.2 Marketing department divided along product lines

break-down by tour operator it will be possible to compare one particular company's performance with that of its competitors and calculate its share of the market. Computerisation has made it easier for companies to keep track of their own year-on-year sales and revenue performance, broken down into appropriate categories. Government and tourist board passenger surveys will also provide useful data.

b) demographics and changing social attitudes. Some of this information will come from research carried out by specialist companies like the Henley Centre for Forecasting or Mintel, some of it from the company's own research.

c) the actual products on offer and pricing trends. Some of this information will come straight from competitors' brochures, some of it from the trade press and some of it from general business reporting.

d) the environment in which the operator is functioning. Some of this information will come from the trade press, some from the national press and some from specialised research.

2. SWOT analysis

Once the starting point has been examined, marketeers should carry out what is called a **SWOT** analysis to identify the company's strengths, weaknesses, opportunities and threats. For a tour operator, **strengths** may include:

- being long-established
- having a well-known, respected name
- being associated with a product that is growing in popularity
- having good, well-trained staff
- having a superior computer reservations system
- having good contacts in the resorts

Weaknesses are often the inverse of the strengths and might include:

- being new and therefore unknown
- being associated with an inferior product
- being associated with a product thought to be past its prime
- having poorly trained and motivated staff
- having a poor distribution system
- having a computer reservations system perceived as slow or inadequate by travel agents

Opportunities may arise from internal changes but may also arise from changes in the external environment; for example, the collapse of the Berlin Wall in 1989 and the ensuing changes in the old Eastern bloc countries offered opportunities for companies to open up new destinations. Opportunities can also arise if another company goes into liquidation, enabling quick-witted and fast-moving rivals to pick up the lost business. In the travel business technological changes, particularly in aircraft and reservations systems, have regularly offered new opportunities to tour operators.

Again, **threats** can come from external factors. Good examples are the price rises brought about by the oil price increases of the 1970s, the threat presented by war and terrorism in the 1980s and 1990s, and the surcharge problems resulting from exchange rate turmoil in 1993. Sometimes a threat can lie latent for many years, before being sparked into life. So the British climate has always presented a potential threat to the domestic holiday industry. However, until improvements in aircraft and falling fares brought the Mediterranean destinations within reach of almost everybody's pocket, it was a potential rather than an actual threat. Now it is hard to see how even the best efforts of the marketeers can reverse the trend away from British seaside holidays.

3. Product analysis

Companies with a wide range of products will need to consider each of them separately to identify strengths and weaknesses of components of the overall programme. After all, the fact that the summer sun programme is still selling well even in a recession does not necessarily mean that the winter sun or winter sports programme will be doing equally well.

In *Marketing for Tourism* (Pitman Publishing), Holloway and Plant draw attention to two methods of looking more closely at individual products. The first consists of drawing up a product-positioning map (*see* Fig. 9.3) which, by showing, how different companies are perceived by potential customers, sometimes helps identify gaps in the market, the snag being that those gaps could exist because there is no market for the products.

The second is the Boston Consultancy Group (BCG) growth-share matrix which enables a company to divide its products into:

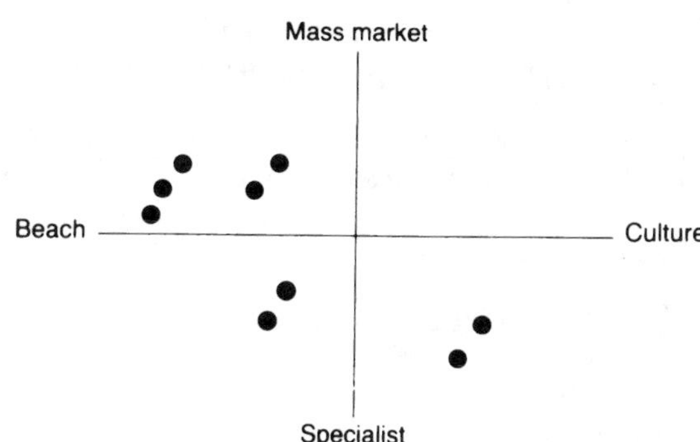

Fig. 9.3 Product-positioning map, showing perceived image of long-haul holidays offered by nine companies
(Source: *Marketing for Tourism*, Holloway and Plant, Pitman Publishing)

1 **Stars** – products which are market leaders and fast-growing. Although these products offer stable profitability, they may not be as highly profitable as might be assumed because their success will quickly attract imitators.
2 **Cash cows** – products with a large market share but in a small or declining market, less likely to attract competitors. Such products are useful because they produce a steady cash flow to cover operating costs but without the high marketing costs necessary when competitors need to be fought off.
3 **Question marks** – products in a high growth market which look likely to succeed.
4 **Dogs** – products in declining markets where the company has only a small market share.

Figure 9.4 shows a typical BCG Growth-Share Matrix with the horizontal axis representing the company's market share (with 10x representing ten times the leading rival's share), and the vertical axis representing the rate of growth.

Clearly a different marketing strategy will be needed for these different product types. For example, it may make sense to pour advertising effort and money into the star and question mark products. To do the same for the dogs would be foolish; instead effort should be focused on devising alternative growth products into which to diversify. It's also important to bear in mind that different types of client usually buy products at different points in their life cycles: 'new' products tend to appeal to adventurous clients and those who like to keep ahead of the Joneses, while products at the end of their life cycle usually appeal to those in search of something cheap and cheerful. Marketing strategies need to take this into account, particularly when it comes to selecting appropriate advertising media.

The marketing plan

1. Forecasting

Once the marketeers have established the company's position, looked at relevant trends and examined individual products in more detail, they will be ready to draw up a marketing plan which will depend on their forecasts for the future. Accurate forecasting is made particularly difficult by the range of external factors that can come into play (*see* Chapter Eleven), and unfortunately tour operators have not proved very good at foreseeing the future. In particular, in the late 1980s and early 1990s, they tended to overestimate the size of the summer sun market, leading to dumping of products at low prices even in high season. However, short-term forecasts, covering the next three to six months, are not as problematic as long-term forecasts.

Forecasters will have to consider both demand for a particular product and its sales potential. Forecasting demand is about looking at the overall

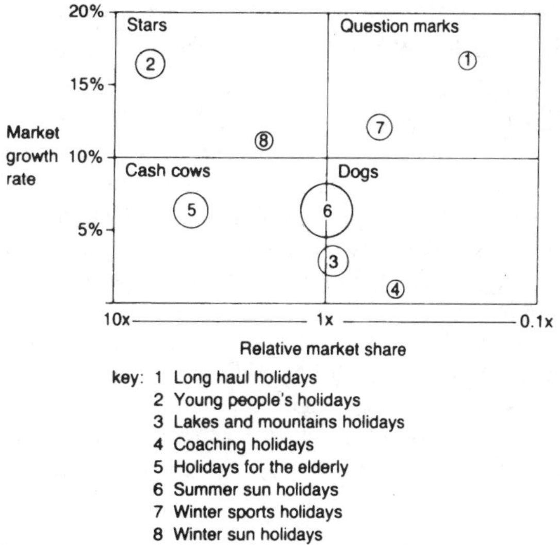

Fig. 9.4 BCG growth-share matrix applied to a major tour operator's package tour programme
(Source: *Marketing for Tourism*, Holloway and Plant, Pitman Publishing)

size of the market, deciding what percentage of it is likely to buy a holiday and of that percentage, how many are likely to buy a particular company's products as opposed to those of a competitor. Forecasting sales potential is about looking at external circumstances which could have an influence on sales, considering such industry-specific factors as new government legislation and its likely impact, and then assessing the company's own sales potential in light of its existing sales pattern and marketing plan. Ideally, the company should consider best and worst case sales scenarios, before arriving at a final estimate of the likely sales performance.

2. Outlining an overall strategy

There are three main strategic approaches an operator can take to marketing.

a) The biggest companies may decide to go for the lowest prices, building on the economies of scale their size brings and on their muscle when it comes to sealing contracts.
b) Smaller companies may decide to concentrate on specific products and on building up a reputation for quality to justify higher prices. Sunvil Holidays is a good example of a company that has pursued this strategy in the early 1990s.
c) Other companies may decide to target specific sectors of the market. Saga Holidays is typical of a company adopting this approach.

Within these overall strategies, companies may take a long- or short-term approach. Some will nurture individual destinations over a period of years, even where they are not immediately profitable. Others may wait until somewhere becomes fashionable and move in quickly to exploit that fact, pulling out again as soon as the immediate cash bonanza starts to fade.

Companies do not always see profits as the sole target of their strategies. In the early 1990s, the UK's largest operators regarded building up their market share as important as short-term profitability, seeing this as a way of ensuring a prosperous future.

3. The marketing mix

In the light of the forecasts and the overall strategy, a marketing plan will be drawn up, utilising what is known as the 'marketing mix', defined by Kotler as

> the mixture of controllable marketing variables that the firm uses to pursue the sought level of sales in the target market.

The 'variables' that make up the marketing mix are usually divided into four categories, known as 'the four Ps'. These four Ps are:

- Product – design, features, range, brand name, quality
- Price – basic price, discounts, surcharges, extras, commissions
- Place – the distribution channel, coverage, location
- Promotion – sales, advertising, promotions, other publicity

One particular marketing plan will not necessarily cover all aspects of the marketing mix, although an effective plan will at least have considered them all. Many aspects of the marketing mix (product design, the brochure, the sales process, arriving at a holiday price) have already been considered in previous chapters, but it is important to be aware that they all form part of a good marketing plan.

Ideally, marketing plans should be drawn up in tightly quantifiable terms so that their effectiveness can be measured. They must also be controlled carefully, particularly to prevent risk of overrunning the budget.

The marketing budget

The marketing budget is drawn up as part of the company's overall financial planning process and will involve discussions between people in marketing and those in other decision-making departments. In theory, the company should first establish its objectives, then draw up a marketing plan to achieve them and then work out how much must be set aside to fulfil the plan. However, just as forecasting is often carried out in a less than scientific fashion, so calculating the marketing budget is often done more on the basis of what the company can afford in light of the previous year's profits than on the basis of identified needs.

Sometimes the budget will be based on an estimate of the number of passengers the company hopes to carry. So, for example, a company expecting to carry 200,000 passengers might have a marketing budget of £300,000, which would add

£1.50 to the average holiday cost. When a new product is being launched the sum involved could be very much higher; so when Thomson launched its 'Freestyle' programme for 20 to 35-year-olds the marketing costs are estimated to have worked out at £75 per holiday sold.

Market research

When deciding on a marketing plan and a budget, tour operators will usually have done *some* market research, even if only looking at their own sales figures for the past year. However, some information can only be found out by secondary research, involving surveys, questionnaires and other methods of communicating with customers and potential customers. Secondary research can be used for other purposes too; for example, to establish trends in the market or to find out how popular particular brochure designs or advertisements are.

Effective secondary research can be very expensive. Consequently, although large tour operators may be able to afford to use outside specialists like the British Market Research Bureau, smaller companies may not bother with any formal research at all beyond what can be done from their desks.

Before embarking on a research project the company needs to:

a) define the problem and the objectives, to ensure that the right questions (and only those questions) are asked.
b) identify all the possible sources of information so money isn't wasted on finding out what was already easily available.
c) develop a research plan.
d) design any necessary survey forms and decide how the research should be conducted. Questions for the survey should never be vague, ambiguous, too testing of the respondent's memory or phrased to encourage only one particular answer.

One of the most popular forms of market research is the survey, whether undertaken on the street or in people's houses. Given that the British population is currently about 56 million, to be statistically valid a survey needs to include the views of about 2,000 respondents, but these must form a representative cross-section either of the population as a whole, or of the group which the research is interested in. It would not, therefore, be adequate to survey all 2,000 students in a college to obtain a meaningful picture of how many holidaymakers went to Spain last year, unless the research was being carried out for a company whose clients were all likely to be students. Instead, a representative sample of people of both sexes, all age groups, from different socio-economic backgrounds and from varying ethnic groups would be required.

Not all secondary research is concerned with surveying techniques, although other methods tend to take longer and are therefore even more expensive. An operator may, for example, set up a panel interview where a group of people are asked their views on a new advert or brochure design. Thomson even ran an experiment in which they asked people to say what sort of personalities they would imagine the different tour operators having if they were to come alive as people. From this it discovered that many people would have seen it as a solid, sensible family man. a finding which might have had implications for its advertising.

Customer service questionnaires (CSQs)

Most large companies give their clients questionnaires (customer service questionnaires or CSQs) to complete at the end of their holiday. These generate a lot of information about various different aspects of the product: how welcoming the hotel reception was, how good the food was, how efficient the resort representative was, etc. However, there are drawbacks to using questionnaires to acquire information:

a) Not everyone will complete them. Some companies encourage them to do so by distributing the forms on the flight home and collecting them back in again before people disembark. Others supply prepaid envelopes to encourage people to reply. British Airways Holidays even offers two free holidays as an incentive to persuade people to complete the form.
b) People with complaints may be more inclined to complete the forms than satisfied customers.
c) Such questionnaires can only be used to find out about existing resorts, hotels that are already in the brochures, etc. They are of no use when it comes to identifying things like gaps in the programme or better hotels.

Further information can be culled from the customer complaints/customer relations department who usually receive letters indicating when something has gone seriously wrong.

The four Ps

Product policies

As we have seen in Chapter One, the package holiday product is unusual in many ways which have implications for marketing. It is also important to realise that when people buy a package holiday they are buying not so much the product or the features of the product, but the benefits that those features offer and the fulfilment of needs through them. Much marketing effort therefore goes into showing how many needs a particular product can satisfy. In a highly competitive market, it is vital to highlight what benefits your particular company's product offers that another's does not. Ideally, it should also highlight any **unique selling propositions** (USPs) that would make it more attractive than the competitor's product; for a company like The Club, specialising in holidays for young people, that might mean the fact that only their clients will be using the hotel, while for long-haul market leaders Kuoni it might mean highlighting a destination not featured in any other brochure.

Among other features of their products that operators may choose to emphasise are:

- low price or 'value for money'
- quality – you pay more but for a good reason
- fashionability, especially of a destination
- reliability – the company has been in business a very long time or has featured a particular destination for a long time
- style or personality of the product – Club Med, for example, prides itself on its distinctiveness and class
- novelty – for example, Voyages Jules Verne offering the first self-drive tours of China and Regent Holidays uniquely featuring trips to Albania

Pricing polices

The UK holiday market is generally thought of as more price-led than is the case in the rest of Europe. This is partly a result of the 1990s recession which has put a lot of emphasis on holidays which are perceived as 'affordable' and as representing good value for money (often a pseudonym for 'cheap'). However, it also has to do with intense competition which has persuaded the operators to engage in price wars over and over again, cutting back on short-term profit margins in the hope of long-term benefit. Furthermore, for several years operators have got their estimates of the size of the market (or their own share of it) wrong, resulting in discounting to shift unsold holidays and an increased expectation by holidaymakers that they would do better to delay booking for as long as possible.

The result of all this has been to make pricing a prime marketing tool, with most of the biggest operators determined to ensure their prices are never undercut by their rivals, even when this sometimes means reissuing brochures and discounting. 'Lead-in' prices, in particular, are very important for their publicity value, either through the media or emblazoned on the front cover. Sometimes the number of holidays actually available at the hyped prices is very small (indeed, in 1992 there was doubt whether any of Airtours' trumpeted £299 deals to the Dominican Republic actually existed). However, clients who have set their heart on going somewhere, enticed by a low price, may be persuaded to settle for something else when they find that their first choice is unavailable; in that way a very few 'loss leaders' can actually generate profit-making bookings.

On top of the operator's own discounts, prices have been kept down by travel agencies offering reductions to try and attract bookings away from their rivals. This is made easier for those multiples which are able to negotiate override commissions (*see* page 183) which they then pass on as discount prices to the customer.

Some destinations, especially the Mediterranean resorts, are particularly price-sensitive; for example, in years when prices to Spain are relatively high, Greece may receive more visitors, and when Greek prices are high, people will flock to Spain, on the assumption that what they are after (i.e. sun and sand) can be found just as readily in one as in the other. After a shaky start, Turkey is also entering this equation. Not only does it have the same combination of sun, sand and antiquities as Greece, but it also has a relatively low cost of living and therefore lower prices for incidentals like meals out and souvenirs. So in 1993 when the market was still fairly flat, Turkey was one of the fastest growing destinations. There also appear to be effective cut-off prices as far as the public are concerned; holidays to Greece for £295 will sell, those for £305 won't. In 1993, a few companies even experimented with 'price guarantees' of the John Lewis type, offering to refund the difference in price to anyone who found the same product on sale at a lower price within a set period of time.

However, not all operators think such low-price-led marketing makes sense. In 1993, Club Med stopped selling its holidays through Lunn Poly because it did not want them discounted. Instead, it felt its products should be marketed on quality in the hope of building up repeat business. Some companies also indulge in 'premium pricing', especially with a new product for which there is little competition, using higher prices to cream off quick profits.

CREATING A BRAND IMAGE

Most package holidays are sold through travel agencies where they are represented by a selection of brochures on the shelves, all competing for the customer's attention. In those circumstances marketeers will have three clear objectives:

a) to ensure that their product stands out from the others
b) to ensure that it is readily identifiable as one particular company's product
c) to ensure that potential customers have a clear idea of what sort of product is being sold

Making the product stand out

The average travel agency may have rack space for about 140 different brochures, which means lots of products all competing to catch the customer's eye. In some ways a company's scope for making their product stand out is being reduced. For example, city-breaks specialist Time Off used to use distinctive leaflet-sized brochures. However, they have now switched to standard A4 format because travel agencies have standard-sized brochure racks; anything that doesn't fit or wastes space is unlikely to get shelved.

Given the limitations of the A4-sized standard brochure, operators mainly fall back on design to make their product stand out. However, this is not at all easy to achieve, especially since the travel agent may put a sticker across even the most attractive front cover. More money tends to be spent on long-haul brochures which often have the most striking images on the glossiest paper. However, the main thing which makes one particular brochure stand out from the others is when it has a picture that differs from those of its neighbour. So in 1993/4 one of the most striking ski brochures was Airtours' which did away with images of skiers altogether in favour of bold blue writing against a grey-white image of snow.

Making the product identifiable as a particular company's

When it comes to ensuring that a product is readily identifiable, several factors play an important role.

1. Name

The simplest way for a client to identify a product is obviously by its name; Thomson may now have a multitude of different brochures on the market but most of them bear the Thomson name so they can be easily recognised. There are a few exceptions, of course; for example, for some time after taking over Horizon, Thomson continued to produce Horizon brochures, but with a small and not always instantly visible Thomson logo; the Skytours product, too, is only identifiable as a Thomson product by a small logo. In 1992 British Airways renamed its 'Speedbird' long-haul product 'British Airways Worldwide Holidays' so that the name would immediately evoke the image of the well-known parent company.

The value of a familiar name is exemplified by the fact that even after taking over OSL Villas, Thomson continued to label some of its villa and apartment holidays as being 'OSL' products. Likewise, after absorbing Holiday Club International, it retained the HCI name. British Airways Holidays also continued to mention 'Speedbird' in its new long-haul brochures.

One of the problems Owners Abroad suffered from in trying to establish its image in the public mind was that its tour operating side has been created out of the amalgamation of all sorts of different companies, most of them (Sunmed, Enterprise, Sovereign, Olympic) with strong images of their own. In 1994 Owners Abroad announced plans to rebrand its products in order to make the parent company more visible (*see* pages 49–50). However, in the short term, it risked losing the brand loyalty to those individual products. What was more, this was likely to be a lengthy exercise since all the different brands had been contracted, priced and marketed separately. In contrast, Airtours, which started life as a tour operator, has Airtours clearly emblazoned on all its products. In 1993 when Sun International (owners of the Bridge Travel Group) bought loss-making German specialists GTF Tours they had to decide whether to stick with a long-established, well-known name or to change it to 'German Travel Service' which would let it slot in alongside their other products in the public's mind. In 1994 Iberotel transferred Neilson's Lakes and Mountains programme to sister-company Sunworld, justifying the change with the argument that the public thought of Neilson as a ski operator and therefore overlooked the second product.

When choosing a name, a company can go for something dull and corporate, like Thomson, or for something more evocative of the product, like Sunvil. Ideally, the name must be easy to pronounce, both for English and non-English speakers, and it must be easy to remember. A company like Tjaereborg is the exception that proves the rule. In choosing a name, companies may also have to choose between the convenience of having one which immediately identifies the product (Amsterdam Travel Service, Olympic Holidays, Yugotours) and one which is less product-linked but which offers greater scope for diversifying into other areas without problem (Cosmos, Pullman Holidays, Panorama).

Apart from the company's own name, the actual product often benefits from an identifying tag as well. Again, wherever possible it's best to pick something distinctive, even when the product is basically similar to everybody else's. So Silk Cut Travel describes its long-haul brochure as its 'World Collection' to distinguish it from Kuoni, Thomson and all the other 'Worldwide' products. Thomson has a 'Faraway Shores' brochure covering its long-haul beach destinations as well as the main long-haul 'Worldwide' brochure.

2. Logos

Almost all companies nowadays have a logo, defined as 'an identifying symbol consisting of a simple picture or design and/or letters'. Tour operators' logos usually consist of their name, sometimes decorated with something thought of as symbolising holidays: the sun, birds, an aeroplane. Occasionally the decoration will relate to the company's name or image rather than to the general holiday atmosphere: so Sovereign uses a stylised crown over the letter 'o'. Sometimes companies don't add in any decoration: Cosmos, for example, sticks with just its name. The logo may become the company's registered trademark, in which case no one is allowed to produce another one that is almost identical.

Colour plays an important role in logos; it's not just chance that so many companies – Thomson, Falcon, Aspro – opt for red, with its connotations of warmth, for their logos. Ideally, red is combined with yellow, another warm colour (Aspro, Thomson). However, if all companies went for red and yellow that would defeat the second objective of making their product stand out from the competition. Companies offering upmarket products in particular may steer clear of these rather garish colours, opting for more stylish blues and greens. Sometimes the choice of colour or image will be dictated by other considerations: British Airways Holidays has the same colours and design as parent company, British Airways, so that the two are instantly linked in the client's mind.

Apart from pictures and colour, companies can make use of the wide variety of different typefaces available to make their own name stand out. For example, when Sunworld launched its new logo in 1993 it incorporated two different typefaces into its own name, beneath a schematic globe.

3. Images

Apart from the logo, a company can select a particular image to link up its products and make them instantly identifiable. In the late 1980s one of the most easily identifiable products was Intasun's which always featured a blonde woman in a bikini who was drawn rather than photographed and cropped up in different poses on all Intasun brochures. In the 1990s, Airtours also started to use a schematic female for the covers of its specialist

Fig. 9.5 A selection of tour operators' logos

brochures. However, the Airtours girl was more varied and imaginative than Intasun's had ever been.

Kuoni has been particularly successful in creating an overall identifying image for its main worldwide products. Its logo, in pure white, is nothing to write home about, but every year the brochures bear striking single photographs, usually of people from the tourist receiving countries, framed in vivid colour.

4. 'Tags' and slogans

Some companies also devise advertising tags and slogans which they can put on their brochures and then reproduce in advertising. Few of these slogans are truly memorable. However, they can be quite useful in summarising how the company sees itself and therefore what market it is likely to be targeting. The following are a few tags that appeared on 1993/4 brochures:

'We go a long way to make you happy' – Airtours

'The A to Z of Long-Haul Travel' – Kuoni

'Ski with the Leaders' – Neilson

'The World from a Different Point of View' – Encounter Overland

'Holidays for Thinking People' – Regent Holidays

5. Identifying the product on offer

Since brochures are expensive to produce, it is important that they are designed to make clear what is on offer, thereby cutting down on waste as much as possible. It is also important that the public can associate a particular type of product with a particular name. Although an established image can certainly be changed (viz. Airtours' effort to reposition itself further upmarket in 1994), this may take time and only larger companies can usually afford such luxury. When Riva Travel was born out of the ILG collapse in 1991, it was originally envisaged and launched as an upmarket company. However, within eight months there was a change of strategy and it was relaunched as a mass-market product. While that alone would not have accounted for its failure, the uncertainty about what was being offered certainly can't have helped.

As usual, it is the front cover that has to make it clear what sort of product is on offer, so family holiday products usually have pictures of happy families on beaches on the front, while long-haul brochures tend to emphasise the exotic appearance of the destinations featured rather than the fun to be had in them. Indeed the director of Silk Cut Travel believed putting a picture of a beach on a brochure full of what were really adventure holidays actually lost the company business. Holidays aimed at the youth market will always show pictures of young people enjoying themselves, often, as with The Club, in a blatantly sexual way. However, holidays aimed at the older end of the market are less likely to feature pictures of the intended consumers; instead, like the long-haul brochures, they usually home in on pictures either of the destinations or of the mode of transport.

Overbranding

Sometimes, however, an operator may feel that a travel agent's name is an even better endorsement than their own, and this has led to the widespread policy of 'overbranding'. Thomas Cook, for example, has an arrangement to overprint other operators' brochures with a flash reading 'Thomas Cook Holidays'; companies favoured in this way feel that the benefit they get from the link-up with such a famous name outweighs any loss of identity involved. For example, after Thomas Cook overbranded Sunworld's summer sun product, the company saw bookings rise significantly. Although in 1993 Thomas Cook relegated Sunworld to its premier selection group, replacing it with the Owners Abroad product, Enterprise, Sunworld continued to sell well and was able to come to a new overbranding agreement with AT Mays.

In 1993 six miniples (John Hilary Travel, Alec Bristow Travel, Ickenham Travel, Dunstan Brearley Travel, Winston Rees Travel and Sam Smith Travel) announced a deal with Ultimate Holidays that would enable them to re-cover their ski and Far East brochures with 'own-brand' labels. In 1993 AT Mays started overbranding Sunworld as their 'own' summer sun product; however, it allowed the company's own name to remain on the front cover alongside its own, unlike the other agencies. By 1994, Thomas Cook was overbranding 14 suppliers, each covering a different sector of the market.

Operators see overbranding as making the chosen brochures stand out, thereby helping them gain maximum exposure in the High Street. However, the more it happens, the less impact it is likely to have.

Brand stretching

When it comes to 'brands', a tour operator may opt for one overall brand name or may develop different brand names to cover different products. Thomson, Cosmos and Sunworld tend to go for the 'one brand' strategy (although Thomson does have its Horizon and Skytours products), while until 1994 Owners Abroad opted to keep the brand names of the different companies it had bought. Until 1994, Airtours also went for a 'one brand' strategy. However, after buying Aspro and Tradewinds, it subdivided its products into three distinct brands: those sold under the Aspro name are the cheap and cheerful packages, those sold as Airtours are more mainstream, and those sold as Tradewinds are most upmarket.

If a company has a really strong brand image, it may be able to indulge in what is called 'brand stretching' – moving into a completely different product area while still using the same name. This was what Airtours was doing in 1994 when it launched a new cruising brochure under the familiar Airtours brand name. An added extra to 'brand stretching' is that it tends to consolidate consumer loyalty to a particular name because the client can buy a wide variety of products from the one company.

Rarely, a company has a name that might be thought to be a problem. Silk Cut Travel (owned by Meon), for example, might be thought to be at risk from a boycott by the anti-smoking lobby. However, research (admittedly in 1984) suggested only 5 per cent of people would find the link sufficiently off-putting to avoid using the company. All the same, the company has been careful to avoid representing the cigarette brand in its brochures.

BROCHURES

Clearly brochures are an operator's main marketing tool. Indeed they are so important that an entire chapter (Chapter Five) has been devoted to their role. However, this chapter looks at some specifically marketing aspects of the brochure, as opposed to its actual creation.

The launch of a new season's brochures acts as the spur for a flurry of promotional activities.

The press

The launch of a new brochure makes the perfect time to send press releases to the media (newspapers, magazines, radio and television) who are always on the lookout for new angles to publicise. Press releases (*see* page 209) will often home in on particular features of the new programme: new destinations, new hotels, cheap lead-in prices. So, in August 1993 the £299 lead-in price for Airtours' holidays to Cuba generated publicity not just on holiday programmes but also in the mainstream news.

Travel agencies

Travel agents must also be informed when a new brochure comes out. If there will be a delay in getting main stocks to them, they should be provided with a file copy to deal with enquiries generated by media activity.

This is also the time when many operators run promotional events for agents. Such events are normally aimed at familiarising agents with the brochures, either by formal teaching sessions or through competitions based on their contents. Events are usually designed to be fun so that agents who've enjoyed themselves (or even won something) may be more inclined to sell the particular company's products (*see* pages 214–215).

Summer sun brochures start to reach the travel agencies in mid-August, while winter sun and winter sports brochures usually arrive in May. Summer sun brochures therefore appear before the previous summer season has finished. In contrast, winter brochures usually appear *after* the previous winter season. However, in 1992 Crystal Holidays launched its 1992/3 brochure before the end of the 1992 winter season, and in 1993 Ingham's followed suit, bringing out a preview 1993/4 brochure in March. In both cases the operators did this by reprinting the previous year's brochure but with a new cover and in both cases it was believed they did it in the hope of increasing their market share.

Companies are sometimes reluctant to be the first to produce their brochures; although this can guarantee scooping the publicity, it also allows competitors to wait until they've seen the prices and then reduce theirs accordingly. Instead they may hang back to see what their competitors are doing before launching their own brochure. So in 1993 Manos delayed producing a Cyprus brochure with its Greece and Turkey programmes; after difficult 1992 and 1993 seasons it wanted to see what other operators would do before deciding whether to continue offering Cyprus.

Sometimes a company will launch brochures concentrating on one part of the programme before the main brochure launch. In publicity terms this is a good way of focusing on specific products. New products may also take longer to sell, so getting the brochure out as soon as possible is very important. However, in 1993 Unijet co-ordinated the launch of all its winter brochures, believing that its failure to do that in previous years had meant customers perceiving it as a specialist in whatever product had just been launched rather than a major operator offering a variety of destinations.

Deciding on the brochure format

In the early 1980s, tour operators usually produced one summer sun and one winter sun brochure, with a separate brochure for winter sports holidays. However, there are several problems with this approach. In the first place, few clients are equally interested in all parts of an operator's programme, which means they are usually only concerned with relatively few pages of the main brochure. This is obviously wasteful in terms of the money spent on producing chunky brochures, most pages of which will be thrown away unread. It is also more costly to transport and post big brochures than small ones. So increasingly operators have tended to break their programmes up and put discrete parts into separate brochures. So the main Thomson summer sun brochure for 1993 had 507 pages, but the Small and Friendly brochure, featuring holidays in small hotels, had a much more manageable 83. Unfortunately, travel agencies have limited rack space, so the more a programme is broken down, the less likely it is that all parts will be shelved.

One answer is for operators to produce separate, or 'dedicated', brochures for particular products they feel need publicity, primarily new ones. So in 1993 Airtours produced a dedicated Cuba brochure to promote its new venture there and Sunworld had a dedicated 'Reflections of Goa' brochure. Travelscene produced a new 'BreakAway to Spain' brochure to publicise both its link with P&O European Ferries and, in particular, its holidays using the new Portsmouth to Bilbao route which even regular clients would not necessarily know about; once the route became familiar they planned to merge it back into the main 'BreakAway to the Continent' brochure. Thomson also had a dedicated 'Mexico' brochure, as it tried to relaunch a product which had not done as well as expected in the past.

Dedicated brochures are also used to differentiate products. Airtours put Tunisia into a separate brochure for summer 1994 in the hope that clients would understand it was a rather different destination to, say, Spain. Having Cuba in a stand-alone brochure was also intended to differentiate it in this way; during 1993 when Thomson included it in the main worldwide brochure they found clients assuming it would compare with other Caribbean holiday islands like Barbados and the Bahamas.

Alternatively, operators can produce separate dedicated destination brochures to go out to independent travel agents, and a comprehensive version to got to the multiples who are unlikely to rack all the separate ones.

Maximising the brochure's selling potential

It has been suggested that the tour operating business produces roughly 120 million brochures a year, of which maybe 48 million are not used at all. Given the cost of producing and distributing brochures, it is vital to operators that they are used effectively to sell their products, which means aiming for a high conversion rate of brochures taken to holidays booked (*see* page 129). Figures are hard to come by but some industry estimates suggest that some holidays are only sold after 28 sets of customers have picked up the brochure featuring them. Unfortunately because most brochures are distributed through the intermediary of travel agencies, operators have only limited control over conversion ratios (*see* Fig. 9.6). They can, however, limit the number of brochures an agent is supplied with, rewarding good sellers with large supplies and punishing poor ones with fewer. So for winter 1993/4 Unijet announced that it would only be sending bulk deliveries of brochures to its top 3,500 agents to try and eliminate waste.

- Only distributing brochures when ordered
- Tightening distribution control in favour of productive agents
- Packing brochures in smaller units for distribution
- Producing one year-round brochure instead of separate winter and sun ones
- Putting prices on a pull-out supplement so that if they need revising it can be done without reprinting the whole brochure

Fig. 9.6 Some ways in which operators can influence brochure conversion ratios

Reissuing the brochure

If all has gone well with an operator's forecasting and sales are proceeding according to plans, then it should not be necessary to reissue the brochure, simply to reprint it if stocks get too low. However, by the early 1990s new editions had become a regular feature of operators' strategies. Sometimes new editions appeared because one operator's prices were too high in comparison with another's and had to be reduced, sometimes because sales were sluggish and price cuts needed to be made to nudge them along. In 1993, for example, some companies produced two or three new editions to shift their summer sun products.

Relaunches are far from ideal, not least because of the administrative inconvenience of having to refund the difference between the original price and the new one to people who have already booked. This involves not only the operator but also the agent in non-productive extra work, and since agents' commission depends on the cost of the holiday, the new lower price means they must do more work for a reduced income, hardly a process to endear the operator to them.

Because of the cost of preparing whole new brochures, some companies now produce their price lists as a separate pull-out supplement, sometimes on cheaper paper. It is then possible to alter the price panels and replace them in the brochures without having to alter the whole thing. For example, Falcon Holidays used a pull-out price panel for its 1993 summer sun brochure which ran to four editions.

ADVERTISING

The ABTA Tour Operators' Code of Conduct defines advertising as 'a means of promoting tours, holidays or travel arrangements by publication other than a brochure'. Most tour operators are involved in some kind of advertising, although the fact that their products are sold through travel agencies means that less advertising is needed than would be the case if they had to depend solely on their own promotional efforts.

ABTA's code of conduct sets out the following rules for advertising.

a) All advertising by tour operators shall observe the requirements of all such Acts of Parliament as may be enacted from time to time and, in particular, of the Trade Descriptions Act, the Misrepresentation Act, the Civil Aviation Act, the Control of Misleading Advertisements Regulations and the Consumer Protection Act.

b) Tour operators who are convicted of offences against these laws shall be deemed to be in breach of the code.
c) All advertising shall comply with the codes or regulations of the recognised organisations or associations. Where a tour operator is reported to have breached such codes or regulations, the code of conduct committee retains the right to reconsider the alleged complaint and to decide in their view if the tour operator has or has not breached this code.
d) A tour operator shall not advertise in such a manner as to suggest that other members of the Association are or may become insolvent.
e) A tour operator shall show his ABTA number in all his press advertisements for travel business, but shall not be obliged to do so where these advertisements are in classified run-on form unless such advertisements contain any reference to ABTA.

Companies may want to advertise two different things:

(i) Their company image. The intention will be to create a generally favourable image of the company rather than to focus on any particular holidays. So in 1993 Thomson ran a very successful advertising campaign on the theme 'We go there. We don't go there' in which the company's customers were shown enjoying themselves in desirable resorts with attractive hotels and efficient transport, in contrast with people who had been foolish enough to travel by other (unspecified) means. During the late 1980s when there was a lot of merger activity in the City, tour operators spent much of their television advertising budget on corporate advertising rather than on advertising aimed at selling holidays. In 1993, when Airtours put in its bid for Owners Abroad, it upped its television advertising budget to try and overcome its rather downmarket image.
(ii) Special offers. Advertisements for special offers on specific holidays are far more common than those for standard brochure holidays.

Designing an advert

Tour operators may budget as much as £20 million a year for advertising. Some will use an advertising agency, like Ogilvy and Mather, WCRS or Saatchi and Saatchi, to come up with ideas and produce their advertisements. Others will use their own marketing departments to do the work.

Advertisements are a form of communication and have three main functions: to inform the viewer about the product, to persuade them to buy it and to remind the viewer of the product or company in general. The message needs to be short, eye-catching and credible, and its appeal can be rational or emotional or both. Advertisers use the acronym AIDA to signify that the advert should

A attract Attention
I create Interest
D foster Desire, and
A inspire Action

Adverts often try to exploit the product's unique selling proposition but, depending on where the product is in its life cycle, may focus on different aspects of it. For example, with a new product, ads will emphasise the benefits it offers, whereas with a long-established product they may prefer to emphasise anything it offers that is better than what the competition is doing. The design of the ad will also depend on the product's features; so Voyages Jules Verne's hefty, informative ads aimed at an adventurous clientele are wholly different from Thomson's more generalised ones.

Because national advertising is expensive, not many tour operators use it. However, those that don't may still benefit from the efforts of those who do. If, for example, a client is inspired to go to an agency to pick up a Thomson brochure which is not then available, they may pick up other brochures instead rather than leave empty-handed.

It is not always easy to assess the impact of an advertising campaign since it's always possible the company would have got the bookings anyway, even without the adverts. However, when special offers aimed at selling slow-moving products are advertised, it is easier to assume extra bookings have come in as a result of the ads.

It's worth adding that tour operators also benefit from indirect forms of advertising. For example, national tourist boards sometimes run advertising campaigns to promote their country. While these rarely if ever mention the tour operators who go there, they will have the general effect of stimulating interest in a destination which should translate indirectly into bookings for relevant tour operators. For example over the winter of 1993/4 the Israel Government Tourist Office ran a £500,000 TV campaign, and all the operators featuring the country expected to benefit. Travel agencies also advertise, although often in far too general terms to benefit particular operators.

Even more influential are the television holiday programmes which are not meant to be advertising but do, of course, have that effect. Particularly important are BBC1's *Holiday* and *Summer Holiday* and ITV's *Wish You Were Here* which focus on specific named products. Radio 4's Saturday morning *Breakaway* is similarly influential with people who prefer the radio to television. In 1994, a new cable and satellite television channel called simply *Travel* was launched. This, too, is likely to offer plenty of indirect advertising opportunities for operators.

In order for operators to take full advantage of adverts, whether direct or indirect, they must ensure all their agents have an adequate supply of brochures to handle the response. Smaller operators sometimes lose out when people pick up their brochures to make comparisons which don't translate into bookings.

Placing advertisements

Adverts can be placed in:

- the national press
- the regional press
- the travel trade press
- national radio
- local radio
- national television channels
- regional television channels
- satellite (BSkyB) and cable television channels

Before deciding where to place an ad, it's essential to determine what sort of people will see it and how often. If an advertisement is to go on television, it's vital to know how many viewers the channel has, what catchment area it covers, and what times and slots are available. For a press ad, the operator needs to know:

a) how many copies will be distributed
b) what the catchment area is
c) how many people read each edition
d) whether people receive it free or have to pay for it
e) how often it's published
f) whether its readership is high or low brow
g) how good the reproductive quality is
h) whereabouts in the paper/magazine the ads will be placed

Scale of advertising

Between 1992 and 1993, tour operators increased their overall advertising budgets by 29 per cent. In 1991 advertising by tour operators had made up 16.5 per cent of the travel industry's total; in 1992 the percentage had risen to 18.5 per cent, as increased competition in a flat market encouraged operators to spend more on publicity.

Compared with travel agencies and airlines, tour operators have a very seasonal advertising pattern, with more than 25 per cent of their total advertising taking place in January which used to be the peak booking season. Conversely, their low point for advertising (5 per cent) is July when most likely clients could be assumed to be already overseas. Although travel agency advertising patterns are largely independent of tour operators, they reach a peak in late August and September, to coincide with the arrival of the operators' new brochures in their shops (*see* Fig. 9.7).

The travel trade press

The three main trade papers which are read by most travel agents are *Travel Weekly*, *Counter Weekly* and *Travel Trade Gazette (TTG)*. All of these carry extensive advertising, mainly by tour operators, and are effective mediums for getting a message to travel agents. Like all advertising, they need to convey a clear, simple message as vividly as possible.

The most striking adverts are full page, colour spreads, those in the centre and on right-hand pages having the most impact. However, sometimes black and white adverts with striking images or slogans can be nearly as effective; so in 1993 British Airways Holidays was advertising with the slogan 'Life's a beach and then you're surcharged', promoting the message that none of their long-haul holidays were subject to surcharges.

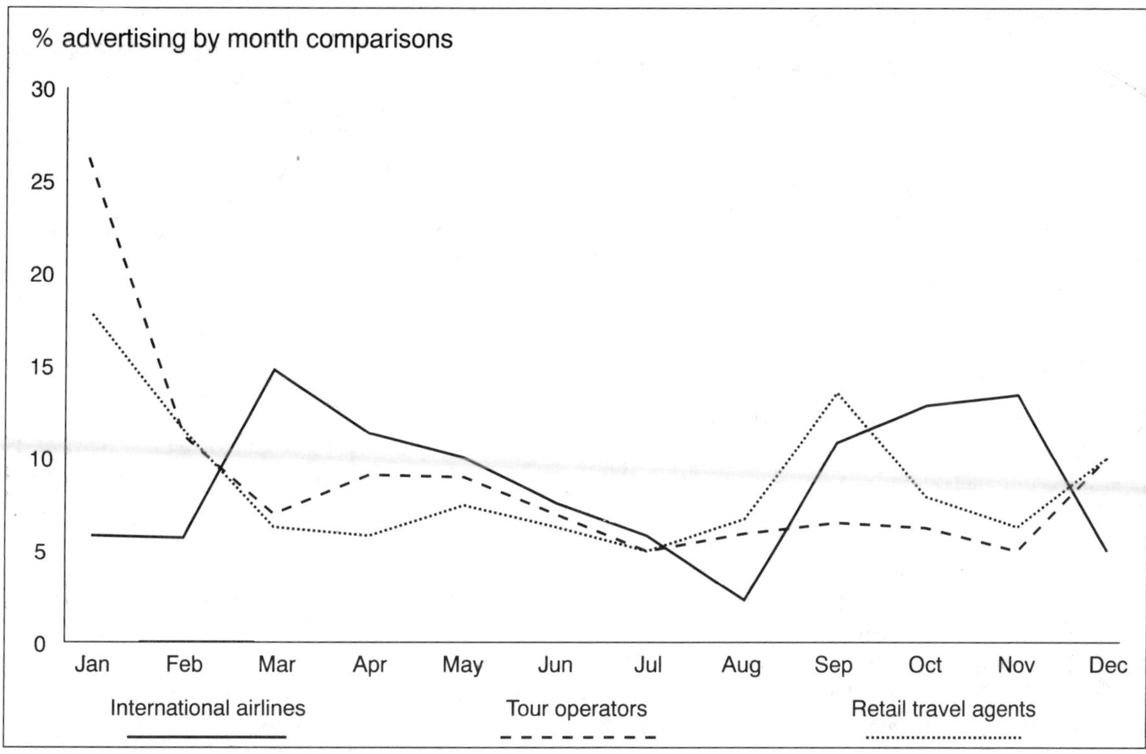

Fig. 9.7 Seasonality of travel industry advertising

To encourage agents to read the ads and absorb their messages, operators often add in competitions or incentive deals.

National newspapers and magazines

Although the same advertisements sometimes appear in both the trade press and the national press, this cannot always be the case because the trade press adverts are meant to encourage sellers while those in the press are aimed directly at potential consumers. Most newspapers have travel pages, usually in their weekend colour supplements but also in the Friday editions, and advertisements appear on those and adjacent pages. The actual features often serve an advertising function as well but operators don't have direct control over their content which can sometimes be negative and which will usually promote more than one company at a time. Nevertheless, companies may decide to place advertisements in issues which cover generally appropriate material; for example, a company might pick out and advertise the Indian holidays in its programme when the main feature on the travel page is about India in general. Magazines, too, usually have a travel page or column and advertising will appear as close to it as possible.

Newspaper advertisements are expensive and are therefore usually quite small and simple. However, Jules Verne Holidays habitually produces adverts that look like pages from a brochure complete with entire holiday itineraries in the quality national papers (*see* page 123). However, companies that wouldn't normally advertise in the nationals may do so to hit a specific target audience; for example, to aim a particular holiday at teachers over half-term.

Ideally adverts should appear in newspapers and magazines likely to be read by a defined target clientele, which means the readership of each one must be analysed carefully before the advert is committed. Since there is some evidence to suggest that women play a major part in making holiday choices, women's magazines are often seen as a good place for tour operators to advertise.

Local newspapers and magazines

Although the same considerations apply to local newspapers and magazines, fewer operators will use them to advertise because they have a much more limited readership. The adverts will cost less to place but may not generate many bookings. However, operators may find it useful to advertise in local papers whose catchment area covers regional airports featured in their programme.

Television advertising

Television stations have accepted advertising since 1955. Most of this advertising is still on the ITV channels, but increasingly it is also on Channel 4, GMTV and Sky. This is by far the most expensive medium on which to advertise both in terms of preparing the materials and in buying space to show them. Nor is it enough to have the advert shown once; repetition will be necessary to hammer the message home. A tour operator may need to budget up to £½ million to have an advert shown enough times to be effective. Of this sum, as much as £100,000 may have been paid out in preparations. Consequently television advertising is only truly a realistic option for the largest tour operators. Nevertheless tour operators are the biggest spenders on television advertising in the travel world; in the first quarter of 1993 they increased their TV advertising expenditure by 38 per cent against the same period in 1992.

In 1992 tour operators spent £5,542,000 between them on television advertising, a marked increase on the total of £2,606,000 spent in 1991. In 1993, they increased their expenditure by a further 161 per cent, Thomson upping its investment by 221 per cent and Airtours by 1,005 per cent. It's important to remember that, as the travel business has become more integrated, what appear to be agency advertisements are often partfunded by the owner-operators too. So when a television campaign was run to relaunch Hogg Robinson and Pickfords as Going Places in 1994, much of the funding for it came from Airtours.

Operators vary in the importance they attribute to television advertising from year to year. In 1991, for example, Airtours spent just over £l million, or 40.9 per cent of all operators' total expenditure, on television advertising. At this time it was a relatively new and unknown company with aggressive expansion plans that needed to get its name across to the public. Better established, in 1992 it cut back its television advertising budget to just 5.8 per cent of the total. Then in 1993, when it put in a hostile bid to take over Owners Abroad, it once again increased its television advertising spend in an effort to improve its somewhat down-market image. In other words, Airtours has used television advertising primarily to put across its corporate image rather than to sell particular holidays.

Conversely, in 1991 market leader Thomson was only responsible for 1.5 per cent of operators' total television advertising budget. However, in 1992 its share soared to 42.8 per cent, making it by far the most visible tour operator on the TV screen, probably in response to a fall in its overall share of the holiday market. Owners Abroad also increased its advertising of its main family holiday brand 'Enterprise' from 3 per cent of the total in 1991 to 10.2 per cent in 1992.

Research indicates that Channel 4 is the travel industry's least popular advertising channel now that it is responsible for its own advertising separate from ITV. In fact advertisers seem to prefer to use BSkyB despite the relatively small number of households able to receive it; by 1993 3.5 million households could receive BSkyB, 700,000 of them via cable rather than satellite dishes.

Teletext

About half the households in Britain now have access to Teletext services, and in 1993 Teletext took over holiday advertising from Oracle. An NOP survey suggested that roughly 2.9 million people a week look at Teletext's holiday adverts (most of them placed by agents rather than operators), mainly for last-minute bargains. This fits with a general trend towards home-based shopping which is even further advanced in the United States. In July 1993, Teletext featured 63 pages of ads for the Mediterranean and Canaries alone.

In 1993, guidelines for teletext advertising said that minimum prices must be quoted for 'bargains of the day', and that in other sections, where a lead-in price was quoted there must be a reasonable supply of accommodation actually available at that price. Prices must also include known taxes and surcharges. To ensure these rules are obeyed, Teletext phones companies at random; any found breaking the rules face a month's ban for which they will still be billed.

Radio advertising

Advertising on radio is a cheaper and therefore more realistic option for most operators. However, since so much of a holiday's appeal is visual, verbal adverts are rarely ideal. They're mainly used by local operators to push special offers.

Posters

Big tour operators often use posters to advertise their holidays. The following are some of the places posters are commonly sited:

- hoardings around building sites
- sides of buses
- sides and interiors of taxis
- on the platforms and along the escalators of the London Underground
- bus shelters

Poster campaigns are often co-ordinated with advertising in the press or on television; so in 1993 Thomson's 'we go there, we don't go there' advertising campaign was featured both on television and advertising hoardings. The ideal sites are ones which people will have time to look at and read, which makes the platforms of the London Underground particularly popular. While the problem here, as anywhere, is to design something eye-catching enough for people to bother to read, one advantage of using station platforms is that people may be standing on them for quite a while, long enough, in fact, to read text as well as absorb a quick message and slogan.

Eye-catching images are obviously crucial to a successful poster campaign. When British Airways relaunched its holiday programme as British Airways Holidays in 1992, it used striking images of a Thai flower market and people eating truffles in a Parisian restaurant, in order to attract attention and impress its new name on the public. However, it is very difficult to assess the impact of even the most expensive poster campaign.

REGULATING ADVERTISING

The Advertising Standards Authority

Formed in 1962, the Advertising Standards Authority (ASA) polices the British Code of Advertising Practice (BCAP) and the British Code of Sales Promotion Practice. These codes require that advertisements and sales promotions should be:

- legal, decent, honest and truthful
- prepared with a sense of responsibility to the consumer and to society
- in line with the principles of fair competition

Fig. 9.8 The Advertising Standards Authority logo

The British Code of Advertising Practice is based on the International Code of Advertising Practice (ICAP) which has been in existence since 1937. The code applies to:

- adverts in newspapers, magazines and other printed publications
- indoor and outdoor posters and other outdoor adverts, including aerial advertisements e.g. on hot-air balloons
- cinema and video commercials
- promotional materials like brochures and leaflets, however they reach the public

This is what the ASA has to say about the requirement for advertisements to be 'legal, decent, honest and truthful':

> **Legality**
> Advertisements should contain nothing which is in breach of the law, nor omit anything which the law requires.
>
> Advertisements should contain nothing which is likely to bring the law into disrepute.
>
> **Decency**
> Advertisements should contain nothing which, because of its failure to respect the standards of

decency and propriety that are generally accepted in the United Kingdom, is likely to cause either grave or widespread offence.

Some advertisements, which do not conflict with the preceding subparagraph, may nonetheless be found distasteful because they reflect or give expression to attitudes or opinions about which society is divided. Where this is the case, advertisers are urged to consider the effect any apparent disregard of such sensitivities may have upon their reputation and that of their product; and upon the acceptability, and hence usefulness, of advertising generally.

The fact that a product may be found offensive by some people is not, in itself, a sufficient basis under the Code for objecting to an advertisement for it. Advertisers are urged, however, to avoid unnecessary offence when they advertise any product which may reasonably be expected to be found objectionable by a significant number of those who are likely to see their advertisement.

Honesty

No advertiser should seek to take improper advantage of any characteristic or circumstance which may make consumers vulnerable; as, for example, by exploiting their credulity or their lack of experience or knowledge in any manner detrimental to their interests.

The design and presentation of advertisements should be such as to allow each part of the advertiser's case to be easily grasped and clearly understood.

Courtesy: Advertising Standards Authority

Furthermore, the code says that where an advertisement deals with matters of fact, the advertiser should have material ready to back up their claim in case there should be any complaint. Where the advert contains information that is a matter of opinion rather than fact, then this should be made clear. Advertisements should never play on people's fear and should never condone or incite violent or antisocial behaviour. Nor should they show or advocate dangerous behaviour or unsafe practices. They must also be designed so that anyone looking at them can tell immediately that they are advertisements. Advertisements shouldn't refer to or portray living people unless those people have given their express permission in advance.

The code permits advertising that makes comparisons between one product and another and between their prices (in 1994, Airtours advertised Tradewinds holidays by making direct comparisons with Kuoni's higher prices to the same destinations). However, it doesn't permit advertisers to try and discredit their competitors by unfair means. Nor should they exploit the goodwill attached to someone else's trade name, mark, or advertising campaign in a way which would unfairly prejudice the other party. Nor should adverts be designed to so closely resemble other adverts that they could mislead or confuse the public.

Although the code has separate sections covering specific areas of advertising, there is not currently one devoted to travel advertising despite the fact that the 1992 Annual Report stated that 'holiday advertising is a regular source of complaint'. This is because, as with all other sectors, the general rules of the code apply to all advertisements. Most complaints relate to special offers, discounts and low prices; for example, where the word 'from' is omitted from a statement about price. Actual itineraries which differ from those advertised are another regular source of complaint.

If an advertisement breaks the code's rules, the ASA can ask the advertiser to amend or withdraw it. If they refuse to do so, the ASA will then publicise their refusal and ask the media to comply with the code by refusing further advertising space to the culprit. If they still fail to comply, the ASA can refer the advert to the Office of Fair Trading which can take out an injunction to prevent the advertiser repeating the false claim or any similar claim in the future. To avoid falling foul of the code, advertisers can ask the ASA's copy advice team to look at their proposed advert and indicate if they foresee any problems.

The ASA details its decisions on individual cases in regular reports. The following are some of the complaints about tour operators' advertising which it has upheld.

Report No. 25 published June '93

S.H. TOURS LTD
t/a Asian Affair Holidays
143/147 Regent Street
London W1R 7LB

Agency:
Edwards Martin Thornton Ltd

press

Complaint from:
Fife

Complaint: Objection to a national newspaper advertisement headlined 'Five nights in Singapore. It's a snip. £499' and which indicated the offer period. The complainant, upon making further enquiries, discovered that a supplement of £120 was applicable for passengers travelling alone and objected that this was not indicated in the advertisement.
B 5.1; B 7.3.4

Adjudication: **Complaint upheld.**
The advertisers stated that it was standard practice in the holiday industry for per person prices to be based on twin reservations and that the full details, including those pertaining to the single supplement, were set out in the follow up literature. The Authority was concerned that the advertisement did not indicate that the price was a base price and was subject to possible additional charges but noted the advertisers' assurance that any future advertisements of a similar nature would include the word 'from'.

Report No. 24 published May '93

Olympic Holidays Ltd
Olympic House
30–32 Cross Street
London N1 2BG

brochure

Complaint from:
Essex

Complaint: Objection to a travel brochure which detailed the 'Galaxy' apartments in Aghios Nikolaos, Crete as 'a peaceful retreat'. On arrival, the complainant found that the apartment was situated at the junction of the main road and the town by-pass road which generated continuous noise throughout the day and night. The complainant therefore considered the claim misleading.
B 5.1

Adjudication: **Complaint upheld.**
The advertisers stated that this was an isolated complaint and the accuracy of their description had never been questioned to date. In view of the photographic evidence submitted by the complainant coupled with the positioning of the apartment, the Authority considered the claim inaccurate and requested that the advertisers omit the claim from future brochures to avoid disappointment.

Report No. 28 published September '93

Inspirations

Coombe House
St John's Road
Isleworth
Middlesex TW7 6NA

brochure

Complaint from:
Warwickshire

Complaint: Objection to an entry for the Agapinor hotel (Paphos, Cyprus) in the Inspirations Winter 92/93 brochure which claimed 'this Little Gem has panoramic views over the harbour . . . twin rooms have a seaview . . . Cocktail bar. . . . Breakfast is Waiter Service'. The complainant, who had stayed at the hotel, questioned the accuracy of the claims.
B5.1

Adjudication: **Complaint upheld.**
The advertisers stated that the harbour could be seen from all seaview rooms. The Agapinor's bar was named 'the Cocktail bar' and might close at the owner's discretion and tea and coffee at breakfast were served by a waiter. The Authority considered that the brochure had given the impression that the Agapinor hotel directly overlooked the harbour, whereas it was situated over two kilometres away. As breakfast was a self service buffet and the advertisers had not shown the cocktail bar generally to be open in the evening, it considered the brochure had

exaggerated the level of services provided. It requested that the claims be amended.

Source: Advertising Standards Authority

However, the ASA doesn't uphold all the complaints made to it. The following is a complaint that was rejected.

Report No. 4 published September '91

Airtours plc
Wavell House
Helmshore
Rossendale
Lancashire BB4 4NB
(Previous complaints upheld in the last 12 months: 1)

brochure

Complaint from:
Sussex

Complaint: Objection to the Florida '91 holiday brochure which claimed 'FREE' CAR FOR YOUR FLORIDA HOLIDAY, 'Subject to compulsory protection coverage package'. The complainant found that the package cost $12.75 per day and thus disputed that the deal could be described as free.
B 8

Adjudication: **Complaint not upheld.**
The advertisers stated that the cover of the insurance package and its cost was broadly similar to terms offered by competitors. The Authority made further enquiries which confirmed this to be the case, and thus found the claim to be unobjectionable. It considered that the Code's requirement that incidental costs incurred in obtaining the 'free' deal had been indicated and that the charge of $12.75 for insurance was not an inflated price.

Source: Advertising Standards Authority

Independent Television Commission (ITC) and Radio Authority

The 1990 Broadcasting Act required the Independent Television Commission to draw up a code of practice for advertising on Channel 3 (ITV and GMTV), Channel 4, BSkyB and cable channels. Broadly, the code follows the ASA guidelines, requiring all television advertising to be legal, decent, honest and truthful. However, it also covers areas specific to television by, for example, laying down rules about the reuse of programme material and of television personalities. Subliminal advertisements (so brief the viewer would not realise they had seem them) are prohibited and advertisers are warned to use typefaces large enough and held on the screen long enough for the average viewer with an average sized set to be able to read them properly. This would particularly apply to travel advertising which often incorporates conditions of an offer in small type at the foot of the screen.

The Radio Authority regulates advertising on the radio along the same principles as the ASA and the ITC.

Independent Television Commission

Fig. 9.9 The Independent Television Commission logo

DIRECT MARKETING THROUGH THE MEDIA

Most advertisements placed by the larger tour operators are aimed at directing clients through travel agency doors. Smaller direct sell companies, however, often rely heavily on advertisements in newspapers and magazines to set their phones ringing. Depending on how specialist they are, they may advertise in national newspapers and general interest magazines or in magazines with a more specialised audience; ornithological holidays, for example, are often advertised in *Bird*, the magazine of the Royal Society for the Protection of Birds.

The Advertising Standards Authority has a set of rules governing direct marketing too. In particular it is concerned with the collection of personal data for direct marketing purposes; for example, when companies build up a database of people who have responded to their advertisements so that they can mail them with details of other holidays instead of waiting for them to see a new advert. It requires that all advertisements aimed at attracting a direct response must include the name and full address of the advertiser.

Furthermore, the code requires that lists should be kept up to date as far as possible and that list holders should be quick to respond to requests for alteration of incorrect details and requests for suppression of details. List holders should also be able to identify which people on the list have asked that their details should not be passed to a third party and those who have not been given the option. All personal details should be safely secured against unauthorised access.

Some companies who use direct mailing will not compile their own lists but will instead rent them from other list compilers. Where they do that, the code requires that they should not make wholly inappropriate mailings e.g. because of the age of the recipients, etc. If a company decides to rent out one of its own lists, it must first run it against the Mailing Preference Service (MPS) Suppression File to ensure it doesn't include the names of people who have asked to be removed from direct mailing lists.

Where a company compiles lists of addresses for direct mailing, it is bound by the terms of the 1984 Data Protection Act (*see* page 226).

Using the media in other ways

Apart from advertising directly, tour operators also use the media to promote their products in other ways. In particular they organise press trips when they take journalists from assorted newspapers, magazines and radio and TV programmes to a particular destination to experience it. The intention is that those so favoured will follow up by writing or broadcasting about the destination, giving a plug for the particular operator who took them there. In general it is thought that the public trust feature articles and editorial programmes about a place more than they trust adverts for the same product because they believe the former to be more objective. For this reason, tour operators hope that the publicity generated in this way will translate into enough bookings to recoup the cost of taking the journalists to the destination in the first place. Some outlets like the BBC Holiday programme are seen as particularly authoritative. However, careful monitoring of booking patterns following publication of an article or the broadcasting of a programme is essential since some question whether press trips do actually achieve their aim.

Journalists are also kept informed of developments through **press releases** which highlight new products, new angles, in fact anything thought newsworthy. Figure 9.10 shows a press release circulated by Meon Villas in September 1993. It announces the launch of the 1994 brochure and draws attention to a growth in the market for villa and apartment holidays. It also mentions improvements to villas to provide private swimming pools 'in line with client demand', and lists the most popular destinations, with a special note about Florida which had been the subject of 'adverse publicity' after nine tourists were murdered there in one year.

Journalists are busy people and often work to tight deadlines. They receive a large number of press releases, so to be effective these must be carefully designed. It's vital that the tour operators get the gist of what they're saying into the first paragraph, preferably stating *what* the press release is about, *when* and *where* it's happening and *why* it should be of interest to the journalist's potential readership. The best press releases are short and to the point, with all the information on no more than two sides of A4 paper. If more information is deemed essential, it can be typed on a separate sheet (*see* Fig. 9.11, page 211). If the press release is written well enough, chunks of it may be incorporated in articles word for word. Often a copy of the relevant brochure will be attached as well; occasionally a photo, perhaps of a brochure cover, will be provided too. Good press releases should be

HIGHLIGHTS OF THE MEON VILLAS 1994 BROCHURE

* Destinations

Algarve - Costa Blanca - Costa del Sol - Lanzarote
Menorca - Majorca - Ibiza - Malta - Gozo - Corfu
Florida - Caribbean

* Rating

Every villa is 'Star Rated by Meon: This is a personal rating based on the judgement of Meon's staff, and ranges from 'Blue Riband' through five, four and three stars: some villas in particularly peaceful locations are marked with a 'Peace & Quiet' symbol of a flying swallow.

* Winter holidays

Lanzarote, Florida and the Caribbean are featured year-round and the Algarve, Malta and Gozo suggested for spring and autumn holidays.

* Facilities

The majority of Meon Villas have private pools; welcome food packs are provided at every property, and maid service is available.

* Flexibility

Meon Villas offers complete flexibility: bookings can be for any length of stay; discounts are offered for parties; no minimum number for villa occupancy.

* Flights

Daytime, mid-week flights on charter or scheduled services are offered from eight UK airports.

* Representation

Top quality representatives, highly experienced and full of local knowledge, are a source of pride to Meon Villas; they are on the spot in every destination featured in the brochure; many have lived in their area for years, and their depth of 'know how' is unrivalled.

* Extra touches ...

Every booking for a Meon Villas holiday entitles clients to two free leather passport holders. For parties of 6-8 adults Meon will offer one free extra car or two free extra cars for parties of 9 or more adults.

Fig. 9.10 Press release for the Meon Villas 1994 brochure

Courtesy: Meon Villas

MEON VILLAS LAUNCHES 1994 PROGRAMME TO CATCH EARLY BOOKERS

The September 6 launch of the 1994 Meon Villas brochure - much earlier than in previous years - aims to capture the attention of villa holiday seekers at a time when an upsurge in bookings for next summer is being seen.

According to Stefan Olszowski, Chairman and Managing Director of The Meon Group of Companies, the timing of the launch seems to be "spot on". He comments: "The last two weeks have seen holidaymakers flocking into agencies to book for summer 1994, and we hope to capitalise on this booking trend by offering the best villa choices at the earliest opportunity."

Meon Villas has increased its ratio of villas per destination, with the majority of properties now having private pools in line with client demand. "Some other operators are cutting back in the villa market," says Stefan Olszowski, "but Meon has actually increased the choice of villas in the destinations we feature."

The 1994 Meon Villas programme highlights top performing destinations Menorca, the Algarve, Majorca and Lanzarote, along with Ibiza, Malta, Gozo, and Corfu; the Costa Blanca and Costa del Sol in Spain, and villas in the Caribbean and Florida.

Stefan Olszowski notes that interest in Florida is particularly strong: "Demand for villas in Florida has grown considerably, despite some adverse publicity for that destination; we fully expect to see growth in this area in 1993/4".

Fig. 9.11 Page of supplementary information to go with the Meon press release
Courtesy: Meon Villas

Meon Villas launches 1994 programme

Commenting on prospects for 1994, Stefan Olszowski sees a period of slow but steady growth: "It's clear that interest for summer 1994 is gaining strength, and with the early launch of our programme we are well poised to provide what our clients are looking for."

- ENDS -

For further information, please contact:

Judy McCluskey
Sugden McCluskey Associates
50 Sulivan Road, London SW6 3DX

tel: 071 371 8900 September 6, 1993

Fig. 9.11 ***Continued***

designed to stand out from all the others. Use of company logos helps by making the source of the information immediately identifiable. Certainly they should be of a quality that reflects well on the company's overall image.

PUBLIC RELATIONS

Press releases may be produced by public relations officers, often themselves ex-journalists. Alternatively some operators will use a specialist public relations company to produce their press releases.

In general, public relations is a rather nebulous function, the results of which are difficult to quantify except in terms of column inches in magazines and newspapers. However, a public relations officer will look after some or all of the following tasks:

a) Press relationships, including creating news stories.
b) Publicising products generally.
c) Publicising the company generally, a task which may involve trying to counteract negative publicity, as when the CAA has delayed granting an ATOL, for example.
d) Lobbying politicians and other influential people.
e) Counselling management and others on potential problems that need to be avoided, etc.

Public relations officers, or specialist press officers, may organise occasional press conferences, providing food and drink to encourage journalists to attend. They may also arrange press facility trips, or themselves write guest columns in magazines or newspapers.

Word of mouth recommendation/repeat business

No matter how much operators spend on advertising and jollying the press along, the best form of advertising actually comes from word of mouth recommendation by satisfied clients; people are more likely to trust what their friends say than what the papers do. Satisfied customers also turn into repeat customers. Boating holiday specialists Hoseasons estimate that two-thirds of their reservations are repeat bookings from satisfied clients. Cruise ships, too, are often more than half full with repeat passengers.

OTHER FORMS OF SALES PROMOTION

Apart from conventional advertising, there are other ways in which tour operators can hope to influence booking patterns. Some sales promotions are aimed at the operator's own staff, some at travel agents and others at potential clients (*see* Fig. 9.12).

ABTA defines promotions as 'activities designed to stimulate the sale or purchase of a tour, holiday or travel arrangements offered by a tour operator by means other than incentives or advertising'. The British Code of Sales Promotion Practice states that much advertising is supported by promotional schemes aimed at making goods or services more attractive to the consumer. It goes on to say that these sales promotions are usually temporary and invariably offer the consumer some additional benefit in cash or kind. It cites examples of sales promotions as being competitions, free gifts and coupons offering reduced price purchase opportunities. All sales promotions need to be designed to reinforce the company's image as projected, for example, in advertisements.

Point of sales materials

When sales representatives visit travel agencies they often take supplies of point of sales materials with them which they hope will raise both the travel agents' and their clients' interest in their holidays. For maximum effect all these things must have the company's name and logo clearly displayed on them to reinforce the company's name and image over time.

Point of sales materials may include any or all of the following:

a) Window display materials. To be effective these generally need to be brightly coloured, imaginative, eye-catching and professionally made. Sometimes they are free-standing displays (e.g. models of skiers), at other times made of thick cardboard. The window display may be put together by the travel agent, by the sales representative or by a display company employed for the purpose.
b) Posters to advertise the company generally or special offers or late availability specifically.
c) Illuminated signs, usually to go in the window.
d) Wallcharts or calendars bearing the company logo.
e) Writing pads to go on agents' desks, again with the company's logo.
f) Open/closed shop signs bearing the company logo.
g) Pens, pencils and telephone pads.
h) Mugs and ashtrays for the staffroom.
i) T-shirts, sweatshirts, cabin bags and luggage straps.
j) Sales certificates to go on the agency wall.

Brochure launches

A different type of promotional activity aimed at travel agents is the brochure launch party which takes place when the year's new brochures come out. When new brochures are launched tour operators often organise big promotional events to which travel agents are invited and which may be

Fig. 9.12 Sales promotional tactics

attended by sales representatives, company directors and reservations staff as well. Such events may take place in local hotels, in nightclubs, even on boats, and will usually involve plenty of free food and alcohol, the emphasis being on offering the agents a good time. Sometimes the event will be themed in accordance with the holidays on sale, with, for example, Mexican tacos and tequila sunrises on offer at a launch focusing on Acapulco and Cancun. Often there will be competitions to win holidays with the company, the prize being based on information culled from the new brochure. There will also be a brief training session on the brochure's contents as well. The hope is that agents who have enjoyed themselves at the brochure launch will be more inclined to sell the company's holidays afterwards.

Other promotional activity aimed at agents

Companies often go to extraordinary lengths to attract attention to their products. So, for example, in 1993 Wallace Arnold ran 'mystery tours' for agents on some of its coaches to try and alter the image of coach tours as boring. Iberotel (owners of Neilson, Skybargains and Sunworld) sponsors the Sunworld Sailing Challenge for travel agents at Cowes on the Isle of Wight.

Joint venture sales promotions

Some promotions involve operators working with companies outside the travel business. In 1992/3 Hoover made an unfortunate offer of free flights to Europe or the USA to purchasers of its products. Despite the fact that this scheme eventually cost Hoover an enormous amount both in cash and bad publicity, it spurred a number of other companies to enter into similar promotional links not just with airlines but also with tour operators. So Cosmos agreed to discount holidays for Hoover customers, Sony gave discounts on Thomas Cook own-brand holidays, and Safeways offered up to 15 per cent off Thomson holidays booked through Page & Moy. All these discounts depended on how much the customer spent. In the face of opposition from travel agents who believed these offers threatened their own sales, Thomson said they had linked up with Safeways because the supermarket chain did not ask them to put in a lot of promotional funds themselves. At most Thomson estimated one per cent of their 1993 bookings, or 30,000 bookings in all, would be redirected through Page & Moy as a result of this promotion. As far as operators are concerned, such promotions give them access to a useful database of customers who can then be mailed in the future.

Incentives

ABTA defines incentives as 'offers in cash or kind to ABTA member companies to sell holidays'. Until 1993 operators offered travel agents incentives to sell their holidays in haphazard fashion. They might, for example, offer Marks and Spencer's vouchers for sales of late-date holidays. However, in 1993 the situation changed as the travel business became increasingly vertically integrated. In February 1993, Airtours started paying Pickfords' staff £3 a head for each Airtours holiday booking they made. In May, Thomson retaliated by paying Lunn Poly staff £3 a head and their managers £1 a head for each Thomson holiday booking they made. In July, when Owners Abroad announced a slump in its forecast profits, it attributed this in part to the effect of these payments in persuading Pickfords' and Lunn Poly staff to switch-sell to incentive-bearing products. The Office of Fair Trading then launched an inquiry into the impact of vertical integration on the industry in the face of increasing concern that the public would not realise that the product advice they were being given was being influenced in this way.

Educationals

A particular type of incentive offered to agents by operators is the educational, a chance to travel abroad and sample a particular operator's products. The theory behind this is that it is easier for agents to sell products which they have experienced firsthand. In a broader sense, agents who have enjoyed themselves on a trip abroad are likely to view the operator who made that possible with favour when it comes to time to sell. Educationals vary in form but usually involved travelling to a popular (or new) resort and then visiting the accommodation the operator uses there. In 1992, Cresta Holidays took 1,000 agents on educational trips to France, while in 1993 Kuoni arranged many long-haul educationals for agents.

Some educationals are completely free, but others require the agent to make a contribution towards the cost. Sometimes the individual agent will have to pay, but sometimes the office as a whole will pick up the tab. In the tougher conditions of the early 1990s wholly free educationals were rarer than they had been in the early 1980s. It was also felt that participants were more inclined to take educationals seriously as a learning exercise when they had had to contribute to their cost. From the point of view of the tax office, operators also need to be able to show that the educationals are work trips in order for them to qualify for tax exemption.

Sometimes operators simply give educationals to reward offices which do a lot of business for them generally or to agents recommended as particularly worthy by their sales representatives. At other times the educational may be offered as an incentive to increase sales of a particular product; so in 1993, Kuoni promised an educational to the finalists who completed its long-haul training modules. Some educationals are promoted specifically for managers, others for agency staff; rarely are they for both groups together since it is felt that the two groups have different needs.

The most effective educationals are well-planned and structured. If too many hotel visits are included, they may end up blurring into one in the agents' memories; on the other hand if there are too few, they may not take the trip seriously enough. Ideally, agents should have to report back to the rest of the office to ensure everyone learns as much as possible from their experiences.

As an alternative to educationals (or in addition to them) some operators also offer agents discounted holidays or two-for-the-price-of-one deals which also enable them to sample their product but as a holiday rather than in a structured way.

Presentations to the public

Occasionally an operator may choose to aim a presentation at the public rather than just at agents; alternatively they may agree to share costs with a travel agent who wants to stage such an event. A good presentation will be expensive because of the need to hire a suitable venue, probably in a good hotel, and to use the best technology, for example, tape-slide dissolving units. To reach the widest audience such events need to take place in the evening and should be aimed at both men and women. Dates should be picked carefully to avoid clashing with holidays or events (like World Cup football matches) which may result in poor attendance. If admission is by ticket only it will make realistic catering possible. Possible guests can be reached either by direct mailing or through placing an advert in a local paper with an RSVP coupon.

All staff attending such a presentation should have name badges and sales materials should be supplied on every seat. To make sure everything goes smoothly the entire presentation should have been rehearsed beforehand, and there should be a supply of spare projector bulbs and other equipment.

Other promoters

Just as operators sometimes benefit indirectly from other people's advertising, so they can also benefit from other people's promotional activities, especially those of the national tourist offices. For example, in 1993/4 when skiing holidays to Austria were selling badly, the Austrian National Tourist Office launched a promotional drive to supplement the operators' own efforts. During the 1980s and 1990s a sequence of 'Visit . . . Years', starting with 'Visit Thailand Year' in 1987, also helped operators by providing a burst of promotional activity focused on one destination. 1994 was 'Visit Korea Year' which was expected to benefit Kuoni, Travel 2 and Jetset, all of whom feature Korea.

Regulation of sales promotions

The Advertising Standards Authority (ASA) polices the British Code of Sales Promotion Practice, a self-regulated Code designed to ensure that, like advertisements, sales promotion are legal, decent, honest and truthful. The Code covers:

- premium offers which promise goods and services in return for money or tokens
- reduced price and free offers
- distribution of vouchers, coupons and samples
- personality promotions
- charity-linked promotions
- prize promotions e.g. competitions, lucky draws, etc.
- incentives aimed at sales staff, retailers, etc.

- promotional offers made by some newspapers and magazines to their readers
- some aspects of sponsorship

In general, sales promotions must always comply with the British Code of Advertising Practice (*see* above), must ensure the public's right to privacy is protected, must avoid making offers that could be regarded as offensive and must never exaggerate. Consumers must be told what kinds of proofs of purchase are needed, whether it will cost them anything to take part in the promotion, how they can contact the promoter in business hours and when the offer will close. Promoters are expected to have adequate stocks to avoid having to disappoint consumers; where supply of the offered product is limited, this fact should be made clear in all publicity.

The code is particularly detailed on the subject of 'free' offers. For example, it states that nothing can be described as 'free' where the consumer has to pay something to obtain it (other than legitimate costs like car hire insurance). Nor must the promoter try to recoup the cost of the free item by inflating the normal cost of other products, or by bumping up the price of anything that must be bought to qualify for the offer.

When it comes to promotions aimed at a sales force, the codes stresses that they should not prevent the salesperson giving honest advice to consumers.

Where a promoter fails to fulfil the conditions of the code this fact will be highlighted in ASA reports. The following is a typical case.

> **Basis of complaint:** A member of the public objected to a mailing which stated '. . . as a valued customer of Ventura, you will find enclosed a special voucher entitling you to secure your Summer 1987 holiday now at our Summer '86 brochure prices, if you book before 30th November 1986.' The voucher stated, 'You may take advantage of this privilege offer on any number of bookings made at the same time and our existing 1986 party, group or children's discounts will still apply.' The complainant booked a holiday under the scheme but was advised:
>
> a) Child discounts had been reduced from those offered in the 1986 brochure.
> b) 'Super Saver' holidays, which the complainant had chosen, were not available for 1987.
>
> The complainant subsequently received the advertisers' 1987 brochure and noted that the conditions relating to child discounts were unchanged, and further that Super Saver holidays were still being offered. The holiday he had selected in place of the Super Saver, at the Bienvenida Apartments, was also featured, although having booked it he was later advised that the apartments had since been withdrawn along with other accommodation in the area. In view of his experience, the complainant questioned the availability of the Super Saver holidays, the apparent withdrawal of the promotional offer, and the availability of the advertised accommodation in the Bienvenida Apartments.
>
> **Conclusion:** The advertisers stated that the holidays were advertised as 'subject to availability' and that approximately 1000 holidays were sold to customers who used the special advance booking voucher and booked 1987 holidays at the 1986 brochure prices. They submitted details showing that child reductions had been made and that Super Saver holidays had been available for 1987. The Authority was unable to ascertain why the complainant had been advised to the contrary.
>
> The advertisers stated that the Bienvenida Apartments had been unavailable for contractual reasons but that other similar properties in the area were available under the same offer.
>
> While the Authority noted that the voucher stated that holidays were 'subject to availability', it considered that this disclaimer would be understood to relate to accommodation restrictions rather than total non-availability of certain listed accommodation. The advertisers were requested to ensure that literature was properly updated to take account of contractual changes such as had occurred in the case of Beinvenida Apartments. (Ventura Holidays)
>
> Courtesy: Advertising Standards Authority

Product endorsement

A few operators include endorsements by famous people or satisfied customers in their brochures. When famous people are used, it helps credibility if they have some sort of link with the product; so for the winter skiing season of 1993/4 Neilson included a photograph of Graham Bell, Britain's national ski champion together with 'Bell's View' comments on each resort in the brochure, while

Airtours included an introduction by Claire de Pourtales, the leading British women's skier (both these skiers are also sponsored by Neilson and Airtours).

In general, it is the smallest companies which include customer endorsements in their brochures. However, in 1994, in relaunching Croatia as a holiday detination, Phoenix printed words of praise from previous travellers in its brochure. These were intended to suggest to potential customers that if others had enjoyed the product, they would too. What's more, they were also intended to allay the concerns of potential clients who still thought of Croatia as a state at war.

Travel markets and fairs

Some travel fairs/markets are aimed at the public, others at the trade. Tour operators may take stands at the ones aimed at the public, although they use trade fairs more as a way of making contact with their principals: hoteliers, airline representatives, tourist office staff, etc. Having a stand can be expensive, not just because of the cost of renting the space, but because of the staff time taken up with installing and running the stand. There is also intense competition to get the best positions (always the most expensive ones), and making a stand stick out among all its competitors will be even more costly. Installing electrical equipment for signs, computers, etc. is expensive, and often food and drink must also be supplied for guests.

The biggest of all the travel markets are the annual International Tourism Exchange (ITB) in Berlin, followed by the World Travel Market in Earls Court. However, increasingly there are trade fairs all around the world, as well as more speciaist events like the Ski Show and Independent Travellers' World. Operators who don't think it's worth their while attending the big events may opt to attend the more specialist ones instead. Some of the main events are shown in the table in the next column.

Name	*Venue*	*Date*
Fitur	Madrid	January
Holiday '94	Manchester	January
BTL	Lisbon	January
BIT	Milan	February
Russian International Show	Moscow	February
International Tourism Exchange	Berlin	March
TUR	Gothenburg	March
International Travel & Tourism Show	Moscow	March
Arabian Travel Market	Dubai	May
TTW	Montreux	October
BTT	Brussels	November
World Travel Market	London	November
Philoxena	Thessaloniki	November
Incoming Workshop	Prague	November

Niche marketing

Niche marketing in retailing was a child of the 1980s boom years. However, in tour operating it has proved a relatively recession-proof strategy. Niche marketing is about homing in on smaller, precise sections of the market rather than trying to cover it all. All specialist operators are therefore in the business of niche marketing. However, many of the bigger companies have also homed in on niche-market products. Two examples would be all-inclusive holidays and overseas wedding packages which now appear in a wide variety of brochures although the market for either of them can only ever be relatively small.

All-inclusive holidays were originally developed to cushion people against the high cost of 'extras' in hotels. Nowadays they are surprisingly popular, despite being more expensive than many other products. Likewise, 'wedding' holidays were originally dreamt up as an exotic way of reducing the cost of a wedding in the UK. However, by 1993 they had become so popular that many Caribbean hotels began catering specifically for them. It is assumed that products like these tend to appeal to a better-heeled clientele who have been less badly hit by the recession and who are less interested in discounts. For operators, therefore, these are good markets to handle because healthy profits can be made from them even when the numbers involved are fairly small. Homing in on a niche within a niche, ITC/Caribbean Connection even markets Catholic and Jewish weddings in the Caribbean.

Tactical decisions in marketing tour operations

Once a programme has been running for at least a year, it should be possible to produce a graph showing the pattern of bookings for each week of the year. It will then be possible to plot the break-even point and the previous year's sales pattern on the graph and match these against the current year's sales activity. Assuming that progress towards achieving the break-even point is proceeding according to pattern, it should not be necessary to make any tactical strategic interventions. If, however, the graph shows sales falling behind their estimated levels, then the marketeers may have to decide on action to speed sales up again.

These are the options they could consider:

- Increased or new advertising.
- Sales promotions aimed at the customer, such as offering child discounts or discounts for booking before a set date. They might also throw in a week's free car hire or car insurance.
- Sales promotions aimed at the retailers, including discounted holidays or actual incentive payments.
- Discounts for weeks that are selling particularly badly.

With luck these promotional activities will stimulate sales until the break-even point is reached. However, if this still doesn't happen, the decision to consolidate flights or even drop some slow-selling holidays may have to be made, bearing in mind that the EC Package Travel Regulations now require operators to compensate holidaymakers if they cancel a holiday without having previously warned that this would happen if they didn't receive a specific number of bookings.

It is when sales are slow that the operators' links with computerised travel agencies are particularly vital; without such links it would be much harder to highlight products that need that extra sales push. When discounting is added to the link with agencies, operators have an even better chance of speeding up sales.

QUESTIONS AND DISCUSSION POINTS

1 Which forms of advertising do you think are likely to be most effective for tour operators and why?

2 Collect specific examples of tour operator advertising and discuss their effectiveness in class. Grade them for effectiveness and then discuss your conclusions.

3 Visit a local travel agency and see what examples of tour operators' promotional activities you can find. See if you can spot any missed opportunities.

4 In 1994, Airtours marketing director Richard Carrick said, 'The Airtours brand name is not ever elastic. It represents value-for-money holidays, mostly for the family market, and we can't put everything we want to offer in this brand'. Discuss the usefulness of brand names as marketing tools in the light of this statement and the trend towards overbranding.

ASSIGNMENTS

1 Each member of the class should select **one** non-specialist tour operator and carry out a SWOT analysis on its products. The raw results should be presented as a chart attached to a report which draws conclusions from the analysis and then makes suggestions for a marketing plan based on those conclusions.

2 A small tour operator is looking for an agency to design an advertising campaign to promote its new destination (what this is can be decided by the class together

or by the lecturer). The class should divide into four groups, each group representing one advertising agency.

Each group should meet to discuss the best ways to advertise the destination. Once this has been done, each member of the group should take responsibility for a different aspect of the campaign (e.g. for designing a poster, coming up with a slogan, making an advert to go on the radio). Once everyone has come up with their ideas, the group should reassemble to discuss what each has done and decide whether together they amount to a suitable campaign. Changes may need to be made as a result of these discussions.

Once all the groups are happy that their ideas have reached presentation standard, the entire class should reconvene and each group should present its campaign to the others. At the end of the presentations the class should vote for the campaign it thinks most promising. Finally the class should discuss the good and bad points of each presentation.

3 It's late August and the operators are getting ready to start the round of brochure launch promotions. You work for a travel consultancy which has been asked to come up with imaginative new ideas for launches. Working in pairs, select a particular brochure from the current year and decide what sort of a launch you would have given it. (Students may find it easier to select a smaller, more specialised programme than to go for one of the main summer or winter sun brochures.)

(Note: If the college has a training travel agency, it may be possible to put at least one of these launch plans into operation, using other college students and lecturers as guinea pigs.)

4 Your manager asks you to write a press release to coincide with the brochure launch. This should highlight any new features of the brochure, any particularly interesting prices and anything else you think newsworthy. Your press release should fit on one side of A4 paper and should be written in language and style appropriate for a local newspaper.

CHAPTER 10

Law for tour operators

LEARNING OBJECTIVES

After reading this chapter you should be able to:

- **understand the unique difficulties tour operators face in ensuring their products comply with UK and EU law**
- **explain how breaches of these laws would be handled**
- **explain the development of consumer protection law**
- **list the main laws of concern to tour operators**
- **describe the content of these laws**
- **describe the industry bodies which have developed to represent the industry and to protect consumers**

INTRODUCTION

As businesses producing holiday programmes, all tour operators are obliged to work within the framework of relevant British and European Union legislation. Operators are affected by the law in the following broad areas:

- law concerned with the organisation of businesses
- contract law
- employment law
- consumer law
- fair trading law
- property law
- insurance law
- law of agency

Laws remain in force until repealed or amended. British law also depends on precedent i.e. how one case is decided will form the basis for interpreting later cases.

BUSINESS ORGANISATION

British business organisations exist in three forms:

- sole traders
- partnerships
- limited companies

1. Sole traders

Sole traders are self-employed individuals, engaged in business activities. Becoming a sole trader is the easiest way to go into business since it doesn't require you to go through any specific legal formalities. The biggest drawback is that sole traders are personally liable for any debts the business incurs; if the business fails they may lose all their possessions and be made bankrupt. If they employ other people, sole traders are bound by the usual employment legislation. If providing goods or services, they are also bound by relevant consumer legislation. Sole traders can bequeath their businesses to their heirs.

Although many tour operators may have started in business as sole traders, only the smallest would continue as such because of the unlimited risks they run if anything goes wrong.

2. Partnerships

If someone wants to go into business with someone else they can set up a partnership, defined by the 1890 Partnership Act as 'the relation which subsists between persons carrying on business in common with a view to profit'. According to the 1985 Companies Act, there cannot normally be more than 20 partners in a partnership. Partnerships suffer from many of the same drawbacks as sole trading; partners are personally liable for all the debts of their business and are also liable for each other's actions. Unless the partners draw up a separate contract, the terms of the partnership are dictated by the 1890 Partnership Act. If one of the partners dies, the partnership will be terminated unless they have previously signed an agreement to the contrary.

Because partnerships involve the same risk of unlimited liability as sole trading, few tour operators would opt for this form of organisation.

3. Limited companies

As in most areas of business, the majority of tour operating businesses are run as limited companies. According to the 1985 Companies Act, limited companies can take two forms:

- public limited companies
- private limited companies

Limited companies exist as legal entities separate from their owners, which means that the owners' liability for their debts can be limited to the amount they have invested in the company. Because the company exists independently of its owners, the death of a founder-member does not mean the company has to cease trading.

Limited companies raise capital by persuading people or institutions to invest in them in return for shares in the company. This is easier for public limited companies which can sell their shares to the public by 'floating' them on the Stock Exchange; private limited companies can only sell to contacts and therefore usually find it harder to raise large sums of money. Normally a company has to have been in existence for three years before its shares can be traded on the Stock Exchange, However, in 1993 Inspirations Holidays was able to float itself after only a year's successful trading on the basis that it was a development of the old direct-sell company Inspirations East. The only other UK companies solely involved with package holidays which are floated on the Stock Exchange are Airtours and First Choice. Once a company has gone public, the only way its original owners can get it back again is by buying back the majority of the shares through the Stock Exchange. Having floated ILG on the Stock Exchange in 1981, Harry Goodman then bought it back again in 1987, believing that it was impossible for him to build up Air Europe in the way he wanted to while having to meet the requirements of anonymous shareholders.

The advantages to a company of being floated on the Stock Exchange include:

- a higher public profile
- greater media interest
- easier access to bank loans
- ability to make money by selling shares
- possibility of issuing new shares

Disadvantages include:

- a higher profile results in closer inspection e.g. of accounts
- responding to increased interest can divert attention from day-to-day running of the business
- shareholders' desire for steady growth in profits and dividends can make it harder to make long-term decisions

The main differences between a public and private limited company are as follows:

a) public companies must have a minimum share capital of £50,000, a quarter of it in fully paid-up shares, while a private company can be set up with only two shares, costing £2 each, as capital.
b) public limited companies can advertise their shares and invite the public to buy them; the public can then buy and sell the shares freely. In contrast, shares in private companies can only be sold privately.

The easiest way to tell if a tour operator is a public or private limited company is to look for its full company name, usually displayed on the booking form at the back of the brochure. Those ending in 'plc' (for public limited company) are public companies, those ending in 'limited' are private companies.

SETTING UP A LIMITED COMPANY

Most tour operations of any size are limited companies. To set up as a limited company it is necessary to apply to the Registrar of Companies and submit two documents: a) a memorandum of association, giving specific details of the company, and b) articles of association, giving details of how the company will be run. These must be accompanied by a fee and a statutory declaration that the requirements of the Companies Acts are being complied with, signed by the company secretary and one of its directors.

The memorandum of association must include:

- the company's name, followed by 'public limited company' or 'limited', as appropriate
- the address of the company's registered office
- a list of the company's objectives
- a statement about the liability of its members
- a note of the amount of capital the company will start trading with and how that is divided up
- the signatures of at least two people (the minimum legal number of members) who have agreed to take at least one share each

Companies can choose to adopt a set of model articles of association or can draw up their own which might include such details as:

- how often meetings of shareholders will be called and how they will be called
- how directors will be appointed to run the company
- the voting rights of shareholders and how shares will be transferred
- how the company will borrow money

Once all this has been received, the registrar will issue the new company with a certificate of incorporation.

Legal requirements for limited companies

The **Companies Act** of 1985 (amended by the Companies Act of 1989) lays down many of the rules which all companies must abide by. They must, for example, file an annual report in a specific form with the Registrar of Companies. This will show what has happened to their capital over the preceding year. They must also lodge a copy of their audited accounts and their profit and loss account with the Registrar. Small and medium-sized private companies are exempted from some of these obligations. Company directors are legally obliged to keep account books, showing details of all financial transactions.

Limited companies must have two registered officers: a director, and a company secretary who is responsible for administering the instructions of the board of directors.

According to the **Business Names Act** of 1985, businesses operating under names other than that of their owners (i.e. most companies) must display the owner's name and the company's address in the UK, and include this information on all their letterheads, invoices, etc. In addition, ABTA requires that ABTA operators shall notify the organisation of any trading names other than the incorporated name that the company may be using.

The **Insolvency Act** of 1986 lays down the rules for winding up an insolvent company. A company can go into voluntary liquidation (if, for example, it wishes to cease trading), as Novotours did in January 1993. More normally it will be compulsorily wound up after a creditor makes a petition to the Court to have it declared insolvent. When this happens the Official Receiver (or another firm of liquidators) may be appointed to act as liquidator, to sort out the company's financial affairs. Once a company is liquidated, its name will be removed from the register at Companies House in Cardiff and London.

CONTRACT LAW

Tour operators are involved in making contracts with:

- their suppliers (hoteliers, airlines, ground handling agents, etc.)
- their retailers (the travel agencies)
- their customers
- their employees

Contracts are agreements freely entered into by at least two parties and intended to be legally binding. They must contain the following elements:

- An offer and acceptance. The offer must be made by one party, communicated to a second and accepted unconditionally by that second party.
- An intention to create a legal relationship, normally indicated in writing for business contracts.
- A consideration, or the exchange of something of value, often goods for money in business.

In addition, the subject matter of the contract must not be illegal, and those entering into the contract must have the capacity to do so. People 'of unsound mind' or under the influence of drink or drugs would not be regarded as having the capacity to enter into a contract. Minors under 18 are also regarded as incapable of entering into a contract, so in the section on tour operators' booking forms which commits the client to a contract with the operator there is usually a clause reading 'I am over 18 years of age'; minors must get their parents or other responsible adults to sign for them.

In the case of the contract between the tour operator and the holidaymaker, the brochure or an advertisement can be seen as the invitation to the customer to do business (i.e. the 'invitation to treat'). The booking form can be seen as the consumer's offer to buy the holiday. In signing the booking form the client (or the travel agent acting on the client's behalf) agrees to the operator's terms and conditions. In theory, that contract is concluded as soon as the operator agrees to the booking, whether or not that agreement is in writing. The booking form simply confirms in writing what has already been agreed verbally and acts as evidence of the intention by both parties to create a legal relationship. Since the 1993 EC Package Travel Regulations lay out in detail what the contract between the tour operator and the client must contain (*see* below) it is likely that booking forms, rather than shrinking as they have tended to do since computerisation, will start to expand again to contain a lot more of the information required. When the booking is made over the telephone it will be necessary for the organiser (or the agent) to draw the customer's attention to the contract conditions in the brochure to comply with the new Regulations.

A breach of contract by the operator may result in one of three possible consequences:

1 The operator has to pay compensation, or damages, as assessed by a court to the injured party. Compensation is usually meant to restore the injured party to the position he/she would have been in had the offender fulfilled its obligations (including reimbursing him/her for 'reasonable' costs incurred, for example, for alternative accommodation) but is intended to take into account not just monetary loss but also disappointment and loss of enjoyment. In that case, it is only the person who has signed the contract who is entitled to compensation for disappointment.

> In 1973, a client arrived for a 'house-party' holiday to find only one other guest. He sued Swans Tours for breach of contract in 'failing to provide the holiday promised' and was awarded compensation not just for the cost of the holiday but for the 'loss of entertainment and enjoyment' as well.

An operator may also have to compensate a client for the distress caused by its failure to fulfil the contract.

> In 1981, a young woman on a Tracks trans-Africa expedition won substantial damages to compensate her not only for loss of earnings incurred when problems resulted in a 14-week trip becoming a 5-month marathon, but also for the distress caused to her by being stranded in particularly difficult circumstances.

2 The injured party may take out an injunction to prevent the operator continuing with the particular breach of contract.

3 A court could issue a decree of specific performance, ordering the operator to fulfil its contractual obligations.

A breach of contract is an offence against the civil law. Minor cases may be settled through the County Court's small claims procedure called arbitration (at present the largest sum that can be disputed through arbitration is £1,000 unless both parties agree to use it). Cases involving sums up to £50,000 are now dealt with in the County Court, while those worth more than £50,000 go to the High Court, Chancery Division.

When a client claims breach of contract by an operator the case may not even come to court, since most businesses would rather avoid the cost of litigation (and the ensuing adverse publicity) if possible. Between 1975 and 1992 ABTA ran their own conciliation scheme aimed at resolving disputes between clients and operators without involving the courts; in 1990, 17,261 cases were referred to conciliation. Faced with an ever growing number of complaints, ABTA withdrew from offering conciliation in 1992.

In 1975, ABTA also set up an arbitration scheme for the travel industry. This is run by the Chartered Institute of Arbitrators, and continues to deal with disputes between operators and their clients provided they are not over a sum of more than £1,500 per person (or £7,500 per booking form) and don't involve illness or physical injury. All ABTA operators must be prepared to go to arbitration and accept the arbitrators' decision.

To use this service, clients must pay a registration fee of £23.50 (plus £7.61 for each additional claimant) for claims worth less than £2,000, and £29.38 (plus £9.66 for each additional claimant) for claims worth £2,001 to £7,500. If the case is decided against the client they are only liable for costs amounting to twice the registration fee. The operator, on the other hand, has to pay not just the registration fee but also £200 plus VAT. The entire case is decided by inspection of documentary evidence and the operator is regarded as having lost the case where the arbitrator awards damages exceeding the last offer of compensation it had made. If the operator wins its case, ABTA pays the £200 fee.

Critics argue that because the scheme is administered by ABTA, it is bound to be biased in favour of the operators, but ABTA feels that the panel of arbitrators appointed to deal with these cases has built up an understanding of the industry's problems which would not be available to a Circuit Court or County Court judge dealing with isolated cases. 'Professional complainers' with frivolous complaints are also likely to be deterred by being asked to refer their complaints to arbitration, thereby avoiding protracted disputes. They also believe that the fact that the arbitrators are appointed by the independent Chartered Institute of Arbitrators ensures their impartiality.

Arbitrators can come to one of three decisions over the case:

- They can make an award in favour of the client, with the operator usually required to refund the client's registration fee and pay them whatever compensation is decided.
- They can dismiss the case, with the client required to pay the operator's registration fee.
- They can make a 'nil award' where no amount is awarded to the client and both parties forfeit their registration fee.

Table 10.1 shows the number of complaints submitted to arbitration between 1987 and 1992, while Table 10.2 shows the known results of those cases.

The Association of Independent Travel Operators (AITO) offers its clients a similar low-cost Independent Dispute Settlement Service.

In 1993, the EC Package Travel Regulations laid down stricter requirements for contracts between operators and clients, meaning that it will probably be easier for clients to win breach of contract cases where something has gone significantly wrong in future.

EMPLOYMENT LAW

Tour operators, as employers, are bound by all the same employment legislation as other employers. Depending on their size, smaller companies may be exempt from some of the requirements for larger companies. It would not be possible to consider all the legislation affecting employment here. However, some of the most important points are considered below.

Table 10.1 The number of complaints referred to arbitration, 1987–92

1987	*1988*	*1989*	*1990*	*1991*	*1992*
551	538	707	670	750	890

Table 10.2 Results of arbitration over holiday complaints, 1987–92

	1987	*1988*	*1989*	*1990*	*1991*	*1992*
Awards favouring client	441	426	529	523	601	769
Cases dismissed	102	112	153	147	149	121

(NB Not all these cases would have involved breach of contract – some cases were withdrawn before adjudication)

1. Employment contracts

The law does not actually insist that employees are given a written contract of employment. However, most large companies will provide written contracts setting out the conditions of employment to avoid any possible misunderstandings. A contract of employment exists when the employer has made an offer of a job which the would-be employee has accepted. The **Employment Protection (Consolidation) Act** of 1978, however, requires that every employee shall be given a Section 1 Notice setting out details of their employment within 13 weeks of starting work. Among other things, this Section 1 Notice should say how much notice must be given by each party when terminating the contract; the minimum period of notice required by law is one week for between four weeks' and a year's employment, with an extra week for each year of employment up to a maximum of 12 years. However, some tour operations' staff, particularly overseas staff and staff working for their airline operations, will be employed on fixed term contracts which automatically expire at the end of the period agreed, frequently at the end of a summer or winter season.

2. Redundancy

The **Employment Protection (Consolidation) Act** also sets out rules for the treatment of redundant staff. Redundancy pay will depend on the age of the member of staff, how long he/she had been employed and what he/she was earning when he/she was made redundant. Sometimes the employer can avoid having to pay redundancy money by offering the employee reasonable alternative employment. Disputes over redundancy are handled by industrial tribunals, with appeals going to the Employment Appeals Tribunal. In the 1980s and 1990s, a major cause of redundancy among tour operating staff was mergers and takeovers: for example, the Airtours buy-out of Aspro on 1993 resulted in job losses in Aspro's Leeds office and among ground-handling staff for Inter European Airways, the company's charter airline.

3. Unfair and wrongful dismissal

The **Employment Protection (Consolidation) Act** also states that employees shall have the right to belong to a trade union and to take part in its activities, and shall be protected against unfair dismissal. Unfair dismissal would occur where an incompetent employee is sacked without being given adequate training or warning of the problem and where the company's own disciplinary procedures have not been followed. In certain circumstances, however, an employee can be dismissed on the spot; such circumstances usually include things like being drunk while on duty and are normally itemised in the company's disciplinary procedures. If the employee is dismissed without being given the proper period of notice, this would constitute wrongful dismissal rather than unfair dismissal. Disputes over unfair or wrongful dismissal are dealt with by industrial tribunals, with appeals to the Employment Appeals Tribunal.

4. Health and safety

The **Health and Safety at Work Act** of 1974 requires employers to provide a high standard of health and safety conditions in the workplace, and to produce a written statement of their policy on health and safety. Health and Safety Inspectors can issue improvement notices to force employers to put right notified problems.

The **Occupiers' Liability Act** of 1957 says occupiers of buildings owe a 'common duty of care' to anyone coming into them, extending the employer's liability beyond its employees to people visiting its premises as well. The **Occupiers' Liability Act** of 1984 extends limited responsibility for care to trespassers as well, although the requirements of this Act can often be fulfilled by posting notices of any obvious dangers.

5. Equal opportunities

The **Race Relations Act** of 1976 makes it illegal to discriminate against employees on the basis of race, colour or ethnic or national origin. The **Equal Pay Act** of 1970, the **Sex Discrimination Act** of 1975 and the **Employment Act** of 1989 also require employers to treat men and women equally in terms of pay (for the same work or work of equal value) and conditions. There is no similar legislation to prevent discrimination against the disabled, although their treatment at work is governed by the **Disabled Persons (Employment) Acts** of 1944 and 1958.

The **Employment Protection (Consolidation) Act**

of 1978 also entitles women who have left work to have babies to return to their old job provided they have notified their employer in writing of their intention to return to work and have exercised their right to do so by the end of the 29th week after the birth.

6. Miscellaneous considerations

Employers are required by law to deduct tax from employees under the Pay As You Earn (PAYE) scheme. Under the **Social Security Act** of 1975 they must also pay Class 1 National Insurance (NI) contributions for their employees and deduct the employees' contributions as well.

Since most tour operators are now computerised, they are also bound by the terms of the **Data Protection Act** of 1984. This requires them to register as data users with a data protection registrar and to ensure that all personal information they keep in their computers is 'collected and held only for purposes specified in [their] current register entry' and that it is 'adequate, relevant, and not excessive in relation to those purposes'. They may store information on members of the travelling public, employees and others (e.g. suppliers) provided it has been collected fairly and lawfully. Some data may have to be stored for six years or more to comply with commercial law. Otherwise, data should not be stored for longer than is necessary for the purposes for which it was obtained. Operators must also take adequate steps to ensure the security of their databases which means considering the positioning of visual display units and ensuring that they only give access to their computers to engineers who have signed a confidentiality agreement. Even when old disks are being disposed of, the security of their contents must be considered.

Companies must also make the information they are holding about individual data subjects available to them within 40 days of their requesting it in writing. They may make a charge of no more than £10 for doing this. They will be committing an offence if they disclose the information to others without the individual's consent.

CONSUMER LAW

It is probably in the very nature of trade that some people in business will always be blinded by the desire to make a quick profit. Since time immemorial there have been attempts to redress the balance between the trader and the consumer; even in the Middle Ages there were officials whose job it was to stamp out attempts to short-change customers. Nevertheless, until relatively recently there was a tendency to cling to the old dictat of *caveat emptor* (buyer beware), whereby the onus fell on the consumer rather than the seller to ensure that what they were buying was what it was meant to be. However, in the 1970s and 1980s the emphasis shifted dramatically, partly as a result of pressure from the media. Nowadays *caveat emptor* only really applies when it comes to personal transactions; where businesses are concerned the law increasingly comes down on the consumer's side.

The first law specifically concerned with the rights of the consumer was the 1893 Sale of Goods Act. Since then a succession of new Acts of Parliament have tried to close loopholes which leave the consumer vulnerable. The most important of these Acts are summarised below.

The consumer

The Fair Trading Act of 1973 defined a consumer as a person:

a) to whom goods or services are supplied, or sought to be supplied, in the course of a business carried on by the supplier; and
b) who does not receive or seek to receive them in the course of a business carried on by him.

Misrepresentation Act 1967

This Act enables consumers to take out a civil case against a business for any loss they suffer as a result of false statements of fact made by the seller or provider of goods or services. To defend themselves against liability, the seller would have to prove that what they said was fair and reasonable in the circumstances.

Trade Descriptions Acts 1968 and 1972

These Acts make it an offence to:

a) apply a false trade description to goods
b) supply goods to which a false trade description has been applied

c) make a false statement knowingly or recklessly as to the provision of service, accommodation or facilities

The Acts cover both oral and written descriptions, although obviously it is easier to prove a written offence than an oral one. Often the most important consideration is whether the false description was made 'recklessly'. What is meant by 'recklessly' is open to interpretation by the courts. In 1990 Crystal Holidays published a brochure in which it stated that there was a new 18-hole golf course in the Austrian village of Schladming. A client later complained that work on building the site had not been completed and that he had been unable to use the course. Buckinghamshire County Council referred the case to Milton Keynes Magistrates Court for prosecution under the Trade Descriptions Act. The magistrates decided that although the description in the brochure was false and Crystal Holidays had known the course was incomplete, the company had nevertheless taken 'all reasonable precautions and exercised all due diligence' in preparing the entry and was not, therefore, guilty of an offence. The County Council appealed against this ruling to the High Court which reversed the original decision and said Crystal Holidays was guilty of an offence under the Act.

In 1994, Airtours, too, escaped conviction over a hotel description in a winter sun brochure which included mention of a non-existent indoor swimming pool. The company admitted misrepresentation but argued that the directors had set up guidelines for copy checking and brochure production and could not therefore be said to have acted 'recklessly'. Under the Trade Descriptions Act it is the 'mind' of a company (usually interpreted as its board of directors) who must be proved reckless. Airtours successfully proved that it was its overseas operations controllers who gave final approval to the brochure copy, and that they were not in a senior enough position to be convicted. In future it will be harder for companies to use such a loophole. Under the EC Package Travel Regulations, to avoid conviction a company will have to be able to prove both that it took all steps to ensure the accuracy of the brochure *and* that it continued to recheck for accuracy throughout the life of that brochure.

Consumer Credit Act 1974

This Act covers all credit agreements involving less than £15,000. It makes it a criminal offence to offer credit or act as a credit broker without a licence. From the consumer's point of view, it makes credit card companies jointly liable with tour operators for any breaches of contract or misrepresentation by the operator where the consumer has used a credit card to pay a cost of no less than £100 and no more than £30,000. As a consequence of this, when a tour operator has collapsed without a bond or with inadequate bonding, clients who have paid for their packages with credit cards have sometimes been able to obtain a refund from the credit card company.

NB: Access/Mastercard and Barclaycard/Visa are credit cards covered by the Act, whereas American Express and Diners Card are charge cards and are not covered by it.

Restrictive Trade Practices Acts 1976 and 1977

Restrictive trade practices can be agreements between suppliers, or between suppliers and distributors or retailers. Because such agreements can be anti-competitive, the Restrictive Trade Practices Acts of 1976 and 1977 were passed, enforcing registration of all such agreements with the Office of Fair Trading. If the OFT thinks the restrictive practice may not be in the public interest, it can refer it to the Restrictive Trade Practices Court for a ruling. If it is found to be contrary to the public interest, the restrictive trade practice can then be prohibited.

To obtain approval for a restrictive practice a trade association has to prove:

a) that the restriction is necessary to protect the public against injury
b) that its removal would deny the public some substantial benefit
c) that the restriction is necessary in order to enable members to negotiate with a third party which holds a majority share of the market

In 1965 ABTA members drew up a rule which came to be known as 'Stabiliser'. Under Stabiliser, ABTA tour operators could only sell their products through ABTA travel agencies and vice versa. As a result of this agreement, most agencies and operators wanted to belong to ABTA which, in turn, meant that the rule covered most of the travel trade. However, Stabiliser was clearly a restrictive practice, working against the interests of operators and agents who didn't belong to ABTA. When service industries were drawn into the ambit of the Restrictive Practices Act in 1976, the OFT referred Stabiliser to the Restrictive Practices Court for discussion. ABTA also had to register all the following with the Office of Fair Trading:

- its articles of association
- the tour operator and travel agent codes of conduct
- its guide to business relationships between tour operators and travel agencies
- its list of recommended service charges

In 1978, before the Court reached its conclusions, ABTA dropped some restrictive practices it recognised would be unsustainable. In particular, it dropped rules which had previously prevented operators and agents discounting brochure prices. In 1984, after a six year investigation, the Restrictive Practices Court ruled that on balance Stabiliser operated in the public interest by providing a safeguard against cowboy holiday companies. However, it decided that other restrictive practices previously permitted by ABTA should be outlawed. In particular, groups of agents and/or operators were forbidden to get together and make 'restrictive' agreements or arrangements which could work against the general public interest (e.g. agreeing to stop racking the brochures of an operator whose commission levels were thought too low).

In the aftermath of a rash of tour operator failures in 1991 and 1992, ABTA was left financially weakened and insurance companies became reluctant to provide the necessary shortfall insurance to enable it to continue to guarantee refunds to all holidaymakers affected by the collapse of ABTA operators. In such circumstances, Stabiliser looked increasingly untenable. ABTA needed to be able to vet the financial status of potential members to avoid such drains on its resources in the future. However, if it were to do that, it would leave itself open to the criticism that it was making it impossible for some companies to trade effectively (i.e. through ABTA agencies) and expose itself to further complaints about restrictive trading practices. In October 1993 ABTA members voted to scrap Stabiliser, after receiving advice that a battle to defend it in court would be expensive and unlikely to succeed. ABTA travel agencies were thus freed to sell the holidays of non-ABTA tour operators. Almost at once, Airtours, Med Choice and Rainbow Holidays signed agreements to retail through the non-ABTA Travel Group (now The Global Travel Group), which planned a chain of franchised agencies.

Unfair Contract Terms Act 1977

This Act makes it impossible to exclude or restrict liability for death or personal injury caused by negligence. Liability for other loss or damage can only be restricted or excluded where the notice stating this is judged to be 'reasonable'.

Sale of Goods Act 1979

The Sale of Goods Act states that there are a number of implied conditions in a contract of sale. These are:

a) that the seller has the right to sell the goods
b) that the goods are free from any charge or encumbrance not disclosed or known to the buyer before or at the time of the sale
c) that the buyer shall have and enjoy quiet possession of the goods
d) that the goods sold shall correspond with any description given of them
e) that the goods are of merchantable quality (i.e. that they are not suffering from defects that make them unusable)
f) that where the seller sells the goods in the course of a business and the buyer, expressly or by implication, makes known to the seller any particular purpose for which the goods are being bought, the goods supplied are reasonably fit for the purpose

Competition Act 1980

In general, in the 1980s it was believed that free and open competition between companies would offer benefits to the consumer by encouraging lower prices and a better quality and range of services.

Under the 1980 Competition Act anything seen as uncompetitive can be referred to the Office of

Fair Trading whose Director-General must decide if there is a case to answer and, if so, set up an inquiry. After the inquiry has taken place, suggestions may be made about how the company can comply with the law. If it still fails to do so, the matter can be referred to the Monopolies and Mergers Commission and the Secretary of State for Trade can order an alteration of the trade practice.

The law doesn't make anti-competitive practices illegal but provides a way to regulate them in circumstances where the OFT decides they are 'contrary to the public interest'.

Between 1978 and 1984, the Restrictive Practices Court undertook a comprehensive investigation of the rules ABTA imposed on its members. When it delivered its verdict in 1984, some of the decisions were based on the Restrictive Trade Practices Act of 1976 (*see* above) and others on the Competition Act.

Supply of Goods and Services Act 1982

This covers much the same ground as the Sale of Goods Act. However, for services it states that sales involve implied terms covering:

a) the use of reasonable care and skill
b) performing within a reasonable time
c) charging a reasonable fee

Since tour operators offer a service, this Act brought them within the scope of the 1979 Act.

Restriction on Agreements and Conduct (Tour Operators) Order 1987

When the Restrictive Practices Court finally announced the results of its inquiry into ABTA's rules and codes of conduct in 1984, the Director General of Fair Trading instructed the Monopolies and Mergers Commission to investigate the agency agreements drawn up between ABTA members. Increasingly, these included conditions barring travel agents from offering discounts or incentives (like free taxis to the airport) to encourage sales of package holidays. In 1986, the Commission reported that such agreements acted against the public interest, and in 1987 the government introduced the Restriction on Agreements and Conduct (Tour Operators) Order which made it illegal to build such restrictions into future agency agreements. It also required operators to withdraw them from existing agreements.

Consumer Protection Act 1987

This Act states that if a defect in a product causes injury to anyone, whether or not they are the purchaser, the producer will be liable for damages whether or not they were negligent or knew the goods were defective. Anyone who puts their own name on a product becomes jointly liable. Producers are required to abide by general safety requirements and local trading standards officers can:

a) make safety regulations
b) make orders for forfeiture
c) serve suspension or prohibition notices
d) serve warning notices

If the supplier then breaches any of the these regulations it becomes liable for any damages caused unless it can show that it had taken all reasonable steps and exercised all due diligence to avoid committing an offence.

The Act also makes it illegal for a business to give consumers misleading information about the price of goods, services, accommodation or facilities available. So, for example, prices must be quoted *inclusive* of VAT.

In 1994 it seemed likely that the Act would be extended to state that tickets for concerts, sports events, etc. must be endorsed with their price in an effort to stamp out ticket touting. They would also be required to state if they offered only a restricted view. Package tours including such tickets would have to mention the cost of the tickets in the brochure.

Control of Misleading Advertisements Regulations 1988

These regulations make it an offence to publish a misleading advertisement if it deceives, or is likely to deceive, the people to whom it is addressed or whom it reaches. It is also an offence to publish a misleading advert if its deceptive nature is likely to affect viewers' economic behaviour, or if it injures, or is likely to injure, competitors of the person whose interests it seeks to promote. Offences are handled by the Director-General of the Office of

Fair Trading, except in the case of television or radio advertising which are dealt with by their regulatory bodies (*see* page 2068).

It's important to remember that law is not something fixed for all time. Old laws are constantly being updated and new ones introduced to meet new needs, so companies must be constantly alert to ensure they trade on the right side of the law. At ABTA's convention in Majorca in 1993 there were discussions about a probable development of the Unfair Contract Terms Act which would regulate package holiday cancellation conditions. It was also possible that a new directive on data protection would require operators to inform clients of how their personal details were being stored, used and accessed.

European Community/European Union law

Great Britain entered the European Economic Community (EEC) in 1973 and since then companies have had to comply with relevant European Community (EC) (now European Union (EU)) legislation as well as with British law. In particular, in December 1992 the EC-directed Package Travel, Package Holidays and Package Tours Regulations (hereafter referred to as the EC Package Travel Regulations) became law in Britain.

The Package Travel, Package Holidays and Package Tours Regulations 1992

Since January 1993, the EC Package Travel Regulations have provided the main legal framework for both overseas and domestic tour operating businesses. In many ways these Regulations simply consolidate existing law and industry codes of conduct. However, although there had been a lengthy period of consultation before the Regulations became law, there were still some initial hiccoughs, and at the end of 1993 doubts still remained about the precise interpretation of parts of the Regulations which awaited settlement by the courts.

In its preamble the new law provides definitions of industry terms like 'brochure' and 'package'. In general these follow definitions long since laid down by ABTA. Perhaps the most important – and fraught with difficulty in interpretation – is the definition of a 'package' which dictates who and what exactly is covered by the new law. According to the Regulations, the term 'package' means:

> the prearranged combination of at least two of the following components when sold or offered for sale at an inclusive price and when the service covers a period of more than 24 hours or includes overnight accommodation:
> a) transport
> b) accommodation
> c) other tourist services not ancillary to transport or accommodation and accounting for a significant proportion of the package,
> and
> (i) the submission of separate accounts for different components shall not cause the arrangement to be other than a package;
> (ii) the fact that a combination is arranged at the request of the consumer and in accordance with his specific instructions (whether modified or not) shall not of itself cause it to be treated as other than prearranged:

According to the Department of Trade and Industry (DTI) the expression 'tourist services' refers to things like excursions, access to a golf course or fishing rights, theatre tickets, guided tours, or a crew on a chartered yacht. It does *not* include educational services, business services, conference services, etc.

The DTI emphasises that a 'package' only falls within the scope of the law when it has been 'sold or offered for sale'. In its view, therefore, groups of people getting together to organise their own holiday and then splitting the cost among themselves are not covered by the law, provided there is no element of profit involved and the organiser is acting on a voluntary basis. School field trips, etc. are also unlikely to be offered for sale in the normal sense of the word and so are also exempt.

Some travel agents who sell tailor-made travel arrangements have worried that the new definition could make them 'organisers' under the terms of the Act which defines an 'organiser' as 'the person who, otherwise than occasionally, organises packages and sells or offers them for sale, whether directly or through a retailer'. The DTI believes the crucial factors are a) whether the package is sold at an inclusive price, and b) whether it was prearranged. It does not believe a package has been created where the consumer buys an air ticket from a travel agent one day and then returns the next day to book accommodation, unless the items have simply been invoiced separately to unmake a package. If the customer asks the agent to book a specific hotel and a specific flight and pays for them at the same time, the DTI still thinks this would not be regarded as a package because it had not been prearranged by the agent as organiser.

There are also some reservations about the exemption for those who 'occasionally' organise packages. The intention behind this choice of wording was presumably to exclude situations like annual school geography excursions from bonding requirements. However, some have argued that there should be no such exemptions because:

a) the consumer does not necessarily realise that the organiser only occasionally arranges trips and is therefore exempt
b) the more rarely an organiser arranges a trip, the more likely mistakes are

To try and simplify things the DTI drew up a sequence of questions that those in doubt about whether they are selling 'packages' under the Regulations could ask themselves:

1 Does what you offer include an overnight stay or last more than 24 hours?
If 'no', then it is not a package.
If 'yes', then go to Q.2.

2 Does what you offer include services other than accommodation and transport?
If 'no', go to Q.5.
If 'yes', go to Q.3.

3 Are these tourist services?
If 'no', go to Q.5.
If 'yes', go to Q.4.

4 Are these services significant? (For a service to be 'significant', its presence would have to be a significant part of the reason for the customer's taking the package.)
Whether 'no' or 'yes', go to Q.5.

5 Does what you offer include accommodation? (e.g. in a hotel, guest house, self-catering accommodation, fixed tent, caravan, boat on inland waterway, berth on cruise ship, etc.)
Whether 'no' or 'yes', go to Q.6.

6 Does what you offer include transport? (e.g. seat on aircraft, train, coach, ferry, cruise ship, etc.)
Whether 'no' or 'yes', go to Q.7.

7 If you answered 'yes' to only one of Q.4, 5 or 6, then it is unlikely that you are offering a package within the scope of the Regulations.
If you answered 'yes' to two or more of Q.4, 5 or 6, then you should answer Q.8.

8 Is what you sell 'pre-arranged' (put together before the conclusion of the contract)?
If 'no', then you are probably not offering a package.
If 'yes', go to Q.9.

9 Is it sold or offered for sale at an inclusive price? (The submission of separate invoices does not prevent something being regarded as being sold at an inclusive price.)
If 'no', then you are probably not offering a package.
If 'yes', then you are likely to be offering a package within the scope of the Regulations.

Despite these attempts to clarify the situation, doubts still remain. The situation with 'seat-only' packages, for example, is uncertain. Often such sales are technically illegal in the destination countries which wish to protect their national airlines from competition. To get round this problem, operators have often provided seat-only customers with 'minimum accommodation' vouchers which name a particular hotel/hostel without there ever being any intention they should actually be used. If 'seat-onlys' are treated as what they really are (i.e. transport-only arrangements), then they don't fulfil the definition of a package under the Regulations and so do not come under its protection. If, however, the accommodation is regarded as being 'real', then it would never match up to the rules on brochure descriptions, etc.

The problems were highlighted when ABTA was accused of breaching the Regulations itself when it organised the travel arrangements for its 1993 conference in Palma. According to *Travel Weekly*, 'ABTA offered delegates packages consisting of flights, accommodation, car hire and rail travel together with tourism and hospitality services at prices available only to those booking for the convention'. However, ABTA refuted this, saying it sold flight and educational services which did not constitute a package, while delegates paid for their accommodation directly.

What the Package Travel Regulations cover

1 Misleading descriptive matter

The Regulations supplement the provisions of the Trade Descriptions Act 1968 and the Consumer Protection Act 1987 in stating that organisers must not supply consumers with any descriptive matter about a package, its price or the conditions relating to the contract of sale which is misleading. If they do, they must compensate the consumer for any loss, including disappointment, incurred as a result. To sue an operator under the Regulations the consumer no longer has to prove the misleading information was provided knowingly or recklessly, as under the Trade Descriptions Act.

2 Brochure requirements

Organisers are required to include information about the price and the following items in their brochures in 'a legible, comprehensible and accurate manner':

a) The destination and the means, characteristics and categories of transport used.
b) The type of accommodation, its location, category or degree of comfort and its main features and, where the accommodation is to be provided in a member State (of the EU), its approval or tourist classification under the rules of that member State.
c) The meals which are included in the package.
d) The itinerary.
e) General information about passport and visa requirements which apply for British citizens and health formalities required for the journey and the stay.
f) Either the monetary amount or the percentage of the price which is to be paid on account and the timetable for payment of the balance.
g) Whether a minimum number of persons is required for the package to take place and, if so, the deadline for informing the consumer in the event of cancellation.
h) The arrangements (if any) which apply if consumers are delayed at the outward or homeward points of departure.
i) The arrangements for security for money paid over and for the repatriation of the consumer in the event of insolvency.

The particulars in the brochure are to be regarded as 'implied warranties' ('implied terms' in Scotland) unless the brochure clearly states that this is not the case until a contract has been concluded.

3 Other information

Before the contract is completed, the tour operator is required to provide information on passport and visa requirements (for British citizens only), and on health formalities for the journey. It is also required to explain how the client's money is being safeguarded and how they would be repatriated, should that become necessary. Before the passenger travels, the operator is also required to provide full details of all stops *en route* and of the accommodation which will be provided. They must also supply a local contact or contact telephone number for emergencies. Where the contract between the tour operator and the client doesn't make it a condition of completion that the client must take out insurance, clients must be provided with details of suitable insurance, specifically to cover cancellation of the holiday, and sickness abroad and possible repatriation.

4 The contract

The Directive states that all clients must be given a copy of the contract in writing and that the contract must contain the following details:

- The travel destination(s) and, where periods of stay are involved, the relevant periods, with dates.
- The means, characteristics and categories of transport to be used and the dates, times and points of departure and return. (The DTI doesn't believe it is necessary to specify the type of aircraft or car.)
- Where the package includes accommodation, its location, its tourist category (where there is a compulsory grading system) or degree of comfort, its main features and, where the accommodation is to be provided in a member State, its compliance with the rules of that member State. In the case of 'square deal' type packages, the

client need not be told the precise hotel which they will be staying in, although they do have to be told its general location and be given an indication of its standard of comfort.

- The meals which are included in the package.
- Whether a minimum number of people is required for the package to take place and, if so, the deadline for informing the consumer in the event of cancellation.
- The itinerary.
- Visits, excursions or other services which are included in the total price agreed for the package.
- The name and address of the organiser, retailer and, where appropriate, the insurer.
- The price of the package and, if the price may be revised in accordance with other terms of the Directive, an indication of the possibility of such price revisions, and an indication of any dues, taxes or fees chargeable for certain services (landing, embarkation or disembarkation fees at ports and airports and tourist taxes) where such costs are not included in the package.
- The payment schedule and acceptable methods of payment.
- Special requirements which the consumer has communicated to the organiser or retailer when making the booking and which both have accepted.
- The periods within which the consumer must make any complaint about failure to perform or inadequate performance of the contract.

Given that 15 per cent of all package holidays are booked over the telephone, the DTI believes the organiser (or retailer) will have fulfilled its obligations under the Regulations provided it checks that the client has a copy of the brochure, drawing attention to the contract details published inside it.

5 Transfer of bookings

The Regulations state that it is an implied term of every contract that consumers should be able to transfer their booking to another person who fulfils the conditions of the package if they are unable to travel, provided they give the organiser 'reasonable notice' of this fact. The DTI points out that simple change of mind is not a good enough reason to transfer a booking; the original clients must be prevented from travelling by circumstances outside their control, like illness, death of a close relative, jury service, or an employer's requirements. The organiser is still allowed to include in a contract a stipulation that if the person making the original booking cancels, it will be transferred to the person at the head of any waiting list and not necessarily to a person of the original client's choice. Where the booking is transferred to another person, the new client and the original client remain 'jointly and severally liable' for all outstanding costs (i.e. if the new traveller doesn't pay, the person who made the original booking will still be liable for the cost of the holiday).

6 Price revision

The Regulations state that contract terms allowing for upward revision of prices must also allow for downward revision too. They must also state how the new price is to be calculated. Price revisions are only permissible to allow for:

- changes in transportation costs, including the price of fuel
- changes in dues, taxes or fees e.g. airport taxes (the DTI believes this would cover changes in general tax rates like VAT too)
- exchange rate fluctuations affecting specific packages

No price revisions may be made less than 30 days before the departure date, and the latest date for revisions must be included in the contract. No increases of less than two per cent can be passed on to the client. If the surcharge is larger, the operator must absorb the first two per cent of it. The Regulations also say that the client must be allowed to cancel without penalty if there is 'significant' alteration to an essential term of the contract, which would include price. However, there is no definition of what is meant by 'significant' in this context. Organisers are obliged to pass on details of all significant alterations to essential terms 'as quickly as possible' so the client can make a decision on whether to cancel or not; once again, however, what is meant by 'as quickly as possible' is not defined.

7 *Withdrawal of the consumer when there is a significant change to the booking/ cancellation of the package by the organiser*

If the organiser makes a significant change to an essential term of the contract, the client is entitled:

a) to a substitute package of equal or superior quality, where this is possible,
b) to a substitute package of lower quality (where this is possible) and a refund of the difference in price between what was booked and what is actually taken, or
c) to a full refund.

The organiser will have to compensate the client for cancelling their holiday except where the contract had stated that a specific number of people were needed before the holiday could take place, or where cancellation is the result of 'unusual and unforeseeable circumstances' beyond the organiser's control. Overbooking is specifically excluded from these unusual and unforeseeable circumstances.

8 *Situations in which a significant proportion of a service is not provided*

If the organiser is unable to provide a 'significant' proportion of the services named in the contract, it must make alternative arrangements at no extra cost to the client and compensate them for any difference between what was contracted and what was supplied. The amount of compensation should normally take into account disappointment and inconvenience as well as purely monetary loss. If it can't make alternative arrangements that are acceptable to the clients, it must return him/her to the place of departure or somewhere else mutually acceptable.

9 *Liability for proper performance of the contract*

One of the most important sections of the Regulations relates to the organiser's liability for the performance of the contract. Tour operating is unusually dependent on third parties for the fulfilment of its contracts. Often a company will be depending on the staff of airlines, hotels and coach companies which it doesn't own to ensure that substantial parts of the contract are carried out satisfactorily. In the past they might have been able to claim that things that went wrong were the fault of, for example, the hotelier. However, under the Regulations the organiser can be held responsible for 'the proper performance of the obligations of the contract' irrespective of whether those obligations were to be carried out by the organisers themselves or by other suppliers of services. If forced to compensate a client for something which has not been carried out by another supplier of services, it is up to the organiser to take action against that supplier for their failure. The organiser is also liable to the consumer for any damage caused by failure to fulfil the contract unless it can prove that the damage was caused neither by itself nor by other suppliers of services with which it had agreements but by 'third parties'. So, for example, a tour operator could not be held liable for an accident one of its clients sustained while riding a moped booked directly with a bike hire company while on holiday. As usual, there is a let-out clause which recognises 'unusual and unforeseeable circumstances' as a defence. Such circumstances might include:

- air traffic control delays
- delays or diversions caused by bad weather which could not have been predicted
- disruption caused by industrial action outside the control of the organiser

Operators are allowed to write limitations in line with international conventions (e.g. the Warsaw Convention limiting airline liability and the Athens Convention limiting shipping liability) into their contractual liability to compensate clients for damage. Where the damage suffered is other than personal injury they can also set written limits on the amount of compensation that will be payable.

10 *Security in the event of insolvency*

One of the biggest concerns of consumers, highlighted by well-publicised collapses, has been that their money should be secure if the tour operator ceases trading. The new Regulations aim to improve on the protection already provided to customers which had proved inadequate to cover all situations, as the collapse of Bath-based coach tour operator Land Travel in 1992 indicated. At first reading the Regulations are clear:

The other party (normally the operator) to the contract shall at all times be able to provide sufficient evidence of security for the refund of money paid over and for the repatriation of the consumer in the event of insolvency.

However, note that no definition of 'sufficient proof' is given.

The Regulations go on to describe three permitted ways to protect the client's money:

- bonding
- trust accounts
- insurance

These are described in detail below (pages 237–43).

The remainder of the Regulations concern enforcement of the rules, which is the responsibility of local authority trading standards officers. However, they were soon attracting criticism for lack of clarity. In particular there were concerns that retailers who sold transport and accommodation might find themselves reclassified as 'organisers' with all that implies in terms of expensive bonding requirements. In May 1993 a small company, SFV Holidays of Oxford, ceased trading and was found to have no bonding to refund its clients. Although it sold tailor-made ferry and self-catering holidays in France, SFV had been advised by the DTI that it was not technically a package operator because it gave its clients a choice about which ferry they took. An AITO spokeswoman pointed out that if this was the case, many AITO members would also qualify to avoid the bonding rules.

The most important features of the new Regulations are:

a) that they extend tour operators' liability for problems with holidays by making it difficult for them to pass the buck to their suppliers
b) that they make legally enforceable what was previously just ABTA required good practice
c) that they alter the basis for bonding of holidays by extending it to all travel organisers offering 'package' arrangements
d) that, in doing this, they reduce the importance of ABTA and make likely changes in the main travel trade association
e) that they make legal what were previously ABTA requirements for brochures
f) that they make it a legal obligation for travel agents to provide additional information on visas, insurance, etc. to clients

Immediate consequences of the EC Package Travel Regulations

During 1993, the travel trade started to adjust to the changed situation created by the Regulations. However, it took a long time for new bonding arrangements to cover non-ATOL-licensed traffic to be put into place. ABTA's future also remained in doubt throughout most of the year. Confusion was also caused by conflicting interpretation, as when President of the Board of Trade, Michael Heseltine, told SFV Holidays that they did not fit the definition of a package holiday and so did not need bonding (*see* above). The Local Authorities Co-ordinating Body on Food and Trading Standards, which advises the 129 British trading standards departments charged with policing the Regulations, had also ruled that operators couldn't pass the buck on protecting clients' money by obliging holidaymakers to take out insurance with a clause covering company failure, only to have the Department of Trade and Industry contradict their advice, creating yet more confusion.

However, the changes did have some immediate consequences:

1. Several large operators, including Thomson, Airtours and Sunworld, agreed to retail their products through The Travel Group (now The Global Travel Group), a non-ABTA company with 5 retail shops and 28 telesales units but with plans to expand rapidly.
2. Le Shuttle Holidays became the first major non-ABTA operator to arrange to retail its products through ABTA agencies, including Lunn Poly. Its clients' money was to be placed in a trust account for protection.
3. Legal firms advertised brochure-checking services to ensure companies kept within the letter of the law.
4. Insurance firms began to develop new bonding arrangements to suit small and medium-sized operators.
5. Some small producer-operators, particularly hotels, decided to drop their operating arms because they didn't want to have to undertake complex bonding arrangements.

BONDING OF HOLIDAYS

ABTA defines a 'bond' as 'an irrevocable guarantee provided by a third party . . . [which] can be enforced in the event of the financial failure of the company in respect of which the bond is provided'. A system for bonding holidays has been put in place so that:

a) customers whose holidays are actually taking place when an operator ceases trading can continue with their holiday as far as possible as originally planned
b) customers whose holidays are actually taking place when an operator ceases trading can be brought back to the UK either immediately or at the end of their holiday
c) customers who have paid for holidays which were yet to commence when the operator ceased trading can be reimbursed
d) alternative holiday arrangements can be made for customers who have paid for trips which were yet to commence when the operator ceased trading

In general, ABTA's view is that each member should be able to stand on its own bonding feet (i.e. that it should put up sufficient bonding to cover its own worst case failure scenario). However, to ensure consumer confidence, arrangements have also been made to cover any shortfall in an individual company's bonding arrangements. Figure 10.1 shows how the bonding of package holidays has three 'lines of defence'.

Licensable activities

Licensable activities are all those involved with holidays including an air transport component for which an Air Transport Organiser's Licence has had to be issued. **Non-licensable activities** are all those involved with holidays which don't include air transport and for which no licence is required. Some operators have both licensable and non-licensable business.

Bonding: the background

In 1993, the EC Package Travel Regulations caused an extensive rethink of the arrangements for bonding holidays. However, bonding is nothing new. After the collapse of Fiesta Tours in 1964 and Omar Khayyam Tours in 1965, ABTA pooled 50 per cent of its membership subscriptions to create a 'Common Fund' which could be used to reimburse holidaymakers following any further failures. ABTA had assumed the government would start regulating who could set up as a tour operator. However, when this didn't happen, it established Operation

	Licensable Activities *Statutory*	**Non-Licensable Activities** *Statutory*
First line of defence ('Each member stands on its own bonding feet')	**CAA bonds** Individual bonds provided to the ATOL-holders	**ABTA bonds** Individual bonds provided to ABTA by all ABTA members conducting non-licensable activities
Second line of defence ('Common fund or insurance scheme')	**Air Travel Trust Fund** Contributed to by all ATOL-holders	**ABTA insurance scheme** Premium contributed to by relevant ABTA members
Third line of defence ('Common fund')		**ABTA Tour Operator's Fund** Contributed to by ABTA tour operators

Fig. 10.1 Bonding requirements for ABTA members, 1994

Source: ABTA

Stabiliser (*see* page 227) so that Common Fund money would only be available to compensate customers who had booked holidays with ABTA tour operators through ABTA travel agencies.

Many travel agencies objected to having to contribute to a fund which was effectively insuring tour operators. It was also clear that the Common Fund alone would not be adequate to cope if there was a major company failure. In 1970, the Tour Operators Study Group (TOSG) set up a new Trust Fund into which members had to pay 5 per cent of their annual turnover ready to compensate clients after another collapse. However, in 1974 the demise of Clarkson's during the peak holiday period revealed that even this degree of insurance was inadequate and the government was forced to help out; between 1975 and 1977, the Air Travel Reserve Fund Act allowed the government to raise a levy of 2 per cent on tour operators' turnovers to make up the shortfall in the Trust Fund. In 1972, the Civil Aviation Act introduced a system of licensing for all-inclusive package holidays using charter flights which, it was hoped, would weed out unviable operators. Since then, all tour operators wishing to create such packages have had to apply to the Civil Aviation Authority (CAA) for an Air Transport Organiser's Licence or ATOL (*see* below).

1965	**Creation of Common Fund to reimburse clients of failed tour companies.** **'Operation Stabiliser' – Common Fund protection restricted to clients of ABTA tour operators trading through ABTA travel agencies.**
1970	**TOSG establishes new Trust Fund to pay out after tour operator failures.**
1972	**Introduction of ATOL licensing system.**
1974	**Government forced to top up Trust Fund after collapse of Clarkson's.**
1975-77	**Government levy on tour operators to recoup top-up funds.**
1982	**ABTA bonding scheme extended to cover non-air tour operators.**
1993	**EC Package Travel Regulations bring about complete rethink on bonding.**

Fig. 10.2 Development of bonding to protect tour operators' clients

THE CAA AND BONDING OF HOLIDAYS WITH AN AIR TRAVEL COMPONENT

Air Transport Organiser's Licences (ATOLs)

To protect the public, all operators selling charter air holidays or charter flight seats are required to obtain an Air Travel Organiser's Licence, or ATOL, from the Civil Aviation Authority (CAA). Since 1992, operators selling packages using scheduled flights have also needed to obtain an ATOL, a change which had greatest impact on long-haul companies.

ATOL-holders are required to display their number on their brochures, leaflets and advertisements, making it possible to check up on them. In 1994 there were 890 companies in the UK which held ATOLs, although most flights were offered by the 30 biggest tour companies. Table 10.3 shows the capacity the CAA licensed for the top 10 tour groups and operators in May 1994 compared with the figures for May 1993.

Companies applying for an ATOL must pay the CAA an application fee of £150. If the application is approved, they must pay an additional £375, plus 4.2 pence per one-way journey.

The ATOL system offers protection to the public in three ways.

1 Financial checks

Every year the CAA has to check that the people holding the ATOL are fit to do so and that their company finances are sound, i.e. that they have a substantial level of assets on their balance sheet and secured funding to meet future cash flow demands. These requirements can be very onerous for small companies, particularly because the CAA usually discounts cash flow that relies on clients' advance payments and assets of a fixed nature (houses, property) which can't easily be realised at short notice. Licences normally run for 12 months from either March or September.

These annual checks can't prevent problems arising between one year and the next, and the fact that all the licences become due for renewal at the same time means that there is often a delay in getting

Table 10.3 Capacity licensed to top 10 groups and operators 1993–4

	Group and licence holders	*Seats licensed*	*% total*	*Seats licensed*	*% total*
		at May 94		*at May 93*	
1	Thomson Group				
	Thomson Tour Operations	3,715,000		3,224,000	
	Portland Holidays	70,000		250,000	
	Airlink International	16,150		13,500	
	Lunn Poly	0		n/a	
	Thomson Group Total	3,801,150	22	3,487,500	24
2	Airtours	2,437,627	14	1,692,253	12
3	Owners Abroad Group				
	Owners Abroad Holidays	1,625,000		1,534,500	
	Owners Abroad Travel	300,000		299,500	
	Olympic Holidays	116,500		105,250	
	Owners Abroad Aviation	0		0	
	Owners Abroad Group Total	2,041,500	12	1,939,250	13
4	Cosmos Group				
	Avro	1,269,200		655,500	
	Cosmosair	490,000		380,000	
	Cosmos Coach Tours	42,000		43,000	
	Archers Tours	3,550		2,200	
	Sure Flights	0		0	
	First Aviation	0		n/a	
	Cosmos Group Total	1,804,750	11	1,080,700	7
5	Iberotravel	633,180	4	400,000	3
6	Unijet Travel	529,250	3	395,500	3
7	Best Travel	347,500	2	350,000	2
8	Sun International Group				
	Cresta Holidays	134,500		105,775	
	Paris Travel Service	85,000		80,000	
	Swiss Travel Service	40,500		31,250	
	Amsterdam Travel Service	22,000		18,250	
	Belgian Travel Service	3,000		3,375	
	London Tours and Travel Service	1,000		n/a	
	Bridge Travel Service	2,800		n/a	
	Sun International Group Total	288,800	2	238,650	2
9	Virgin Holidays	190,300	1	158,758	1
10	Kuoni Travel	180,964	1	175,320	1
	Total seats licensed to above ten groups	12,225,021	72	9,917,931	68
	Seats licensed to all ATOL-holders	17,136,366	100	14,544,721	100

THIS IS WHY MORE AND MORE OF YOUR CUSTOMERS WILL BE ASKING YOU FOR ATOL NUMBERS THIS YEAR.

NATIONAL PRESS CAMPAIGN STARTS 10th FEBRUARY

Thursday 10th February marks the start of a new national press campaign for the Civil Aviation Authority's ATOL scheme.

The campaign, which will be seen by over 75% of all adults, advises anyone planning a holiday abroad to ask two vital questions. Does this trip need an ATOL and if so, what is the ATOL number of the Tour Operator?

ATOL IS A LEGAL REQUIREMENT

It is a legal requirement for every tour operator offering charter flights, package holidays including charter flights, virtually all package holidays which include a scheduled flight and many discounted fares on scheduled flights to have an ATOL licence. *It is the ATOL scheme which provides customers with the guarantee of full financial cover.*

The ATOL number must be featured in all advertisements and literature produced by the licensed Tour Operators.

TRAVEL AGENTS AND ATOL

To make sure customers are protected by ATOLs, Travel Agents must give them the ATOL holder's booking confirmation. This is the guarantee of financial cover.

HOW TO GET FURTHER INFORMATION

Write to the Civil Aviation Authority, ATOL Section, CAA House, 45-59 Kingsway, London WC2B 6TE or telephone us on 071-832 6600.

Fig. 10.3 The CAA advert for the ATOL system showing the ATOL logo

them all processed. This can cause difficulties for operators, not least if the press picks up on the delay. There is six months' leeway but it is illegal for a company to continue to trade without an up-to-date ATOL.

2 Bonding

Before operators are granted ATOLs, they must arrange a bond with a bank or insurance company which will make it possible to reimburse customers in the event of the business failing. The amount of bonding required has to rise in line with the company's turnover and will amount to 10 per cent of the operator's licensable turnover. Non-ABTA operators applying for an ATOL licence have to pay 15 per cent of their turnover to the CAA as a bond. If the company does fail, the bond money will be paid to the CAA, ABTA or FTO (*see* below) who will arrange for customers who are already abroad to continue with their holiday and then fly home. They will also reimburse clients who have paid for but not yet taken their holiday.

3 Air Travel Trust Fund (ATTF)

In the event of the bond not producing enough cash to meet all the claims (most likely at the height of summer when the maximum number of clients will have booked and travelled), the CAA will make up the shortfall from the Air Travel Trust Fund (previously the Air Travel Reserve Fund), which has 'substantial invested funds' for this purpose. In 1990 these reserves stood at £27.6 million, but by mid-1993 a succession of payouts had reduced them to £9.8 million (in the year March 1991 to March 1992 the Air Travel Trust Fund paid out £13.56 million to meet shortfalls in bonds, with another £5.98 million used to bale out a further 12 companies between March 1992 and March 1993).

An ATOL-holding tour operator is required to send a written confirmation of booking shortly after the reservation is made, and certainly before the flight departs. This must show:

- the ATOL-holder's registered name and address
- the ATOL number
- the details of what is to be provided and the price to be paid

Direct sell operators send these details direct to the client, but most operators send it to a travel agent who must then forward it to the client. The invoice confirms the contract existing between the operator and the client and will be vital if the operator does fail and a claim has to be made against its bond. ATOL-holders must also send the CAA a copy of all their brochures, leaflets, etc., and details of their holiday prices as soon as they are published.

The CAA can limit the number of flights an ATOL-holder can offer, and can also limit the geographical area to which they can offer flights. This doesn't prevent ATOL-holders requesting extra capacity as and when needed, provided they can also increase their bonding as required.

The record number of ATOL licenses issued in 1994 reflected the fact that, for the first time, companies using scheduled air services to create their packages were also required to take out licences.

Bonding for package holidays without an air transport component

In 1982, ABTA extended the bonding scheme to cover domestic and overseas package holidays using surface transport, provided the company offering the holiday was a member of ABTA. However, in 1992 the collapse of Land Travel, a non-ABTA coach tour company, highlighted loopholes in the existing arrangements.

When the EC Travel Regulations became law in 1993, it was intended that these loopholes would be closed. According to the Regulations, all package tour organisers, regardless of the mode of transport they are using, are required to protect their clients' money against the risk of failure. Since attempts to set up a new Travel Protection Association to handle bonding arrangements for non-air tour operators failed in 1993, ABTA has been acting as a CAA equivalent to handle bonding for member companies offering holidays using surface transportation. (Some are also bonded by the Passenger Shipping Association or the Confederation of Passenger Transport UK.) Relevant companies are also expected to contribute to insurance arranged by ABTA as further protection against financial risk. Finally, the ABTA Tour Operators' Fund acts as an equivalent to the Air Travel Trust Fund, providing money to make up any remaining shortfall in the individual company's bonds.

Non-ABTA tour operators offering non-air packages are required to take out insurance to protect their clients' money or to put it into a separate trust account. Local authority trading standards officers are supposed to monitor these arrangements. However, it is likely that some small companies will manage to circumvent them.

Where bonds come from

Most larger operators provide their bonds through their banks. In practice this means that the bank opens a special account into which the operator pays a sum representing an agreed percentage of their annual turnover. They will not be able to touch this money so that, in the event of their ceasing trading, it will be available to meet their liabilities. Although they will earn interest on the money while it is invested, they will also have to pay the bank a management fee (perhaps one per cent of the total sum) to manage it for them.

Before agreeing to provide the bond, the bond *obligor* may ask the operator to provide additional information beyond what was required for licensing purposes. The bond obligor may also agree to take on only part of the risk, in which case the total bond may have to be provided from more than one source. Bonds are valid for the period of the operator's annual licence and must stay in force for six months to one year after it expires to give time for all outstanding liabilities to be uncovered. However, since the period of the licence (and the bond) runs from March of one year to March of the following year, there can be problems with autumn holidays. These are on sale in October of the first year, during the period of the bond's validity. However, the bond will only continue to be valid until the end of September of the following year, leaving holidays sold for October of that year unprotected.

How much bonding must be provided

According to the EC Package Travel Regulations, bonds must cover 25 per cent of a company's annual turnover, or the maximum amount that it expects to be holding in respect of uncompleted contracts at any one time, whichever sum is the smaller. However, where the company belongs to an 'approved body' which has its own reserve fund or insurance to compensate a member company's clients for all contracts which have not been fully completed when it becomes insolvent, then the company itself need only put up a bond equal to 10 per cent of anticipated turnover. In this context, ABTA and AITO count as 'approved bodies' with appropriate cover to protect members against the steep 25 per cent levy.

New companies without a proven track record may be asked to put up a bond of 15 per cent of their projected turnover. Where most of a company's programme takes place within a short period of time and prepayments are made a long way ahead, they may even be asked for bonds of more than 15 per cent (school ski tour operators are likely to fall into this latter category). In cash terms, what this means is that a company with a projected annual turnover of £1 million will be expected to put up a bond of between £100,000 and £150,000. Since this must be in cash rather than secured assets like property, it represents a considerable hurdle for a new company starting up in the business.

Other methods of protecting clients' money

The EC Package Travel Regulations recognise two other ways for tour operators to protect their clients' money which were likely to be of most interest to smaller operators who would have difficulty meeting ABTA's terms for bonding.

1 Trust accounts

The smallest operators, including some hotel chains offering short-break packages, can opt to put clients' money into a specially opened trust, or escrow, account where it will have to stay until the clients have finished their holidays. Trustees must be nominated to administer these accounts. Ideally, they should be independent of the operator although the Regulations don't insist on this.

One problem with this system is that small operators may need access to clients' deposit and balance payments to prepay hoteliers, etc. to secure their bookings.

2 Insurance

Instead of taking out a bond, operators can also take out insurance with an 'insurer authorised in respect of such business in a member State (of the EU)'. The insurer would then indemnify clients for all losses as a result of the operator's insolvency. However, smaller operators are finding it hard to persuade insurers to take on what is seen as high risk business.

Tour operators' bonds and 'agents'

Before the passing of the 1993 Regulations, travel agents sometimes took deposits from customers before they had actually confirmed the availability of a particular holiday: for example, when the accommodation was on request, or there was a waiting list for places, or when would-be holidaymakers wanted to register in advance of the brochure appearing for popular periods like Christmas, or for the limited number of free child places. However, the Department of Trade and Industry doesn't believe a client's money will be protected in such circumstances since a retailer can only be said to be acting as an agent for the operator when a booking has been confirmed. Money taken in circumstances other than that will only be protected where the agent is also bonded as a travel organiser.

In February 1993, ABTA announced that travel agents who also do some tour operating (which could mean selling a ferry ticket and accommodation) would need to assess the scale of the tour operating side of their business and then take out a bond to cover it like other operators. Where they offered air packages, they would also need to apply to the CAA for an ATOL.

What happens when a company ceases trading

If a bonded tour operator collapses, the bond obligor must pay over the value of the bond to the trustee responsible for repatriating and reimbursing holidaymakers. This trustee is usually the CAA which has permitted ABTA and FTO to act as its agents in administering its bonds. This arrangement works particularly well because ABTA and FTO are in a strong position to rally support for speedy repatriation, etc.

ABTA's rules require that its members should be prepared to make any surplus flight seats available to help repatriate the clients of a failed member. If the bonding arrangements don't provide enough funds to cover all the company's outstanding liabilities, members will be expected to provide this repatriation service free of charge.

A closer look at the problem of bonding school tours

In the 1980s, an increasing number of companies went into business offering tours for school groups, often to the ski resorts. Such tours often had to be booked much further in advance than normal holidays because a) school children often needed time to save up for the trips, and b) the trips normally took place over peak periods when late capacity was hard to come by. As a result, companies were taking deposits and sometimes further payments more than a year ahead of the booked departure date. What's more, this was a very competitive market with prices pared to the bone to enable children to pay them. At the same time the profit margin needed to be enough to cover one or more free places for teacher-escorts.

In the difficult trading conditions of the early 1990s, several school tour operators collapsed, leaving ABTA to bale them out from bonds which sometimes turned out to be inadequate; over three years, school tour operator failures are thought to have cost ABTA £12 million. As a result ABTA found itself in financial difficulties. In the general shake-out of bonding arrangements following the passing of the 1993 Regulations, ABTA wrote to schools saying that in future it could only guarantee refunds on deposits of £25 paid no more than a year ahead of the departure date and balances paid no more than 10 weeks in advance. It was then forced to issue a clarification note explaining that these limitations only applied to tours by surface transport and not to air tours which continued to be bonded by the CAA.

A group of school tour operators (Travelbound, Ski Partners, Campus Centres, Seasun Tentrek, STS and Equity) then went to court to try and force ABTA to continue the old guarantees. They won their case. (Seasun Tentrek has since gone into liquidation.)

AGENCY LAW

Although some tour operators sell their products direct to the public, most use travel agencies as intermediaries for the majority of their sales. When they decide to do this, they enter into agency agreements with the travel agents. Such agreements are then governed by the general principles of agency law.

An agent can be defined as anyone (in this case, the travel agent) who has an express or implied authority to act on behalf of a principal (in this case, the tour operator) to create a contractual relationship between the principal and a third party (in this case, the would-be holidaymaker). Anyone who is able to enter into a contract (*see* above) can appoint an agent. In the case of the tour operator's relationship with the travel agent, authority will usually be expressly given in writing.

Agents have the following duties:

- to perform tasks with reasonable skill and diligence
- to avoid conflicts of interest
- not to accept secret bribes or profits
- not to delegate their authority

In return, agents have the following rights:

- to be remunerated by the principal (in this case, in the form of commission on sales)
- to be indemnified against losses incurred by the operator
- of lien (i.e. the right to hold onto the operator's property until they are reimbursed)

Travel agents can become personally liable in place of the tour operator where they sign a contract in their own name without indicating that they are acting as an agent for the principal.

An agency agreement can be terminated in the following ways:

- by mutual agreement
- if the agent renounces it
- if the operator revokes it
- if the operator becomes bankrupt
- if the agency ceases trading
- if it becomes illegal (for example, because trade sanctions have been imposed)
- at the end of a pre-agreed fixed period

In 1987, the Restriction on Agreements and Conduct (Tour Operators) Act forbade operators to write clauses preventing agents from offering discounts or incentives to help sell package holidays into their agency agreements.

INSURANCE LAW

Like most businesses, tour operators need to take out insurance against standard business risks which might include:

- the destruction of buildings and contents as a result of a fire or other cause
- the loss of goods and property as a result of theft
- problems caused by the death, disability or sickness of important members of staff

In addition, most businesses insure themselves against claims made by third parties as a result of accidents. Tour operators are in particular need of this sort of **public liability insurance** because the nature of their business exposes them to claims for compensation by customers who can be dissatisfied with their holidays for all sorts of reasons. The 1993 EC Package Travel Regulations extended an operator's responsibility to indemnify customers for losses incurred even when they themselves had not been immediately responsible for the loss (e.g. in situations where the hotel did not live up to descriptions of it provided in good faith by the operator). ABTA's Code of Conduct for Tour Operators requires them to take out adequate public liability insurance to indemnify themselves against such claims, while the Association of Independent Tour Operators (AITO) now requires members to take out public liability insurance to the value of at least £1 million.

The future?

In 1994, operators were concerned about the possibility of an EU Directive on the Protection of Consumers in Respect of Contracts Negotiated at a Distance. The draft directive defined 'distance selling' as all transactions where the buyer and seller didn't have face-to-face contact. It would mean that clients who booked holidays other than through agencies (primarily by phone or through the post) would not have to pay for them until they returned home. Some commentators even thought some conventional agency business might be affected. Operators argued that the inevitable results of such a directive being made law would be to deprive them of clients' payments to earn interest and ensure smooth cash flow, and to guarantee unrecovered debt with all the expense of pursuing it.

Inevitably, holiday prices would rise to absorb these additional costs.

The directive also envisaged a seven-day 'cooling off' period for all distance contracts, even where there was no specific problem. Clients would also be able to cancel credit card transactions made at a distance.

ABTA believed up to 90 per cent of holiday sales could be affected by these proposals, although they were particularly likely to hit direct-sell operators and the expanding number of agency telesales units. The Department of National Heritage was pressing for all references to tourism to be deleted from the draft directive.

TOUR OPERATORS' TRADE ASSOCIATIONS

Most tour operators belong to one of the following trade associations.

Association of British Travel Agents (ABTA)

Founded in 1950, the Association of British Travel Agents was turned into a limited company in 1955 and now represents both travel agents and tour operators. By 1994, it had 746 tour operator members. Unusually for a trade association, ABTA is also supposed to represent the consumer's interest in travel matters. Probably because of the role it has played in helping to develop protection for consumers when tour companies collapse, ABTA has a very high public profile. Indeed, a 1993 MORI survey found that 91 per cent of the general public are familiar with the ABTA logo, making it one of the best-known of all symbols.

In its memorandum of association ABTA's stated objectives are:

- to promote and develop the general interests of all members of the Association

Fig. 10.4 The ABTA logo

- to do all such things as may be deemed necessary or expedient to raise the prestige and status of members of the Association

ABTA sees its commercial role as being 'to influence events, for instance at government and EC level and in commercial affairs in a general way, so as to create as favourable a business environment as is possible consistent with its members' right to compete freely with other sectors of trade and industry and with each other'. Among other things, ABTA:

a) opposes legislation which it sees as damaging to members' interests
b) provides a united public face to present industry-wide views to the media
c) supports the National Training Board which runs travel industry youth training schemes

What ABTA does *not* do is interfere with individual members' commercial decisions over:

a) discounting
b) brochure relaunches
c) overcapacity
d) direct selling
e) the proliferation of travel agencies
f) advertisements comparing one member favourably in relation to other members
g) which ABTA agents ABTA operators should appoint to sell their products

ABTA has drawn up codes of good industry practice backed up by the threat of disciplinary measures for non-compliance. Membership of ABTA is therefore supposed to imply a high standard of trading practice, so it can also be seen as a consumer protection body.

ABTA members are divided into members of the Tour Operators' Class or the Travel Agents' Class. To join the Tour Operators' Class, an operator must satisfy the Tour Operators' Council that:

a) it is engaged in business as a tour operator
b) it publishes promotional materials to market its holidays
c) that none of its directors, partners or company managers is, or has been, an undischarged bankrupt; involved in a business which failed to meet its liabilities; or was guilty of conduct which rendered them unfit for ABTA membership.

Once accepted as a member, a tour operator must pay a membership fee, put up a bond or other security against company failure and agree not to trade under the name of any previous ABTA member which had failed to meet its liabilities.

The operator must also agree to abide by ABTA's Tour Operator's Code of Conduct. When first introduced in February 1960, this laid down a few basic rules of good business practice but these gradually expanded as the industry developed. In 1972, when ABTA was reconstituted with separate classes of membership for travel agents and tour operators, the Tour Operators' and Travel Agents' Councils were required to draw up new codes of conduct which would become binding on members once they had been approved and published by the National Council. The new codes were revised in 1975, in consultation with the Office of Fair Trading (OFT), and then again in 1976 when restrictive practices legislation was first applied to service industries. The codes were revised again in 1978 and in May 1990 after further consultation with the OFT. Although the Tour Operator's Code of Conduct has no legal standing, failure to comply with it can lead to the operator being reprimanded, fined or having its membership terminated.

The preamble to the Code of Conduct sets out its aims as follows:

1 To ensure that the public receive the best possible service from tour operators.
2 To maintain and enhance the reputation, standing and good name of the Association and its membership.
3 To encourage initiative and enterprise in the belief that properly regulated competitive trading by and between tour operators will best serve the public interest and the well-being of the travel industry.
4 To ensure that the public interest shall predominate in all consideration of the standards of competitive trading between tour operators.
5 To encourage growth and development of the travel industry, consistent with the above aims.

It also establishes the following broad principles for the Code:

A That it is designed to regulate the activities of tour operators between themselves and members of the public; between themselves and their travel agents; and between themselves.
B That it recognises and embodies the relevant parts of those Acts of Parliament and Government Regulations which relate to Trade Descriptions and Civil Aviation and the Codes and Regulations of recognised organisations or associations such as the Advertising Standards Authority, the Code of Advertising Practice Committee, the Independent Broadcasting Authority, the Independent Television Companies Association and the Association of Independent Radio Contractors which regulate the standards and practices of tour operators in relation to advertising.
C That it embodies measures for the regulation of the standards and practices of tour operators generally. These measures are included in recognition of the need to regulate competitive commercial practices where such practices are considered by the Association to conflict with the public interest.
D That it embodies definitions of commercial practices and nomenclature used by tour operators. These definitions are designed to specify and clarify beyond reasonable doubt the intentions of the code.
E That it recognises the necessity for enforcement of its standards and practices and embodies measures and procedures by which tour operators can uphold observance of the code under the authority of the Tour Operators' Council.

The Code of Conduct covers:

- minimum standards for brochures
- procedures for alterations to holidays, overbooking, cancellations and surcharges
- procedures for complaints, etc.

In the early 1990s ABTA, along with so many other businesses, hit financial hard times. However, cutbacks in most areas of expenditure meant that by 1993 its financial position was once again reasonably secure.

During the 1990s these were some of the activities ABTA was involved with:

- training – mainly through the ABTA National Training Board in Woking
- technology – in 1993 it announced a nationwide survey of the technology being used by its members with the aim of improving understanding between members

- public relations – promoting the industry as a whole to the media
- lobbying Westminster, Brussels and Strasbourg on all matters concerning the travel industry
- providing information to members through:
  - Abtel, a viewdata service which keeps members informed about members who have ceased trading, legal matters, regional news and events, and the latest Foreign and Commonwealth Office advice for travellers
  - the ABTA/ANTOR Factfinder, a glossy book with details of every country in the world
- offering members legal advice

In 1993, the EC Package Travel Regulations gave some aspects of the ABTA Tour Operators Code of Conduct the force of law, while at the same time undermining ABTA's own importance to the industry by providing for other methods of protecting clients' bookings.

The Tour Operators' Council

Members of ABTA's tour operators' class elect 20 representatives to form a Tour Operators' Council. For purposes of deciding who should sit on the Council, operators are grouped according to 'turnover bracket', with those turning over more than £29,534,000 at the top and those handling less than £3,626,000 at the bottom. Seventeen members are nominated from these groups. One each is nominated by the Northern Ireland Tour Operators' Region, the Scottish Tour Operators' Region and the Northern and Midland Tour Operators' Region. In turn, the Tour Operators' Council appoints its chair, vice-chair and three other members to ABTA's ruling body, the National Council.

If a tour operator commits an offence against the relevant code of conduct, it will be considered initially by the ABTA Secretariat. If they think there is a *prima facie* case, it will be referred to the code of conduct committee of the Tour Operator's Council. Sometimes the operator will simply present its case in writing. At other times someone will appear in person, perhaps with legal representation. Possible punishments include a reprimand, a fixed penalty or a fine. If the offence is such that they are likely to be suspended or expelled from ABTA, then it will be referred to a full meeting of the Tour Operators' Council. Operators can, if they wish, appeal against the Council's decision to an independent appeal board.

Association of Independent Tour Operators (AITO)

Fig. 10.5 The AITO logo

The Association of Independent Tour Operators was established in 1976 to represent smaller tour operators which increasingly found themselves in difficulties as the amount of bonding ABTA required steadily rose after the Court Line collapse. Until the late 1980s, it was a fairly low-key association. However, as the large tour operators asserted a stronger grip on the market, AITO became more high-profile and proactive, especially under the enthusiastic chairmanship of Noel Josephides of Sunvil Holidays (1990-93). In 1990, it introduced its own bonding scheme which is administered by AITO Trust Limited (AITOT) and approved under the EC Package Travel Regulations; in 1993 the AITO Trust held bonds for 45 member companies. By 1994 AITO had 142 member companies, the largest of them carrying just under 200,000 passengers a year, but the majority of them far smaller. Roughly 40 per cent of member companies are direct-sell operators. But in 1993 an ABTA/MORI survey found that only 6 per cent of the public had heard of AITO, compared with 91 per cent who were familiar with ABTA.

Companies applying for membership of AITO must be able to meet the following criteria:

a) They should be bona fide tour operators engaged first and foremost in the sale of inclusive holidays (departing from the UK) involving both transport and accommodation.
b) They should be able to demonstrate independence from mainstream tour operating companies.

c) They should conduct a minimum of 50 per cent overseas business.
d) They should have been trading as tour operators for a minimum of two years.
e) They should be UK-based and all their literature/brochures should be in English.
f) They should have a proper, creative brochure rather than an overprinted shell or photocopied leaflets (i.e. a good standard of presentation is required).
g) They should match the profile of AITO members, i.e. should be specialist companies at the smaller end of the spectrum, with hands-on management as far as the day-to-day running of the company is concerned.
h) They should be fully bonded for the financial protection of clients (whether with ABTA, TOSG, the AITO Trust or the CAA (ATOL)).
i) They should have public liability insurance offering minimum cover of £1 million.
j) They should be prepared to abide by the terms of the AITO quality charter (*see* page 72) and code of business practice.
k) Their booking conditions and methods of operation should meet all the requirements of the EC Package Travel Regulations and other applicable laws.

AITO has the following aims:

a) To ensure that the public can book AITO members' holidays with every confidence.
b) To inform members of the issues of the day and to encourage higher standards and greater professionalism among members.
c) To encourage members and their clients to be aware of environmental issues and to promote environmentally sustainable tourism.
d) To help members market their wares more effectively to customers.
e) To ensure that the views and problems of the smaller, specialist tour operators are understood and that the interests of their clients are protected.

In the event that a client is not satisfied with his/her holiday, AITO has its own low-cost, independent dispute settlement service: for £30 an AITO mediator will talk to the client and the tour operator by phone in an attempt to provide 'arbitration in the spirit of conciliation'.

AITO plays an important lobbying role as one central voice representing 142 companies with, between them, a carrying capacity of about 1.5 million passengers a year. It has been consulted by the Monopolies and Mergers Commission (over Thomson's takeover of Horizon), by the Office of Fair Trading (over Airtours' proposed takeover of Owners Abroad) and by the Department of Trade and Industry (over the implementation of the EC Package Travel Regulations). It also plays an important PR role, aiming to emphasise the vital part smaller tour operators play in Britain's overall travel industry.

AITO also produces the annual *Directory of Real Holidays*, listing all member companies, and the smaller *Ski Directory*. With the *Observer*, it sponsors an annual award for the best brochure. It also uses its collective buying power to negotiate favourable insurance rates for members, to cover needs like insuring overseas representatives and public liability insurance.

In 1990 AITO helped in the formation of Green Flag International (GFI), whose purpose is to advise tour companies on environmental issues and to work with individual companies on projects to achieve environmentally sustainable tourism (see Chapter Eleven).

In June 1994, in a new initiative to help its members reach a wider clientele, AITO set up the **AITO 100 Club**, an elite group of independent travel agencies licensed to rack 45 specialist company brochures, as well as *The Guide to Real Holidays*, for the first time. It also created a series of **AITO Business Partnerships** with 400 independent (mostly owner-managed) travel agents who would also be able to rack the *Real Holidays* guide and display AITO point of sale materials.

Federation of Tour Operators (FTO)/Tour Operator's Study Group (TOSG)

The Federation of Tour Operators was set up in 1967, as the Tour Operator's Study Group (TOSG), to provide a forum for the largest tour operators to discuss topics of mutual interest. It currently consists of representatives of the 17 largest tour companies, who, between them, handle 80 per cent of all British overseas holidaymakers. A non-commercial body, it is a voluntary association, with membership by invitation only.

From the start, FTO has been an influential pressure group, working to improve conditions for holidaymakers. For example, in 1970 it was responsible for the creation of a Trust Fund into which ABTA members paid 5 per cent of their turnover as a bond against their collapse. Pressure from them also persuaded the government to scrap the Provision 1 arrangement which prevented tour operators selling packages for less than the lowest normal scheduled air fare. More recently, in 1992 the TOSG persuaded operators to cut the number of bed spaces they had contracted in Cyprus from 500,000 to 450,000 after the Cyprus Tourism Organisation highlighted the risk of overbooking as operators rushed into a newly fashionable destination. They also lobbied to dissuade Balearics tourist authorities from imposing new limits on how many people could stay in hotel rooms in an attempt to reposition the islands' image more upmarket, and tried to persuade Corfu authorities to improve refuse collection and sewage disposal, and to restrict the sale of brands of alcohol responsible for the worst bouts of drunken disorder on the island.

FTO members often attend meetings with their European equivalent, the International Federation of Tour Operators (IFTO).

British Incoming Tour Operators Association (BITOA)

The British Incoming Tour Operators Association was founded in 1977. Members are incoming tour operators and suppliers of services to British tourism. BITOA has the following objectives:

a) To improve the quality of service provided by members for the benefit of visitors to Britain, and to encourage the maintenance of a high standard of facilities from all British providers of tourism services.
b) To develop and uphold a generally accepted code of conduct in the supply of services by members.
c) To establish and maintain a recognised status for members, by informing the travel industry, the British government and associated agencies, and the public of members' activities and objectives.
d) To provide a forum for the exchange of ideas and information relevant to members' activities.
e) To provide members with an opportunity to express a corporate voice on matters of common interest e.g. on the exchange rate which can contribute to the impression that the UK is an expensive holiday destination.
f) To consult with central government and the European Union on matters of common and commercial interest to members.
g) To provide incoming tour operators with an opportunity to form, express and promulgate an independent corporate voice on matters of common interest.
h) To maintain regular liaison with central government, the British Tourist Authority, national and regional tourist boards, and other trade bodies, to develop policies to assist members' commercial activities.
i) To create recognised training programmes and develop recognised qualification standards.

Fig. 10.6 The BITOA logo

Associate membership of BITOA is open to:

- accommodation providers (both hotel groups and individual properties)
- arts, heritage and leisure venues
- conference venues
- ecclesiastical foundations
- restaurants and caterers
- services like printers and English language schools
- shops and stores
- regional and national tourist boards/organisations
- attraction operators
- transportation companies

In 1994, some issues of concern to BITOA members were:

a) the impact of the EC Package Travel Regulations
b) commission charges for accepting credit card payments
c) the surcharges put on theatre tickets booked over the phone
d) restaurant 'service' charges
e) the threat that local authorities might impose a tourism tax to pay for infrastructural improvements

f) the idea of harmonising British and European time zones

Confederation of Passenger Transport UK/Bus and Coach Council (BCC)

The Confederation of Passenger Transport UK, formerly the Bus and Coach Council, was founded in 1974. All professional bus and coach operators are eligible to join it, and it acts as an industry-wide voice in discussions on national and international legislation, operational practices and mechanical standards. It also represents the industry to the media.

The Bonded Coach Holiday Group (BCH) of the Confederation has drawn up a code of conduct for bus tour operators which demands that they should be bonded against the risk of financial failure, as required by the 1993 EC Package Travel Regulations.

Fig. 10.7 The Confederation of Passenger Transport UK logo

The Passenger Shipping Association (PSA)

Originally set up in 1958 as Ocean Travel Development (OTD), the Passenger Shipping Association

Fig. 10.8 The Passenger Shipping Association logo

represents British shipping and ferry companies, now separated into two discrete sections. It sees its role as liaising with the government and with ABTA on subjects of general interest to the industry like pilotage and duty-free sales on-board ship. In 1986 the PSA organised bonding for member companies along the same lines as ABTA's. It also offers independent arbitration and conciliation services like AITO's.

In 1987 the PSA set up the Passenger Shipping Association Retail Agents Scheme (PSARA) to encourage agency sales of shipping products through better education. It is funded by the cruise industry and by retail travel agents and is seen as having been instrumental in the growth of cruise traffic in the UK.

As well as these major trade associations, there are also smaller associations representing subdivisions of the trade who meet together to discuss topics of common interest. Typical of such associations is the Association of British Tour Operators to France, or ABTOF, which represents all the many small, specialist companies involved in selling France to the British market.

QUESTIONS AND DISCUSSION POINTS

1 Do you think it is possible for ABTA to continue to represent tour operators, travel agents *and* holidaymakers? If it is to be restructured, how do you think that might best be achieved?

2 How realistic and reasonable do you think the EC Package Travel Regulations on tour operators' liability towards their clients are? Discuss the sorts of situations which operators might have been able to pass off on their suppliers in the past but which they will no longer be able to. How do you think they will deal with the increased responsibility?

3 When companies collapse, their creditors often lose their money. Discuss why successive governments have seemed more concerned to protect holidaymakers' money than that of other consumers.

4 'The client will enjoy *real choice*. The independent agent will win *new* business. The independent operator will win *new* business.' How far do you think that the AITO 100 Club and the AITO Business Partnerships have opened up the prospect of 'a win-win-win scenario', as 1994 Chair, Christopher Kirker, hoped?

ASSIGNMENTS

1 The definition of a 'package holiday' as given in the 1993 EC Package Travel Regulations has proved more difficult to interpret than expected. Make a list of what you think are the key features of a 'package holiday'. Then try to write your own definition that will include all those features. Bear in mind that vagueness is what has caused difficulty with the original definition and that legal documents must always be written in formal language.

2 You are approached by one of the travel trade newspapers to write a summary of the main features of the EC Package Travel Regulations. The piece should be no longer than 1,000 words. Since it is to be written for the trade it can make reference to industry jargon (e.g. ABTA, CAA, ATOL) which would not be appropriate in a non-trade article. The piece should highlight the main consequences of the Regulations for a) the tour operator, and b) the travel agent. Before starting work, make sure you have read a recent copy of either *TTG* or *Travel Weekly* and understand the style of writing they employ.

3 You have just been appointed Chair of AITO. Write a briefing paper to take to the first meeting you will attend, laying out your proposals for:

a) raising AITO's profile with travellers in the light of the finding that only 6 per cent of the public have heard of it, and

b) generally improving the position of independent tour operators in the market-place

CHAPTER 11

Tour operating and its environment

LEARNING OBJECTIVES

After reading this chapter you should be able to:

- **identify those factors outside the tour operators' control which can nevertheless have a major impact on their businesses**
- **assess the socio-economic, cultural and environmental impacts tour operators' actions have on the destinations they feature**
- **suggest ways in which the adverse effects of tour operating can be reduced**

INTRODUCTION

Like all businesses, tour operations take place within a wider context than just the company itself; factors like domestic interest rates and government employment policies over which the company has little control can nevertheless have a considerable impact on its plans and forecasts. What's more, the very nature of non-domestic tour operating, which is all about interacting with other countries, means that companies are uniquely vulnerable to external factors, like wars and fluctuating exchange rates, as well.

Because tour operating involves an intimate relationship with other countries, decisions made by the companies can also have a much more direct impact on those countries, some of them with very different cultures and standards of living, than is the case with other businesses. For example, when charter flights to Goa in India became available, several tour operators started offering package holidays there, thus encouraging the development of large hotels complete with all the mod cons western tourists are accustomed to, including swimming pools. Since Goa suffers from water shortages, the tour operators were in part responsible for creating a situation in which scarce resources were diverted from local people to outsiders.

EXTERNAL FACTORS WHICH CAN AFFECT A TOUR OPERATOR'S PROGRAMME

There are many different external factors which can influence a tour operator's programme. Some will have an impact on prices, some will determine whether there is any market for its holidays and others may dictate which countries can and cannot be featured in its brochures or in what ways they can be featured. Some of these things can reasonably be foreseen, but others arise unexpectedly and can cause problems even with holidays which are already taking place. The tour operator's ability to forecast what will happen is made particularly difficult because of the need to sell its products from brochures which will have been prepared up to 18 months before the departure date.

Among the external factors which regularly have an impact on operators' decisions are:

- foreign exchange rates
- interest rates at home and abroad
- inflation rates at home and abroad
- the cost of aviation fuel
- levels of unemployment in the tourist generating country
- outbreaks of disease in resorts
- natural disasters
- war and civil war involving either the tourist generating or receiving country
- political change in the tourist generating or receiving country

- terrorist activities
- airport delays and aircraft accidents
- fashion
- the weather at home and abroad
- crime in a resort
- general bad publicity – algae off the Italian coast, lager louts in Spain, etc.

Figure 11.1 shows how the number of tourists travelling to Greece varied between 1960 and 1984. Although the overall pattern was of a steadily increasing number of visitors, nevertheless it is possible to see sporadic falls which relate to external factors over which tour operators would have had no control. So in 1967 the number of tourist arrivals dropped by 12 per cent after the Greek army staged a *coup d'état* against the elected government resulting in considerable uncertainty. By 1969 numbers were once again on the increase. Then in 1974 they dipped back by 31.3 per cent, falling to below the 1971 figure. This fall was brought about by a combination of the Turkish invasion of Cyprus, which led to fears of war between Greece and Turkey, and by the oil crisis when the Arab embargo on oil exports forced up prices, including that of aviation fuel. Faced with higher costs, some people were forced to cut back on holiday expenditure too. This fall-off was shortlived, and by 1975 the number of tourist arrivals was again on the increase. In 1980 the second oil crisis once again led to a hike in the price of aviation fuel at the same time as recession was beginning to affect the UK. Tourist arrivals to Greece slumped by 9.1 per cent. Although the figure picked up in 1981, it then fell again in 1982, and even more in 1983 as world economic recession took a grip and would-be tourists stayed at home or traded down to cheaper holidays. (These figures are, of course, for *all* tourist arrivals, and not just package holidaymakers).

Foreign exchange rates

In general, the rate of exchange between one country's currency and another's fluctuates according to the political and economic circumstances of the two countries. Strong economies will have strong currencies. So for most of the 1980s the German mark and the Japanese yen were among the world's strongest currencies because both Germany and Japan had strong, expanding economies. Someone

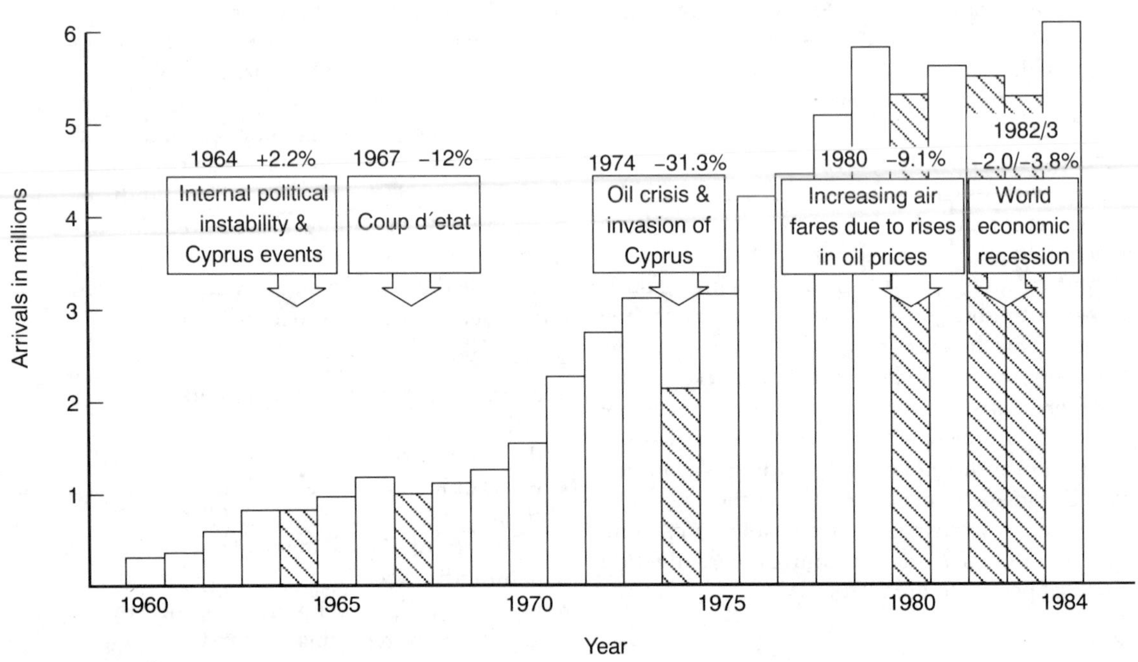

Fig. 11.1 Foreign tourist arrivals in Greece 1960–84
Courtesy: Tourism Management

wanting to buy marks in exchange for sterling would therefore have to pay more for them than someone wanting to use marks to buy sterling would, reflecting the relative strength of the German economy *vis-à-vis* the British one.

However, the relative strength of two currencies can fluctuate dramatically. An example of this is the rate of exchange of the pound against the US dollar which rises and falls according to the perceived strength of the American economy. At the start of the 1980s, the pound was worth around US$2, whereas in the early 1990s it fetched only US$1.50, making a visit to the States considerably more expensive.

The European Exchange Rate Mechanism (ERM) was supposed to help take the guesswork out of calculating exchange rates within the EC. Currencies were assessed against each other and their value fixed, after which they were only supposed to move up and down within a specified range of the agreed exchange rate. However, in 1992/3 the ERM came under pressure which it was not able to withstand. In September 1992 Britain left the ERM which it had joined in 1990, and at once the exchange rate of sterling against the other EC countries plummeted. Italy, Spain and Portugal were also forced to devalue their currencies or leave the ERM.

Tour operators delay calculating final prices to go in the brochures until the latest possible moment to try and take account of as many exchange rate changes as possible. However, for summer of any one particular year prices will have had to be fixed in July of the previous year, leaving plenty of time for exchange rates to alter significantly. To protect themselves against this risk, the bigger operators will buy the currencies they need at the time the rates are agreed if they look encouraging. Smaller companies may not be able to afford to do this, in which case they stand to lose out if exchange rates move unfavourably. In 1993, the pound's devaluation after its departure from the ERM in September 1992 meant that some smaller companies were forced to levy unpopular currency surcharges or face losing enormous sums of money.

Some countries' currencies are so weak that they may not actually be convertible outside their country of issue. However, in most cases these countries have such weak economies or are so unstable politically that few tour operators are interested in them.

Interest rates at home and abroad

Interest is charged for borrowing money and the rate of interest may vary over time, often according to government or Bank of England decisions. Following deregulation of the money markets in the mid-1980s, the British government used interest rates from 1988 to 1993 as a method of regulating the economy. From a low of 7.5 per cent in 1988, interest rates rose steadily to 15 per cent in 1989, with devastating effects for everyone with loans. In the mid-1980s the government had encouraged people to take out mortgages to buy their own homes. Other policies had also caused property values to rise dramatically with the result that in 1988 and 1989 many people took on very high mortgages which they then had trouble paying as interest rates rose. Although this was not the only reason for the recession of the early 1990s, it was an important contributory factor, squeezing people's net disposable income and ensuring less was available to pay for holidays and other luxuries.

Some tour operators were also directly affected by interest rate hikes where they had taken out large loans. Because in general they don't need to buy in stock, operators suffered less than manufacturers because they had made less investment. However, those with airline operations had sometimes taken out loans to pay for the aircraft. It was in part the size of loans for expanding Air Europe that contributed to the International Leisure Group's (ILG) collapse in 1991 (*see* page 46).

Inflation rates at home and abroad

Inflation is defined as a progressive increase in the general level of prices and is generally seen as something damaging to the economy which must be restrained. Different countries will have different inflation rates depending on all sorts of factors to do with their economies. On the whole, though, the stronger an economy, the lower the rate of inflation is likely to be. Conversely rates of inflation of several hundred per cent have not been uncommon, for example, in South American countries with unstable economies like Brazil.

The result of inflation pushing up prices can make people poorer unless they are able to negotiate pay increases on a similar scale. So when inflation is high (as it was in Britain in the early

1980s) it can mean that people are forced to economise. However, price wars have prevented British package holiday companies putting up their prices in line with inflation so that packages have become cheaper in real terms.

Where there is a high rate of inflation in the tourist receiving country it means that prices will be going up all the time. However, favourable exchange rates usually ensure that foreign visitors with hard currencies are protected from the worst impact of rising prices.

Levels of unemployment in the tourist generating country

One important consequence of recession tends to be increasing unemployment as a country's economy contracts. During the 1980s the UK suffered two periods of recession, one at the start of the decade, the other, more serious of the two, at the end. With more people out of work and the level of unemployment pay very low, the potential market for tour operators' products tended to be reduced. However, the fall off in the number of holidaymakers in the early 1990s was not as great as might have been expected, suggesting that many people now see holidays as necessities rather than luxuries.

Outbreaks of disease in resorts

While most long-haul holidaymakers take the risk of disease in their stride and take sensible precautions against it, short-haul tourists don't expect to have to worry too much about their health while on holiday. It's therefore particularly galling when there is an outbreak of disease in any of the Mediterranean resorts. In the summer of 1983 an outbreak of cholera in Kos was traced back to a waiter in one particular hotel. Twenty-nine holidaymakers were affected but *The Times* warned against 'a bad epidemic of news hysteria'. Although Thomson offered its clients the chance of an alternative holiday or their money back, only 11 of those on Kos at the time asked to be moved. Horizon received one cancellation which was more than compensated for by two late bookings!

In the summer of 1989 a typhoid epidemic broke out in Salou on the Costa Brava, blamed on a sewage outlet near a hotel used by Thomson clients. After five tourists fell ill, Thomson stopped sending clients to the hotel and offered alternatives to those who had already booked. This is what *The Times* editorial of 3 August 1989 had to say about the incident:

> Typhoid is a cause of fear. Like cholera, it is part of a continuing British folk memory of the health hazards of the nineteenth century, It will be little comfort to holidaymakers in Spain this summer to know that biologically it is no more than a particularly severe form of salmonella, or that nowadays it usually responds to drugs.
>
> Thomson Holidays is the main tour operator to the Spanish resort under most suspicion, Salou. It has announced that it is offering alternative holidays to those booked to go there, largely on a circumstantial connection between typhoid cases and poor public health facilities.
>
> It is reported, for example, that raw sewage is pumped into the sea not far from the beach and visitors have described the general condition as filthy. So far, however, the exact link has not yet been established, and the British health authorities are co-operating with the Spanish to try and build up a picture to locate the source more exactly.
>
> As the inadequacy of the methods of sewage disposal on Salou should have been apparent before the typhoid scare . . . and may turn out to have no connection with it . . . Thomson Holidays seems to owe an explanation why it did not spot the problem sooner. The risks should have been obvious enough.
>
> So far five British holidaymakers who visited Salou have been confirmed as cases of typhoid. Meanwhile the only sound advice to those still to go to Spain for their holidays is to treat the water . . . whether sea water for bathing or shell fish, or tap water for drinking, washing and food preparation . . . as highly suspect. Perhaps they may consider somewhere other than Spain next year.
>
> Ultimately it is only because of the fear of such a reaction from tourists that Spain will be forced to clean up its act. The Spanish tourism industry of which the British sector has a majority share, is a vital part of their economy, and many Spanish themselves are becoming increasingly critical of the neglect of sewage treatment facilities along some parts of the Spanish coastline.
>
> British tour operators are in a good position to exert pressure themselves, should they choose to do so, and it is certainly in their commercial interests. There are signs this year that the market for

overseas holidays is stagnant or beginning to decline, mainly as a result of domestic economic pressures and the near-Mediterranean summer season that Britain itself has been enjoying. That should increase competition among the operators and between resorts, not only on price but also on quality.

(Courtesy: The Times)

In 1993 reported outbreaks of diphtheria and other health problems in Russia caused Thomson to cancel all programmes there and give refunds to those who had already booked.

Natural disasters

Tour operators also face problems when destinations they feature are hit by natural disasters like earthquakes, tidal waves, hurricanes and volcanic eruptions. Although some popular tourist destinations, like San Francisco in the United States, lie in earthquake zones so far there have been no real difficulties. In fact, tour operators could be said to have benefited from the terrible earthquake that hit Agadir in Morocco in 1960, since a purpose-built resort which was easy to package as a winter sun destination quickly grew up in its place.

War and civil war

Perhaps the worst of all problems tour operators have to handle is an outbreak of war or civil war. Sadly, the early 1990s furnished two striking examples of the way in which war can interfere with even the best run holiday business.

The Gulf War (1991)

In August 1990 Iraq invaded Kuwait. Six months later a combined army of Americans, British and Arabians attacked Iraq and forced it to retreat. The actual war lasted only seven weeks but because of the extended period of build-up to it, the damage it did to tourism businesses was enormous.

Neither Kuwait nor Iraq is a conventional tourist destination so the number of programmes to either country that had to be cancelled was minimal. However, adjacent countries with big tourist industries like Turkey and Israel were badly hit as tour operators withdrew programmes from them to be on the safe side. Cyprus also suffered a big drop in tourist arrivals, as operators and holidaymakers avoided the entire Eastern Mediterranean. Worst affected were specialist companies like Transglobal which had a programme featuring Turkey, Israel and Egypt – all three, countries which no one wanted to visit. Eventually Transglobal was forced out of business altogether. In general all Muslim countries were thought risky for western holidaymakers and suffered a decline in tourist arrivals. By 1993 Morocco had still not recovered its pre-Gulf War position in the tourism stakes; in 1987 it received 187,000 visitors from the UK, in 1992 only 96,000. It is even thought that the Caribbean gained in popularity *vis-à-vis* the Far East, as people redirected their holiday plans westwards to avoid flying over the Gulf.

Since the war broke out in low season, very few passengers needed to be repatriated. However, what should have been the operators' peak booking season for the summer was blighted as holidaymakers waited to see what would happen. International Leisure Group alone reckoned that it had lost £24 million in deposits. Simultaneously many companies grounded their travelling executives, leading to a decline in passengers for Air Europe's business flights. These two factors were in large part responsible for ILG's collapse in March 1991, just after the war ended.

However, for all the companies and countries that suffered as a result of the Gulf War, there were a few that actually benefited from it. For example, as customers boycotted the Eastern Mediterranean, the Western Mediterranean picked up trade; Portugal alone reported 1991 tourist arrivals 8.7 per cent up on the 1990 figure. Of course for tour operators to benefit from the switch in direction they had to be in a position to secure new aircraft seats and hotels rooms at short notice.

Unlikely though it might sound, some of the overland countries have actually found it easier to operate the old routes through Western and Central Asia since the end of the Gulf War.

Civil war in 'Yugoslavia'

In 1991, civil war broke out in Yugoslavia, until then one of Europe's most popular holiday destinations in Europe where 600,000 British tourists had holidayed in 1990. Initially, Slovenia and Croatia, two of the six republics making up the old Yugoslavia, declared themselves independent and were recognised by the European Community. Slovenia managed to make the transition to independence relatively smoothly. However, war quickly broke out between Croatia and what became known as rump Yugoslavia (i.e. Serbia and Montenegro). During the course of this war, in addition to all the people who died, Dubrovnik in Croatia, the so-called 'pearl of the Adriatic' was attacked and many erstwhile popular tourist hotels were destroyed.

No sooner did the situation between Croatia and Serbia start to calm down, than Bosnia-Herzegovina also declared itself independent. Once again this led to fighting, this time on an even worse scale, with many more fatalities. During the course of this war, Mostar – another popular tourist destination, this time inland – was attacked and virtually destroyed as Bosnian Croats struggled to make it the new capital of their own mini-state.

All the operators featuring 'Yugoslavia' were forced to withdraw their programmes as a result of the fighting, although by 1993 Slovenia had started to re-establish itself as a lakes and mountains destination. Worst hit was Yugotours, the state-owned tour company founded in 1956 whose entire programme had been to Yugoslavia. Not only were many of the hotels it used destroyed or taken over to house refugees, but some of its resort representatives joined the armies as well. The company was forced to repatriate 12,000 holidaymakers. Building on tentative diversification attempts dating back to 1987, in 1992 Yugotours relaunched itself as 'Med Choice' with a programme to a conventional choice of Mediterranean resorts as well as Slovenia; in 1992 it took 3,000 people to Slovenia compared with 35,290 in 1990. The United Nations had imposed economic sanctions against Serbia/Montenegro in an attempt to force the Serbian President, Slobodan Milosevic, to put pressure on the Bosnian Serbs to end the fighting. There was some discussion about whether Med Choice could be seen as sanctions busting. However, the company argued that it was 100 per cent UK-registered and that its payments were cleared through the Bank of England and not repatriated to Serbia. Phoenix Holidays had also specialised in Yugoslavia. In June 1991 it suspended its programme and refunded the 12,000 people who had booked to travel there. Half the staff in its UK office had to be laid off, and those remaining became primarily agents for the new Croatia Air. However, in 1993 the company relaunched its programme with support from the Croatian tourism authorities, after confirmation that bomb and gunfire damage to hotels in Dubrovnik and other centres had been repaired. Although the 1994 'Welcome to Croatia' brochure made oblique reference to what had happened when it talked of visitors 'returning' and to coastline and islands 'untouched by recent events', the word 'war' didn't appear once.

As a result of the war, the number of package holidays sold to 'Yugoslavia' from the UK slumped to 103,000 in 1991 and 7,000 in 1992. Once again, however, other destinations picked up the slack. Prime winners were Cyprus and Turkey; in 1992 Cyprus jumped from seventh to fourth most popular destination and Turkey from fourteenth to tenth. It is perhaps worth noting that continental Europeans returned to Croatia more readily than the British; by 1993 arrivals from Austria were back to 67 per cent of the pre-war figures and those from Italy back to 40 per cent, although those from Germany had fallen to 20 per cent.

These are only two instances of how war has forced tour operators to alter their plans. In April 1994 civil war also broke out in the central African state of Rwanda which had been popular with holidaymakers hoping to see its mountain gorillas. As in 'Yugoslavia', tourism to Rwanda ceased altogether, although the number of potential tourists affected was much smaller than had been the case with the Mediterranean country. Delving further into the past, another example would be Sri Lanka, once seen as a paradise island in the Indian Ocean but which, during the 1980s, was embroiled in a vicious civil war between the Singhalese and the Tamils in the north who wanted an independent Tamil state. Although the situation has calmed down enough for tourism to resume in the south part of the island, in 1993 both the President and the Leader of the Opposition were blown up by suicide bombers within a week of each other, suggesting that the idyllic image presented in the brochures is far from telling the whole story.

Political unrest

While wars are the most dramatic forms of political unrest, there are other forms, usually shorter in duration, which may also force operators to change their plans. For example, in 1992 hitherto peaceful Bangkok suddenly exploded in rioting, leading to the temporary suspension of holidays there. In June 1989, television viewers watched the Chinese army crush the student uprising in Beijing's Tiananmen Square; for some time afterwards operators found it harder to sell China as the best place for a holiday. In December 1981 500 tourists were briefly stranded in the Seychelles following an attempted *coup* which led to the airport being shut down. Again, holiday programmes were temporarily suspended.

South Africa is a more extreme example of a destination that, while not technically at war, has suffered from serious political unrest. Throughout the 1970s and 1980s, the apartheid system of government, which isolated blacks and whites from each other, made South Africa an international pariah; in the 1970s when Thomas Cook business travel held the United Nations account, a condition of doing so was that it should not rack brochures for holidays in South Africa. In 1986/7, haphazard boycotting of South Africa was formalised into proper international sanctions, including a ban on promoting holidays to South Africa. During the late 1980s many of the outward manifestations of apartheid were abolished. Then in 1989 the ANC leader Nelson Mandela was released from jail to begin talks with the De Klerk government on a new multi-racial system of government. By 1993 sanctions against tourism had been lifted and tour operators were looking at South Africa with greater interest.

However, the situation remained very unstable. In 1993 Thomson withdrew a trial programme after three months of poor sales. Following the murder of black opposition leader Chris Hani, British Airways Holidays also began to consider whether to keep running its programme, and Airwaves and Jetsave reported a slump in bookings. The general view was that the mainly older, visiting friends and relatives market was not put off by reports of violence on television and in the papers but that the wider holiday market was. Those operators that continued to feature South Africa mainly concentrated on its game parks, or on two-centre holidays, teaming it with Zimbabwe (for Victoria Falls), Mauritius or Sun City in the unrecognised 'homeland' of Bophuthatswana. In April 1994 the first multi-racial elections in South Africa's history took place and Mandela became president. Provided there are no new outbreaks of violence, South Africa looks set to become a popular new long-haul tourist destination.

Following a period of unrest, tour operators can react in various different ways. After the attempted *coup* in Moscow in September 1993, some companies let clients rebook for a later date, remove Moscow from a multi-centre itinerary or cancel without penalty. Some withdrew Moscow from sale altogether; others continued to sell it on the assumption that the situation would be back to normal by the time clients actually travelled.

Terrorism

From the mid-1960s onwards, terrorism (and, perhaps more importantly, the fear of terrorism) began to pose a threat to international tourism. It was the fear of terrorist attacks as much as specific incidents that led to the grounding of business travellers after the Gulf War. Likewise, in the immediate aftermath of the war many holidaymakers decided not to risk visiting *any* of the Arab countries, which was unfortunate for operators with programmes to Morocco and Tunisia which were nowhere near the fighting and yet saw a drop in their trade. In 1985 the Americans bombed Tripoli in Libya as a reaction to what they saw as Colonel Gaddafi's sponsorship of state terrorism. The planes used in the attacks took off from American air bases in England. Following that episode, many tourists (most of them American but some of them British) decided to stay at home rather than risk revenge attacks. Again, countries like Morocco, Tunisia and Egypt saw their visitor numbers fall. After attacks at Rome and Athens' airports and the hijacking of the cruise ship *Achille Lauro* in 1985, President Reagan warned Americans against trips to Europe; that time it was Europe's incoming tour operators who suffered worst.

In 1992 the nature of the threat changed, as terrorists increasingly targeted not just tourist sites but also tourists themselves, as a way of sabotaging the economies of countries whose governments they opposed. In 1992 Islamic fundamentalists in Egypt, previously thought of as a moderate Arab country, announced that they saw tourists as a legitimate target in their struggle to create an Islamic state. Shortly afterwards a cruise boat full of Germans was raked with gunfire, British holidaymakers

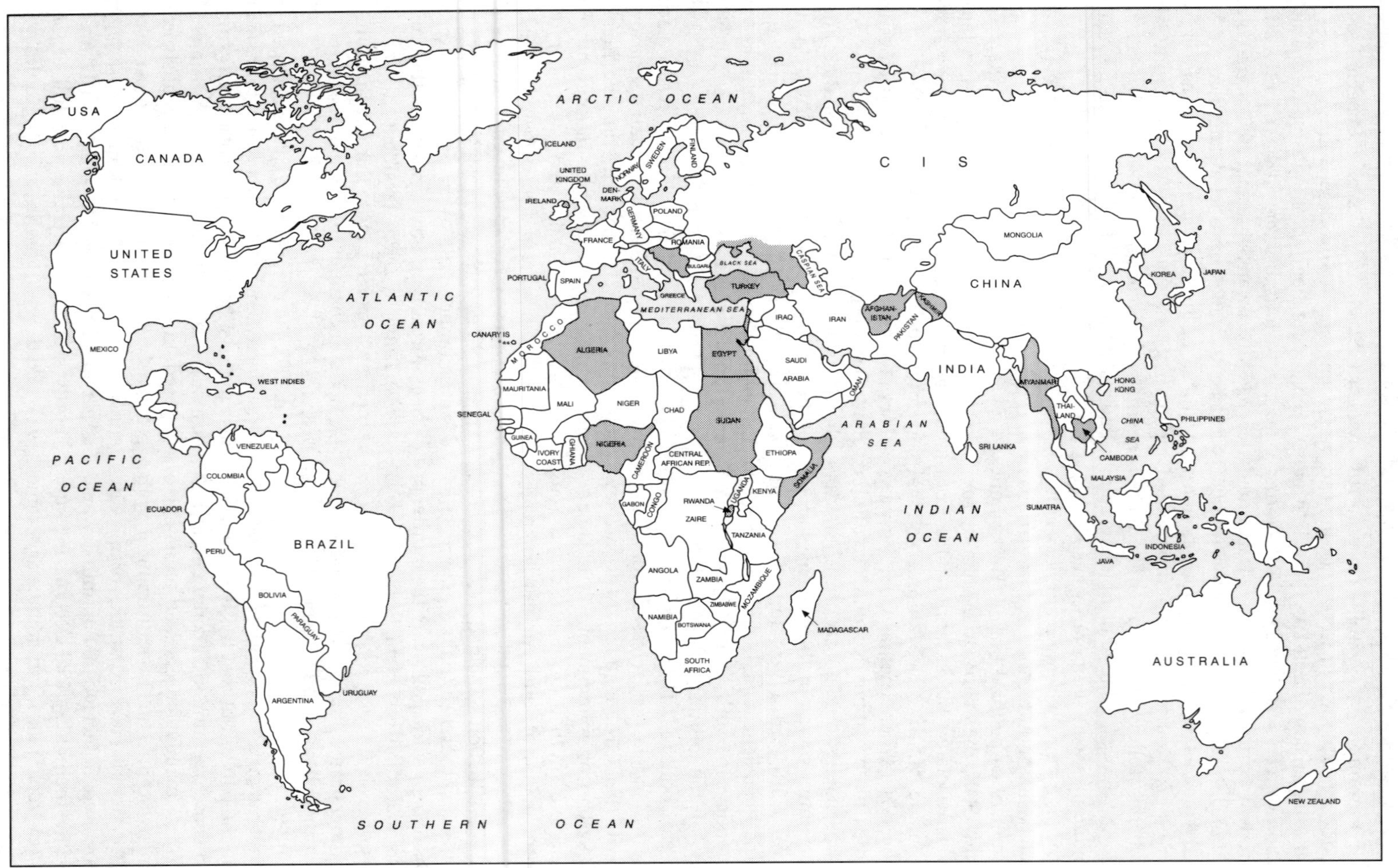

Fig. 11.2 Trouble spots of particular interest to tour operators in 1994

were wounded when a bomb was thrown at a tour bus on its way to the Pyramids, and a British woman was shot dead in a tour bus near Dairut. Not surprisingly, tour operators found it much harder to sell holidays to Egypt, even when they slashed prices dramatically. In 1993 Inghams pulled out of the market altogether, and by the end of the year companies were reporting a drop of 25-30 per cent in sales. Egypt had once been the biggest seller for Bales Travel. However, between 1990 and 1994 the number of bookings to Egypt slumped from around 6,000 to under 1,000, causing them to refocus their attentions on India, China and South America instead.

In summer 1993 members of the PKK (People's Party of Kurdistan), seeking independence for the Kurdish eastern half of Turkey, planted bombs in popular Turkish coastal resorts, including Kusadasi and Antalya. In 1994 they followed up with bombs in Istanbul, Fethiye and Marmaris which killed three tourists and injured many others. The PKK leafleted in Germany and the Netherlands, warning would-be holidaymakers to stay away from Turkey. After the 1994 bombs, several British tour operators offered to let people who had already booked trips to Turkey switch to other destinations without penalty. In doing so, they agreed to absorb the administrative costs of the necessary changes.

But whereas war has an immediate impact on tourism (in part because governments issue directives that tourists should not travel to war zones, in part because insurance companies won't insure those who do), fear of terrorism can be slower to show itself in the booking figures, not least because operators can levy cancellation fees on holidaymakers who want to pull out of their contracts; only when the Foreign Office has issued advice against travelling to a particular destination do most operators waive such fees, so it can take six to nine months before the full impact of publicised terrorist incidents shows itself in booking figures. Despite the 1993 bomb outrages in Turkey, Lunn Poly was still able to report Turkey as the fastest growing country in terms of popularity with British holidaymakers.

Case study: India

India is an example of a country where tour operators have had to contend with a variety of external considerations, including political disturbances, terrorism and government taxation. Although the country's poverty and underdeveloped infrastructure make it an unlikely mass-market destination, nevertheless old colonial associations, its rich culture and the opening up of the Goan beaches for sun and sand holidays guarantee it a steady package holiday market. Traditionally it was the province of specialist operators like Cox and Kings, established in 1758. However, in the 1990s large mainstream operators began to include it in their long-haul brochures, usually offering tours of Delhi, Agra, Jaipur and Udaipur (the 'Golden Triangle'), with a second week tacked on for sunbathing in Goa.

India is so large and has such varied climatic conditions that until the late 1980s operators had been able to market it as a year-round destination; in the summer when the Golden Triangle became unbearably hot they could redirect clients to cooler Kashmir, with its lakes, mountains and ski resorts. However, in the late 1980s what had been relatively low-key skirmishing by militants demanding an independent Kashmir (or union with Pakistan) became much more serious. This came on top of long-standing terrorist activity in the Punjab which had forced Amritsar's Golden Temple off the tourism map, as Sikh militants struggled to win an independent Khalistan. Eventually the government was forced to declare Kashmir and its popular houseboats a tourism no-go area. Deprived of the obvious destination for summer tours, operators have been forced to look for alternatives, including the foothills of Himachal Pradesh and Ootacamund, a southern Indian hill-station which has proved harder to market, in part because the southern infrastructure is less developed than the north's.

In 1993 a series of bombs in Calcutta and Bombay did nothing to help India's tarnished image, and some tours had to be cancelled. Further disruption followed when a strike by pilots on Indian Airlines, the domestic carrier, forced cancellations and reroutеings. The government also introduced a 20 per cent hotel tax, forcing operators to hike their prices for 1994. Operators were also finding it increasingly hard to secure flight seats and hotel allocations in Goa, which seemed immune to these problems. Their difficulties were not helped by Thomson's decision to start offering charter flights to Goa for stay-put holidays where beforehand it had only featured Goa as an add-on to northern holidays and had used scheduled flights throughout. Thomson's huge buying power enabled it to secure all the rooms it required at the cost of squeezing out smaller operators.

Fashion

Like so many things, the tourism product can be seen as having a distinct life cycle. Most destinations are discovered not by tour operators but by small groups of independent travellers. As word begins to spread, small, specialist operators may move in and start to package the destination. All things being equal it will become increasingly popular and well-known, attracting the big name operators as well. As they move in, those in search of something more exclusive will tend to move out. All too often the destination quickly becomes overdeveloped and associated with the problems of downmarket tourism.

So tour operators are also affected by fashion. Certainly by the late 1980s, countries seemed to go in and out of fashion alarmingly quickly, making it very difficult for operators to keep up. Turkey and Cyprus are two countries which have been affected by fashionable whim. In 1989 Turkey was the 'in' place to go. Tour operators rushed to find suitable beds to contract and the Turks rushed to oblige, building new hotels at a phenomenal speed and with a blithe disregard for their design or the damage they were doing to the landscape. Tourists arrived to find their hotels surrounded by building sites, and standards lower than they were used to in other Mediterranean destinations. In 1990 the number of people wanting to go to Turkey started to fall, before plummeting in 1991 after the Gulf War. In 1992 the fashionable elite decided they would rather go to Cyprus and a similar scramble for beds took place there, with claims of double bookings rife. In 1993 the Cypriots in turn found that they had fallen from favour.

All sectors of the market can be affected by fashion. It might have been assumed that popular city-break destinations like Paris and Amsterdam would be immune to such whims. However, figures for 1993 suggested that these cities should now be viewed as mature products, with newcomers like Prague and Budapest nibbling away at the edges of their popularity.

In theory, the companies best placed to take advantage of swings in fashion are the smaller specialists who already serve those destinations. However, once the big operators move in, smaller companies often find themselves underpriced and threatened with being squeezed out altogether. Their smaller, more discerning clientele may also be put off as the mass market descends, bringing with it changes which may be difficult to reverse even after the newcomers have grown bored and moved on again (for example, hotels once erected, are there for the foreseeable future, however much of an eyesore they may be).

At the opposite end of the spectrum to the fashionable destinations are the unfashionable ones. Benidorm, for example, is a resort which was fashionable in the 1970s but slid rapidly downmarket in the 1980s. By 1990 not only was the surrounding area so built up that its original beauty was buried beneath concrete but it had also earned an unenviable reputation for attracting the type of holidaymaker with not much money but who spent what they did have on drink. Tour operators will not continue to feature a resort that they believe has become unsaleable. Faced with the prospect of seeing the town dropped by companies like Thomson, Benidorm's authorities have since done their best to clean up their act and there are signs that it may be recovering some of its old popularity. Majorca, too, has responded to criticism and the threatened loss of visitors by attempting to attract a different, more monied clientele.

The weather

The weather in Great Britain can have a small but nevertheless discernible affect on tour operators. For example, when England is basking in a rare heat wave some would-be holidaymakers (mainly late bookers) may decide to stay at home instead of going abroad, bringing an unexpected bonus for domestic operators. Conversely, after a typically wet and unpleasant English summer, more people may be ready to part with their cash early in the following year to ensure themselves their two weeks in the sun. If the weather is bad, people who have not taken a holiday at all or who have had a wet one at home may also opt for a late-booked one week abroad towards the end of the season, particularly in September.

Winter sports holidays are among the most sensitive to adverse weather. After a year in which resorts suffer either little or no snow, clients may be reluctant to commit themselves until late in the day when they can be sure the pattern won't repeat itself. Late bookings are also unlikely to materialise when the weather reports are all indicating no snow in the resorts.

Of course, extreme weather in overseas destinations can also have an adverse effect on operators' programmes. For example, in 1988 Hurricane Gilbert did enormous damage to Jamaica and the Yucatan peninsula of Mexico, causing some holidays to be cancelled.

Price increases

Although tour operators obviously have some control over their prices, they may also be forced to pass on price increases which are outside their control but which may make a programme harder to sell. Such increases can be caused by rises in the cost of aviation fuel (as in 1974 and 1979), by new or increased taxes or by currency fluctuations. In 1993 many operators were struggling with price rises brought about by the withdrawal of the pound from the European Exchange Rate Mechanism in 1992 and the consequent 14 per cent devaluation of the pound. For the first time in years, many operators were forced to levy unpopular surcharges on their brochure prices or risk significant losses on currency deals.

In November 1992 Greece increased its tourist tax to £15 a head, too late in the year for it to have been costed into 1992/3 winter holidays. Operators featuring Greece, especially those specialising in Greece, were also very reluctant to price it into summer 1993 holidays at a time when the market was still very uncertain. A month before, India had introduced a 20 per cent tourism tax which operators protested would cause long-term damage by making India seem more expensive. However, relatively few British holidaymakers visit India which may also be seen as a 'once-in-a-lifetime' destination and one which people expect to pay a lot to visit because it is so far away. Greece, however, is just one of several Mediterranean sun and sand destinations all competing for much the same mass market clientele. Anything that makes Greece look more expensive could cause would-be holidaymakers to switch to Spain, Italy or Turkey instead. For the biggest operators offering all these destinations, it might just mean one destination selling instead of another, but for specialists it could mean people forsaking their programme for another, cheaper one with a different operator. How a tax is collected can be very important. Turkey also has a tourist tax but this is collected from passengers in cash at the airport and so doesn't affect the brochure price. In contrast the Greek tax must be collected from passengers in advance. British tour operators reacted to it in different ways. Sunvil Holidays opted to increase holiday prices by £9, Airlink Holidays dropped its no surcharge guarantee to allow them to recoup the tax, while Greek specialists Olympic Holidays decided to absorb the cost of the tax themselves instead of putting up their prices, even though, on sales of 80,000 holidays, that represented an increase in costs of over £1 million. Airlink Holidays also launched a new programme to Turkey, the country which it believed was most likely to benefit from a price-driven switch away from Greece. In summer 1993 sales of holidays to Greece declined in favour of those to Spain.

In 1994 tour operators had to start costing into their holidays a new UK airport tax of £5 to destinations within the EU and £10 to places outside it.

Miscellaneous considerations

Through their brochures and their own advertising, tour operators do their best to create an image of the destinations they serve which will entice tourists to visit. However, they are perhaps uniquely at the whim of the media. In 1988 and 1989 lurid reports of the misdeeds of lager louts on the Spanish Costas did nothing to encourage more discerning customers, with perhaps more cash to spend, to visit coastal Spain. Exaggerated reports of the risk of crime in places like Jamaica can also be very damaging to operators; indeed bookings to Kenya declined so much as a result of reported attacks on tourists that Inghams pulled out of the country altogether in 1993. As a result of the scare over muggings and murder in Florida in 1993, Swinards renamed its American accommodation-only brochure to remove 'Florida' from the title after six years. At the same time some companies reported an increased interest in escorted trips to Florida which could be seen as safer.

In the early 1990s the 'green' environmental movement was of growing importance which made pollution scares like the one in the 1980s when an algae bloom appeared in the sea off the Italian coast all the more damaging.

In 1992/3 city-break operators also lost sales as a result of free flights offered to customers by supermarket Sainsbury's. Travelscene did its best to compensate by offering agents commission for accommodation-only bookings.

Although all tour operators are affected by at least some of these external considerations, long-haul operators are probably most at risk and of those, the overland 'adventure tour' operators are most at risk of all because, by the very nature of what they offer, they venture into parts of the world which are politically unstable, with dodgy currencies and poor standards of public hygiene. This is what Encounter Overland says in its brochure about the potential extra cost of possible alternative routes:

> Occasional tense political situations are a fact of life for overlanders. When one does arise it is either a border dispute and/or hostilities or it is due to a country en route rejecting visa applications from nationals of at least one country with which it is currently having some sort of diplomatic disagreement.
>
> We really are very attuned to such matters and have a reputation (very much lived up to during the recent 'Gulf Situation') for finalising the best alternative plan if a project cannot . . . or is ill-advised to . . . proceed exactly as planned.
>
> As this is seldom required, it would be unfair to provide for it unnecessarily in our prices. On the other hand it would be somewhat irresponsible not to provide for it at all, for the fact is there could be political forces or other *force majeure* situations capable of barring every realistic/responsible land route.
>
> In such a circumstance, after thorough investigation, the best possible alternative will be implemented. If that calls for the use of a plane or ship, then that in turn is bound to call for cash. In that case the first US$300 per person will be met by Encounter Overland. Should more than that be needed, a contribution from you of up to, but not exceeding US$250 would be required, while any further amount beyond that will be met by Encounter Overland.
>
> Your possible contribution is therefore a clearly limited amount to be called on to assist with exceptional and essential extra expenditure only if, for reasons beyond Encounter Overland's control, a plane or ship has to be used.
>
> (Courtesy: Encounter Overland)

LIMITING FACTORS

Tour operators are not necessarily free to develop programmes to anywhere in the world either. In particular they may be limited by:

a) political considerations
b) socio-economic circumstances in the receiving country

Political considerations

Concerned that their culture may be diluted through contact with foreigners, some governments make it difficult for outsiders to visit. Until 1989 all the countries of the so-called Eastern bloc (i.e. the Communist countries) discouraged visitors to prevent their oppressive political systems being undermined. They did this by making visa applications slow and costly, by insisting that visitors changed fixed amounts of money into their currency and by restricting foreigners in where they could stay and travel. Since the momentous changes of 1989, however, these restrictions are easing. Hungary, Poland, the Czech Republic and Slovakia no longer charge British visitors for visas. Nor do they force them to change fixed sums of money or limit where they can travel or stay. Consequently the number of operators featuring these countries (and in particular featuring Prague and Budapest for city breaks) has risen dramatically. Restrictions are also being lifted in what was the old Soviet Union, although the situation there remains too unsettled to know what will be the final outcome. Even China is making it easier for visitors: it is no longer necessary to get special permission to visit most towns (though tours to Tibet are still strictly controlled), although in theory tourists can still only stay at certain hotels and are still charged higher prices for transport and admission to sights. However, some of the few remaining Communist countries (Laos, North Korea) continue to make it very difficult for foreign visitors. In such circumstances only specialist tour operators find it worth their while to develop programmes to these destinations. Even Regent Holidays gave up featuring North Korea after tours which had been complicated to arrange were cancelled at short notice as a result of such things as military manoeuvres along the border with South Korea.

Other countries also try to exclude tourists to protect their culture. So, for example, the tiny Himalayan Kingdom of Bhutan strictly limits the number of visas it will issue to foreigners each year. Myanmar (Burma) will only issue visitors' visas for one month stays which has stopped it becoming as popular a place to visit as neighbouring Thailand. Ecuador also limits the number of visitors who can travel to the Galapagos Islands to try and protect their fragile flora and fauna. However, every year the number of permits allowed to be issued goes up, suggesting they are not as sure of their policy as the Bhutanese are.

Socio-economic conditions in the receiving country

In theory, there is nothing to stop Thomson or Sovereign launching a programme of tours to Chad, Sudan or Bangladesh. In practice, however, the desperate poverty in these countries, combined with the lack of infrastructure, the appalling heat and the limited number of specific sights, mean that again it is only the specialist operators, mainly the overland adventure companies, that bother with them.

Case study: Cuba

Cuba is an example of a Caribbean island with lovely beaches, a good climate and interesting historical sights but where a combination of political factors and socio-economic circumstances have tended to deter tour companies from developing holiday programmes. This is how Thomson described it in its worldwide brochure in 1993:

> A multi-faceted island, Cuba offers something for everyone. You'll find little to spend your money on by way of souvenirs, but the prices in hotels are good, the atmosphere is wonderfully friendly and the sun shines happily down.

Before Castro came to power in 1959 and established a Communist regime there in 1961, Cuba had been a popular holiday destination, particularly for North Americans. After 1959, however, Castro discouraged tourists as firmly as did other Communist leaders. A few specialist companies, mainly with left-wing interests, like Regent Holidays and Progressive Tours, continued to run primarily sightseeing programmes to Cuba, and in the early 1980s Pegasus tried to relaunch a more conventional beach holidays programme. In doing so, however, it came up against bureaucratic obstacles and problems with transfers; what's more, with no charter flights available, it was forced to use the scheduled services of Cubana, not one of the world's most efficient airlines. Eventually it abandoned the effort. In an attempt to undermine Castro's regime, the United States started a trade embargo against Cuba which meant that what had once been a fairly developed economy gradually deteriorated. When the Soviet Union stopped supplying it with oil on preferential terms in the 1990s, the situation became dramatically worse, with bullocks replacing tractors on farms and huge numbers of bicycles being imported from China to replace cars for which there was no petrol. With his back against the wall, Castro was forced to reconsider tourism as a potential source of hard currency.

In 1992 Thomson launched a programme of beach holidays to Varadero in the north, using charter flights to get there. Despite some consumer resistance, it sold about 2,000 holidays in the first year. The programme reappeared in 1993 brochures, using scheduled flights. However, by the end of the summer 1993 season Thomson had sold only about 200 holidays and decided to drop Cuba for 1994. They attributed some of the problems to the fact that tourists didn't expect the near Third World conditions in sharp contrast to those in some other popular Caribbean destinations. However, Airtours then launched a programme to Cuba for 1994, using its own Boeing 767s to fly customers direct to Varadero. To publicise this new service it used lead-in prices of £299 for a two-week stay, inclusive of air fare and accommodation. However, its brochure was still forced to comment:

> Please be aware that there are shortages of certain items. It is not unusual to see locals queuing outside the shops in Havana. However, in the hotels, there are no such shortages of items for holidaymakers.

By 'shortages of certain items' it was referring to

shortages of food, fuel and medicine, among other things.

In 1994 Leisure International started operating charters to Holguin and Varadero for Owners Abroad and Sunworld.

THE IMPACT OF TOUR OPERATIONS ON RECEIVING COUNTRIES

It would not be possible for tour operators to move millions of people around the world every year without their activities having some effect on the tourist receiving countries. The question of the impact of tourism on host countries is a complex one. Sometimes it can have a desirable impact, but at other times it can be decidedly damaging. In most cases the picture is more mixed. This section merely highlights tourism's impact in the following broad areas:

- economic
- social
- environmental
- political

Economic impact of tour operations on receiving countries

Money

Considering the amount of disruption the invasion of thousands of holidaymakers can have on a country, it is unlikely that any governments would welcome the tourism industry if they didn't believe that their country stood to benefit from it economically. It is assumed that huge sums of money will flow into the country, paid by the operators to hotels, ground handlers and sometimes national airlines, and by their clients to bars, restaurants, shops, etc. Certainly, it is clear that money generated from tourism has helped Spain's economy expand enormously since the 1950s. Likewise the areas of Portugal, Greece and Turkey most visited by package holidaymakers are also the wealthiest parts of those countries.

However, it would be simplistic to assume that all or even most of the money paid out by tourists finds its way into the pockets of people in the host countries. The tour companies are usually owned by people in the tourist generating rather than the tourist receiving country, and obviously they cream off some of the money as profit. Increasingly within Europe, the tour companies also own their own airlines which means that the money paid for flight seats simply finds its way back into company hands. A few operators also own resort hotels which, once again, means they can prevent money leaking out to anybody else. At least in developed countries, hotels will sell locally bought and paid for food, and money spent on film, souvenirs, drink and meals out will mainly go to local people. However, in developing countries, even some of the food, drink and film will have been imported into the host country for tourists to buy, because the host country either doesn't produce the goods at all or doesn't produce them to the quality tourists would expect. In such circumstances the amount of the holiday price that actually remains in the host country can be very small indeed. Where a package tour uses its own airline but pays for accommodation and food locally, as little as 40 per cent of the retail holiday price may actually stay in the host country; if the hotel is also owned by the tour operator or a foreign company it may be as little as 25 per cent. Caribbean cruises offer an extreme example of what can happen. In theory, since these holidays are expensive, it could be assumed the receiving countries would do very well out of them. In fact the ships are owned by big international companies. Because they act as floating hotels the tourists don't actually 'stay' in their destination at all, depriving it of any benefit from the accommodation payment element of their holiday. Since they're not staying, visitors won't often eat expensive meals out either. In fact, the islanders may only benefit from money spent on excursions, souvenirs, snacks and drinks. Likewise, a 1987 study of tourism in the Pacific islands suggested that almost two-thirds of the holiday price leaked straight back out of the Pacific to the foreign owners and operators.

Jobs

Most of the staff actually employed by UK-based tour operators, including their resort representatives, will have been recruited in the UK. However, indirectly tour operators are responsible for providing local employment, particularly in hotels whose staff will mainly be recruited locally. Critics point out that the best paid and most prestigious jobs tend to be reserved for UK staff. For example, even a company like Yugotours which employed local people as its hotel representatives nevertheless had a British senior representative supervising them. In Britain work in hotels and restaurants tends to be seen as low-status employment. However, this view is not universal and, certainly in many developing countries, hotel work, even with its seasonality and unsociable hours, can seem distinctly preferable to the alternative, often backbreakingly hard agricultural work.

Social impact of tour operations on receiving countries

Tourism's impact on the social aspects of life in receiving countries is mainly the result of the behaviour of individual tourists rather than of the tour operators directly. However, inasmuch as the operators are responsible for the tourists being there in the first place, they cannot duck all blame for the problems that arise.

Changed social opportunities

In poorer countries those local people who do find work in tourism, either in the hotels or working as guides, may have much greater opportunities than their compatriots. They are likely to be better paid and work in more pleasant circumstances. What's more, their contact with tourists may also offer them opportunities not available to others.

Male-female relationships

What impact tourism has socially depends to a large extent on the indigenous culture. In Muslim countries where local women are all but invisible it is men who work in the tourism industry, even in jobs that would be filled by women in western countries. This can be very disruptive of traditional social relationships. For example, in Tunisia many of the jobs in tourism are concentrated in hotels along the coast causing ambitious men to desert inland villages in search of better paid work. Sometimes this means there are barely enough men left in the villages to do all the agricultural work. A few of the men marry tourist women, reducing the pool of potential husbands for local women. Even where they don't actually marry foreigners, many local men have relationships with them, while it would be out of the question for their own women to behave in a similar fashion. Such behaviour can make it hard for them to settle down again in the role of traditional husbands and breadwinners.

Land for homes

In countries with a large tourist industry, land appropriate for hotel development becomes extremely valuable. Although a few lucky landowners are able to make a fortune out of selling property, for most local people what tends to happen is that the price of land is pushed up beyond their means. Worse still, local people are sometimes forcibly moved to make way for tourism developments. This was what happened when Acapulco in Mexico was being developed as a resort.

Crime and prostitution

Another unfortunate side effect of tourism tends to be a rise in the crime rate. Although the problem is at its most acute in developing countries where the difference between local people's living standards and those of the tourists is greatest (e.g. Kenya, Ecuador), tourists are often seen as targets for thieves in Italy, Spain and the United States as well.

In some poor countries which receive a lot of tourists, begging has become a serious problem. It starts with children requesting pens and sweets from visitors and progresses to straight demands for cash which can be persistent, even menacing. Variations on this are demands for payment for photographs which have become routine among tribal groups like the Masai who argue, not altogether unreasonably, that they are providing a 'service' for which the tourist should expect to pay; the Tanzanian government, however, objects to tourists paying for photographs, arguing that it is a disincentive to the recipients ever taking up more meaningful work. Other people offer themselves as unofficial guides which sounds harmless and sometimes is; all too often however, as in Morocco, these 'guides' impose their services on unwilling customers and resort to tricks like leading people deep into the warren-like streets of the medinas and then demanding money before they will show them the way out again. At one remove from the 'guides' are the 'friends' who hang around beaches in places like Gambia and Sri Lanka and attach themselves to tourists; frequently they are young men who attach themselves to lone western females, half hoping to be invited back to live with them in their home countries.

Worse than any of these problems is the rise in prostitution linked to tourism in some poorer countries, notoriously in Thailand but also in Kenya, Sri Lanka and the Philippines. Prostitution of adult men and women to tourists is bad enough, but increasingly there is evidence, particularly in Thailand, of child prostitution, some of it linked to a search for 'virgins' to minimise the risk of catching AIDS.

The 'human zoo'

Another problem associated with tourism in some countries is the way in which local people are viewed in much the same way as the local wildlife. Flick through brochures featuring African safaris and you'll find the Masais and Samburus and, even more, the pygmies, depicted alongside lions and leopards and with very little distinction made between them. 'Tribal treks', primarily in Thailand but also in Sarawak in Eastern Malaysia and a few other areas, encourage tourists to look at local inhabitants as exotic 'others'; cut off from meaningful exchange by language barriers, visitors stare at the colourful 'tribals', take pictures of them, perhaps buy some of their handicrafts and then move on.

Tourist behaviour and dress

In some countries, the behaviour of tourists can be offensive to local people. For example, in Muslim countries women are always completely covered up, so the sight of female tourists in skimpy clothing is very offensive. Even greater offence is given by visitors who thoughtlessly enter mosques in shorts or with their heads and shoulders uncovered. Even in more laidback Thailand, local people dress conservatively and don't always approve of the way tourists disregard their customs.

Environmental impact of tour operations on receiving countries

Critics of the tourism industry have identified the following adverse impacts of tourism on the environment:

- Inappropriate development, with ugly buildings which fail to take the local landscape into account and which are sometimes built with a disregard for inadequate infrastructure (roads, sewage disposal, water supply, etc.). In some cases, particularly in Hawaii, hotels have even been built over sacred sites to which local people are then denied access.
- Destruction of the natural habitat, particularly along the coast and in ski resorts. This can lead to threats to wildlife, as in the much publicised cases of the monk seal in the Eastern Mediterranean and the loggerhead turtles at Dalyan in Turkey and Zante in Greece. Fragile coral reefs, in particular, can be damaged by thoughtless tourism development.
- Increased land and sea pollution.
- Damage to flora and fauna to produce souvenirs e.g. ivory ornaments, snakeskin belts.

On the other hand, desire to attract visitors may encourage poorer countries to conserve wildlife and beautiful scenery in national parks. Old buildings which might otherwise have been pulled down may also be restored or found new uses (perhaps as hotels or restaurants) in an attempt to make the environment more appealing.

Because tour operators are not responsible for a country's infrastructure and infrequently build their own hotels, they are rarely directly responsible for the effects of tourism on a local environment. Instead, it is usually governments or governmental bodies that designate and run national parks or decide to preserve historical monuments, and it is individual hoteliers, building companies and governments that decide where hotels will go up and what they will look like. Local government bodies usually have responsibility for ensuring sewage systems, road networks and other facilities are appropriate to the number of people expected in any one area.

Nevertheless, it could be argued that tour operators are in a strong position to influence such matters. If they decide not to use a hotel which has been designed with no thought for its impact on the environment, then other developers will have less incentive to behave in such cavalier fashion. If they decide to boycott hotels with inadequate sewage disposal facilities, then the local authorities will be given considerable incentive to do something about it. It is not the tour operators but their clients who drop litter in areas of natural beauty, but the operators are in a unique position to educate their clients about appropriate behaviour abroad, perhaps through their brochure or through the information they send out with their tickets. Where they own the airline that will fly the clients to a resort, they even have access to the plane's video system, a perfect potential tool for putting across important messages about how to protect the environment, how to dress without offending local people and so on.

TOUR OPERATORS' REACTIONS

Increasingly, operators are waking up to the worst results of uncontrolled tourist development and becoming aware of the need to develop 'greener' or more sustainable tourism products. In part this is because self-interest dictates that they should take greater interest. There is a danger, for example, that holidaymakers will stop buying packages to resorts they perceive as 'spoilt' or dangerous. In the short term this is mainly a problem for resort managers because tour operators can always diversify into other areas. It has been suggested that even the most spoilt resorts may still have a few years life left in them, as the newly-liberated people of Eastern Europe start taking holidays with the same sort of expectations as British holidaymakers had in the 1970s; even so authorities in the Costa Brava and Majorca have made considerable efforts to improve the image of their resorts to stop operators cancelling their programmes and to try and regain some of the more lucrative upper end of the market. However, there must come a point when operators cannot simply switch to a new area (there are, after all, few undeveloped stretches of the Mediterranean left). In any case, in switching to a new area, they forego the benefit of the years of familiarity they may have built up with hoteliers and other local suppliers, so operators do have some vested interest in seeing the situation improve too.

Some smaller specialist operators already have an admirable record of taking the environment into account. For example, before its demise in 1992, Turkish Delight supported the campaign to protect the turtles at Dalyan in southern Turkey whose breeding practices were threatened by careless

FRIENDS OF CONSERVATION

Kenya is home to some of the most spectacular game parks in the world – it is here that many of our client's experience the thrill of seeing at first hand, wildlife roaming free.
But if the parks and the wildlife they support are to survive, the Kenya Wildlife Service needs help. The Game Parks and Reserves of Kenya are under intensive pressure from a rapidly increasing human population and unless they can be proven to be worth saving, they will be forced to yield to this pressure. We believe that tourism can help stop this disaster from happening.

In conjunction with the registered UK charity **Friends of Conservation,** Kuoni supports the joint projects of Friends of Conservation and the Kenya Wildlife Service, under the personal management of Dr. Richard Leakey.
A donation of £2 on behalf of every passenger travelling on safari with us to Kenya will be our 1993 contribution to the Kenya Wildlife Service.
This enables us to support the following projects:
* Wildlife Protection Unit. This unit's tasks include anti-poaching activities, rescuing injured animals, monitoring of tourist vehicles relative to animal harrassment and care of wildlife.
* Rhino Translocation and Wildlife Veterinarian Programme – support for veterinary expertise and the translocation of endangered rhinos into protected sanctuaries.
* Community Conservation and Educational Projects – support for local conservation groups and the production of educational material for use in schools.

Should you wish to make an additional contribution to the Kenya Wildlife Service, more information is available from:
Friends of Conservation
Sloane Square House
Holbein Place
London SW1W 8NS
Telephone: 071 730 7904
Registered Charity No: 328176
(Patron: HRH The Prince of Wales)

... Thank you for your help in supporting Kenya's Wildlife.

Fig. 11.3 Kuoni's work with Friends of Conservation
Courtesy: Kuoni

development of the beach. Guerba has set up a company in Nairobi which employs local people, supports a Worldwide Fund for Nature conservation project and gives money to the charity, Action Aid (that it includes information about these activities in its brochure suggests it sees them as a selling bonus). Kuoni works with the UK charity Friends of Conservation to support the Kenya Wildlife Service, donating £2 per safari passenger booked to the Service (*see* Fig. 11.3). The Association of Independent Tour Operators even helped set up Green Flag International (*see* page 269), and its 1993 brochure also contained 'green tips' to help tourists become more sensitive to their environment (*see* Fig. 11.4). In 1993 AITO was also carrying out a detailed study of the impact of skiing on the environment, with a view to drawing up guidelines for more sensitive use of the ski resorts to protect both skiers and the slopes themselves. In 1992, Thomson appointed an environment manager to be responsible for monitoring the impact of its programmes on the host countries. Its 1993 summer sun brochure included the following guidelines for being a better tourist:

- **Don't litter**
  Discarded rubbish is an eyesore, so even if you see others litter, be sure to take yours away for proper disposal.
- **Do save water**
  Water is a precious resource in hot climates, so take care to use water sparingly.

GREEN TIP:
Find out about the food of the area and its specialities – you could make your holiday more enjoyable and expand your own repertoire of dishes on your return.

GREEN TIP:
Buy a phrase book before you go, and take the time to learn a few words of the language. A little knowledge about the places you intend to visit, their culture and natural history, will enhance your holiday experience.

GREEN TIP:
Take only sun creams and lotions that are environmentally friendly – again, this will help to prevent unnecessary pollution of water supplies.

GREEN TIP:
Respect local sensitivities to dress and behaviour.

GREEN TIP:
If you have ideas which might help your tour operator to become more environmentally friendly, take the trouble to write to the company with suggestions.

GREEN TIP:
Get your holiday off to a green start – travel to and from your airport by public transport, if possible.

GREEN TIP:
Choose natural oils and skin preparations – buying natural products can help a third world economy.

GREEN TIP:
Please don't drop litter – keep the world tidy!

GREEN TIP:
Use your camera to record plants and animals seen. Never be tempted to bring back living material.

GREEN TIP:
Try to use public transport, a bicycle or shanks's pony to get around while on holiday.
You'll meet people and see far more than you would from a car.

GREEN TIP:
Try not to waste power unnecessarily.

GREEN TIP:
Take only environmentally friendly detergents and shampoos with you to help keep rivers and the sea – and thus the water – free from pollution.

Fig. 11.4 Some of the 'green tips' included in AITO's *1993 Real Holidays Directory*
Courtesy: AITO

- **Don't waste energy**
  Always switch off lights and electrical or gas appliances when not in use.
- **Do guard against fire**
  In hot, dry countries a carelessly discarded cigarette or unquenched picnic fire could easily start a fire.
- **Remember the countryside code**
  Fasten all gates, keep to paths when crossing farmland, avoid damaging fences, walls or hedges, and respect the life of the countryside.
- **Do respect the rights of others**
  We all enjoy some peace and quiet on holiday. Loud noise can be annoying, so please think of your fellow guests.
- **Do protect local wildlife**
  Don't collect coral, shells, reef animals or other marine 'treasures'. Remember many animals are protected by law. Please don't buy souvenirs made of tortoiseshell, ivory, reptile skins, furs or exotic feathers.

British Airways also co-sponsors the Tourism for Tomorrow award which aims to encourage and promote 'green tourism'. Not surprisingly, therefore, the British Airways Holidays brochure contains similar advice for tourists. It says:

- Remember that wherever you go, there are opportunities to learn more about your surroundings, the landscape, flora, fauna and people.
- If you hike or bike in wilderness areas, please take away with you whatever you brought in and leave the areas you visit clear of litter.
- Please resist the temptation to take 'souvenirs' from historical sites and beauty spots and please leave exotic plants in their own habitat where they belong.
- Leave only footprints and take only photographs.
- If you go snorkelling or diving, please remember that coral is a sensitive living organism. Touching it or bruising it can turn the kaleidoscope of colours into a lifeless ashen grey.
- Above all, do not encourage the trade in products from endangered species by buying items such as ivory, shells, tortoiseshell, animal skins and feathers. If your conscience fails to guide you in this matter, you should be aware that the importation of many of these items into the UK is illegal.

The customer service questionnaire handed out by British Airways Holidays also has a section devoted to finding out the public's attitude to environmental considerations as they affect their holidays.

One problem has been the difficulty in even defining what is meant by a sustainable, eco-friendly or environmentally sensitive holiday. In its *1993 Directory of Real Holidays* AITO suggested it meant small-scale tourism which would have a low impact on the host environment, and which took into account the needs of local people and of the local wildlife. Furthermore 'green' tourism would encourage reuse of traditional buildings (rather than the building of brand-new hotels), and would seek to conserve traditional ways of life and traditional crafts.

Some companies have responded by producing new 'environmentally aware' programmes. For example, Cox and Kings has a new 'Environmental Journeys' brochure featuring botanical tours of areas as diverse as South Africa and Majorca. However, it might be argued that there always were such tours and that they make little difference to the overall problems created by mass tourism. It could also be argued that some eco-tourism is, itself, dubious because it involves taking people to fragile environments which may not be equipped to deal with more than very limited numbers of visitors.

THE TOURISM PRESSURE GROUPS

As tourism grew rapidly in the 1980s and 1990s and its detrimental effects became more obvious, pressure groups dedicated to doing something about this appeared. First was **Tourism Concern**, set up in 1989, which has devoted its energies to publicising the downside of tourism and educating the public about how to be better tourists, Although representatives of many tour operators are individual members of Tourism Concern, companies are not allowed to actually join the organisation so that it can remain free of commercial pressures. Amongst other things, Tourism Concern has designed a Himalayan Tourist Code (see Fig. 11.5), offering advice to tourists on how to protect the fragile Himalayan environment. A few companies like High Places, featuring treks in the Himalayas, have agreed to print the Code in their brochures.

In contrast, **Green Flag International (GFI)**, set

THE HIMALAYAN TOURIST CODE

By following these simple guidelines, you can help preserve the unique environment and ancient cultures of the Himalayas.

Protect the natural environment

▲ **Limit deforestation – make no open fires** and discourage others from doing so on your behalf. Where water is heated by scarce firewood, use as little as possible. When possible choose accommodation that uses kerosene or fuel efficient wood stoves.

▲ **Remove litter, burn or bury paper** and carry out all non-degradable litter. Graffiti are permanent examples of environment pollution.

▲ **Keep local water clean and avoid using pollutants** such as detergents in streams or springs. If no toilet facilities are available, make sure you are at least 30 metres away from water sources, and bury or cover wastes.

▲ **Plants should be left to flourish in their natural environment** – taking cuttings, seeds and roots is illegal in many parts of the Himalayas.

▲ **Help your guides and porters to follow conservation measures.**

▲ **When taking photographs, respect privacy** – ask permission and use restraint.

▲ **Respect Holy places** – preserve what you have come to see, never touch or remove religious objects. Shoes should be removed when visiting temples.

▲ **Giving to children encourages begging.** A donation to a project, health centre or school is a more constructive way to help.

▲ **You will be accepted and welcomed if you follow local customs.** Use only your right hand for eating and greeting. Do not share cutlery or cups, etc. It is polite to use both hands when giving or receiving gifts.

▲ **Respect for local etiquette earns you respect** – loose, light weight clothes are preferable to revealing shorts, skimpy tops and tight fitting action wear. Hand holding or kissing in public are disliked by local people.

▲ **Observe standard food and bed charges** but do not condone overcharging. Remember when you're shopping that the bargains you buy may only be possible because of low income to others.

▲ **Visitors who value local traditions encourage local pride and maintain local cultures,** please help local people gain a realisitic view of life in Western Countries.

The Himalayas may change you
please do not change them.
As a guest, respect local traditions,
protect local cultures, maintain local pride.
Be patient, friendly and sensitive
Remember – you are a guest

Tourism Concern
Froebel College, Roehampton Lane, London SW15 5PU
Tel: 081-878-9053

Fig. 11.5 Tourism Concern's Himalayan Tourist Code
Courtesy: Tourism Concern

up in 1990, works with individual tour operators, identifying projects in the host countries that they can become involved with and perhaps invest in. The following companies are full members of GFI:

Air Travel Group	Arctic Experience
Bladon Lines	British Airways
Business Green	Campus Centres
Club Cantabrica	Countrywide Holidays
Cox & Kings	CV Travel
Elysian Holidays	Espirit Holidays
Eurocamp	Explore
Grecofile	Greek Islands Club
Guerba Expeditions	Individual Traveller Co.
Holidays for the Barefoot Traveller	Journey Latin
Intourist America	Kirker Holidays
Le Ski	Meon Travel
Moswin Tours	NSR Travel
Panorama Holiday Group	Pure Crete
RCI	Rainbow Holidays
Simply Travel	Select Site Reservations
Sun Blessed Holidays	Sunspot Tours
Sunvil Travel	Travel and General Insurance Co.
Travel Club of Upminster	VFB Holidays
Voyages Ilena	Wildlife Safari
Wildlife Travel	YHA

In addition, a few companies are associate members of GFI. Altogether 51 companies selling over 2 million holidays a year now belong to GFI. The following are the sort of projects it is involved in:

- Carrying out an environmental audit and introducing a programme of environmental play for children and of green tourism advice for Eurocamp clients.
- Providing an article on environmental considerations in India, Kenya and Thailand for British Airways (Speedbird).
- Writing a booklet for Timsway clients to selected Greek islands.
- Working with representatives of the printing industry to help reduce wastage through recycling schemes, etc.

In 1991 John Elkington and Julia Hailes contacted about 200 tour operators to find out their attitudes to environmental issues for their book, *Holidays that Don't Cost the Earth*. Roughly 40 per cent replied, and from these replies Elkington and Hailes concluded that 'in most firms it was clear that environmental issues had not yet been seriously addressed', although the smaller and medium-sized firms appeared to be doing better than their larger rivals. They also noted that the recession had put paid even to some of those environment-protecting measures already in place. At the end of the book they included a lengthy checklist to help customers decide how 'green' a tour operator was.

Elkington and Hailes identified ten broad areas of interest:

1. Information for tourists

This should include:

- a written environmental policy in the company brochure . . . and details of how it is being carried out
- general guidelines on what the tourist can do to minimise environmental damage and to blend in with local cultures
- fact sheets on environmental issues and projects relating to specific destinations, and information on what can be done to help
- details of endangered species . . . animal or plant . . . and the laws and regulations concerning the export of products made from them
- advice on the potential environmental impact of sporting and leisure activities . . . and on how to minimise them

2. Community projects

The company should:

- participate in local initiatives and projects in tourist destinations, for example litter clean-ups
- help to plan resorts to suit local needs, not just the needs of tourists
- support local crafts, so long as they don't rely on endangered or banned species for raw materials
- encourage communication between local people and visitors, to help promote a better understanding between them

3. Environmental and conservation projects

The company should:

- promote environmental organisations and initiatives in its holiday brochures
- make donations to environmental projects and organisations, perhaps linking donations to the number of bookings or profits
- give active support to conservation and environmental projects focusing on nature, culture or architecture, both worldwide and in tourist destinations
- consider setting up environmental projects where none exist
- encourage clients to monitor environmental projects and improvements . . . and provide feedback to operators
- make sure that all tour groups abide by local regulations or relevant codes of conduct

4. Transport

The company should:

- be aware of the environmental impact of the transport systems it uses
- put pressure on the transport companies it uses, such as airlines and car rental firms, to ensure they move towards better fuel efficiency, recycling and other environmental measures
- consider switching to more environment-friendly alternatives, such as public transport, using trains rather than planes . . . or supporting local transport systems, where applicable
- enforce strict guidelines for coach operators to ensure that they do not drive too fast, do not leave their engines on whilst the coach is stationary and ensure that the vehicles are well-maintained
- create a policy for hire cars, which should be diesel-powered or fitted with catalytic converters and be fuel-efficient
- provide guidelines on greener motoring
- make sure that coaches or cars do not drive into sensitive areas, for example the hearts of medieval towns
- provide information on local bicycle hire companies, where appropriate

5. Planning and development

The company should:

- promote greater pedestrianisation in town or city

centres . . . by supporting and encouraging local government initiatives, or even suggesting them
- help to ensure that sewage facilities in resorts are adequate for the increased numbers brought in through tourism
- use and improve on existing facilities, rather than constantly switching to new resorts or encouraging new developments
- make sure that any new development is sympathetic to the environment, using traditional local materials and local styles

6. Hotels and accommodation

The company should:
- use local accommodation where possible, so that the income goes to the local economy rather than being siphoned off to international corporations
- request that large hotel chains carry out an environmental audit of their operations . . . and that they make the necessary improvements when it is completed
- question the need for modern conveniences, for example air conditioning, particularly in less developed countries
- encourage energy and water efficiency, particularly where these resources are in short supply, and support initiatives that use alternative energy sources, such as solar power
- specify that the recycling of waste is . . . or will soon become . . . a requirement
- support innovative green accommodation, either where it already exists or where it is planned

7. Governments and tourism agencies

The company should:
- alert governments and national tourism agencies to its interest in environmental initiatives
- specify measures that should be taken by governments if it is to continue bringing tourists . . . and therefore tourist revenue . . . into the country
- establish straightforward, above-board contact with government ministers in the countries visited
- protest to national governments, tourist bodies and in international circles about any corruption encountered, especially where money for environmental projects is affected

8. Leisure activities

The company should:
- be aware of the potential environmental impacts of any leisure activities it promotes or organises
- check all operators it uses . . . or whom its clients are likely to use . . . to make sure that they are behaving responsibly
- provide guidelines for tourists on how to minimise damage
- actively discourage activities that are excessively damaging to the environment, favouring activities with a minimal impact

9. Company greening

The company should:
- produce a written environmental policy statement
- carry out an environmental audit of its activities, implementing changes where necessary
- look at the best of the competition to see . . . and, where appropriate, emulate . . . what they are doing
- start greening its office(s), including initiating a recycling scheme for paper, glass and cans, cutting down on waste and using recycled paper for office stationery and brochures where appropriate
- operate a staff and client suggestion scheme for environmental improvements in running both the office and the company's holidays

10. Communications

The company should:
- be in a position to provide information for clients who enquire about its environmental initiatives
- create a code of practice for tour leaders
- keep a regular flow of information to travel agents to make sure they are well informed about environmental issues
- report other tour operators if they are not complying with environmental or conservation regulations
- present a real picture of the host country rather than a 'packaged' and 'distorted' version for tourists

Courtesy: Victor Gollancz Ltd

Political impact of tourism

It is much harder to quantify any political impact of tourism or to decide how much of it is due to independent travellers and how much to organised package tourism. Nevertheless Neil Taylor of Regent Holidays, long-term organiser of packages to the Eastern bloc countries, believes tourism did play an important role in planting the seeds for change in the minds of those in the ex-Communist countries who came into contact with foreigners. That this is likely to be true is suggested by the lengths to which Communist regimes traditionally went to limit and control tourism. The government of Laos continues to argue that it doesn't want its culture diluted by mass-market tourism. However, arguably the greatest dilution would be that its people come to envy the greater freedom and material wealth of westerners.

QUESTIONS AND DISCUSSION POINTS

1 On a map of the world, mark those areas which rarely appear in mainstream holiday brochures. Discuss the reasons why these countries are missed out. Which of them do you think might soon appear in the brochures?

2 Make a list of all the events which have occurred in the world during the last 12 months which have had significant consequences for tour operators. Which of these do you think they could reasonably have been expected to anticipate? Which of these events was likely to have had the greatest disruptive effect?

3 Read through the guidelines for being a better tourist which appeared in the Thomson Summer Sun 1993 brochure, the British Airways Holidays 1993 Worldwide brochure and the 1993 AITO *Real Holidays Directory*. In what ways are they similar and in what ways different? Do you think they are adequate? In what, if any, ways could they be improved?

4 Look at the two 'Juxtapositions' features taken from the Tourism Concern newsletter *In Focus* (Fig. 11.6). The first looks at 'the human zoo' in Thailand, and contrasts how tribal groups are described in package holiday brochures, guidebooks and other sources. The second looks at attempts to revive tourism in war-torn Croatia, again taking extracts from newspaper accounts and comparing them with what the brochures, etc. have to say. Discuss the moral issues raised by the concept of the human zoo and by the idea of holidays to war zones.

5 Following bad publicity about the mugging and murder of tourists in Florida in 1993, the Miami authorities stepped up police patrols and put armed police in the airport, erected clearer road direction signs, and removed the requirement that hired cars should have a letter signifying that fact in their registration plates. They also launched the 'TRAP' programme, with police aiming to intercept motorists they believed were lost and redirect them to safety. Airtours reacted by offering price reductions and coach transfers to the hotel for people who no longer wanted to pick up a hired car at Miami airport. Consider what operators could do to counteract the damage done by six of the events you identified above (2). What should local authorities do to help?

ASSIGNMENTS

1 Choose **one** tour operator offering a programme to more than one country and try to find out what it is doing to meet the criteria laid down by Elkington and Hailes for promoting responsible tourism. (Note to lecturers: all class members should select a different tour operator.) Write up your findings in the form of a report to the rest of your group. Ask your lecturer to photocopy all the reports and circulate them to the rest of the class. Allow time for everyone to read through the reports and then organise a class discussion to talk about which of the chosen operators is doing the most to encourage responsible tourism.

2 The subject of responsible tourism and the tour operator's role in promoting it is very controversial. Organise a class debate on the motion that 'Tourism can only survive if tour operators take a more active role in encouraging responsible tourism'. Two members of the class should represent the tour operators (one large operator and one smaller, specialist one – they need not be real companies as long as the people representing them have a clear idea what sort of holidays they would be selling, to what market and on what scale). One member of the class should be a spokesperson for the pressure group Tourism Concern and another should be an independent traveller who believes most of the damage is being caused by package tourists. A fifth member of the class should chair the debate on behalf of an identified local organisation (Friends of the Earth, Chamber of Commerce, Women's Institute, etc.). Other members of the class should represent interested holidaymakers; each of them should prepare a question to put to the panel after the main speeches and before a vote is taken. One member of the class will have to act as teller to count the votes at the end of the debate. Another should keep a written record of what is said and of the decision reached.

3 The class should divide into pairs. Each pair should pick **one** of the following destinations and prepare a 'Juxtapositions' feature, similar to those produced by Tourism Concern, to highlight the particularly controversial aspects of tourism in these areas. Before starting work, it is important that each pair considers what particular issues need examining for their chosen destination, so lecturers should allow plenty of research time and be ready to 'guide' groups towards suitable source materials.

- Eastern Turkey
- Hawaii
- the Caribbean
- Goa
- the Australian Outback
- South Africa
- the Amazon
- China
- Cyprus (North and South)
- Ecuador

JUXTAPOSITIONS

JUXTAPOSITIONS

Own Name of Tribe: Hmong 'free people'
Thai Name of Tribe: Meo 'barbarian'

'Trekking in the mountains of north Thailand differs from trekking in most other parts of the world, in that the emphasis is not primarily on the scenery but on the region's inhabitants.

Originating in various parts of China and Southeast Asia, the hill tribes are often termed Fourth World people, in that they are migrants who continue to migrate without regard for established national boundaries.

In recent years, with the effects of rapid population growth and ensuing competition for land, of discrimination and exploitation by lowland Thais, and of tourism, their ancient culture has come under threat, but the integrity of their way of life is as yet largely undamaged . . . '

P Gray & L Ridout, The Rough Guide to Thailand 1992

Come and experience these amazing people. Primitive hill tribe villages that are totally untouched and in their natural surroundings. See their culture and live among them in their timelessness.

1977 advertisement on fence of Guest House in Chaing Mai, Thailand

---

The Meo are considered to be intelligent people. Legend tells us that long, long ago there was a famine. The Meo had to eat their books. Now the Meo consider it unnecessary to learn to read and write. After all, they already have the words inside them!

Tourist Authority of Thailand brochure, no date

HILLTRIBES

The region is, however, most strongly coloured by the various hilltribes who make their homes in the highlands. Comprising seven major tribes – Meo, Karen, Yeo, Lisu, Lawa, Lahu and Akha, each with its own distinct culture, religion, language and colourful style of dress – these people maintain independent lifestyles. They are nonetheless hospitable and welcome visitors to their villages where their singular cultures are mostly untouched by the 20th century.

Chiang Mai & Northern Thailand Tourism Authority of Thailand, 1990

Today, we visit the village of the Padong. This unique and primitive tribe are spirit worshippers and many of its women still wear neck, leg and arm rings. The giraffe-neck women are a spectacular sight and they consider a 'long neck' as symbols of grace and beauty.

Thailand Adventures, Exodus, 1991

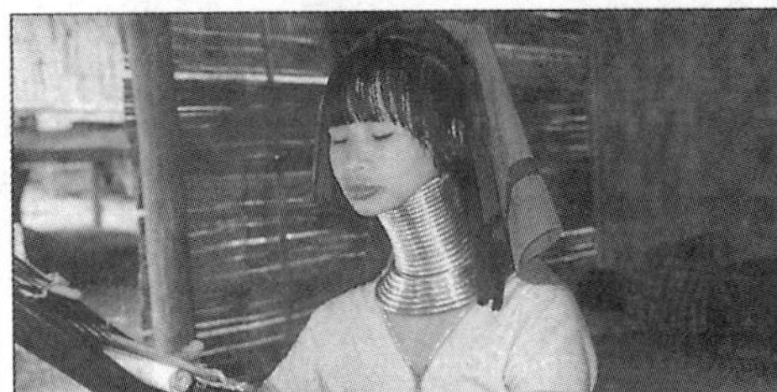

Kayan woman weaving in Nam Pin Den – *photo by Tim Forsyth*

Some people worry that tourism on this scale might damage the culture of the Yao. Hill tribes are the primary tourist attraction of northern Thailand, and anthropologists have questioned whether the poorly developed groups may lose identity.

But Leh Tsan Kway is optimistic. 'There is no problem,' he says. 'Most tourists stay on the main street next to the stalls. Sometimes important wedding festivals are held in houses nearby, but few tourists find out. In fact, we would prefer more interest in our culture. Besides, if I see villagers wearing modern clothes, I get angry and say they will stop the tourists coming. If anything, tourism enforces tradition.'

Tim Forsyth, Traveller's Tales Far Eastern Economic Review 6 May 1993

Eagle House

Pon & Annette Trekking
From Comment Book

'To begin with, I wasn't sure if I wanted to go on a trek. The stories I hear made it sound like foreigners stomping into a quiet village changing the lifesyle and imposing a foreign culture. Friends convinced me it would be different and it was!

This was not a trek where villages line up in traditional dress (especially for tourists) and try and sell you things. It is a real look at village life. A real insight into a life we have left too far behind.'

Shana, Perth, Australia
Eagle House Trekking Brochure, 1992

The Akha is one of about a half-dozen hill tribes who eke out an existence in the inhospitable but scenic Thai uplands.

Generally they have simple lives of unremitting tedium, enlivened by two things: addiction to opiates and being used as a tourist attraction.

Tourist on a Tribal Detour, The Weekend Guardian, 8-9/8/92

Our Thai Rama Tour is an opportunity to see something of 'real' Thailand. Waterfalls, wild jungle, rustic life, ruins of ancient towns, adventurous boat trips, hill tribe people with their colourful costumes and a tradition and culture all their own . . .

Worldwide, British Airways Holidays, 1993

Fig. 11.6

Courtesy: Tourism Concern

Glimpse of the Padong/Pa-daung/Padaung

. . . some tribal people left Burma and Laos only about twenty years ago, because of the fighting there . . .to have an ID card is difficult for them, but not for those who have lived there a long time.

Even though they say we are underdeveloped, we are dirty and things like that, they promote the tourists to come and see.

About ten years ago, the government became very concerned about the hill-tribe people. Before, the people lived very peacefully in the forest . . . So the government tried to develop the country through building roads, schools and public health centres. The idea is to unite all tribal people to become one Thai nation.

The fact is that the people in the city are used to looking down on our tribal people. They might say we are dirty because we don't take a bath every day, so we smell. They don't know the real situation in the hillside. The mountain people have to carry water from a long way to take a bath.

Sunny Danpongee, Government Offices and the People Coming Together to Discuss the Problem, Asian Consultation on Tourism and Aboriginal

THE TRAVEL SICKNESS

Seven women, blessed or cursed with being born on a Thursday at full moon which allows them to wear the tall chokers of brass rings, languidly nurse their babies, gazing blankly into camera lenses. We try to ease our discomfort with conversation through a translator, endeavouring to find out names, to build bridges but the Long-neck women have heard it all before. Until last year, the Longnecks refused to allow video recordings in the village for cultural reasons. Now, if you want a video of the Longnecks to show the folks back home, you must pay a premium of £5. Poverty cannot afford principles.

Kristina Woolnough, Scotland on Sunday, 24 January 1993

Although most tribal refugees from Burma's frontier war are unwelcome in Thailand, two women of the Padaung tribal group who sought refuge have been encouraged to stay on – as tourist attractions. Thai authorities actually 'negotiated' to keep them in Thailand, while repatriating other tribespeople to the Burma war zone. The Padaung is the tribal group of the 'long-necked women', and two of them had become, through a series of coercions, a lucrative tourist draw at Thailand's Mae Hong Son Resort.

Edith T Mirante, Hostages to Tourism
Cultural Survival Quarterly, 1990, No 1

In trekking, participants demand 'the Real Thing'. As the Real Thing comes into contact with tourists it becomes a little less of the Real Thing, as the mixing of cultures brought by tourists changes the original culture. Tourists are no longer satisfied with this diluted culture, partly of their own making, and want to go to see the Real Thing elsewhere. This leads to a constant process of trekking companies expanding their range throughout the hilltribe villages as the Real Thing is consumed behind them.

Many of the ills involved in the tourist industry in Northern Thailand originate with the myths and false images presented by marketing people in the lowlands, say experts at the Tribal Research Institute of Chiang Mai University.

Some experts suggest that more hilltribes should be allowed to manage tourism to their villages, though they admit that this presents an added problem as most hilltribes do not have Thai Citizenship.

Tourism: A cash crop that can hurt the hilltribes
Contours - December 1988

Stretching It A Bit

When the Pa-daung women in Nai Soi Village in Burma first started wearing the rings around their necks, one story goes, it was to protect their necks from a tiger-god fang's. The tiger-god, it was said, was sent to them by the deities to punish the women for being materialistic.

Another story has it that the rings were meant to make the village women ugly so that they would not be recruited as concubines for the Burmese King.

Nowadays, however, without the threat of a tiger-god or a hostile Burmese king, the Pa-daung women have found that the metal rings they wear around their necks serve as a great attraction to tourists.

Nipa Pheuksawas,
The Nation
19/2/89

It can be seen everyday when youngsters, some just five, rush up to the tourists in their traditional black costumes and head dress. They smile when cameras are pulled out and chirp: 'Ten Baht, ten Baht'. If the money is not forthcoming they cover their faces with their hands and disappear back into their homes.

Philip, a Canadian, has spent seven years researching the impact of tourism on the hilltribe cultures. Hilltribe trekking mushroomed in popularity in the 80s and Philip estimates that here are now more than 100,000 mostly Western tourists taking part every year. In the process it swells the national coffers by Bt50 million a year. In 1977 there were just a dozen trekking companies operating from Chiang Mai, by 1985 there were 54 and two years ago the number had zoomed to over 100.

Suda Kanjanawanawan, Feeding Time at the Human Zoo, The Nation, 26/3/92

Fig. 11.6 (continued)

JUXTAPOSITIONS

JUXTAPOSITIONS

I was forced to restrain a smile when Vi was asked by an elderly gentleman if he would be able to holiday in Split again soon.

He was most anxious to discover some part of the former Yugoslavia where the "Smurfs and the Crotes" weren't fighting. Also, was it likely to be over by September?

Vi's remark that if Lord Owen and Cyrus Vance didn't know then she stood little chance was met by an earnest plea for their telephone numbers.

Maureen Hill, in *View from the South – Travel Weekly*, February 17, 1993.

DEAR HOLIDAYMAKER,
We are pleased to forward you the first holiday brochure specialising in the best of Croatia and Slovenia.

Nobody knows Croatia as well as Phoenix and for the first time this year we are offering clients both old and new a choice of more than 80 hotels, self-catering apartments and Holiday Clubs situated in 26 of the best loved Adriatic coastal resorts.

Old favourites like Porec, Opatija, Makarska, Dubrovnik, Cavtat, Hvar, Brac and Korcula are offered . . . Prices were always hard to beat and never more so than for this coming summer . . .

Many thousands of clients have contacted us during the last eighteen months anxious to travel again to their particular favourite resort and hotel so we are delighted to advise the opening of a 'tailor made' department which can quote for hotels and/or odd duration holidays not featured within this brochure.

We look forward to being of service to you.

Yours faithfully,
PHOENIX HOLIDAYS LTD

CROATIA has relaunched itself into the conference and incentive market 18 months after its industry was destroyed by civil war.

The Croatian National Tourist Organisation has set up the Croatian Convention Bureau to promote and organise conferences and meetings and attract foreign capital.

CNTO deputy director Vic Radjic said Croatia hosted more than 280 international meetings and incentives in 1990, but none during the conflict.

"Croatia is now in the process of literally laying new foundations for its tourist and business industries and we are open for business in 1993," he said . . . "There is a perception in the UK that southern Croatia is bombed and destroyed but it is now 50 per cent functioning. The only way we can change this perception is to get people out there to experience it."

The CNTO is spending £100,000 in the UK this year on familiarisation trips, marketing and exhibitions.

TRAVEL WEEKLY,
March 3, 1993.

CROATIA '91

WHO GIVES *A DAMN*!

SUADA RAHIC, EIGHT MONTHS PREGNANT WITH HER THIRD CHILD, spends her days on a foam mattress in a gymnasium that reeks of urine. Her view of the near future is a sea of floor mats and hundreds of fellow victims of war.

Mrs. Rahic, a 26 year old Muslim, fled the embattled Herzegovinian city of Mostar with her two young daughters two months ago. She has lived in the gym at Vid Mihaljevic Central Elementary School for more than two weeks because there is no more hotel space . . .

"It's a miracle that everything is functioning here," the refugee co-ordinator Ivica Lelas said at the Hotel Riviera, where 910 people share 290 rooms, and another 217 more live in vans outside . . . Croatia's government feeds and houses refugees at resort hotels, hostels, and school gyms at a coast of about $10 a day for each person.

Maud Beelman,
Associated Press, June 1992.

Fig. 11.6 (continued)

Croatian Postcards

SERBIA

The Civil War has seriously dented plans for tourism development in Serbia. This country as well as currently being an unattractive destination is suffering a serious recession which has affected capital investment. Because of the loss of the Adriatic coastline the Serbs are planning to upgrade their own tourist infrastructure, particularly in relation to the Danube and mountain areas.

A new winter tourist centre in Serbia represents one of these plans. A hotel complex with 9,000 beds will be built in the Babin Zub tourist centre on Mount Stara Planina, near Knjazevac, eastern Serbia. The project will provide for 30 kilometres of ski lifts, 100 kilometres of ski slopes and other facilities at an altitude of over 1,200 metres. The total investment is estimated at US$520 million, of which foreign firms are expected to provide around 65 per cent. The Vlacin Lake area is also planned to have increased tourist accommodation (greater than previous planned levels), which is of concern to environmentalists, although according to officials this will not be detrimental to the environment.

The development plan for the Danube features high on the Serbian list of expansion. The Serbian Ministry of Trade and Tourism do counter any worries about these developments with the assurance that environmental impact assessments are to be used for all proposals.

Tourism investment in Central and Eastern Europe: Structure, Trends and Environmental Implications

The Ecological Studies Institute, Robert Atkinson and Duncan Fisher, April 1992.

WELCOME TO CROATIA!

We are very pleased to announce that our beautiful country, Croatia, is an independent and sovereign state . . .

The destruction of the tourist facilities has been most intensive in Dubrovnik. Each of the 35 hotels in the town and its vicinity have suffered major or minor damage. Hotel complexes in Sibenik, Zadar, Vodice were also damaged. The tourist facilities in Osijek and Vinkovci have been almost totally demolished, not to mention Vukovar and Plitvice Lakes.

CROATIAN MINISTRY OF TOURISM,
Zagreb, January 1992

ZADAR AUTUMN **1991**

HELP CROATIA!

CROATIA:

The war that broke out between ethnic Serbs and Croatians in the autumn of 1991 appeared to have been settled a year ago after 6,000 had been killed. But the conflict started up again recently when Croats invaded the Serb-held district of Krajina.

The Independent on Sunday
(14 March, 1993)

7th December, 1992 . . .

We loaded the van yet again, this time to go to Posusja. The trip was a lot better than the previous day, with magnificent scenery along the coastal route and then up into the mountains. In fact one could almost forget there was a war going on a few miles away. Needless to say we soon came across destroyed buildings and very quickly came back to reality.

from 'Report from the Front-line: Visit to Croatia and Bosnia' made by the Director of Fundraising for Feed The Children.

"Nearly every hotel is being used or has been used. But as summer is approaching refugees are being told to move from the better hotels. Hotels which are up to standard for foreign visitors. 750,000 displaced people and refugees in Croatia are living in shared accommodation or hotels or pensions."

"22 per cent of Croatia is occupied by Serbs and a lot of it is along the Dalmatian coast. An hour's journey inland will get you to the fighting."

Alan Waller
Aid Co-ordinator
Feed The Children
31 March 1993

Fig. 11.6 (continued)

BIBLIOGRAPHY

Bailey, J. *Tour Operating: Ticketing and Documentation* (ABTA, 1990)
Beardshaw & Palfarman *Organisation in its Environment* (Pitman Publishing, 1990)
Buckley, P.J. & Papadopoulos, S.I. *Marketing Greek Tourism: The Planning Process* (Tourism Management, June 1986)
Holloway, J.C. *The Business of Tourism* (Pitman Publishing, 1988)
Holloway, J.C. & Plant, R.V. *Marketing for Tourism* (Pitman Publishing, 1988)
Hussey, J. (ed.) *Understanding Business and Finance* (DP Publications Ltd, 1991)
Kotler, P. *Marketing Management: Analysis Planning and Control* (Prentice Hall International)
Lavery, P. *Travel and Tourism* (Elm Publications 1990)
Middleton, Victor T.C. *Marketing in Travel & Tourism* (Heinemann, 1988)
Pedrick, J. *Tour Operating: The Background* (ABTA, 1986)
Perez, S. & East, M. *The EC Directive: An Analysis* (Travel Industry Digests Ltd, 1991)
Salt, A. *Tour Operating: Business Aspects* (ABTA, 1986)
Yale, P. *Tourism in the UK* (Elm Publications, 1992)

The Package Travel, Package Holidays and Package Tours Regulations 1992 (HMSO, 1993)
The Package Travel, Package Holidays and Package Tour Regulations 1992 Guidance Notes (Department of Trade and Industry, 1992)
ABTA Handbook 1994
British Code of Advertising Practice (ASA, 1988)

INDEX